Solutions Manual to Accompany

Statistics for Bu
and Econom

Fifth Edition

David R. Anderson
University of Cincinnati

Dennis J. Sweeney
University of Cincinnati

Thomas A. Williams
Rochester Institute of Technology

West Publishing Company
Minneapolis/St. Paul   New York   Los Angeles   San Francisco

WEST'S COMMITMENT TO THE ENVIRONMENT

In 1906, West Publishing Company began recycling materials left over from the production of books. This began a tradition of efficient and responsible use of resources. Today, up to 95% of our legal books and 70% of our college texts are printed on recycled, acid-free stock. West also recycles nearly 22 million pounds of scrap paper annually—the equivalent of 181,717 trees. Since the 1960s, West has devised ways to capture and recycle waste inks, solvents, oils, and vapors created in the printing process. We also recycle plastics of all kinds, wood, glass, corrugated cardboard, and batteries, and have eliminated the use of styrofoam book packaging. We at West are proud of the longevity and the scope of our commitment to our environment.

Production, Prepress, Printing and Binding by West Publishing Company.

Contents

Preface

The purpose of *Statistics for Business and Economics* is to provide students, primarily in the fields of business administration and economics, with a sound conceptual introduction to the field of statistics and its many applications. The text is applications oriented and has been written with the needs of the nonmathematician in mind.

The solutions manual furnishes assistance by identifying learning objectives and providing detailed solutions for all exercises in the text. Specific sections of the manual are as follows:

Learning Objectives

Solutions to Exercises

Solutions to Computer Cases

Acknowledgements

We would like to provide special recognition to Catherine J. Williams for her efforts in preparing the solutions manual. We are also indebted to our editor Mary C. Schiller for her support during the preparation of the fifth edition.

David R. Anderson
Dennis J. Sweeney
Thomas A. Williams

Chapter 1
Introduction

Learning Objectives

1. Obtain an appreciation for the breadth of statistical applications in business.

2. Understand the meaning of the terms elements, variables, and observations as they are used in statistics.

3. Obtain an understanding of the four scales of measurement: nominal, ordinal, interval, and ratio.

4. Learn about the sources of data for statistical analysis both internal and external to the firm.

5. Be aware of how errors can arise in data used for statistical inference.

6. Know the meaning of descriptive statistics and statistical inference.

7. Be able to distinguish between a population and a sample.

8. Understand the role the sample plays in making statistical inferences about the population.

Solutions:

1. Statistics can be referred to as the numerical facts or data themselves. Statistics as a discipline or field of study refers to the body of knowledge dealing with the design of surveys, research projects, and so on as well as the collection, analysis, interpretation, and presentation of the data collected.

2. a. 7 elements

    b. 4 variables

    c. 7 observations; Each row of data is an observation

    d. Pay vs. Corporation Profit Rating is qualitative; others are quantitative

    e. Pay vs. Corporation Profit Rating is ordinal; others are ratio

3. a. $923,714

    b. $5/7 = 0.71$ of the firms

    c. Because this variable is qualitative

4. a. 10 elements

    b. The Fortune 500 companies

    c/d. $2,673.4 or $2,673,400,000

5. a. 5 variables

    b. Rank and Industry code are qualitative. Sales, profit, and assets are quantitative.

    c. Ratio for sales, profit, and assets; ordinal for rank; nominal for industry code.

6. Questions a, c, and d are quantitative.

    Questions b and e are qualitative.

7. a. Worker occupation is a qualitative variable.

    b. A nominal scale is being used.

8. a. 1,000

    b. Nominal with six response categories

    c. Percentages since we have nominal or qualitative data

    d. $170/1,000 = 0.17$ or 17%

9. a. Qualitative

    b. An ordinal scale is being used.

    c. Percentages since arithmetic operations including averages are not valid with qualitative data.

10. a. Quantitative, ratio scale

    b. Qualitative, nominal scale

    c. Qualitative, ordinal scale

    d. Qualitative; nominal scale

    e. Quantitative, ratio scale

11. a. Quantitative, ratio scale

    b. Qualitative, ordinal scale

    c. Qualitative, ordinal scale

    d. Quantitative, ratio scale

    e. Qualitative, nominal scale

12. a. The population is all visitors coming to the state of Hawaii.

    b. Since airline flights carry the vast majority of visitors to the state, the use of questionnaires for passengers during incoming flights is a good way to reach this population. The questionnaire actually appears on the back of a mandatory plants and animals declaration form that passengers must complete during the incoming flight. A large percentage of passengers complete the visitor information questionnaire.

    c. Questions 1 and 4 are quantitative data indicating the number of visits and the number of days in Hawaii. Questions 2 and 3 are qualitative indicating the nominal scale categories of reason for the trip and where the visitor plans to stay.

8. a. 1,000

    b. Nominal with six response categories

    c. Percentages since we have nominal or qualitative data

    d. $170/1,000 = 0.17$ or 17%

13.   Internal data on salaries of other employees can be obtained from the personnel department. External data might be obtained from the Department of Labor or industry associations.

14. a.   We would like to see data from product taste tests and test marketing the product.

    b.   Such data would be obtained from specially designed statistical studies.

15. a.   The population is all adults that could have been included in the sample - probably all adults in the United States.

    b.   The variable being studied is favorite evening activity.

    c.   The variable is qualitative.

    d.   The sample size is 1500.

    e.   A descriptive statistic used is that 70% of the adults sampled prefer spending an evening at home.

    f.   The process of statistical inference could be used to infer that 70% of all adults prefer spending an evening at home.

16. a.   (48/120)100% = 40% in the sample died from some form of heart disease. This can be used as an estimate of the percentage of all males 60 or older who die of heart disease.

    b.   The data on caluse of death is qualitative.

17. a.   56% of shoplifters were male

         51% of shoplifters were "under 30"

    b.   The incidence of shoplifting in Southern California may not be representative of national trends.

19. a.   The two populations are the population of women whose mothers took the drug DES during pregnancy and the population of women whose mothers did not take the drug DES during pregnancy.

    b.   It was a survey.

    c.   63 / 3.980 = 15.8 women out of each 1000 developed tissue abnormalities.

    d.   The article reported "twice" as many abnormalities in the women whose mothers had taken DES during pregnancy. Thus, a rough estimate would be 15.8/2 = 7.9 abnormalities per 1000 women whose mothers had *not* taken DES during pregnancy.

    e.   In many situations, disease occurrences are rare and affect only a small portion of the population. Large samples are needed to collect data on a reasonable number of cases where the disease exists.

20. a.   All adult viewers reached by the Denver, Colorado television station.

    b.   The viewers contacted in the telephone survey.

    c.   A sample. It would clearly be too costly and time consuming to try to contact all viewers.

21. a. Percent of television sets that were tuned to a particular television show and/or total viewing audience.

    b. All television sets in the United States which are available for the viewing audience. Note this would not include television sets in store displays.

    c. A portion of these television sets. Generally, individual households would be contacted to determine which programs were being viewed.

    d. The cancellation of programs, the scheduling of programs, and advertising cost rates.

22. a. This is a statistically correct descriptive statistic for the sample.

    b. An incorrect generalization since the data was not collected for the entire population.

    c. An acceptable statistical inference based on the use of the word "estimate."

    d. While this statement is true for the sample, it is not a justifiable conclusion for the entire population.

    e. This statement is not statistically supportable. While it is true for the particular sample observed, it is entirely possible and even very likely that at least some students will be outside the 65 to 90 range of grades.

Chapter 2
Descriptive Statistics I: Tabular and Graphical Approaches

Learning Objectives

1. Learn how to construct and interpret summarization procedures for qualitative data such as :

   frequency and relative frequency distributions

   bar graphs and pie charts

2. Learn how to construct and interpret tabular summarization procedures for quantitative data such as:

   frequency and relative frequency distributions

   cumulative frequency and cumulative relative frequency distributions

3. Learn how to construct a dot plot, a histogram, and an ogive as graphical summaries of quantitative data.

4. Learn about the role of the computer in descriptive statistics.

5. Be able to use and interpret the exploratory data analysis technique of a stem-and-leaf display.

Chapter 2

Solutions:

1.

Class	Frequency	Relative Frequency
A	60	60/120 = 0.50
B	24	24/120 = 0.20
C	36	36/120 = 0.30
	120	1.00

2. a. $1 - (0.22 + 0.18 + 0.40) = 0.20$

   b. $0.20(200) = 40$

   c.

Class	Frequency
A	0.22(200) = 44
B	0.18(200) = 36
C	0.40(200) = 80
D	0.20(200) = 40
	200

3. a. $360° \times 58/120 = 174°$

   b. $360° \times 42/120 = 126°$

   c.

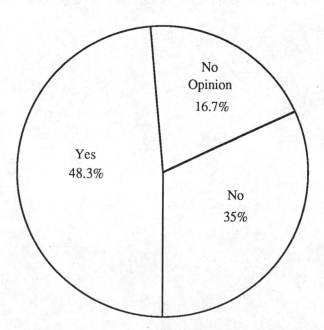

d.

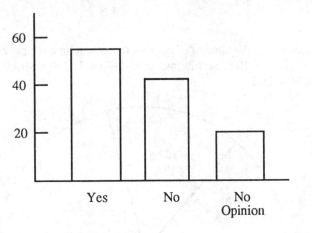

4. a. The data simply describe the category the element belongs to. The scale of measurement is nominal.

    b.

Beverage	Tally	Frequency	Relative Frequency
Milk		3	0.10
Fruit Juice		4	0.13
Soft Drink		13	0.43
Beer		8	0.27
Bottled Water		2	0.07
	Totals:	30	1.00

    c. Bar Graph

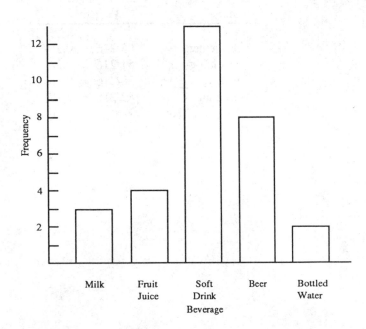

Pie Chart: First compute the number of degrees to allocate to each beverage. Milk: 0.10(360) = 36, Fruit Juice: 0.13(360) = 46.8, Soft Drink: 0.43(360) = 154.8, Beer: 0.27(360) = 97.2, Bottled Water: 0.07(360) = 25.2.

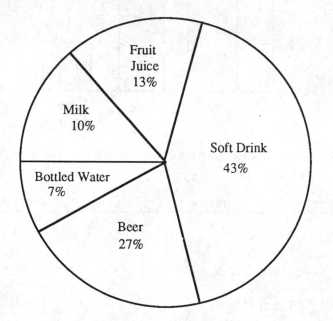

d. America's favorite beverage is a soft drink.

5. a.

Major	Relative Frequency
Management	55/216 = 0.25
Accounting	51/216 = 0.24
Finance	28/216 = 0.13
Marketing	82/216 = 0.38
Total	1.00

b.

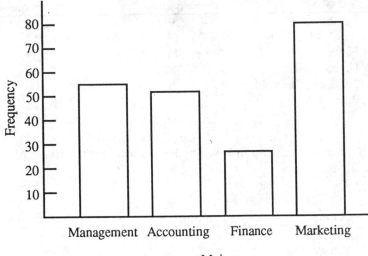

c.   Pie Chart

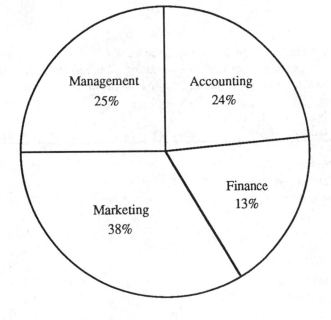

6. a.

Video	Frequency	Relative Frequency
Bambi	9	0.150
ET	13	0.217
Fantasia	14	0.233
Home Alone	8	0.133
The Little Mermaid	6	0.100
Batman	10	0.167
	60	1.000

b. Fantasia is the most successful followed by ET, Batman, Bambi, Home Alone, and The Little Mermaid.

7.

Rating	Frequency	Relative Frequency
Outstanding	19	0.38
Very Good	13	0.26
Good	10	0.20
Average	6	0.12
Poor	2	0.04
	50	1.00

Management should be pleased with these results. 64% of the ratings are very good to outstanding. 84% of the ratings are good or better. Comparing these ratings with previous results will show whether or not the restaurant is making improvements in its ratings of food quality.

8. a.

Position	Frequency	Relative Frequency
Pitcher	17	0.309
Catcher	4	0.073
1st Base	5	0.091
2nd Base	4	0.073
3rd Base	2	0.036
Shortstop	5	0.091
Left Field	6	0.109
Center Field	5	0.091
Right Field	7	0.127
	55	1.000

b. Pitchers (Almost 31%)

c. 3rd Base (3 - 4%)

d. Right Field (Almost 13%)

e. Infielders (16 or 29.1%) to Outfielders (18 or 32.7%)

9. a/b.

Starting Time	Tally	Frequency	Relative Frequency
7:00		3	0.15
7:30		4	0.20
8:00		4	0.20
8:30		7	0.35
9:00		2	0.10
	Totals	20	1.00

c.   Bar Graph

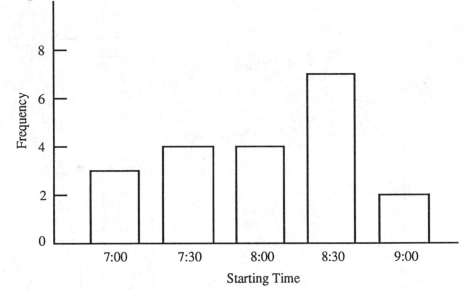

d.

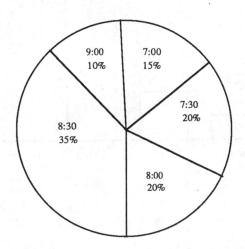

e. The most preferred starting time is 8:30 a.m.. Starting times of 7:30 and 8:00 a.m. are next.

10. a. Because the number merely describes the category the element belongs to. The scale of measurement is ordinal.

b.

Rating	Tally	Frequency	Relative Frequency
Poor		2	0.03
Fair		4	0.07
Good		12	0.20
Very Good		24	0.40
Excellent		18	0.30
	Totals	60	1.00

c.

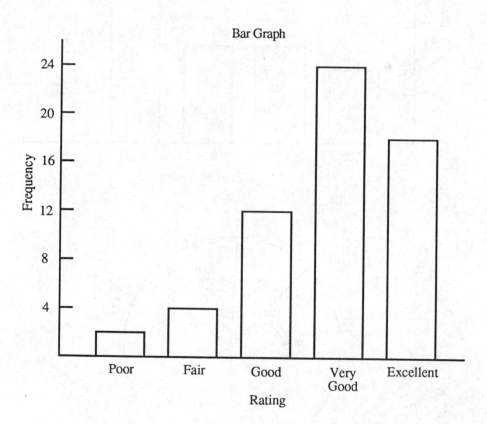

Bar Graph

Pie Chart

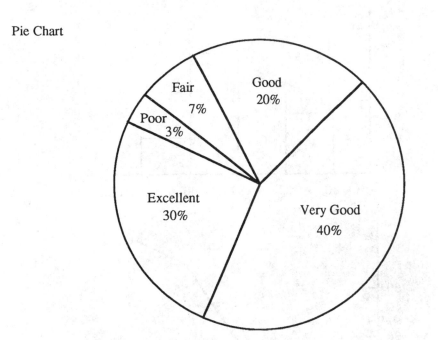

d. The course evaluation data indicate a high quality course. The most common rating is very good with the second most common being excellent.

11.

Class	Frequency	Relative Frequency
0 - 4	2	0.20
5 - 9	4	0.40
10 - 14	3	0.30
15 - 19	1	0.10
	10	1.00

12.

Class	Cumulative Frequency	Cumulative Relative Frequency
less than or equal to 19	8	0.200
less than or equal to 29	20	0.500
less than or equal to 39	35	0.875
less than or equal to 49	40	1.000

13.

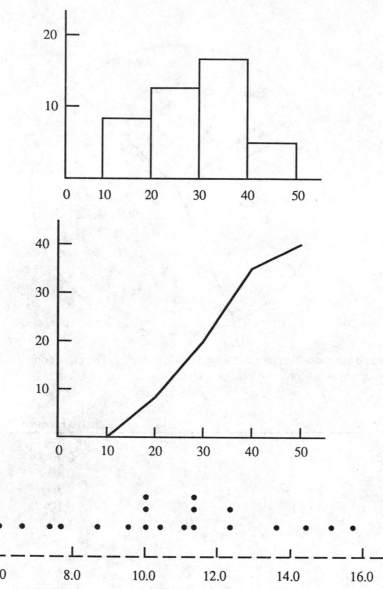

14. a.

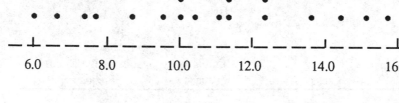

b/c.

Class	Frequency	Relative Frequency
6.0 - 7.9	4	0.20
8.0 - 9.9	2	0.10
10.0 - 11.9	8	0.40
12.0 - 13.9	3	0.15
14.0 - 15.9	3	0.15
	20	1.00

15. a/b.

Waiting Time	Frequency	Relative Frequency
0 - 4	4	0.20
5 - 9	8	0.40
10 - 14	5	0.25
15 - 19	2	0.10
20 - 24	1	0.05
Totals	20	1.00

c/d.

Waiting Time	Cumulative Frequency	Cumulative Relative Frequency
Less than or equal to 4	4	0.20
Less than or equal to 9	12	0.60
Less than or equal to 14	17	0.85
Less than or equal to 19	19	0.95
Less than or equal to 24	20	1.00

e. 12/20 = 0.60

16.

	New		Used	
Prices	Frequency	Relative Frequency	Frequency	Relative Frequency
0.0 - 4.9	0	0.000	3	0.25
5.0 - 9.9	1	0.071	6	0.50
10.0 - 14.9	5	0.357	3	0.25
15.0 - 19.9	5	0.357	0	0.00
20.0 - 24.9	3	0.214	0	0.00
	14		12	

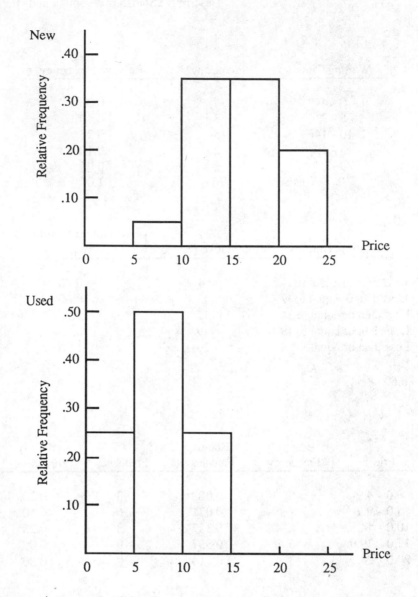

Several comparisons are possible. For example, new car prices are more frequently in the 10 - 19.9 range, with 21.4% 20 or more. Used car prices are more frequently in the 5.0 - 9.9 range.

17.

Call Duration	Frequency	Relative Frequency
2 - 3.9	5	0.25
4 - 5.9	9	0.45
6 - 7.9	4	0.20
8 - 9.9	0	0.00
10 - 11.9	2	0.10
Totals	20	1.00

Histogram

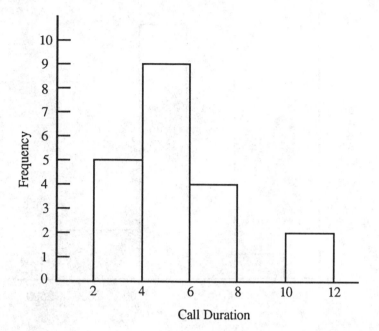

18. a/b.

Salary ($1000s)	Tally	Frequency	Relative Frequency
0 - 499		1	0.04
500 - 999		9	0.36
1000 - 1499		11	0.44
1500 - 1999		2	0.08
2000 - 2499		2	0.08
	Totals	25	1.00

c.

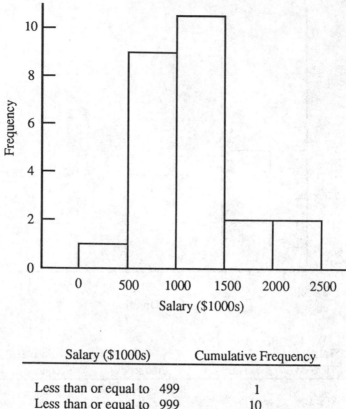

d.

Salary ($1000s)	Cumulative Frequency
Less than or equal to 499	1
Less than or equal to 999	10
Less than or equal to 1499	21
Less than or equal to 1999	23
Less than or equal to 2499	25

e. The majority of the CEOs earn between $500,000 and $1,499,000. A few (four) earn over $1,500,000 and one earns less than $500,000.

19. a/b.

Number	Frequency	Relative Frequency
140 - 149	2	0.10
150 - 159	7	0.35
160 - 169	3	0.15
170 - 179	6	0.30
180 - 189	1	0.05
190 - 199	1	0.05
Totals	20	1.00

c/d.

Number	Cumulative Frequency	Cumulative Relative Frequency
Less than or equal to 149	2	0.10
Less than or equal to 159	9	0.45
Less than or equal to 169	12	0.60
Less than or equal to 179	18	0.90
Less than or equal to 189	19	0.95
Less than or equal to 199	20	1.00

e.

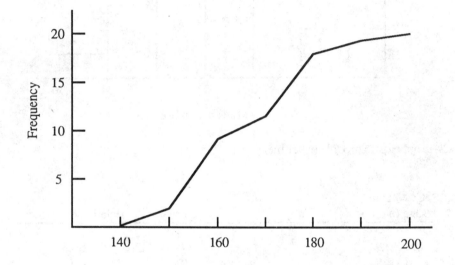

20. a/b.

Miles per Gallon	Tally	Frequency	Relative Frequency
24.0 - 25.9		2	0.07
26.0 - 27.9		5	0.17
28.0 - 29.9		10	0.33
30.0 - 31.9		9	0.30
32.0 - 33.9		3	0.10
34.0 - 35.9		1	0.03
		30	1.00

c.

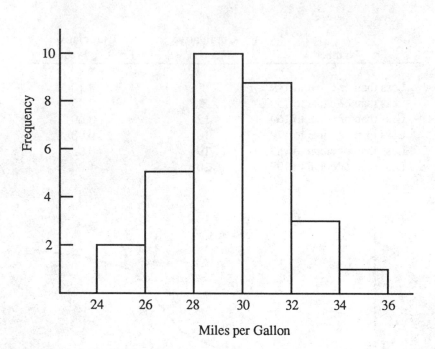

d.   The Civic appears to provide better fuel economy.

21.   a/b.

Computer Usage (hours)	Tally	Frequency	Relative Frequency
0.0 - 2.9		14	0.28
3.0 - 5.9		6	0.12
6.0 - 8.9		6	0.12
9.0 - 11.9		7	0.14
12.0 - 14.9		14	0.28
15.0 - 17.9		3	0.06
	Totals	50	1.00

c.

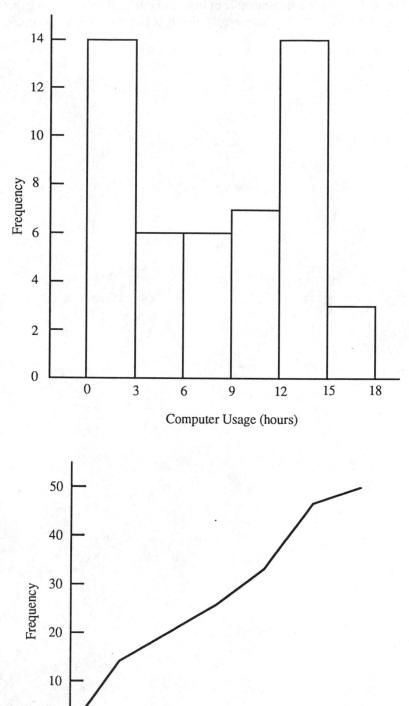

d.

e.   Usage is bimodal. There is a large number of light users (0 - 2.9 hours) and a large number of heavy users (12 - 14.9 hours). Usage is fairly evenly distributed over the rest of the users.

22.

```
5 | 7 8
6 | 4 5 8
7 | 0 2 2 5 5 6 8
8 | 0 2 3 5
```

23.

```
 6 | 3
 7 | 5 5 7
 8 | 1 3 4 8
 9 | 3 6
10 | 0 4 5
11 | 3
```

24.

```
11 | 6
12 | 0 2
13 | 0 6 7
14 | 2 2 7
15 | 5
16 | 0 2 8
17 | 0 2 3
```

25.

9	8 9
10	2 4 6 6
11	4 5 7 8 8 9
12	2 4 5 7
13	1 2
14	4
15	1

26.

-1	3 7
0	1 8
1	3 4 5 6
2	0 1 4 5 5 6
3	0 3 3
4	5 9
12	0

$2.00 - 2.99 is the most frequent range for the data. 13(65%) of the data are in the $1.00 - 3.99 range. Eli Lilly's $4.50 and Procter and Gamble's $4.92 are high earnings per share. General Dynamic's $12.06 is extremely high.

27.

```
4 | 1  3  6  6  7
5 | 0  0  3  8  9
6 | 0  1  1  4  4  5  7  7  9  9
7 | 0  0  0  1  3  4  4  5  5  6  6  6  7  8  8
8 | 0  1  1  3  4  4  5  7  7  8  9
9 | 0  2  2  7
```

or

```
4 | 1  3
4 | 6  6  7
5 | 0  0  3
5 | 8  9
6 | 0  1  1  4  4
6 | 5  7  7  9  9
7 | 0  0  0  1  3  4  4
7 | 5  5  6  6  7  8  8
8 | 0  1  1  3  4  4
8 | 5  7  7  8  9
9 | 0  2  2
9 | 7
```

28. a. Note that the decimal points do not appear in the stem and leaf display.

```
1 | 5 6 8 9
2 | 1 2
3 | 4
4 | 1 6 8
5 |
6 | 5 6 8
7 | 1
8 | 9 9
9 | 2 8
```

b.

Profit Margin	Frequency	Relative Frequency
1.0 - 1.9	4	0.22
2.0 - 2.9	2	0.11
3.0 - 3.9	1	0.06
4.0 - 4.9	3	0.17
5.0 - 5.9	0	0.00
6.0 - 6.9	3	0.17
7.0 - 7.9	1	0.06
8.0 - 8.9	2	0.11
9.0 - 9.9	2	0.11
Totals	18	1.00

Note: The total for the relative frequency actually adds to 1.01 due to rounding.

29. a/b.

Sport	Frequency	Relative Frequency
Baseball	7	0.175
Basketball	6	0.150
Football	14	0.350
Ice Hockey	1	0.025
Tennis	1	0.025
Other	11	0.275
	40	1.000

c.

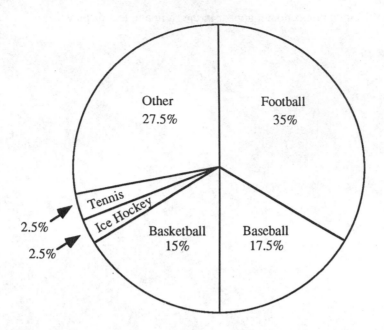

30. a/b.

Industry	Tally	Frequency	Relative Frequency
Beverage		2	0.10
Chemicals		3	0.15
Electronics		6	0.30
Food		7	0.35
Aerospace		2	0.10
	Totals	20	1.00

c.

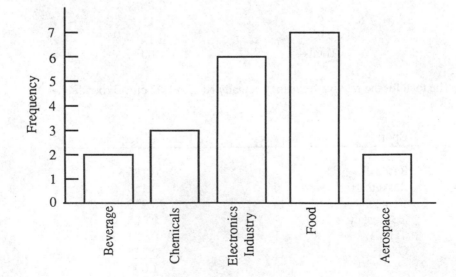

31. a/b.

Airline	Frequency	Relative Frequency
American Air	8	0.200
East Coast Air	13	0.325
Suncoast	8	0.200
Great Western	<u>11</u>	<u>0.275</u>
Totals	40	1.000

c.

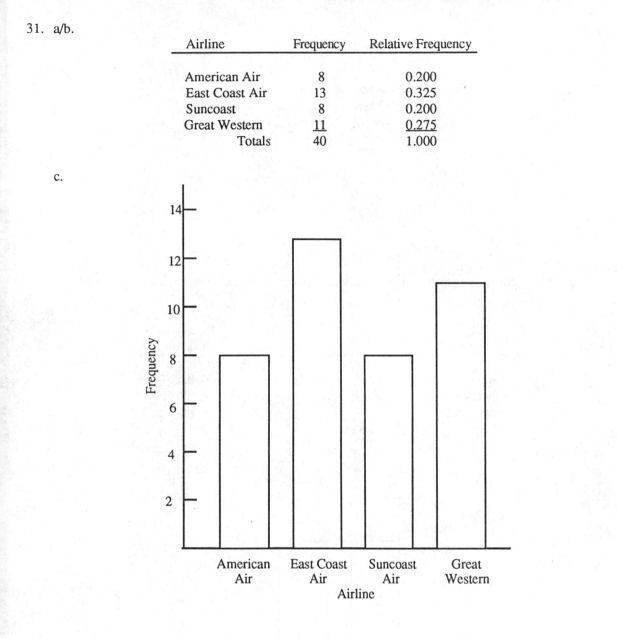

d.

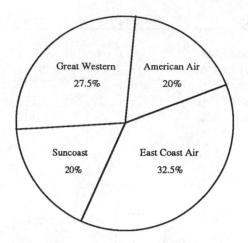

e. East Coast Air appears to provide the best service; Great Western is not far behind.

32. a.

Party Affiliation	Tally	Frequency	Relative Frequency
Democrat		17	0.425
Republican		17	0.425
Independent		6	0.150
Totals		40	1.000

b.

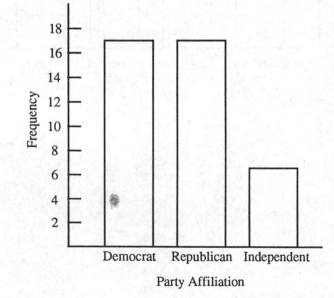

c. The strengths of the political parties are about even. But, the number of independents is smaller than the number affiliated with either party.

33. a.

Movie	Frequency	Relative Frequency
Coming To America	13	0.22
Big	11	0.18
Crocodile Dundee II	5	0.08
Who Framed Roger Rabbit	18	0.30
Good Morning Viet Nam	10	0.17
Other	3	0.05
	60	1.00

b.

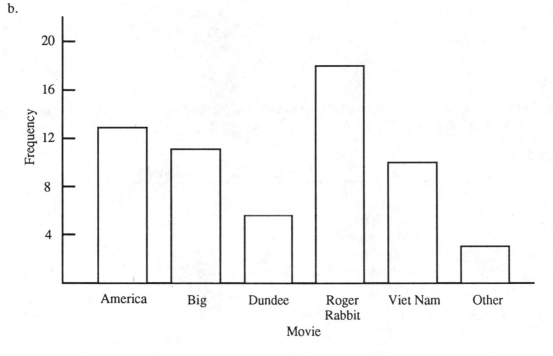

c. 1. Who Framed Roger Rabbit
    2. Coming To America
    3. Big
    4. Good Morning Viet Nam
    5. Crocodile Dundee II

34. a/b.

Hourly Wage	Frequency	Relative Frequency
4.00 - 5.99	1	0.04
6.00 - 7.99	3	0.12
8.00 - 9.99	8	0.32
10.00 - 11.99	6	0.24
12.00 - 13.99	5	0.20
14.00 - 15.99	2	0.08
	25	1.00

c.

Hourly Wage	Cumulative Frequency	Cumulative Relative Frequency
Less than or equal to 5.99	1	0.04
Less than or equal to 7.99	4	0.16
Less than or equal to 9.99	12	0.48
Less than or equal to 11.99	18	0.72
Less than or equal to 13.99	23	0.92
Less than or equal to 15.99	25	1.00

d. Most hourly wages are between $8.00 and $13.99. Only 2 (8%) earn over $14.00 per hour. Four (16%) earn less than $8.00 per hour.

35. a/b.

Sales	Frequency	Relative Frequency
0 - 999	11	0.647
1,000 - 1,999	1	0.059
2,000 - 2,999	3	0.176
3,000 - 3,999	1	0.059
4,000 and over	1	0.059
	17	1.000

c/d.

Sales	Cumulative Frequency	Cumulative Relative Frequency
Less than or equal to 999	11	0.647
Less than or equal to 1,999	12	0.706
Less than or equal to 2,999	15	0.882
Less than or equal to 3,999	16	0.941
Less than or equal to 6,999	17	1.000

e.

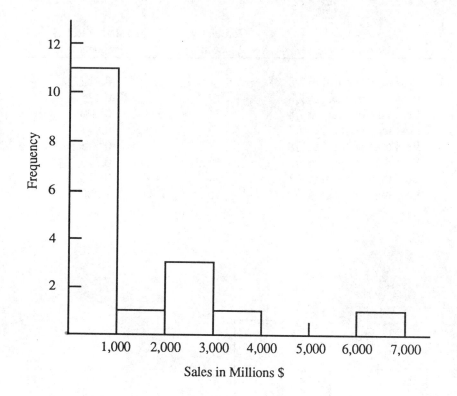

36. a.

Closing Price	Tally	Frequency	Relative Frequency
0 - 9 7/8		9	0.225
10 - 19 7/8		10	0.250
20 - 29 7/8		5	0.125
30 - 39 7/8		11	0.275
40 - 49 7/8		2	0.050
50 - 59 7/8		2	0.050
60 - 69 7/8		0	0.000
70 - 79 7/8		1	0.025
	Totals	40	1.000

b.

Closing Price	Cumulative Frequency	Cumulative Relative Frequency
Less than or equal to 7/8	9	0.225
Less than or equal to 7/8	19	0.475
Less than or equal to 7/8	24	0.600
Less than or equal to 7/8	35	0.875
Less than or equal to 7/8	37	0.925
Less than or equal to 7/8	39	0.975
Less than or equal to 7/8	39	0.975
Less than or equal to 7/8	40	1.000

c.

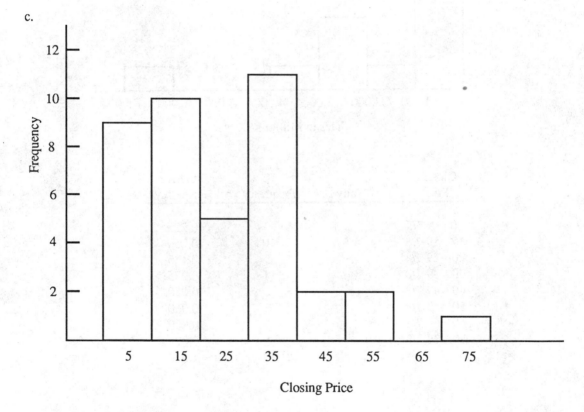

d. Over 87% of common stocks trade for less than $40 a share and 60% trade for less than $30 per share.

37. a.

Grade Point Average	Frequency	Relative Frequency
1.6 - 1.89	1	0.033
1.9 - 2.19	3	0.100
2.2 - 2.49	6	0.200
2.5 - 2.79	10	0.333
2.8 - 3.09	6	0.200
3.1 - 3.39	3	0.100
3.4 - 3.69	1	0.033
		1.000

b.

Grade Point Average	Cumulative Relative Frequency
Less than or equal to 1.89	0.033
Less than or equal to 2.19	0.133
Less than or equal to 2.49	0.333
Less than or equal to 2.79	0.666
Less than or equal to 3.09	0.866
Less than or equal to 3.39	0.966
Less than or equal to 3.69	1.000

c.

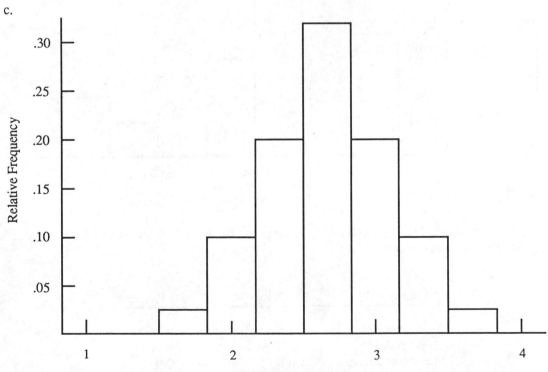

38. a/b.

Cost	Frequency	Relative Frequency
2,000 - 2,499	2	0.04
2,500 - 2,999	7	0.14
3,000 - 3,499	16	0.32
3,500 - 3,999	11	0.22
4,000 - 4,499	5	0.10
4,500 - 4,999	4	0.08
5,000 - 5,499	2	0.04
5,500 - 5,999	3	0.06
	50	1.00

c.

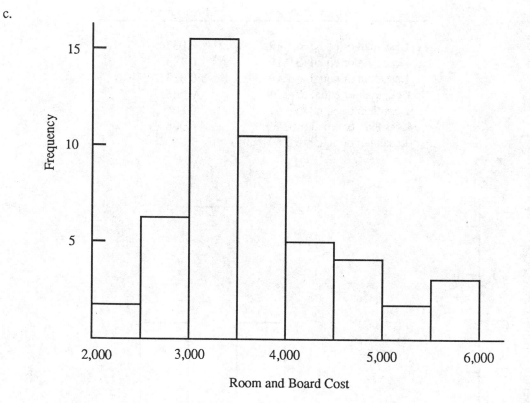

d. The large group is in the $3,000 - $3,499 range (32%). Only 18% are under $3,000. Five schools (10%) are $5,000 or more.

39. a.

Exchange	Frequency	Relative Frequency
American	5	0.33
New York	1	0.17
Over the Counter	9	0.60
	15	1.00

Over the Counter carries the most shadow stocks.

b.

Earnings per Share	Frequency	Relative Frequency
0.00 - 0.49	7	0.47
0.50 - 0.99	4	0.27
1.00 - 1.49	2	0.13
1.50 - 1.99	1	0.07
2.00 - 2.49	0	0.00
2.50 - 2.99	0	0.00
3.00 - 3.49	0	0.00
3.50 - 3.99	0	0.00
4.00 - 4.49	1	0.00
	15	1.00

Almost half of the shadow shocks (47%) have EPS of 0.00 - 0.49. Eleven of the 15 shadow stocks have EPS of less than $1.00. Low EPS should be expected. The EPS of 4.13 for CE Software is unusual.

Price - Earnings Ratio	Frequency	Relative Frequency
0.0 - 9.9	2	0.13
10.0 - 19.9	5	0.33
20.0 - 29.9	3	0.20
30.0 - 39.9	2	0.13
40.0 - 49.9	1	0.07
50.0 - 59.9	1	0.07
60.0 - 69.9	0	0.00
70.0 - 79.9	1	0.07
	15	1.00

P - E ratios vary considerably from 7.1 to 73.4. 33% were in the 10.0 - 19.9 range. Twelve of the 15 shadow stocks have P - E ratios of 39.9 or less.

40.

Income	Frequency	Relative Frequency
12,000 - 13,999	1	0.020
14,000 - 15,999	10	0.196
16,000 - 17,999	17	0.333
18,000 - 19,999	11	0.216
20,000 - 21,999	6	0.118
22,000 - 23,999	3	0.059
24,000 - 25,999	3	0.059
	51	1.000

41.

```
0 | 8 9

1 | 0 2 2 2 3 4 4 4

1 | 5 5 6 6 6 6 7 7 8 8 8 8 9 9 9

2 | 0 1 2 2 2 3 4 4 4

2 | 5 6 8

3 | 0 1 3
```

b/c/d.

Number Answered Correctly	Frequency	Relative Frequency	Cumulative Frequency
5 - 9	2	0.050	2
10 - 14	8	0.200	10
15 - 19	15	0.375	25
20 - 24	9	0.225	34
25 - 29	3	0.075	37
30 - 34	3	0.075	40
Totals	40	1.000	

e. Relatively few of the students (25%) were able to answer 1/2 or more of the questions correctly. The data seem to support the Joint Council on Economic Education's claim. However, the degree of difficulty of the questions needs to be taken into account before reaching a final a conclusion.

42. a.

```
4 | 4
4 | 7
5 | 0 0 0 2 2
5 | 5 6 6 8
6 | 1 1 2 3
6 | 6 7 8 9
7 | 1 3
7 | 9
8 | 0 0
```

b.

```
2 | 5 8 8 9 9 9
3 | 2
3 | 5 5 5 5 5 7 9
4 | 0 1 1
4 | 9
5 | 0 0 3
5 | 6 7 8
```

c. High temperatures were mostly in the 50's and 60's. Five cities had a high over 70° and two cities had highs of 80. Low temperatures were mostly in the 35 to 45 degree range. Six cities have low temperatures in the twenties.

d. 7 cities.

e.

Temperature	Frequency Distribution High	Low
20 - 29	0	6
30 - 39	0	8
40 - 49	2	4
50 - 59	9	6
60 - 69	8	0
70 - 79	3	0
80 - 89	2	0

Solution To Computer Case:

Note to Instructor:

Encourage your students to use the computer to explore the data set and gain as much insight as possible about the Consolidated Foods, Inc. situation. In the case assignment, we suggested some of the standard statistical summaries students should consider in a managerial report. However, they should not feel limited to the items we suggest.

In addition, encourage your students to review the statistical printouts and make judgements and/or interpretations about Consolidated Foods. We have found that many students feel that they have finished with the report once they have obtained the printout of the statistical summaries. Discussion and interpretation presented in the managerial report should be a major component of the computer case assignments.

If your students are using Minitab or The Data Analysis software packages, the data sets for all computer applications are already on a data disk in a format compatible with these packages. If your students are using another software system, the data will need to be input by the students. In the solutions to the computer cases, we will show the Minitab output.

Solution:

The Minitab commands COUNT C1, COUNT C2, and COUNT C3 can be used to count the number of data entries for each method of payment. Doing so provides the following frequency and relative frequency results:

Method of Payment		Frequency	Relative Frequency
CASH		38	0.38
PERSONAL CHECK		40	0.40
CREDIT CARD		22	0.22
	Total	100	1.00

A bar graph or a pie chart can be used to show graphical summarizations of the above results.

Based on the information given in the case that historically 50% of Consolidated's customers paid cash and 50% paid by personal check, we see that the credit card usage by 22% of the customers has reduced both the cash and personal check usage. In fact it appears that both some cash users and some personal check users have opted for the new credit card charging policy. Care should be given to these observations in the sense that we are basing the statements on a sample of 100 customers rather than the entire population of customers. Issues of statistical inference will be treated later in the text.

Minitab histograms, stem-and-leaf plots and dot plots are shown as follows. Students should make some observations about both personal check and credit cards being used on the larger dollar amounts.

Additional insights and observations are as follows:

1. Cash purchases are $20 or less.

2. The majority of personal check purchases are in the $30 - $60 range.

3. The majority of credit card purchases are in the $40 to $60 range.

4. The credit card purchases are more similar to the personal check purchases than the cash purchases.

5. The largest purchase of approximately $78 was by personal check. The largest credit card purchase was approximately $70 while the largest cash purchase was approximately $20.

Histogram of CASH   N = 38

Midpoint	Count	
5.0	24	* *
15.0	13	* * * * * * * * * * * * *
25.0	1	*

Histogram of CHECK   N = 40

Midpoint	Count	
5.0	1	*
15.0	2	* *
25.0	4	* * * *
35.0	11	* * * * * * * * * * *
45.0	8	* * * * * * * *
55.0	11	* * * * * * * * * * *
65.0	1	*
75.0	2	* *

Histogram of CREDIT N = 22

Midpoint	Count	
5.0	0	
15.0	2	* *
25.0	6	* * * * * *
35.0	1	*
45.0	5	* * * * *
55.0	7	* * * * * * *
65.0	1	*

Stem-and-leaf of CASH N = 38

```
0    1 1 1
0    2 2 2 3 3
0    4 4 5 5 5 5
0    6 7 7 7 7 7 7
0    8 8 9
1    1 1 1
1    2 3
1    4 5 5 5
1    6 6 6
1    8
2    0
```

Stem-and-leaf of CHECK N = 40

```
0    2
0
1
1    7 8
2    1
2    5 7 8
3    0 1 1 4
3    5 5 6 6 7 7 9
4    0 1 1 2 2 3
4    8 9
5    0 1 2 2 4
5    5 7 8 8 8 9
6
6    9
7    2
7    8
```

Stem-and-leaf of CREDIT N = 22

```
1    4
1    9
2    2
2    5 6 6 7 7
3    3
3
4    3 4
4    6 6 8
5    0 2 2 3 4
5    5 7
6
6    9
```

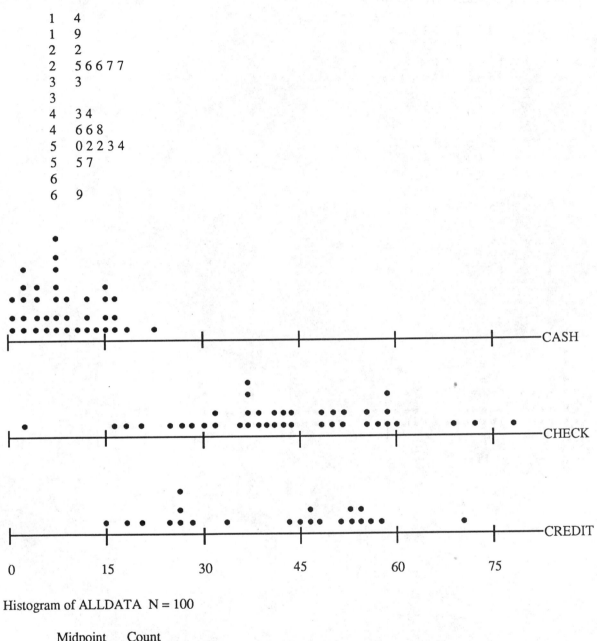

Histogram of ALLDATA N = 100

Midpoint	Count	
5.0	25	* *
15.0	17	* * * * * * * * * * * * * * * * *
25.0	11	* * * * * * * * * * *
35.0	12	* * * * * * * * * * * *
45.0	13	* * * * * * * * * * * * *
55.0	18	* * * * * * * * * * * * * * * * * *
65.0	2	* *
75.0	2	* *

Stem-and-leaf of ALLDATA N = 100

```
0   1 1 1 2 2 2 2 3 3 4 4
0   5 5 5 5 6 7 7 7 7 7 7 8 8 9
1   1 1 1 2 3 4 4
1   5 5 5 6 6 6 7 8 8 9
2   0 1 2
2   5 5 6 6 7 7 7 8
3   0 1 1 3 4
3   5 5 6 6 7 7 9
4   0 1 1 2 2 3 3 4
4   6 6 8 8 9
5   0 0 1 2 2 2 2 3 4 4
5   5 5 7 7 8 8 8 9
6
6   9 9
7   2
7   8
```

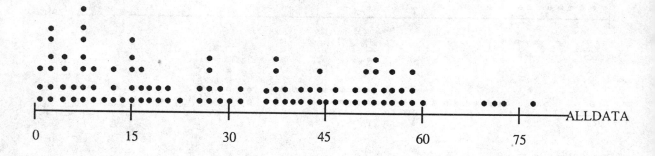

Chapter 3
Descriptive Statistics II: Measures of Location and Dispersion

Learning Objectives

1. Understand the purpose of measures of location.

2. Be able to compute the mean, trimmed mean, median, mode, quartiles, and various percentiles for a set of data.

3. Understand the purpose of measures of dispersion.

4. Be able to compute the range, interquartile range, variance, standard deviation, and coefficient of variation for a set of data.

5. Understand how z scores are computed and how they are used as a measure of relative location of an item in a data set.

6. Know how Chebyshev's theorem and the empirical rule can be used to determine the percentage of items within a specified number of standard deviations of the mean.

7. Learn how to construct a 5-number summary and a box plot.

8. Be able to compute the mean, variance, and standard deviation for grouped data; i.e., when data is only available in frequency distribution form.

9. Learn how the computer is used to summarize data and provide output for a variety of descriptive measures of location and dispersion.

Chapter 3

Solutions:

1.

$$\bar{x} = \frac{\sum x_i}{n} = \frac{75}{5} = 15$$

$$10, 12, 16, 17, 20$$

Median = 16 (middle value)

2.

$$\bar{x} = \frac{\sum x_i}{n} = \frac{96}{6} = 16$$

$$10, \; 12, \; 16, \; 17, \; 20, \; 21$$

$$\text{Median} = \frac{16 + 17}{2} = 16.5$$

3.   15, 20, 25, 25, 27, 28, 30, 32

$$i = \frac{20}{100}(8) = 1.6$$ 2nd position = 20

$$i = \frac{25}{100}(8) = 2$$ $\frac{20 + 25}{2} = 22.5$

$$i = \frac{65}{100}(8) = 5.2$$ 6th position = 28

$$i = \frac{75}{100}(8) = 6$$ $\frac{28 + 30}{2} = 29$

4. $0.05(36) = 1.8$ Remove 2 from each end. The trimmed mean uses the middle 32 data values.

5.   a. $\bar{x} = \frac{\sum x_i}{n} = 24.37$ or $24,370

   b.   Position 13; median = $24,000

   c. $24,000 (occurs 3 times)

   d. $i = 25/100 \,(25) = 6.25$

       Q_1 (7th position) = $22,500

   e. $i = 75/100 \,(25) = 18.75$

       Q_3 (19th position) = $26,200

6. a. $\sum x_i = 145 + 135 + \cdots + 180 = 2055$

$$\bar{x} = \frac{\sum x_i}{n} = \frac{2055}{12} = 171.25$$

Arranging the data in ascending order yields:

100   135   145   145   155   170   180   190   200   205   210   220

$$\text{Median} = \frac{170 + 180}{2} = 175$$

mode: 145

b.   For Q_1,

$$i = \left(\frac{25}{100}\right) 12 = 3$$

Since i is integer,

$$Q_1 = \frac{145 + 145}{2} = 145$$

For Q_3,

$$i = \left(\frac{75}{100}\right) 12 = 9$$

Since i is integer,

$$Q_3 = \frac{200 + 205}{2} = 202.5$$

7.   mean = 17.44

Data in ascending order

11   13   13   13   14   14   17   17   17   18   18   19   21   21   25   28

$$\text{Median} = \text{average of \#8 and \#9} = \frac{17 + 17}{2} = 17$$

The data are bimodal: 13 and 17 occur 3 times

90th percentile

$$i = \frac{90}{100}(16) = 14.4$$

$\therefore$ 90th percentile is in the 15th position; hence, the 90th percentile is 25.

8. a. $\sum x_i = 775$

$$\bar{x} = \frac{\sum x_i}{n} = \frac{775}{20} = 38.75$$

The modal age is 29; it appears 3 times.

b. The 5% trimmed mean is the mean of the middle 18 items.

$$5\% \text{ Trimmed Mean} = 38.61$$

The 10% trimmed mean is the mean of the middle 16 items

$$10\% \text{ Trimmed Mean} = 38.38$$

c. Median is average of 10th and 11th items.

$$\text{Median} = \frac{37 + 40}{2} = 38.5$$

Data suggest at - home workers are slightly younger.

d. For Q_1,

$$i = \left(\frac{25}{100}\right)20 = 5$$

Since i is integer,

$$Q_1 = \frac{29 + 30}{2} = 29.5$$

For Q_3,

$$i = \left(\frac{75}{100}\right)20 = 15$$

Since i is integer,

$$Q_3 = \frac{46 + 49}{2} = 47.5$$

e.

$$i = \left(\frac{32}{100}\right)20 = 6.4$$

Since i is not an integer, we round up to the 7th position.

$$32\text{nd percentile} = 31$$

9. a. $\bar{x} = \dfrac{\sum x_i}{n} = 6.53$

    Median (Positions 10 and 11) $= (6.4 + 6.5) / 2 = 6.45$

    b. $i = (25 / 100)\, 20 = 5$

    Q_1 (Positions 5 and 6) $= (6.0 + 6.2) / 2 = 6.1$

    $i = (75 / 100)\, 20 = 15$

    Q_3 (Positions 15 and 16) $= (7.0 + 7.0) / 2 = 7.0$

    c. For 30 minute program, $6.45 / 30 = .215$ or 21.5%.

    78.5% of time is spent on the program.

10. a.

$$\bar{x} = \frac{1068}{6} = 178$$

    b.

$$168 \quad 170 \quad 174 \quad 182 \quad 184 \quad 190$$

$$\text{Median} = \frac{174 + 182}{2} = 178$$

    c. Do not report a mode. Each data value occurs once.

    d. $i = \dfrac{75}{100}\, (6) = 4.5$

    Q_3 (5th Position) $= 184$

11.

$$\text{Mean} = \frac{1139}{12} = 94.92$$

$$80 \quad 82 \quad 88 \quad 89 \quad 90 \quad 91 \quad 94 \quad 95 \quad 102 \quad 105 \quad 108 \quad 115$$

$$\text{median} = \frac{91 + 94}{2} = 92.5$$

Do not report a mode. Each data value occurs once.

12. a. $\sum x_i = 435$

$$\bar{x} = \frac{\sum x_i}{n} = \frac{435}{9} = 48.33$$

Data in ascending order:

28 42 45 48 49 50 55 58 60

Median = 49

Do not report a mode; each data value occurs once.

The index could be considered good since both the mean and median are less than 50.

b.

$$i = \left(\frac{25}{100}\right)9 = 2.25$$

Q_1 (3rd position) = 45

$$i = \left(\frac{75}{100}\right)9 = 6.75$$

Q_3 (7th position) = 55

c.   The data in positions less than or equal to the median position are

28 42 45 48 49

The median of this data is the lower hinge.

Lower hinge = 45

The data in positions greater than or equal to the median position are

49 50 55 58 60

The median of this data is the upper hinge.

Upper hinge = 55

13.

$$\bar{x} = \frac{526}{20} = 26.3$$

15 16 18 19 20 21 22 22 24 24 26 26 27 27 30 31 33 33 34 58

Median = 25

Do not report a mode since five values appear twice.

For Q_1,

$$i = \left(\frac{25}{100}\right)20 = 5$$

$$Q_1 = \frac{20 + 21}{2} = 20.5$$

For Q_3,

$$i = \left(\frac{75}{100}\right)20 = 15$$

$$Q_3 = \frac{30 + 31}{2} = 30.5$$

14.   Using the mean we get

$$\bar{x}_{city} = 15.58, \quad \bar{x}_{country} = 18.92$$

For the samples we see that the mean mileage is better in the country than in the city.

City

13.2 14.4 15.2 15.3 15.3 15.3 15.9 16 16.1 16.2 16.2 16.7 16.8

↑

Median

Mode: 15.3

Country

17.2 17.4 18.3 18.5 18.6 18.6 18.7 19.0 19.2 19.4 19.4 20.6 21.1

↑

Median

Mode: 18.6, 19.4

The median and modal mileages are also better in the country than in the city.

15. a. Mean = 261/15 = 17.4

$$14\ 15\ 15\ 15\ 16\ 16\ 17\ 18\ 18\ 18\ 18\ 19\ 20\ 21\ 21$$
$$\uparrow$$
$$\text{Median}$$

Mode is 18 (occurs 4 times)

Interpretation: the average number of credit hours taken was 17.4. At least 50% of the students took 18 or more hours; at least 50% of the students took 18 or fewer hours. The most frequently occurring number of hour taken was 18.

b. For Q_1,

$$i = \left(\frac{25}{100}\right)15 = 3.75$$

Q_1 (4th position) = 15

For Q_3,

$$i = \left(\frac{75}{100}\right)15 = 11.25$$

Q_3 (12th position) = 19

c. The lower hinge is the median of the first 8 items; the upper hinge is the median of the last 8 items.

lower hinge = 15.5
upper hinge = 18.5

The hinges are near in value to the quartiles but are not exactly equal to Q_1 and Q_3.

d. For the 70th percentile,

$$i = \left(\frac{70}{100}\right)15 = 10.5$$

Rounding up we see the 70th percentile is in position 11.

70th percentile = 18

16. a. The sample mean is

$$\bar{x} = 210/16 = 13.13$$

$$4\ 5\ 6\ 8\ 9\ 10\ 12\ 14\ 15\ 15\ 15\ 16\ 17\ 18\ 20\ 26$$

$$\text{Median} = \frac{14 + 15}{2} = 14.5$$

Mode: 15

b. 10th percentile

$$i = \frac{10}{100}(16) = 1.6$$

∴ 2nd item or 5

80th percentile

$$i = \frac{80}{100}(16) = 12.8$$

∴ 13th item or 17

c. For Q_1,

$$i = \left(\frac{25}{100}\right)16 = 4$$

Q_1 = (4th and 5th positions) = $\frac{8+9}{2} = 8.5$

For Q_3,

$$i = \left(\frac{75}{100}\right)16 = 12$$

Q_3 = (12th and 13th positions) = $\frac{16+17}{2} = 16.5$

$$\text{Lower hinge} = \frac{8+9}{2} = 8.5$$
$$\text{Upper hinge} = \frac{16+17}{2} = 16.5$$

17. Range 20 - 10 = 10

10, 12, 16, 17, 20

$$i = \frac{25}{100}(5) = 1.25$$

Q_1 (2nd position) = 12

$$i = \frac{75}{100}(5) = 3.75$$

Q_3 (4th position) = 17

IQR = $Q_3 - Q_1$ = 17 - 12 = 5

18.

$$\bar{x} = \frac{\sum x_i}{n} = \frac{75}{5} = 15$$

$$s^2 = \frac{\sum (x_i - \bar{x})^2}{n - 1} = \frac{64}{4} = 16$$

$$s = \sqrt{16} = 4$$

19.   15, 20, 25, 25, 27, 28, 30, 34

Range = 34 - 15 = 19

$$i = \frac{25}{100}(8) = 2 \qquad\qquad Q_1 = \frac{20 + 25}{2} = 22.5$$

$$i = \frac{75}{100}(8) = 6 \qquad\qquad Q_1 = \frac{28 + 30}{2} = 29$$

IQR = $Q_3 - Q_1$ = 29 - 22.5 = 6.5

$$\bar{x} = \frac{\sum x_i}{n} = \frac{204}{8} = 25.5$$

$$s^2 = \frac{\sum (x_i - \bar{x})^2}{n - 1} = \frac{242}{7} = 34.57$$

$$s = \sqrt{34.57} = 5.88$$

20. a.   New: $\bar{x}$ = $16.05   Median $16.40

Used: $\bar{x}$ = $7.53   Median $7.35

   b.   New: Range = 24.7 - 9.8 = 14.9
              IQR   = 17.8 - 13.8 = 4.0
              s = 4.21

        Old: Range = 11.7 - 4.2 = 7.5
              IQR   = 9.9 - 4.75 = 5.15
              s = 2.80

   c.   Difference between means: 16.05 - 7.53 = 8.52

        Difference between medians: 16.40 - 7.35 = 9.05

        New cars are on average $8000 - $9000
        more expensive than used cars.

        There is a larger dispersion or variation in prices for the new cars.

21. Range = 587 - 52 = 535

$$\bar{x} = \frac{1211}{5} = 242.2$$

$$\sigma^2 = \frac{\sum (x_i - \bar{x})^2}{N} = \frac{165,778.8}{5} = 33,155.76$$

$$\sigma = \sqrt{33,155.76} = 182.09$$

22. a. Range = 60 - 28 = 32

  IQR = $Q_3 - Q_1$ = 55 - 45 = 10

  b.
  $$\bar{x} = \frac{435}{9} = 48.33$$

  $$\sum (x_i - \bar{x})^2 = 742$$

  $$s^2 = \frac{742}{8} = 92.75$$

  $$s = \sqrt{92.75} = 9.63$$

  c. The average air quality is about the same. But, the variability is greater in Anaheim.

23.
$$\bar{x} = \frac{2000}{5} = 400$$

x_i	$\bar{x}$	$x_i - \bar{x}$	$(x_i - \bar{x})^2$
410	400	10	100
420	400	20	400
390	400	-10	100
400	400	0	0
380	400	-20	400
2000			1000

$$s^2 = \frac{\sum (x_i - \bar{x})^2}{n - 1} = \frac{1000}{4} = 250$$

$$s = \sqrt{250} = 15.81$$

$$\sum x_i^2 = 801,000$$

$$s^2 = \frac{\sum x_i^2 - n\bar{x}^2}{n - 1} = \frac{801,000 - 5(400)^2}{4}$$

$$= \frac{1000}{4} = 250$$

$$s = \sqrt{250} = 15.81$$

The same answer is found either way.

24.   Dawson Supply: Range = 11 - 9 = 2

$$s = \sqrt{\frac{4.1}{9}} = 0.67$$

J.C. Clark: Range = 15 - 7 = 8

$$s = \sqrt{\frac{60.1}{9}} = 2.58$$

25. a.   Range = 190 - 168 = 22

b. $\sum (x_i - \bar{x})^2 = 376$

$$s^2 = \frac{376}{5} = 75.2$$

c. $s = \sqrt{75.2} = 8.67$

d.   Coef. of Var $= \left(\frac{8.67}{178}\right) 100 = 4.87$

26. a.
$$\bar{x} = \frac{\sum x_i}{n} = \$10.40$$

b.   13th item = $10.05

c.   Range = 15.35 - 5.85 = 9.5

d. Q_1: 0.25(25) = 6.25   Use 7th value = 8.45

Q_3: 0.75(25) = 18.75   Use 19th value = 12.05

IQR = 12.05 - 8.45 = 3.6

e. $s^2 = 6.75$

f. $s = 2.60$

27. $s^2 = 0.021$ Production should not be shut down since the variance is less than .005.

28.
Quarter milers
$s = .0564$
Coef. of Var. $= (s / \bar{x})\ 100 = (.0564 / .966)\ 100 = 5.8$

Milers
$s = .1295$
Coef. of Var. $= (s / \bar{x}) \, 100 = (.1295 / 4.534) \, 100 = 2.9$

Yes; the coefficient of variation shows that as a percentage of the mean the quarter milers' times show more variability.

29.

$$\bar{x} = \frac{\sum x_i}{n} = \frac{75}{5} = 15$$

$$s = \sqrt{\frac{\sum (x_i - \bar{x})^2}{n - 1}} = \sqrt{\frac{64}{4}} = 4$$

10 $\quad z = \dfrac{10 - 15}{4} = -1.25$

20 $\quad z = \dfrac{20 - 15}{4} = +1.25$

12 $\quad z = \dfrac{12 - 15}{4} = -0.75$

17 $\quad z = \dfrac{17 - 15}{4} = +.50$

16 $\quad z = \dfrac{16 - 15}{4} = +.25$

30.

$$z = \frac{520 - 500}{100} = +.20$$

$$z = \frac{650 - 500}{100} = +1.50$$

$$z = \frac{500 - 500}{100} = 0.00$$

$$z = \frac{450 - 500}{100} = -0.50$$

$$z = \frac{280 - 500}{100} = -2.20$$

31. a.

$$k = \frac{40 - 30}{5} = 2 \quad \left(1 - \frac{1}{2^2}\right) = 0.75 \quad \text{At least 75\%}$$

b.

$$k = \frac{45 - 30}{5} = 3 \quad \left(1 - \frac{1}{3^2}\right) = 0.89 \quad \text{At least 89\%}$$

c.

$$k = \frac{38 - 30}{5} = 1.6 \quad \left(1 - \frac{1}{1.6^2}\right) = 0.61 \quad \text{At least 61\%}$$

d.

$$k = \frac{42 - 30}{5} = 2.4 \quad \left(1 - \frac{1}{2.4^2}\right) = 0.83 \quad \text{At least 83\%}$$

e.

$$k = \frac{48 - 30}{5} = 3.6 \quad \left(1 - \frac{1}{3.6^2}\right) = 0.92 \quad \text{At least 92\%}$$

32. a. Approximately 95%

b. Almost all

c. Approximately 68%

33.

$$z = \frac{25,000 - 41,747}{12,200} = -1.37$$

$$z = \frac{125,000 - 41,747}{12,200} = 6.82$$

The first income is 1.37 standard deviations below the mean. The second income is 6.82 standard deviations above the mean. The income of $125,000 is an outlier size since it is more than three standard deviations from the mean.

34. a.

$$\bar{x} = \frac{775}{10} = 77.5 \quad s = 9.86$$

b.

$$z = \frac{110 - 77.5}{9.86} = 3.30$$

Yes, it should be considered on outlier since it is more than three standard deviations from the mean.

c.

$$z = \frac{87 - 77.5}{9.86} = 0.96$$

Since 87 corresponds to a z-score of approximately 1, we would estimate that (100% - 68%) / 2 = 16% of the winning teams will score 87 or more points.

$$z = \frac{58 - 77.5}{9.86} = -1.98$$

Since 87 corresponds to a z-score of approximately -2, we would estimate that (100% - 95%) / 2 = 2.5% of the winning scores will be 58 points or less.

35. a.

$$z = \frac{8100 - 28,085}{4500} = -4.44$$

This is an outlier since it is more than three standard deviations from the mean.

  b.

$$z = \frac{33,500 - 28,085}{4500} = 1.20 \quad \text{not an outlier}$$

$$z = \frac{25,200 - 28,085}{4500} = -0.64 \quad \text{not an outlier}$$

$$z = \frac{28,985 - 28,085}{4500} = .20 \quad \text{not an outlier}$$

$$z = \frac{39,000 - 28,085}{4500} = 2.43 \quad \text{not an outlier using the } \pm 3 \text{ rule}$$
$$\text{but perhaps worth reviewing.}$$

36. a.   28,085 - 2(4500) = 19,085 $k = 2$

$$\left(1 - \frac{1}{2^2}\right) = .75$$

At least 75% of salaries must be in this interval.

  b.   28,085 - 3(4500) = 14,585 $k = 3$

$$\left(1 - \frac{1}{3^2}\right) = .89$$

At least 89% of salaries must fall within this interval.

  c. $19,085 to $37,085 contains approximately 95% of the salaries

$14,585 to $41,585 contains almost all the salaries.

37. a. Approximately 68% of scores are within 1 standard deviation from the mean.

    b. Approximately 95% of scores are within 2 standard deviations from the mean.

    c. Approximately (100% - 95%) / 2 = 2.5% of scores are over 130.

    d. Yes, almost all IQ scores are less than 145.

38. a. 20.5 to 34.5

    $$k = \frac{34.5 - 27.5}{3.5} = 2$$

    $$\left(1 - \frac{1}{2^2}\right) = .75, \text{ at least } 75\%$$

    18.75 - 36.25

    $$k = \frac{36.25 - 27.5}{3.5} = \frac{8.75}{3.5} = 2.5$$

    $$\left(1 - \frac{1}{2.5^2}\right) = .84, \text{ at least } 84\%$$

    17 to 38

    $$k = \frac{38 - 27.5}{3.5} = 3$$

    $$\left(1 - \frac{1}{3^2}\right) = .89, \text{ at least } 89\%$$

    b. 20.5 to 34.5 2 standard deviations
       Approximately 95%

       17 to 38 3 standard deviations
       Almost all.

39. a.

    $$\bar{x} = \frac{\sum x_i}{n} = 88.85 \quad \text{median} = (\text{positions 10 and 11}) = 91$$

    b. Q_1 (Positions 5 and 6) = 87

       Q_3 (Positions 15 and 16) = (93 + 94) / 2 = 93.5

    c. $s = 8.46$

d.

$$z = \frac{76 - 88.85}{8.46} = -1.52$$

$$z = \frac{62 - 88.85}{8.46} = -3.17$$

These two lowest rated ships are 1.52 and 3.17 standard deviations below the mean.

e. Pegasus, with $z = -3.17$, is an outlier.

40. 15, 20, 25, 25, 27, 28, 30, 34

Low = 15

$i = \frac{25}{100}(8) = 2$ $Q_1 = \frac{20 + 25}{2} = 22.5$

Median = $\frac{25 + 27}{2} = 26$

$i = \frac{75}{100}(8) = 6$ $Q_3 = \frac{28 + 30}{2} = 29$

High = 34

41.

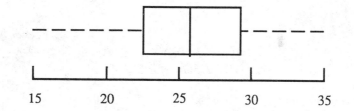

42. 5, 6, 8, 10, 10, 12, 15, 16, 18

Low = 5

$i = \frac{25}{100}(9) = 2.25$ $Q_1 = 8$ (3rd position)

Median = 10

$i = \frac{75}{100}(9) = 6.75$ $\left(Q_3 = 15\right)$ (7th position)

High = 18

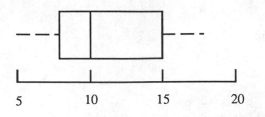

$$5 \quad\quad 10 \quad\quad 15 \quad\quad 20$$

43.   IQR = 50 - 42 = 8

   Inner Fences: Q_1 - 1.5 IQR = 42 - 12 = 30
                   Q_3 + 1.5 IQR = 50 + 12 = 62

   Outer Fences: Q_1 - 3 IQR = 42 - 24 = 18
                   Q_3 + 3 IQR = 50 + 24 = 74

   68 is a mild outlier

44. a. Five Number Summary

   1.9   10.0   14.5   20.4   55.9

   b. Inner Fences

   10.0 - 1.5(10.4) = -5.6
   20.4 + 1.5(10.4) = 36.0

   Outer Fences

   10.0 - 3(10.4) = -21.2
   20.4 + 3(10.4) = 51.6

   c. 46.1 and 49.9 are mild outliers

   55.9 is an extreme outlier

   The outliers identify corporations that are showing unusually high growth in sales.

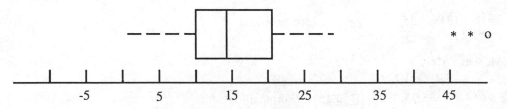

$$-5 \quad\quad 5 \quad\quad 15 \quad\quad 25 \quad\quad 35 \quad\quad 45$$

45. a. Five Number Summary

   484   1061   2472   4514   32,249

b.   Inner Fences

$$1061 - 1.5(3453) = -4118.5$$
$$4514 + 15(3453) = 9693.5$$

Outer Fences

$$1061 - 3(3453) = -9298$$
$$4514 + 3(3453) = 14,873$$

c.   Yes. Dow Chemical and Du Pont are extreme outliers.

d.

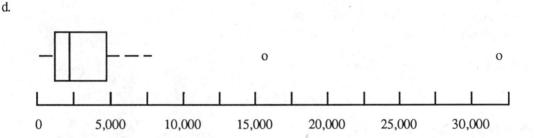

46. a.

$$\bar{x} = \frac{\sum x_i}{n} = 79.31; \quad \text{median (Positions 8 and 9)} = \frac{78 + 79}{2} = 78.5$$

b.

$$Q_1 = (\text{positions 4 and 5}) = \frac{76 + 77}{2} = 76.5$$

$$Q_3 = (\text{positions 12 and 13}) = \frac{80 + 81}{2} = 80.5$$

c.   72, 76.5, 78.5, 80.5, 90

d.   The camcorders had the higher rating with mean 82.56 compared to 79.31 for VCRs and median 82 compares to 78.5 for VCRs. The camcorders showed slightly more variation or dispersion among the models tested with $s = 6.39$ compared to $s = 5.12$ for VCRs. The box plots are as follows.

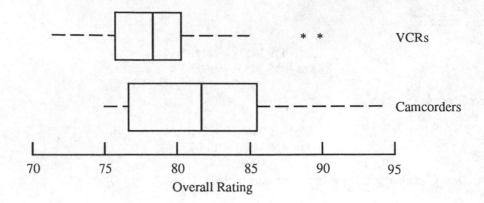

Overall Rating

e. Inner Fence = 80.5 + 1.5 (80.5 - 76.5) = 86.5.
   Yes; Hitachi 89 and Mitsubishi 90 are mild outliers.

47. a. Five Number Summary (Midsize)

   51   71.5   81.5   96.5   128

   Five Number Summary (Small)

   73   101   108.5   121   140

   b. Box Plots

   Midsize

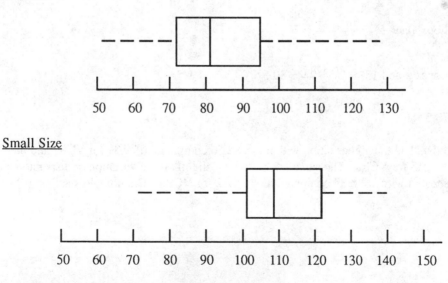

   Small Size

   c. The midsize cars appear to be safer than the small cars.

48. a.

$$\bar{x} = \frac{\sum x_i}{n} = 9.32 \quad \text{Median (Positions 12 and 13)} = \frac{9.6 + 10.0}{2} = 9.8$$

b. Q_1 (Positions 6 and 7) = $(6.3 + 6.7)/2$ = 6.5

Q_3 (Positions 18 and 19) = $(13.9 + 15.3)/2$ = 14.6

c. Inner Fences: IQR = 14.6 - 6.5 = 8.1

Q_1 - 1.5IQR = 6.5 - 1.5(8.1) = -5.65
Q_3 + 1.5IQR = 14.6 + 1.5(8.1) = 26.75

Outer Fences

Q_1 - 3IQR = 6.5 - 3(8.1) = -17.8
Q_3 + 3IQR = 14.6 + 3(8.1) = 38.9

Mild Outliers:

Austria	-13.4	USA	27.2
Finland	-16.7	Australia	29.1
Norway	-15.4		
Portugal	- 7.2		

Extreme Outlier: Hong Kong 42.8

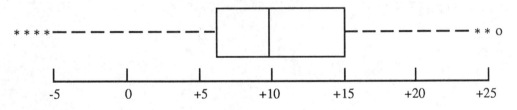

d. 22/24 = 0.9166 Say 91st Any percentile 88 to 91 is acceptable.

49.

f_i	M_i	$f_i M_i$
4	5	20
7	10	70
9	15	135
5	20	100
25		325

$$\bar{x} = \frac{\sum f_i M_i}{n} = \frac{325}{25} = 13$$

50.

f_i	M_i	$M_i - \bar{x}$	$(M_i - \bar{x})^2$	$f_i(M_i - \bar{x})^2$
4	5	-8	64	256
7	10	-3	9	63
9	15	+2	4	36
5	20	+7	49	245
				600

$$s^2 = \frac{\Sigma f_i (M_i - \bar{x})^2}{n - 1} = \frac{600}{24} = 25$$
$$s = \sqrt{25} = 5$$

51.

No. of Present.	f_i	M_i	$f_i M_i$	$M_i - \bar{x}$	$(M_i - \bar{x})^2$	$f_i(M_i - \bar{x})^2$
10 - 12	5	11	55	-6.482143	42.018178	210.09089
13 - 15	9	14	126	-3.482143	12.125320	109.12788
16 - 18	22	17	374	-0.482143	0.232462	5.114164
19 - 21	12	20	240	2.517857	6.339604	76.075248
22 - 24	8	23	184	5.517857	30.446746	243.57397
	56		979			643.98215

a.

$$\bar{x} = \frac{979}{56} = 17.482143$$

b.

$$s^2 = \frac{643.98}{55} = 11.71$$

$$s = 3.41$$

52.

f_i	M_i	$f_i M_i$	$M_i - \bar{x}$	$(M_i - \bar{x})^2$	$f_i(M_i - \bar{x})^2$
3	44.5	133.5	-29.516	871.194	2613.583
5	54.5	272.5	-19.516	380.874	1904.371
11	64.5	709.5	-9.516	90.554	996.097
22	74.5	1,639.0	0.484	0.234	5.154
15	84.5	1,267.5	10.484	109.914	1648.714
6	94.5	567.0	20.484	419.594	2517.566
62		4,589.0			9685.485

$$\bar{x} = \frac{4589}{62} = 74.02$$
$$s^2 = \frac{9685.485}{61} = 158.78$$
$$s = 12.60$$

53.

f_i	M_i	$f_i M_i$	$M_i - \bar{x}$	$(M_i - \bar{x})^2$	$f_i (M_i - \bar{x})^2$
364	8.5	3,094.0	-25.8547	668.4655	243,321.45
1249	14.5	18,110.5	-19.8547	394.2091	492,367.18
3392	23.5	79,712.0	-10.8547	117.8245	399,660.75
3962	44.5	176,309.0	10.1453	102.9271	407,797.22
865	70.0	60,550.0	35.6453	1270.5874	1,099,058.10
9832		337,755.5			2,642,204.70

a.

$$\bar{x} = \frac{337,775.5}{9832} = 34.4 \text{ years}$$

b.

$$s^2 = \frac{2,642,204.70}{9831} = 268.76$$

$$s = 16.39$$

54.

f_i	M_i	$f_i M_i$	$M_i - \bar{x}$	$(M_i - \bar{x})^2$	$f_i (M_i - \bar{x})^2$
74	2	148	-8.742647	76.433877	5,656.1069
192	7	1,344	-3.742647	14.007407	2,689.4221
280	12	3,360	1.257353	1.580937	442.6622
105	17	1,785	6.257353	39.154467	4,111.2190
23	22	506	11.257353	126.728000	2,914.7439
6	27	162	16.257353	264.301530	1,585.8092
680		7,305			17,399.9630

$$\bar{x} = \frac{7305}{680} = 10.74$$

$$s^2 = \frac{17,399.9630}{679} = 25.63$$

$$s = 5.06$$

Estimate of total gallons sold: $(10.74)(120) = 1288.8$

55.

f_i	M_i	$f_i M_i$	$M_i - \overline{x}$	$(M_i - \overline{x})^2$	$f_i(M_i - \overline{x})^2$
3	29.5	88.5	-35.2	1239.04	3717.12
1	39.5	39.5	-25.2	635.04	635.04
2	49.5	99.0	-15.2	231.04	462.08
6	59.5	357.0	-5.2	27.04	162.24
4	69.5	278.0	4.8	23.04	92.16
6	79.5	477.0	14.8	219.04	1314.24
2	89.5	179.0	24.8	615.04	1230.08
1	99.5	99.5	34.8	1211.04	1211.04
25		1,617.50			8824.00

a.

$$\overline{x} = \frac{1,617.50}{25} = 64.7$$

b.

$$s^2 = \frac{8824}{24} = 367.67$$

c. $s = 19.17$

56. a. $\overline{x} = \frac{\sum x_i}{n} = 3.19$

Median (13th position) = 3.30

Mode 3.70 (4 times)

b. Q_1 (7th position) = 2.90

Q_3 (19th position) = 3.50

c. Range = 4.60 - 1.80 = 2.80

IQR = $Q_3 - Q_1$ = 3.50 - 2.90 = .60

d. s^2 = .30 s = .54

e. z-scores 4.60 $z = (4.60 - 3.19) / .54 = 2.61$

1.80 $z = (1.80 - 3.19) / .54 = -2.57$

Inner Fences: $Q_3 + 1.5$ IQR = 3.50 + 1.5 (.60) = 4.40

$Q_1 - 1.5$ IQR = 2.90 - 1.5 (.60) = 2.00

Both 1.8 and 4.60 are mild outliers.

57.

	x_i	$x_i - \bar{x}$	$(x_i - \bar{x})^2$
	12.5	0.10	0.01
	13.2	0.80	0.64
	11.2	-1.20	1.44
	13.0	0.60	0.36
	12.0	-0.40	0.16
	12.5	0.10	0.01
Totals	74.4		2.62

a.

$$\bar{x} = \frac{74.4}{6} = 12.4$$

b.
$$11.2 \quad 12.0 \quad 12.5 \quad 12.5 \quad 13.0 \quad 13.2$$

$$\text{Median} = 12.5$$

c.   Mode = 12.5

d.

$$i = \left(\frac{25}{100}\right)6 = 1.5 \qquad Q_1 \text{ (Position 2)} = 12.0$$

e.   Range = 13.2 - 11.2 = 2

f.

$$i = \left(\frac{75}{100}\right)6 = 4.5 \qquad Q_3 \text{ (Position 5)} = 13.0$$

$$IQR = Q_3 - Q_1 = 13 - 12 = 1$$

g.

$$s^2 = \frac{2.62}{5} = 0.52$$

h.

$$s = \sqrt{0.52} = 0.72$$

i.

$$\text{Coef. of Var.} = \left(\frac{0.72}{12.4}\right)100 = 5.8$$

58.

x_i	$x_i - \bar{x}$	$(x_i - \bar{x})^2$
1100	71.8182	5157.8539
970	-58.1818	3385.1219
1000	-28.1818	794.2139
1250	221.8182	49,203.3140
880	-148.1818	21,957.8460
790	-238.1818	56,730.5700
1300	271.8182	73,885.1340
1050	21.8182	476.0339
900	-128.1818	16,430.5740
950	-78.1818	6,112.3939
1120	91.8182	8,430.5819
11,310		242,563.64

a.

$$\bar{x} = \frac{11,310}{11} = 1028.18$$

Data in ascending order

790 880 900 950 970 1000 1050 1100 1120 1250 1300

Median = 1000

Do not report mode. No value appears more than once.

b. Range = 1300 - 790 = 510

$$i = \left(\frac{25}{100}\right) 11 = 2.75 \quad Q_1 \text{ (Position 3)} = 900$$

$$i = \left(\frac{75}{100}\right) 11 = 8.75 \quad Q_3 \text{ (Position 9)} = 1120$$

IQR = $Q_3 - Q_1$ = 1120 - 900 = 220

c.

$$s^2 = \frac{242,563.64}{10} = 24,256.36$$

$$s = 155.74$$

d. z-score for largest value

$$z = \frac{1300 - 1028.18}{155.74} = 1.75$$

Since this is not an outlier, none of the values greater than the mean are outliers.

z-score for smallest value

$$z = \frac{790 - 1028.18}{155.74} = -1.53$$

Since this is not an outlier, none of the values less than the mean are outliers.

59.   First arrange the data in ascending order.

12.5	13,0	20.0	20.2	23.8
25.2	25.4	25.9	27.5	28.4
30.5	30.5	30.9	31.0	33.0
33.5	33.5	34.0	36.2	37.5
38.1	38.5	39.0	40.5	42.5
43.2	44.8	45.5	51.6	52.0

a.

$$\bar{x} = \frac{988.2}{30} = 32.94$$

$$\text{Median} = \frac{33.0 + 33.5}{2} = 33.25$$

The data set is bimodal: 30.5 and 33.5.

b.

$$i = \left(\frac{25}{100}\right) 30 = 7.5 \quad Q_1 \text{ (Position 8)} = 25.9$$

$$i = \left(\frac{75}{100}\right) 30 = 22.5 \quad Q_3 \text{ (Position 23)} = 39.0$$

60.   Data in ascending order:

$$3 \quad 8 \quad 9 \quad 10 \quad 12 \quad 13 \quad 18 \quad 18 \quad 20$$

a.

$$\bar{x} = \frac{111}{9} = 12.33$$

b. Median (Position 5) = 12

c. Mode = 18

d. $i = \left(\frac{40}{100}\right) 9 = 3.6$ (Position 4)

    40th percentile = 10

e. Range = 20 - 3 = 17

    f. $s^2 = 30.75$

    g. $s = 5.55$

61.   Data in ascending order

$$3 \quad 4 \quad 4 \quad 4 \quad 6 \quad 6 \quad 7 \quad 7 \quad 9 \quad 11$$

$$\bar{x} = \frac{61}{10} = 6.1$$

Median = 6

Mode = 4

Range = 11 - 3 = 8

$s^2 = 6.32$

$s = 2.51$

62.   Use the empirical rule.

    a.   Approximately 68% will be within one standard deviation from the mean.

    b.   Approximatley 95%

    c.

$$z = \frac{225 - 102}{27} = 4.56$$

It should be considered an outlier.

63. a.   The z-score for a home selling for $200,000 is

$$z = \frac{200,000 - 100,000}{40,000} = 2.5$$

Do not consider it an outlier.

    b.   This is an interval from 1.5 standard deviations below the mean to 1.5 standard deviations above the mean.

At least $1 - \dfrac{1}{(1.5)^2}$ of the items must lie in this interval.

$$1 - \frac{1}{(1.5)^2} = 0.56$$

We can say that at least 56% of the homes must sell for between $40,000 and $160,000.

64. a.

Public Transportation: $\bar{x} = \dfrac{320}{10} = 32$

Automobile: $\bar{x} = \dfrac{320}{10} = 32$

b.

Public Transportation: $s = 4.64$

Automobile: $s = 1.83$

c. Prefer the automobile. The mean times are the same, but the auto has less variability.

d. Data in ascending order:

Public: 25 28 29 29 32 32 33 34 37 41

Auto: 29 30 31 31 32 32 33 33 34 35

Five number Summaries

Public: 25 29 32 34 41

Auto: 29 31 32 33 35

Box Plots:

Public:

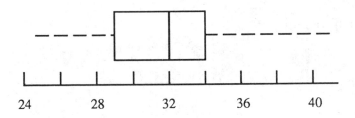

Auto:

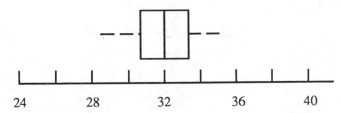

The box plots do show lower variability with automobile transportation and support the conclusion in part c.

65.   Data in ascending order:

$$\begin{array}{cccccccccc}
42 & 44 & 53 & 56 & 58 & 61 & 62 & 62 & 75 & 76 \\
77 & 78 & 79 & 82 & 84 & 84 & 85 & 88 & 89 & 89 \\
93 & 95 & 96 & 97 & 98 & & & & &
\end{array}$$

a.   Five Number Summary

42   62   79   89   98

b.   Box Plot

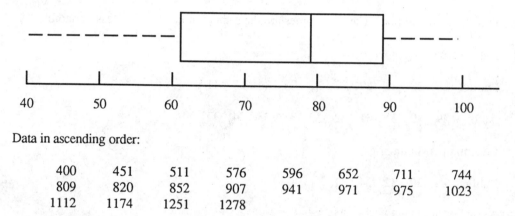

66.   Data in ascending order:

$$\begin{array}{cccccccc}
400 & 451 & 511 & 576 & 596 & 652 & 711 & 744 \\
809 & 820 & 852 & 907 & 941 & 971 & 975 & 1023 \\
1112 & 1174 & 1251 & 1278 & & & &
\end{array}$$

$i = (25 / 100)\ 20 = 5$

$i = (75 / 100)\ 20 = 15$

$i = (50 / 100)\ 20 = 10$

$$Q_1 = \frac{596 + 652}{2} = 624$$

$$Q_3 = \frac{975 + 1023}{2} = 999$$

$$Median = \frac{820 + 852}{2} = 836$$

a.   Five Number Summary

400   624   836   999   1278

b.

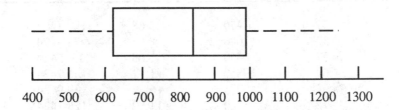

c. There are no values outside the inner fences. Thus no outliers are identified.

Lower inner fence = 624 - 1.5(999 - 624) = 61.5

Upper inner fence = 999 + 1.5(999 - 624) = 1561.5

67.

f_i	M_i	$f_i M_i$	$M_i - \bar{x}$	$(M_i - \bar{x})^2$	$f_i (M_i - \bar{x})^2$
4	5.5	22.0	-6.8	46.24	184.96
5	9.5	47.5	-2.8	7.84	39.20
7	13.5	94.5	1.2	1.44	10.08
2	17.5	35.0	5.2	27.04	54.08
1	21.5	21.5	9.2	84.64	84.64
1	25.5	25.5	13.2	174.24	174.24
20		246.0			547.20

$$\bar{x} = \frac{246}{20} = 12.3$$
$$s^2 = \frac{547.20}{19} = 28.8$$
$$s = 5.37$$

68.

f_i	M_i	$f_i M_i$	$M_i - \bar{x}$	$(M_i - \bar{x})^2$	$f_i (M_i - \bar{x})^2$
2	29.5	59.0	-22	484	968
6	39.5	237.0	-12	144	864
4	49.5	198.0	-2	4	16
4	59.5	238.0	8	64	256
2	69.5	139.0	18	324	648
2	79.5	159.0	28	784	1568
20		1,030.0			4320

$$\bar{x} = \frac{1030}{20} = 51.5$$
$$s^2 = \frac{4320}{19} = 227.37$$
$$s = 15.08$$

69.

f_i	M_i	$f_i M_i$	$M_i - \bar{x}$	$(M_i - \bar{x})^2$	$f_i (M_i - \bar{x})^2$
10	47	470	-13.68	187.1424	1871.42
40	52	2080	-8.68	75.3424	3013.70
150	57	8550	-3.68	13..5424	2031.36
175	62	10850	+1.32	1.7424	304.92
75	67	5025	+6.32	39.9424	2995.68
15	72	1080	+11.32	128.1424	1922.14
10	77	770	+16.32	266.3424	2663.42
475		28,825			14,802.64

a.

$$\bar{x} = \frac{28,825}{475} = 60.68$$

b.

$$s^2 = \frac{14,802.64}{474} = 31.23$$

$$s = \sqrt{31.23} = 5.59$$

Duke: $\bar{x} = 87.97$ Median $= \frac{88 + 89}{2} = 88.5$

70. a.   Opponent: $\bar{x} = 72.64$ Median $= \frac{71 + 72}{2} = 71.5$

b. Duke: Range $= 118 - 68 = 50$

   IQR $= Q_3 - Q_1 = 97 - 75.5 = 21.5$

   Opponent: Range $= 103 - 51 = 52$

   IQR $= Q_3 - Q_1 = 79.5 - 64 = 15.5$

c.

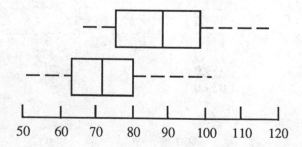

3 - 32

d. Duke had a high scoring team with mean and median scores about 88 points per game. Duke's third quartile was 97. Seven times (22%) Duke scored 100 or more points per game. The opponent's mean 72.64 and median 71.50 show that Duke outscored its opponents by an average of 15 to 16 points per game. Only once did an opponent score over 100 points in a game. The opponent's first quartile was 64 points. There were no outliers in either Duke's or it opponents scores. The lowest points Duke allowed in a game was 51 points by Michigan which occurred in the NCAA championship game.

Solution to Computer Case 1

The descriptive statistics provided by the Minitab command DESCRIBE are as follows:

	N	MEAN	MEDIAN	TRMEAN	STDEV	SEMEAN
CASH	38	8.840	7.405	8.676	5.280	0.856
CHECK	40	42.73	41.34	42.73	15.62	2.47
CREDIT	22	40.88	45.33	40.75	14.87	3.17

	MIN	MAX	Q1	Q3
CASH	1.090	20.480	4.648	13.387
CHECK	2.67	78.16	32.47	54.35
CREDIT	14.44	69.77	26.83	52.80

Using the sample means, we see that personal check has the largest mean amount of $42.73 per customer. This is followed rather closely by the credit card which had a mean of $40.88. The payment by cash is reserved for the smaller dollar purchase amounts with the mean of $8.84. The noncash payment methods (personal check or credit card) have a sample mean purchase amounts that are four to five times larger than the cash payment.

The sample median shows credit card as the largest at $45.33. This is followed by the sample medians of $41.34 for personal check and $7.41 for cash.

The range and standard deviations for the three methods of payment are as follows:

Method of Payment	Range	Standard Deviation
CASH	19.39	5.28
PERSONAL CHECK	75.49	15.62
CREDIT CARD	55.33	14.87

These measures of dispersion show that cash has the least variation among payments amounts. Personal check has slightly more variation than credit card.

The five-number summaries are as follows:

Method of Payment	Min	Q1	Median	Q3	Max
CASH	1.09	4.65	7.41	13.39	20.48
PERSONAL CHECK	2.67	32.47	41.34	54.35	78.16
CREDIT CARD	14.44	26.83	45.33	52.80	69.77

The students may choose to make a variety of comments about the five-number summary. Cash is certainly used for the smallest purchase amount of $1.09, while credit card was not used for purchase amounts of $14.00 or less. The highest cash payment was $20.48 while over 75% of the personal check and credit card purchases were greater than this amount.

50% of the cash payments were between $4.65 and $13.39. The middle 50% for personal check were between $32.47 and $54.35 while the middle 50% for credit card were between $26.83 and $52.80. These observations point to the personal check as the method of payment for the largest purchases. The largest data value of $78.16 was paid for by personal check. The box plots show the distribution of data for each method of payment.

The fact that 22% of the purchases were by the new credit card method and the fact that credit card purchase amounts appear to be similiar to personal check amounts are positive indicators that the new credit card method of payment is beneficial.

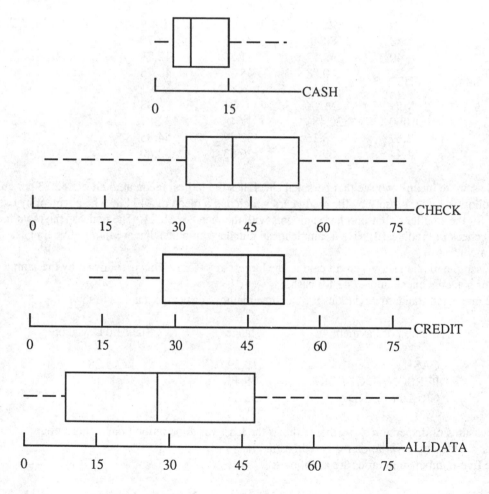

Solution to Computer Case 2

Descriptive Statistics are as follows:

	N	MEAN	MEDIAN	TRMEAN	STDEV	SEMEAN
WORK	50	79.80	82.00	79.98	8.29	1.17
PAY	50	54.46	55.50	54.18	14.75	2.09
PROMOTE	50	58.48	58.50	58.80	16.00	2.26

	MIN	MAX	Q1	Q3
WORK	63.00	95.00	72.00	87.00
PAY	25.00	90.00	44.50	60.50
PROMOTE	16.00	92.00	50.50	68.00

Overall, the nurses show the highest level of satisfaction with their work (mean = 79.80 and median = 82). The stem - and - leaf display shows 40 of the 50 nurses rated work satisfaction in the 70 to 90 range. Six nurses rate work satisfaction 90 or better. Satisfaction with pay (mean = 54.46 and median = 55.50) was the lowest rated followed closely by promotion (mean = 58.48 and median = 58.50). Improvements in the areas of pay and promotion may be worth further consideration.

Measures of dispersion show the following:

Variable	Range	IQR	Standard Deviation
Work	32	15	8.29
Pay	65	16	14.75
Promotion	76	17.5	16.00

The largest dispersion is associated with promotion indicating that this variable has the largest differences among the nurses. Some nurses are apparently very satisfied with the promotion opportunities with 11 nurses rating promotion 90 or better. On the other hand, 5 nurses rated promotion less than 40 including one very dissatisfied nurse who rated promotion 16. The least dispersion existed for the work satisfaction variable, indicating a more consistent opinion among nurses that being satisfied with their work is not the major problem or concern.

Descriptive statistics can be broken down by type of hospital using the HELATH-2 data set. Many comments and observations are possible. Focusing on the mean for the variables, we note the following:

1. Nurses at all three types of hospitals show very similar and high levels of satisfaction with their work (means of 79.32, 80.41, and 79.71 respectively).

2. There is some disagreement among the nurses at the three types of hospitals as to their satisfaction with their pay. In fact, pay at university hospitals ranked the highest with university hospital nurses showing a mean satisfaction of 61.71. The lowest rated variable in the study is the pay of nurses in the private sector. The mean rating of 48.95 indicates a good deal of dissatisfaction.

3. There is also some disagreement among the nurses at the three types of hospitals as to their satisfaction with promotion opportunities. Promotion was rated best at private hospitals (mean = 62.42), followed by VA hospitals (mean = 58.94). Promotion was the major area of concern of nurses in university hospitals (mean = 52.57).

Nurses in private and VA hospitals are least satisfied with their level of pay, while nurses in university hospitals are least satisfied with promotion. This suggests some improvements in levels of satisfaction of the nurses could be made by studying the differences in operations and policies at the three types of hospitals. Specifically, university hospitals may want to consider the promotion policies in place at private and VA hospitals. In addition, bringing pay levels in private and VA hospitals in line with the university hospitals may improve the satisfaction scores reported by the nurses.

The box plots of the data show no outliers in the work satisfaction scores. However, the pay satisfaction scores show two mild outliers associated with the high ratings of 89 and 90. Both of these nurses were in university hospitals. These outliers support the previously noted higher satisfaction with pay and lower satisfaction with promotion for nurses in university hospitals.

Chapter 4
Introduction to Probability

Learning Objectives

1. Obtain an appreciation of the role probability information plays in the decision making process.

2. Understand probability as a numerical measure of the likelihood of occurrence.

3. Know the three methods commonly used for assigning probabilities and understand when they should be used.

4. Know how to use the laws that are available for computing the probabilities of events.

5. Understand how new information can be used to revise initial (prior) probability estimates using Bayes' theorem.

6. Know the definition of the following terms:

experiment	addition law
sample space	mutually exclusive
event	conditional probability
complement	independent events
Venn Diagram	multiplication law
union of events	prior probability
intersection of events	posterior probability
	Bayes' Theorem

Solutions:

1.   Number of experimental Outcomes = (3) (2) (4) = 24

2. $\binom{6}{3} = \dfrac{6!}{3!\ 3!} = \dfrac{6 \cdot 5 \cdot 4 \cdot 3 \cdot 2 \cdot 1}{(3 \cdot 2 \cdot 1)(3 \cdot 2 \cdot 1)} = 20$

ABC	ACE	BCD	BEF
ABD	ACF	BCE	CDE
ABE	ADE	BCF	CDF
ABF	ADF	BDE	CEF
ACD	AEF	BDF	DEF

3. a. Let: p = purchase
              np = no purchase

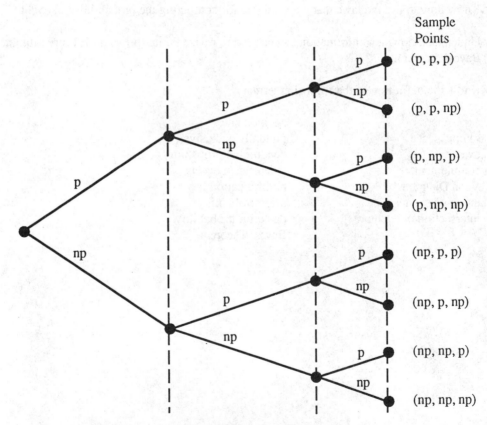

Sample Points
(p, p, p)
(p, p, np)
(p, np, p)
(p, np, np)
(np, p, p)
(np, p, np)
(np, np, p)
(np, np, np)

   b. This is a 3-step experiment with eight sample points.

   c. There are 16 sample points with 4 sales calls.

4. a. There are 3 x 3 = 9 outcomes for this 2-step experiment.

   b. Let: BA = below average
           A = average
           AA = above average

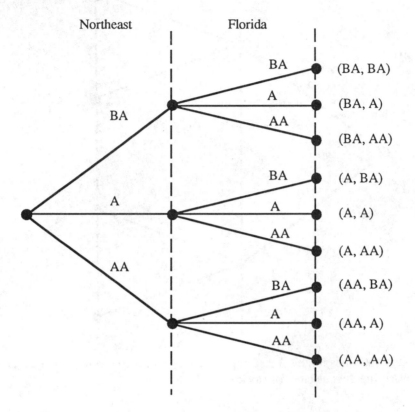

5. a. There are four outcomes possible for this 2-step experiment; planning commission positive - council approves; planning commission positive - council disproves; planning commission negative - council approves; planning commission negative - council disapproves.

b. Let   p = positive, n = negative, a = approves, and d = disapproves

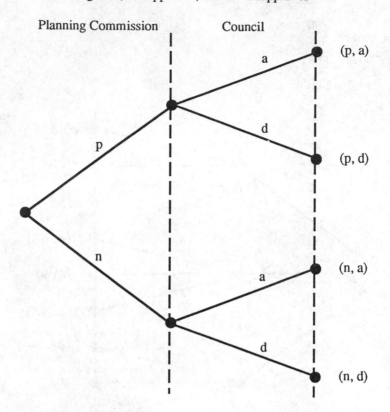

6. a. There are nine outcomes for this 2-step experiment. Step 1 is observing the outcome for stock A; Step 2 is observing the outcome for stock B.

b.

I = increase, U = unchanged, D = decrease

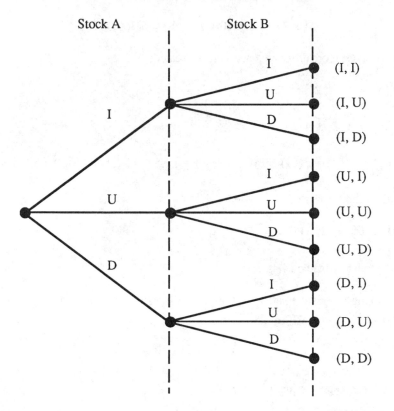

c.   Five outcomes result in an increase for at least one of the stocks: (I, I), (I, U), (I, D), (U, I), (D, I).

d.   One outcome shows an increase in value for both stocks: (I, I).

7. $\binom{6}{2} = \dfrac{6!}{2!\,4!} = \dfrac{6 \cdot 5 \cdot 4 \cdot 3 \cdot 2 \cdot 1}{(2 \cdot 1)(4 \cdot 3 \cdot 2 \cdot 1)} = 15$

8. $\binom{52}{5} = \dfrac{52!}{5!\,47!} = \dfrac{52 \cdot 51 \cdot 50 \cdot 49 \cdot 48}{5 \cdot 4 \cdot 3 \cdot 2 \cdot 1} = 2{,}598{,}960$

9. $\binom{50}{4} = \dfrac{50!}{4!\,46!} = \dfrac{50 \cdot 49 \cdot 48 \cdot 47}{4 \cdot 3 \cdot 2 \cdot 1} = 230{,}300$

10. $\binom{7}{3} = \dfrac{7!}{3!\,4!} = \dfrac{7 \cdot 6 \cdot 5}{3 \cdot 2 \cdot 1} = 35$

11. $\binom{8}{2} = \dfrac{8!}{2!\,6!} = \dfrac{8 \cdot 7}{2 \cdot 1} = 28$

12. a.   This can be thought of as a 6-step experiment with 10 outcomes on each trial.

$$10 \times 10 \times 10 \times 10 \times 10 \times 10 = 1{,}000{,}000$$

b. The number of outcomes on two of the trials increases to 24.

$$24 \times 24 \times 10 \times 10 \times 10 \times 10 = 5,760,000$$

c. More letters because more different plates can be created.

13. $P(E_i) = 1/5$ for $i = 1, 2, 3, 4, 5$

$P(E_i) \geq 0$ for $i = 1, 2, 3, 4, 5$

$P(E_1) + P(E_2) + P(E_3) + P(E_4) + P(E_5) = 1/5 + 1/5 + 1/5 + 1/5 + 1/5 = 1$

The classical method was used.

14. $P(E_1) = .40$, $P(E_2) = .26$, $P(E_3) = .34$

The relative frequency method was used.

15. No. Requirement (4.3) is not satisfied; the probabilities do not sum to 1. $P(E_1) + P(E_2) + P(E_3) + P(E_4) = .10 + .15 + .40 + .20 = .85$

16. a. 52; one for each card.

b. Classical; each outcome is equally likely.

c. 1 / 52 for each sample point or card selected.

d. $0 \leq P(E_i) \leq 1$ since $P(E_i) = 1/52$ for each sample point.

$$\Sigma P\ (E_i)\ =\ 1/52 + 1/52 + \cdots + 1/52\ =\ 1$$

52 terms

17. $P \text{ (never married)} = \dfrac{1106}{2038}$

$P \text{ (married)} = \dfrac{826}{2038}$

$P \text{ (other)} = \dfrac{106}{2038}$

Note that the sum of the probabilities equals 1.

18. a. Six, one for each possible number of refrigerators sold: 0, 1, 2, 3, 4, 5.

b. Relative frequency based on the historical data.

c.

E_1 = 0 sales	$P(E_1) =$	6/50 =	.12
E_2 = 1 sale	$P(E_2) =$	12/50 =	.24
E_3 = 2 sales	$P(E_3) =$	15/50 =	.30
E_4 = 3 sales	$P(E_4) =$	10/50 =	.20
E_5 = 4 sales	$P(E_5) =$	5/50 =	.10
E_6 = 5 sales	$P(E_6) =$	2/50 =	.04
			1.00

The probabilities are all greater than or equal to zero and they sum to one so the two basic requirements are satisfied.

19. a. No, the probabilities do not sum to one. They sum to .85.

b. Owner must revise the probabilities so they sum to 1.00.

20. No, the probabilities do not sum to 1, they sum to 1.10.

21. No. There are four equally likely outcomes, not three; (H, T), (T, H), (T, T), (H, H).

22. Initially a probability of .20 would be assigned if selection is equally likely. Data does not appear to confirm the belief of equal consumer preference. For example using the relative frequency method we would assign a probability of 5 / 100 = .05 to the design 1 outcome, .15 to design 2, .30 to design 3, .40 to design 4, and .10 to design 5.

23. a. $P(E_1 \text{ or } E_2) = P(E_1) + P(E_2) = .35 + .40 = .75$

b. $P(E_1 \text{ or } E_3) = P(E_1) + P(E_3) = .35 + .25 = .60$

c. $P(E_1 \text{ or } E_2 \text{ or } E_3) = P(E_1) + P(E_2) + P(E_3) = .35 + .40 + .25 = 1.00$

24. a. $P(E_2) = 1 / 4$

b. P(any 2 outcomes) = 1 / 4 + 1 / 4 = 1 / 2

c. P(any 3 outcomes) = 1 / 4 + 1 / 4 + 1 / 4 = 3 / 4

25. a. S = {ace of clubs, ace of diamonds, ace of hearts, ace of spades}

b. S = {2 of clubs, 3 of clubs, . . . , 10 of clubs, J of clubs, Q of clubs, K of clubs, A of clubs}

c. There are 12; jack, queen, or king in each of the four suits.

d. For a: 4 / 52 = 1 / 13 = .08

For b: 13 / 52 = 1 / 4 = .25

For c: 12 / 52 = .23

26. a. (6) (6) = 36 sample points

b.

Die 2

		1	2	3	4	5	6
	1	2	3	4	5	6	7
	2	3	4	5	6	7	8
	3	4	5	6	7	8	9
Die 1	4	5	6	7	8	9	10
	5	6	7	8	9	10	11
	6	7	8	9	10	11	12

←—— Total for Both

c. 6 / 36 = 1 / 6

d. 10 / 36 = 5 / 18

e. No. P(odd) = 18 / 36 = P(even) = 18 / 36 or 1 / 2 for both.

f. Classical. A probability of 1 / 36 is assigned to each experimental outcome.

27. a. (4, 6), (4, 7), (4 , 8)

b. .05 + .10 + .15 = .30

c. (2, 8), (3, 8), (4, 8)

d. .05 + .05 + .15 = .25

e. .15

28. a. 0; probability is .05

b. 4, 5; probability is .10 + .10 = .20

c. 0, 1, 2; probability is .05 + .15 + .35 = .55

29. a. Yes, the probabilities are all greater than or equal to zero and they sum to one.

   b. $P(A) = P(0) + P(1) + P(2) = .08 + .18 + .32$

$$= .58$$

   c. $P(B) = P(4) = .12$

30. a. $P(A) = P(\$150 \text{ but less than } \$200) + P(\$200 \text{ and over})$

$$= \frac{26}{100} + \frac{5}{100}$$

$$= .31$$

   b. $P(B) = P(\text{less than } \$50) + P(\$50 \text{ but less than } \$100) + P(\$100 \text{ but less than } \$150)$

$$= .13 + .22 + .34$$

$$= .69$$

31. a. $P(A) = P(1) + P(2) + P(3) + P(4) + P(5)$

$$= \frac{20}{50} + \frac{12}{50} + \frac{6}{50} + \frac{3}{50} + \frac{1}{50}$$

$$= .40 + .24 + .12 + .06 + .02$$

$$= .84$$

   b. $P(B) = P(3) + P(4) + P(5)$

$$= .12 + .06 + .02$$

$$= .20$$

   c. $P(2) = 12 / 50 = .24$

32. a. $P(A) = .40, P(B) = .40, P(C) = .60$

   b. $P(A \cup B) = P(E_1, E_2, E_3, E_4) = .80$. Yes $P(A \cup B) = P(A) + P(B)$.

   c. $A^c = \{E_3, E_4, E_5\}$ $C^c = \{E_1, E_4\}$ $P(A^c) = .60$ $P(C^c) = .40$

   d. $A \cup B^c = \{E_1, E_2, E_5\}$ $P(A \cup B^c) = .60$

   e. $P(B \cup C) = P(E_2, E_3, E_4, E_5) = .80$

33. a. $P(A) = P(E_1) + P(E_4) + P(E_6) = .05 + .25 + .10 = .40$

   $P(B) = P(E_2) + P(E_4) + P(E_7) = .20 + .25 + .05 = .50$

   $P(C) = P(E_2) + P(E_3) + P(E_5) + P(E_7) = .20 + .20 + .15 + .05 = .60$

   b. $A \cup B = \{E_1, E_2, E_4, E_6, E_7\}$

   $P(A \cup B) = P(E_1) + P(E_2) + P(E_4) + P(E_6) + P(E_7)$

   $= .05 + .20 + .25 + .10 + .05$

   $= .65$

   c. $A \cap B = \{E_4\}$ $P(A \cap B) = P(E_4) = .25$

   d. Yes, they are mutually exclusive.

   e. $B^c = \{E_1, E_3, E_5, E_6\}$; $P(B^c) = P(E_1) + P(E_3) + P(E_5) + P(E_6)$

   $= .05 + .20 + .15 + .10$

   $= .50$

34. $P(\text{No Recession}) = 1 - .74 = .26$

35. Let: E = event patient treated experienced eye relief.
       S = event patient treated had their skin rash cleared up.

   Given:

$$P(E) = \frac{90}{250} = .36$$

$$P(S) = \frac{135}{250} = .54$$

$$P(E \cap S) = \frac{45}{250} = .18$$

$$P(E \cup S) = P(E) + P(S) - P(E \cap S)$$

$$= .36 + .54 - .18$$

$$= .72$$

36.   Let: J = event student had a part-time job.

        D = event student had made the Deans' List.

Given:

$$P(J) = \frac{40}{100} = .40$$

$$P(D) = \frac{25}{100} = .25$$

$$P(J \cap D) = \frac{15}{100} = .15$$

$$P(J \cup D) = P(J) + P(D) - P(J \cap D)$$

$$= .40 + .25 - .15$$

$$= .50$$

37.   Let: A = event subscriber has mutual fund

        B = event subscriber has money market fund

Given: $P(A) = .46, P(B) = .63, P(A \cup B) = .74$

$$P(A \cap B) \quad = P(A) + P(B) - P(A \cup B)$$

$$= .46 + .63 - .74$$

$$= .35$$

$$P(A^c \cap B^c) = 1 - P(A \cup B)$$

$$= 1 - .74$$

$$= .26$$

38.   Let: B = rented a car for business reasons

        P = rented a car for personal reasons

a. $P(B \cap P) = P(B) + P(P) - P(B \cup P)$

$$= .54 + .51 - .72$$

$$= .33$$

b. P(did not rent) = 1 - P(B ∪ P)

= 1 - .72

= .28

c. P(business only) = P(B ∩ P^c) = P(B) - P(B ∩ P)

= .54 - .33

= .21

39. a. A and B are not mutually exclusive. There is not enough information to compute P(A ∩ B).

b. B and C are mutually exclusive assuming both could not be identified as the primary cause of death.

P(B ∪ C) = P(B) + P(C) = .25 + .20 = .45

c. P(C^c) = 1 - P(C) = 1 - .20 = .80

40. a. Let: A = event that the first car starts

B = event that the second car starts

Given: P(A) = .80, P(B) = .40, P(A ∩ B) = .3

b. P(A ∪ B) = P(A) + P(B) - P(A ∩ B)

= .8 + .4 - .3 = .9

c.

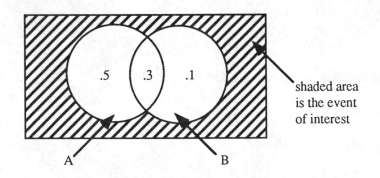

shaded area
is the event
of interest

1 - P(A ∪ B) = 1 - (.5 + .3 + .1) = .1

41. a. Yes; the person cannot be in an automobile and a bus at the same time.

P(A ∪ B) = P(A) + P(B) = .45 + .35 = .80

b. P(B^c) = 1 - P(B) = 1 - .35 = .65

42. a. $P(A\,|\,B) = \dfrac{P(A \cap B)}{P(B)} = \dfrac{.40}{.60} = .6667$

b. $P(B\,|\,A) = \dfrac{P(A \cap B)}{P(A)} = \dfrac{.40}{.50} = .80$

c. No because $P(A\,|\,B) \neq P(A)$

43. a. $P(A \cap B) = 0$

b. $P(A\,|\,B) = \dfrac{P(A \cap B)}{P(B)} = \dfrac{0}{.4} = 0$

c. No. $P(A\,|\,B) \neq P(A)$; $\therefore$ the events, although mutually exclusive, are not independent.

d. Mutually exclusive events are dependent.

44. a.

	Single	Married	Total
Under 30	.55	.10	.65
30 or over	.20	.15	.35
Total	.75	.25	1.00

b. 65% of the customers are under 30.

c. The majority of customers are single: P(single) = .75.

d. .55

e. Let: A = event under 30

B = event single

$$P(B\,|\,A) = \dfrac{P(A \cap B)}{P(A)} = \dfrac{.55}{.65} = .8462$$

f. $P(A \cap B) = .55$

$$P(A)P(B) = (,65)(.75) = .49$$

Since $P(A \cap B) \neq P(A)P(B)$, they cannot be independent events; or, since $P(A \mid B) \neq P(B)$, they cannot be independent.

45. a.

	Reason for Applying				
	Quality	Cost/Convenience	Other		
Full Time	.218	.204	.039		.461
Part Time	.208	.307	.024		.539
	.426	.511	.063		1.00

b.   It is most likely a student will cite cost or convenience as the first reason - probability = .511. School quality is the first reason cited by the second largest number of students - probability = .426.

c. $P(\text{Quality} \mid \text{full time}) = .218 / .461 = .473$

d. $P(\text{Quality} \mid \text{part time}) = .208 / .539 = .386$

e.   For independence, we must have $P(A)P(B) = P(A \cap B)$.

From the table, $P(A \cap B) = .218, P(A) = .461, P(B) = .426$

$$P(A)P(B) = (.461)(.426) = .196$$

Since $P(A)P(B) \neq P(A \cap B)$, the events are not independent.

46. a.

		Do you own a US car?		
		Yes	No	Total
Do you own a foreign car?	Yes	.15	.05	.20
	No	.75	.05	.80
	Total	.90	.10	1.00

b. 20% own a foreign car, 90% own a US car

c. .15

d. Let: A = foreign car

B = US car

$$P(A \cup B) = P(A) + P(B) - P(A \cap B)$$

$$= .20 + .90 - .15 = .95$$

e. $P(A \mid B) = \dfrac{P(A \cap B)}{P(B)} = \dfrac{.15}{.90} = .17$

f. $P(B \mid A) = \dfrac{P(A \cap B)}{P(A)} = \dfrac{.15}{.20} = .75$

g. $P(A)P(B) = (.2)(.9) = .18$; since $P(A \cap B) = .15$, the events are not independent.

47. a. Let: A = event Ms. Smith gets the first job offer

B = event Ms. Smith gets the second job offer

Given: $P(A) = .50, P(B) = .6, P(A \cap B) = .15$

b. $P(B \mid A) = \dfrac{P(A \cap B)}{P(A)} = \dfrac{.15}{.50} = .30$

c. $P(A \cup B) = P(A) + P(B) - P(A \cap B)$

$$= .5 + .6 - .15 = .95$$

d.

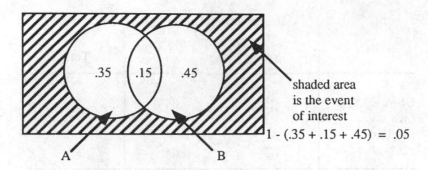

e. $P(B \mid A) \neq P(B)$; the events are not independent.

48. a.

		Son		
		Attended College	Did Not Attend College	Total
Father	Attended College	.2250	.0875	.3125
	Did Not Attend College	.2750	.4125	.6875
	Total	.5000	.5000	1.0000

b.   Son has a higher probability of having attended college.

c.   Let: A = son attends college

B = father attends college

$$P(A \mid B) = \frac{P(A \cap B)}{P(B)} = \frac{.2250}{.3125} = .72$$

d. $P(A \mid B^c) = \dfrac{P(A \cap B^c)}{P(B^c)} = \dfrac{.2750}{.6875} = .40$

e. $P(A \mid B) = .72$ and $P(A) = .50$.
$P(A \mid B) \neq P(A)$; therefore, the events are not independent.

49.   Let: A = event of a well drilled in a type A structure

B = event a well is productive

Given: P(A | B) = .4, P(A) = .50, P(B) = .3

a. $P(A \cap B) = P(A \mid B)P(B)$

$= (.4)(.3) = .12$

b. $P(B \mid A) = \dfrac{P(A \cap B)}{P(A)} = \dfrac{.12}{.50} = .24$

c.   not independent

$P(B \mid A) = .24 \neq P(B) = .3$

50. a. $P(\text{Recovery} \mid \text{Recession}) = \dfrac{P(\text{Recovery} \cap \text{Recession})}{P(\text{Recession})} = \dfrac{.41}{.74} = .5541$

b.

		Recovery		
		Y	N	Total
Recession	Y	.41	.33	.74
	N	.26	.00	.26
	Total	.67	.33	

c.   P(Recovery) = .67

51. a. $P(A \cap B) = P(A)P(B) = (.55)(.35) = .19$

a. $P(A \cup B) = P(A) + P(B) - P(A \cap B) = .55 + .35 - .19 = .71$

c. $P(\text{shutdown}) = 1 - P(A \cup B) = 1 - .71 = .29$

52.   Let H = buy a house, and C = buy a car

a. $P(H \cup C) = P(H) + P(C) - P(H \cap C) = .033 + .168 - .004 = .197$

b. $P(C \mid H) = \dfrac{P(C \cap H)}{P(H)} = \dfrac{.004}{.033} = .121$

c. No. $P(C \mid H) = .121 \neq .168 = P(C)$

53. a. Yes, since $P(A_1 \cap A_2) = 0$

    b. $P(A_1 \cap B) = P(A_1)P(B \mid A_1) = .40(.20) = .08$

       $P(A_2 \cap B) = P(A_2)P(B \mid A_2) = .60(.05) = .03$

    c. $P(B) = P(A_1 \cap B) + P(A_2 \cap B) = .08 + .03 = .11$

    d.
    $$P(A_1 \mid B) = \frac{.08}{.11} = .7273$$
    $$P(A_2 \mid B) = \frac{.03}{.11} = .2727$$

54. a. $P(B \cap A_1) = P(A_1)P(B \mid A_1) = (.20)(.50) = .10$

       $P(B \cap A_2) = P(A_2)P(B \mid A_2) = (.50)(.40) = .20$
       $P(B \cap A_3) = P(A_3)P(B \mid A_3) = (.30)(.30) = .09$

    b. $P(A_2 \mid B) = \dfrac{.20}{.10 + .20 + .09} = .51$

    c

Events	$P(A_i)$	$P(B \mid A_i)$	$P(A_i \cap B)$	$P(A_i \mid B)$
A_1	.20	.50	.10	.26
A_2	.50	.40	.20	.51
A_3	.30	.30	.09	.23
	1.00		.39	1.00

55. S_1 = successful, S_2 = not successful and B = request received for additional information.

    a. $P(S_1) = .50$

    b. $P(B \mid S_1) = .75$

    c. $P(S_1 \mid B) = \dfrac{(.50)(.75)}{(.50)(.75) + (.50)(.40)} = \dfrac{.375}{.575} = .65$

56. M = missed payment

    D_1 = customer defaults
    D_2 = customer does not default

    $P(D_1) = .05 \quad P(D_2) = .95 \quad P(M \mid D_2) = .2 \quad P(M \mid D_1) = 1$

a.

$$P(D_1 \mid M) = \frac{P(D_1)P(M \mid D_1)}{P(D_1)P(M \mid D_1) + P(D_2)P(M \mid D_2)}$$

$$= \frac{(.05)\,(1)}{(.05)\,(1) + (.95)\,(.2)}$$

$$= \frac{.05}{.24}$$

$$= .21$$

b.   Yes, the probability of default is greater than .20.

57.   Let: A = event driver is 30 or older

B = event driver had a traffic violation in a 12 month period.

Given: $P(A) = .60, P(A^c) = .40$

$P(B \mid A) = .04, P(B \mid A^c) = .10$

$$P(A^c \mid B) = \frac{P(A^c \cap B)}{P(B)}$$

$$= \frac{P(A^c)P(B \mid A^c)}{P(A)P(B \mid A) + P(A^c)P(B \mid A^c)}$$

$$= \frac{(.4)\,(.10)}{(.6)\,(.04) + (.4)\,(.10)}$$

$$= \frac{.040}{.024 + .040}$$

$$= \frac{.040}{.064} = .625$$

58.   Let: H = event this game is at home

W = event the team wins

Given: $P(H) = .55, P(H^c) = .45$

$P(W \mid H) = .80, P(W \mid H^c) = .65$

$$P(H \mid W) = \frac{P(H \cap W)}{P(W)}$$

$$= \frac{P(H)P(W \mid H)}{P(H)P(W \mid H) + P(H^c)P(W \mid H^c)}$$

$$= \frac{(.55)(.8)}{(.55)(.8) + (.45)(.65)}$$

$$= \frac{.4400}{.4400 + .2925}$$

$$= \frac{.4400}{.7325} = .6007$$

59. a.

Events	$P(D_i)$	$P(S_1 \mid D_i)$	$P(D_i \cap S_1)$	$P(D_i \mid S_1)$
D_1	.60	.15	.090	.2195
D_2	.40	.80	.320	.7805
	1.00	$P(S_1) =$	.410	1.0000

$P(D_1 \mid S_1) = .2195$

$P(D_2 \mid S_1) = .7805$

b.

Events	$P(D_i)$	$P(S_2 \mid D_i)$	$P(D_i \cap S_2)$	$P(D_i \mid S_2)$
D_1	.60	.10	.060	.500
D_2	.40	.15	.060	.500
	1.00	$P(S_2) =$	.120	1.000

$P(D_1 \mid S_2) = .50$

$P(D_2 \mid S_2) = .50$

c.

Events	$P(D_i)$	$P(S_3 \mid D_i)$	$P(D_i \cap S_3)$	$P(D_i \mid S_3)$
D_1	.60	.15	.090	.8824
D_2	.40	.03	.012	.1176
	1.00	$P(S_3) =$	.102	1.0000

$P(D_1 \mid S_3) = .8824$

$P(D_2 \mid S_3) = .1176$

d. Use the posterior probabilities from part (a) as the prior probabilities here.

Events	$P(D_i)$	$P(S_2 \mid D_i)$	$P(D_i \cap S_2)$	$P(D_i \mid S_2)$
D_1	.2195	.10	.0220	.1582
D_2	.7805	.15	.1171	.8418
	1.0000		.1391	1.0000

$P(D_1 \mid S_1 \text{ and } S_2) = .1582$

$P(D_2 \mid S_1 \text{ and } S_2) = .8418$

60. a. Three, one for each category

b. $P(A) = 3 / 30 = .10$

$$P(B) = \frac{15}{30} = .50$$

$$P(C) = \frac{12}{30} = .40$$

61. a. $(2)(2) = 4$

     b.   Let   s = successful

          u = unsuccessful

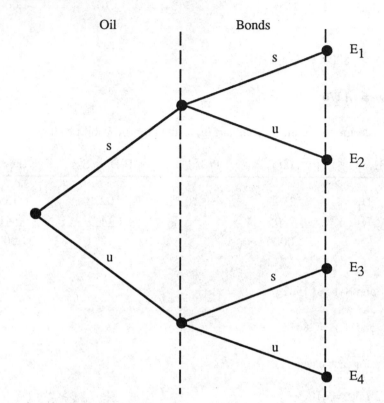

     c. $O = \{E_1, E_2\}$

          $M = \{E_1, E_3\}$

     d. $O \cup M = \{E_1, E_2, E_3\}$

     e. $O \cap M = \{E_1\}$

     f.   No; since $O \cap M$ has a sample point.

62. a. $A \cup B = \{E_1, E_2, E_3, E_4\}$

     b. $C \cup D = \{E_1, E_5, E_6, E_7, E_8\}$

     c. $A \cap B = \{E_2\}$

     d. $C \cap D = \{E_7, E_8\}$

e. $B \cap C$ = no sample points (empty)

f. $A^c = \{E_4, E_5, E_6, E_7, E_8\}$

g. $D^c = \{E_1, E_2, E_3, E_4\}$

h. $A \cup D^c = \{E_1, E_2, E_3, E_4\}$

i. $A \cap D^c = \{E_1, E_2, E_3\}$

j. No, $A \cap B = \{E_2\}$

k. Yes, $B \cap C = \emptyset$

63. a. $P(A) = 3/8$, $P(B) = 1/4$, $P(C) = 3/8$, $P(D) = 1/2$

b. $P(A \cap B) = 1/8$

c. $P(A \cup B) = P(A) + P(B) - P(A \cap B) = 3/8 + 1/4 - 1/8 = 1/2$

d. $P(A \mid B) = P(A \cap B)/P(B) = (1/8)/(1/4) = 1/2$

e. $P(B \mid A) = P(A \cap B)/P(A) = (1/8)/(3/8) = 1/3$

f. $P(B \cap C) = 0$

g. $P(B \mid C) = 0$

i. No, since $P(B \mid C) \neq P(B)$

64. a. $P(\text{No cards}) = 1 - \dfrac{2083}{2125} = 1 - .98 = .02.$

b. $P(\text{American Express Card}) = \dfrac{1360}{2125} = .64$

c. $P(\text{MstrCard} \cup \text{VISA}) = P(\text{MstrCard}) + P(\text{VISA}) - P(\text{MSTRCard} \cap \text{VISA})$

$$= \dfrac{1466}{2125} + \dfrac{1679}{2125} - .55$$

$$= .69 + .79 - .55$$

$$= .93$$

d. $P(AX \cup VISA) = P(AX) + P(VISA) - P(AX \cap VISA)$

$$= .64 + .79 - P(AX \cap VISA)$$

$$= 1.43 - P(AX \cap VISA)$$

Note the probability of having one or more cards is .98. Therefore,

$$1.43 - P(AX) \cap VISA) \leq .98$$

and

$$P(AX \cap VISA) \geq 1.43 - .98 = .45$$

Yes, it makes sense.

65. a. $P(1) = \dfrac{1230}{2046} = .6012$

$P(2) = \dfrac{304}{2046} = .1486$

.
.
.

$P(12) = \dfrac{6}{2046} = .0029$

b. $P(1) = .6012$

c. $P(3) + P(4) + \cdots + P(12) = 1 - P(1) - P(2) = 1 - .6012 - .1486 = .2502$

d. $P(7) + P(8) + \cdots + P(12) = .0396$

66. a. Probability of the event $= P(\text{average}) + P(\text{above average}) + P(\text{excellent})$

$$= \frac{11}{50} + \frac{14}{50} + \frac{13}{50}$$

$$= .22 + .28 + .26$$

$$= .76$$

b. Probability of the event $= P(\text{poor}) + P(\text{below average})$

$$= \frac{4}{50} + \frac{8}{50} = .24$$

67. a. P(A) = P(0 - 99) + P(100 - 199)

$$= \frac{62}{200} + \frac{46}{200}$$

$$= .31 + .23$$

$$= .54$$

  b. P(B) = P(300 - 399) + P(400 - 499) + P(500 - 599)

$$= \frac{30}{200} + \frac{26}{200} + \frac{12}{200}$$

$$= .34$$

	Yes	No	Total
23 and Under	.1026	.0996	.2022
24 - 26	.1482	.1878	.3360
27 - 30	.0917	.1328	.2245
31 - 35	.0327	.0956	.1283
36 and Over	.0253	.0837	.1090
Total	.4005	.5995	1.0000

68. a.

  b. .2022

  c. .2245 + .1283 + .1090 = .4618

  d. .4005

69. a. P(24 to 26 I Yes) = .1482 / .4005 = .3700

  b. P(Yes I 36 and over) = .0253 / .1090 = .2321

  c. .1026 + .1482 + .1878 + .0917 + .0327 + .0253 = .5883

  d. P(31 or more I No) = (.0956 + .0837) / .5995 = .2991

e. No, because the conditional probabilities do not all equal the marginal probabilities. For instance,

$$P(24 \text{ to } 26 \mid Yes) = .3700 \neq P(24 \text{ to } 26) = .3360$$

70. a. $P(A \cup B) = P(A) + P(B) - P(A \cap B) = .30 + .25 - .20 = .35$

$$P(A \mid B) = \frac{P(A \cap B)}{P(B)} = \frac{.20}{.25} = .80$$

$$P(B \mid A) = \frac{P(A \cap B)}{P(A)} = \frac{.20}{.30} = .67$$

b. $P(A \mid B) = .80 \neq P(A) = .30$

They are not independent.

71. a. $P(A \cap B) = P(A)P(B \mid A) = (.40)(.30) = .12$

$$P(B) = \frac{P(A \cap B)}{P(A \mid B)} = \frac{.12}{.60} = .20$$

b. $P(A)P(B) = (.40)(.20) = .08 \neq P(A \cap B) = .12$

They are not independent.

72. a. $P(A \cup B) = P(A) + P(B) = .60 + .30 = .90$

$P(A \cap B) = 0$

b,c. No, mutually exclusive events can only satisfy the definition of independence if the probability of one of the events is zero.

73. a. $P(T) = .50, P(B) = .30, P(T \cap B) = .20$

b. No, since $P(T \cap B) \neq 0$.

c. $P(B \mid T) = \frac{P(T \cap B)}{P(T)} = \frac{.20}{.50} = .40$

d. No, $P(B \mid T) = .40 \neq P(B) = .30$

e. Probability of buying the product increases to .40 from .30.

74. a.

	Smoker	Nonsmoker	Total
Record of Heart Disease	.10	.08	.18
No Record of Heart Disease	.20	.62	.82
Total	.30	.70	1.00

b. $P(S \cap H) = .10$

c. 30% are smokers, 70% are nonsmokers; 18% have a record of heart disease. 82% have no record of heart disease.

d. $P(H \mid S) = \dfrac{P(H \cap S)}{P(S)} = \dfrac{.10}{.30} = .333$

e. $P(H \mid S^c) = \dfrac{P(H \cap S^c)}{P(S^c)} = \dfrac{.08}{.70} = .114$

f. $P(H \mid S) \neq P(H)$; therefore the events are not independent

g. Smokers have a higher probability of having a record of heart disease.

75. a. $P(B \mid S) = \dfrac{P(B \cap S)}{P(S)} = \dfrac{.12}{.40} = .30$

   We have $P(B \mid S) > P(B)$.

   Yes, continue the ad since it increases the probability of a purchase.

   b. Estimate the company's market share at 20%. Continuing the advertisement should increase the market share since $P(B \mid S) = .30$.

   c. $P(B \mid S) = \dfrac{P(B \cap S)}{P(S)} = \dfrac{.10}{.30} = .333$

   The second ad has a bigger effect.

76. Let B = purchase, A = aware of promotion and A^c = not aware of promotion.

   a. $P(B \mid A) = \dfrac{P(B \cap A)}{P(A)} = \dfrac{.20}{.80} = .25$

b. $P(A \cap B) = .20 = P(A)P(B) = (.80)(.25) = .20$

The events are independent.

c. No, it doesn't seem to have any effect on purchase behavior.

77. a. $P(A) = 200 / 800 = .25$

b. $P(B) = 100 / 800 = .125$

c. $P(A \cap B) = 10 / 800 = .0125$

d. $P(A \mid B) = P(A \cap B) / P(B) = .0125 / .125 = .10$

e. No, $P(A \mid B) \neq P(A) = .25$

78. a. $P(B) = .25$

$$P(S \mid B) = 20 / 50 = .40$$

$$P(S \cap B) = .25\,(.40) = .10$$

b. $P(B \mid S) = \dfrac{P(S \cap B)}{P(S)} = \dfrac{.10}{.40} = .25$

c. B and S are independent. The program appears to have no effect.

79.   Let   A = lost time accident in current year

B = lost time accident previous year

Given: $P(B) = .06, P(A) = .05, P(A \mid B) = .15$

a. $P(A \cap B) = P(A \mid B)P(B) = .15(.06) = .009$

b. $P(A \cup B) = P(A) + P(B) - P(A \cap B)$

$$= .06 + .05 - .009 = .101 \text{ or } 10.1\%$$

80. a. $P(H) = .25$

$$P(W) = .30$$

$$P(W \mid H) = .80$$

Therefore $P(W \cap H) = P(W \mid H)P(H) = .80(.25) = .20$

b. $P(W \cup H) = P(W) + P(H) - P(W \cap H)$

$= .30 + .25 - .20 = .35$

c. P(No Regular Viewer) $= 1 - P(W \cup H) = .65$ or 65%

81. Let: H = event that a student did the homework

A = event that a student passes the course

Given: $P(A \mid H)) = .90, P(A \mid H^c) = .25, P(H) = .75$

$$P(H \mid A) = \frac{P(H \cap A)}{P(A)}$$

$$= \frac{P(A \mid H)P(H)}{P(A \mid H)P(H) + P(A \mid H^c)P(H^c)}$$

$$= \frac{(.90)(.75)}{(.90)(.75) + (.25)(.25)}$$

$$= \frac{.6750}{.6750 + .0625}$$

$$= .9153$$

82. Let   C = call back

Events	$P(A_i)$	$P(C \mid A_i)$	$P(A_i \cap C)$	$P(A_i \mid C)$
Sale (A_1)	.10	.40	.040	.21
No Sale (A_2)	.90	.17	.153	.79
	1.00		.193	1.00

P(Sale I Call back) $= .21$. Since probability of sale, while still reasonably small, has approximately doubled, the salesperson should call back.

83. Let: A = sales are greater than 25,000 units
B = winter conditions are severe
C = winter conditions are moderate

Given: $P(A \mid B) = .8, P(A \mid C) = .5, P(B) = .7, P(C) = .3$; find $P(A)$.

$P(A) = P(A \cap B) + P(A \cap C)$
$= P(B)P(A \mid B) + P(C)P(A \mid C)$
$= (.7)(.8) + (.3)(.5) = .71$

84.   Let: A = return is fraudulent
             B = exceeds IRS standard for deductions

Given: $P(A \mid B) = .20$, $P(A \mid B^c) = .02$, $P(B) = .08$, find $P(A) = .3$. Note $P(B^c) = 1 - P(B) = .92$

$$P(A) = P(A \cap B) + P(A \cap B^c)$$
$$= P(B)P(A \mid B) + P(B^c)P(A \mid B^c)$$
$$= (.08)(.20) + (.92)(.02) = .0344$$

We estimate 3.44% will be fraudulent.

85. a. $P(Oil) = .50 + .20 = .70$

     b.   Let S = Soil test results

Events	$P(A_i)$	$P(S \mid A_i)$	$P(A_i \cap S)$	$P(A_i \mid S)$
High Quality (A_1)	.50	.20	.10	.31
Medium Quality (A_2)	.20	.80	.16	.50
No Oil (A_3)	.30	.20	.06	.19
	1.00	$P(S) =$	.32	1.00

P(Oil) = .81 which is good; however, probabilities now favor medium quality rather than high quality oil.

86. a,b. Let   D = first part tested is defective
                 G = second part tested is good

Events	$P(A_i)$	$P(D \mid A_i)$	$P(A_i \cap D)$	$P(A_i \mid D)$
Correct Adjustment	.90	.05	.045	.375
Incorrect Adjustment	.10	.75	.075	.625
	1.00	$P(D) =$	.120	1.000

P(Defect) = .12

P(Incorrect | Defect) = .625

Check machine adjustment. Finding a defective item increases the probability of an incorrect adjustment from .10 to .625.

c.

Events	$P(A_i)$	$P(G \mid A_i)$	$P(A_i \cap G)$	$P(A_i \mid G)$
Correct Adjustment	.375	.95	.356	.695
Incorrect Adjustment	.625	.25	.156	.305
	1.00	$P(G) =$	.512	1.000

Now the probability of incorrect adjustment is .305. This is still high. Either check adjustment now, or perhaps preferred, continue sampling and revising probabilities until probabilities show a clear-cut decision.

87.

Events	$P(A_i)$	$P(D \mid A_i)$	$P(A_i \cap D)$	$P(A_i \mid D)$
Supplier A	.60	.0025	.0015	.23
Supplier B	.30	.0100	.0030	.46
Supplier C	.10	.0200	.0020	.31
	1.00	$P(D) =$	.0065	1.00

a. $P(D) = .0065$

b. B is the most likely supplier if defects are found.

88. a. A_1 = field will produce oil

A_2 = field will not produce oil

W = well produces oil

Events	$P(A_i)$	$P(W^c \mid A_i)$	$P(W^c \cap A_i)$	$P(A_i \mid W^c)$
Oil in Field	.25	.20	.05	.0625
No Oil in Field	.75	1.00	.75	.9375
	1.00		.80	1.0000

The probability the field will produce oil given a well comes up dry is .0625.

b.

Events	$P(A_i)$	$P(W^c \mid A_i)$	$P(W^c \cap A_i)$	$P(A_i \mid W^c)$
Oil in Field	.0625	.20	.0125	.0132
No Oil in Field	.9375	1.00	.9375	.9868
	1.0000		.9500	1.0000

The probability the well will produce oil drops further to .0132.

c. Suppose a third well comes up dry. The probabilities are revised as follows:

Events	$P(A_i)$	$P(W^c \mid A_i)$	$P(W^c \cap A_i)$	$P(A_i \mid W^c)$
Oil in Field	.0132	.20	.0026	.0026
Incorrect Adjustment	.9868	1.00	.9868	.9974
	1.0000		.9894	1.0000

Stop drilling and abandon field if three consecutive wells come up dry.

Chapter 5
Discrete Probability Distributions

Learning Objectives

1.   Understand the concepts of a random variable and a probability distribution.

2.   Be able to distinguish between discrete and continuous random variables.

3.   Be able to compute and interpret the expected value, variance, and standard deviation for a discrete random variable.

4.   Be able to compute probabilities using a binomial probability distribution.

5.   Be able to compute probabilities using a Poisson probability distribution,

6.   Know when and how to use the hypergeometric probability distribution.

Chapter 5

Solutions:

1. a. Head, Head (H,H)
        Head, Tail (H,T)
        Tail, Head (T,H)
        Tail, Tail (T,T)

    b. x = number of heads on two coin tosses

    c.
Outcome	Values of x
(H,H)	2
(H,T)	1
(T,H)	1
(T,T)	0

    d. Discrete. It may assume 3 values: 0, 1, and 2.

2. a. Let x = time (in minutes) to assemble the product.

    b. It may assume any positive value: $x > 0$.

    c. Continuous

3.   Let Y = position is offered
             N = position is not offered

    a. S = {(Y,Y,Y), (Y,Y,N), (Y,N,Y), (Y,N,N), (N,Y,Y), (N,Y,N), (N,N,Y), (N,N,N)}

    b. Let N = number of offers made; N is a discrete random variable.

    c.
Experimental Outcome	(Y,Y,Y)	(Y,Y,N)	(Y,N,Y)	(Y,N,N)	(N,Y,Y)	(N,Y,N)	(N,N,Y)	(N,N,N)
Value of N	3	2	2	1	2	1	1	0

4.   The random variable may assume the values 0, 1, 2, 3, 4, 5.

5. a. S = {(1,1), (1,2), (1,3), (2,1), (2,2), (2,3)}

    b.
Experimental Outcome	(1,1)	(1,2)	(1,3)	(2,1)	(2,2)	(2,3)
Number of Steps Required	2	3	4	3	4	5

6. a. values: 0,1,2,...,20
        discrete

    b. values: 0,1,2,...
        discrete

    c. values: 0,1,2,...,50
        discrete

    d. values: $0 \leq x \leq 8$
        continuous

    e. values: $x > 0$
        continuous

7. a. $f(x) \geq 0$ for all values of x.

        $\Sigma f(x) = 1$ Therefore, it is a proper probability distribution.

    b. Probability $x = 30$ is $f(30) = .25$

    c. Probability $x \leq 25$ is $f(20) + f(25) = .20 + .15 = .35$

    d. Probability $x > 30$ is $f(35) = .40$

8. a.

x	$f(x)$		
1	3/20	=	.15
2	5/20	=	.25
3	8/20	=	.40
4	4/20	=	.20
	Total		1.00

    b.

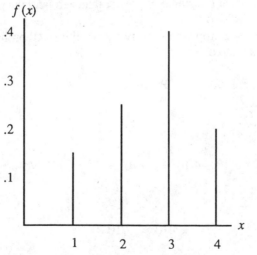

c. $f(x) \geq 0$ for $x = 1,2,3,4$.

$\Sigma f(x) = 1$

9. a.

x	f(x)	
1	.298	Here we have
2	.092	$x = 1$ if IBM
3	.066	$x = 2$ if Apple
4	.035	.
5	.066	.
6	.019	.
7	.424	$x = 7$ if other
	1.000	

b.

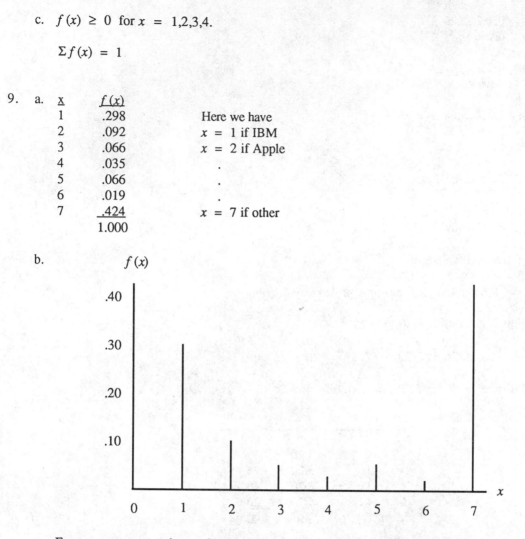

c. From part a, we see that each probability is greater than zero and the probabilities sum to one.

10. a. $.20 + .40 + .40 = 1$. It is a proper probability distribution. All probabilities are greater than or equal to zero and they sum to one.

b. P($150,000 or less) = P($148,000) + P($150,000)
= $.20 + .40 = .60$

11. a. $f(x) \geq 0$ for all values of x

$\Sigma f(x) = 1/10 + 2/10 + 3/10 + 4/10 = 10/10 = 1$

b. $f(2) = 2/10$

c. $P(x \geq 3) = f(3) + f(4) = 3/10 + 4/10 = 7/10$

d.

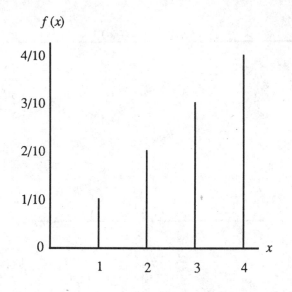

12. a. Yes; $f(x) \geq 0$ for all x and $\Sigma f(x) = .15 + .20 + .30 + .25 + .10 = 1$

   b. P(1200 or less) $= f(1000) + f(1100) + f(1200)$
   $= .15 + .20 + .30$
   $= .65$

13. a. Yes, since $f(x) \geq 0$ for $x = 1,2,3$ and $\Sigma f(x) = f(1) + f(2) + f(3) = 1/6 + 2/6 + 3/6 = 1$

   b. $f(2) = 2/6 = .333$

   c. $f(2) + f(3) = 2/6 + 3/6 = .833$

14. a. $f(200) = 1 - f(-100) - f(0) - f(50) - f(100) - f(150)$
   $= 1 - .95 = .05$

   This is the probability MRA will have a $200,000 profit.

   b. P(Profit) $= f(50) + f(100) + f(150) + f(200)$
   $= .30 + .25 + .10 + .05 = .70$

   c. P(at least 100) $= f(100) + f(150) + f(200)$
   $= .25 + .10 + .05 = .40$

15. a.

x	$f(x)$	$xf(x)$
3	.25	.75
6	.50	3.00
9	.25	2.25
	1.00	6.00

   $E(x) = \mu = 6.00$

b.

x	$x - \mu$	$(x - \mu)^2$	$f(x)$	$(x - \mu)^2 f(x)$
3	-3	9	.25	2.25
6	0	0	.50	0.00
9	3	9	.25	2.25
				4.50

Var $(x) = \sigma^2 = 4.50$

c. $\sigma = \sqrt{4.50} = 2.12$

16. a.

y	$f(y)$	$y f(y)$
2	.20	.40
4	.30	1.20
7	.40	2.80
8	.10	.80
	1.00	5.20

E$(y) = \mu = 5.20$

b.

y	$y - \mu$	$(y - \mu)^2$	$f(y)$	$(y - \mu)^2 f(y)$
2	-3.20	10.24	.20	2.048
4	-1.20	1.44	.30	.432
7	1.80	3.24	.40	1.296
8	2.80	7.84	.10	.784
				4.560

Var $(y) = 4.56$

$\sigma = \sqrt{4.50} = 2.14$

c. E $(x + y) = $ E $(x) + $ E $(y) = 6.00 + 5.20 = 11.20$

d. Var $(x + y) = $ Var $(x) + $ Var $(y) = 4.50 + 4.56 = 9.06$

$\sigma_{x+y} = \sqrt{9.06} = 3.01$

Note: The standard deviation of the sum is not the sum of the standard deviations.

17. a,b.

x	$f(x)$	$xf(x)$	$x - \mu$	$(x-\mu)^2$	$(x-\mu)^2 f(x)$
0	.10	.00	-2.45	6.0025	.600250
1	.15	.15	-1.45	2.1025	.315375
2	.30	.60	- .45	.2025	.060750
3	.20	.60	.55	.3025	.060500
4	.15	.60	1.55	2.4025	.360375
5	.10	.50	2.55	6.5025	.650250
		2.45			2.047500

$E(x) = \mu = 2.45$
$\sigma^2 = 2.0475$
$\sigma = 1.4309$

18. a. $E(x) = 26.0 (.31) + 8.6 (.23) + 7.7 (.45) - 2.9 (.01)$
$= 13.474$

The expected return of $1.00 for an individual investor is 13.474%.

b.

$x - 13.474$	$(x - 13.474)^2$	$f(x)$	$(x - 13.474)^2 f(x)$
12.526	156.900680	.31	48.639211
-4.874	23.755876	.23	5.463851
-5.774	33.339076	.45	15.002584
16.374	268.107880	.01	2.681079
			71.786725

Var $(x) = 71.7867$ $\sigma = 8.4727$

c.

x	$f(x)$	$xf(x)$	$x - \mu$	$(x-\mu)^2$	$(x-\mu)^2 f(x)$
5.0	.31	1.550	-1.964	3.857296	1.19570
8.6	.23	1.978	1.636	2.676496	.615594
7.7	.45	3.465	.736	.541696	.243763
-2.9	.01	-.029	-9.864	97.298496	.972985
		6.964			3.028042

$E(x) = 6.964$
Var $(x) = 3.028042$
$\sigma = 1.7401$

19. a. $E(x) = \Sigma xf(x) = 0 (.50) + 2 (.50) = 1.00$

b. $E(x) = \Sigma xf(x) = 0 (.61) + 3 (.39) = 1.17$

c. The expected value of a 3 - point shot is higher. So, if these probabilities hold up, the team will make more points in the long run with the 3 - point shot.

20. a.

x	$f(x)$	$xf(x)$
0	.90	0.00
400	.04	16.00
1000	.03	30.00
2000	.01	20.00
4000	.01	40.00
6000	.01	60.00
	1.00	166.00

$E(x) = 166$. If the company charged a premium of $166.00 they would break even.

b.

Gain to Policy Holder	f(Gain)	(Gain)f(Gain)
-260.00	.90	-234.00
140.00	.04	5.60
740.00	.03	22.20
1,740.00	.01	17.40
3,740.00	.01	37.40
5,740.00	.01	57.40
		-94.00

E(gain) = -94.00. The policy holder is more concerned that the big accident will break him than with the expected annual loss of $94.00.

21. a. $f(x) \geq 0$

$\Sigma f(x) = 1/6 + 1/6 + 1/6 + 1/6 + 1/6 + 1/6 = 1$

b.

c. $E(x) = \Sigma xf(x)$

$= 1(1/6) + 2(1/6) + 3(1/6) + 4(1/6) + 5(1/6) + 6(1/6)$

$= 21/6 = 3.5$

Over the long run (repeated rolls), the average number of dots on the upward face of a die will be 3.5.

d.

x	$f(x)$	$x - \mu$	$(x - \mu)^2$	$(x - \mu)^2 f(x)$
1	1/6	-2.5	6.25	1.0417
2	1/6	-1.5	2.25	.3750
3	1/6	-.5	.25	.0416
4	1/6	+.5	.25	.0416
5	1/6	+1.5	2.25	.3750
6	1/6	+2.5	6.25	1.0417

$$\sigma^2 = 2.9166$$
$$\sigma = \sqrt{2.9166} = 1.7078$$

22. a. $E(x) = \Sigma x f(x)$

$= 300 (.20) + 400 (.30) + 500 (.35) + 600 (.15)$

$= 445$

The monthly order quantity should be 445 units.

b. Cost: 445 @ \$50 = \$22,250
Revenue: 300 @ \$70 = 21,000
\$ 1,250 Loss

23.

x	$f(x)$	$x - \mu$	$(x - \mu)^2$	$(x - \mu)^2 f(x)$
300	.20	-145	21025	4205.00
400	.30	-45	2025	607.50
500	.35	+55	3025	1058.75
600	.15	+155	24025	3603.75

$$\sigma^2 = 9475.00$$
$$\sigma = \sqrt{9475} = 97.34$$

$\mu = 445$

24. a. Medium $E(x) = \Sigma x f(x)$

$= 50 (.20) + 150 (.50) + 200 (.30) = 145$

Large: $E(x) = \Sigma x f(x)$

$= 0 (.20) + 100 (.50) + 300 (.30) = 140$

Medium preferred.

b. <u>Medium</u>

x	$f(x)$	$x - \mu$	$(x - \mu)^2$	$(x - \mu)^2 f(x)$
50	.20	-95	9025	1805.0
150	.50	5	25	12.5
200	.30	55	3025	907.5
				$\sigma^2 = 2725.0$

<u>Large</u>

y	$f(y)$	$y - \mu$	$(y - \mu)^2$	$(y - \mu)^2 f(y)$
0	.20	-140	19600	3920
100	.50	-40	1600	800
300	.30	160	25600	7680
				$\sigma^2 = 12,400$

Medium preferred due to less variance.

25. a. $E(x + y) = E(x) + E(y) = \$2,000 + \$1,500 = \$3,500.$

b. $Var(x + y) = Var(x) + Var(y)$
$= 90000 + 160000$
$= 250000$

Std. dev. $= \sqrt{250000} = \$500$

26. a. $E(A + B + C) = E(A) + E(B) + E(C)$
$= 5.4 + 3.2 + 8.4$
$= 17$

b. $Var(A + B + C) = Var(A) + Var(B) + Var(C)$
$= 1.00 + .64 + 1.69$
$= 3.33$

Std. dev. $= \sqrt{3.33} = 1.82$

27. a.

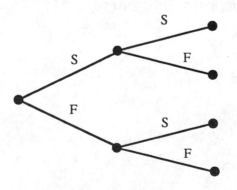

b. $f(1) = \binom{2}{1}(.4)^1(.6)^1 = \dfrac{2!}{1!\,1!}(.4)(.6) = .48$

c. $f(0) = \binom{2}{0}(.4)^0(.6)^2 = \dfrac{2!}{0!\,2!}(1)(.36) = .36$

d. $f(2) = \binom{2}{2}(.4)^2(.6)^0 = \dfrac{2!}{2!\,0!}(.16)(1) = .16$

e. $P(x \geq 1) = f(1) + f(2) = .48 + .16 = .64$

f. $E(x) = np = 2(.4) = .8$

   $\text{Var}(x) = np(1-p) = 2(.4)(.6) = .48$

   $\sigma = \sqrt{.48} = .6928$

28. a. $f(0) = .3487$

   b. $f(2) = .1937$

   c. $P(x \leq 2) = f(0) + f(1) + f(2) = .3487 + .3874 + .1937 = .9298$

   d. $P(x \geq 1) = 1 - f(0) = 1 - .3487 = .6513$

   e. $E(x) = np = 10(.1) = 1$

   f. $\text{Var}(x) = np(1-p) = 10(.1)(.9) = .9$

   $\sigma = \sqrt{.9} = .9487$

29. a. $f(12) = .1144$

   b. $f(16) = .1304$

   c. $P(x \geq 16) = f(16) + f(17) + f(18) + f(19)\ f(20)$
   $= .1304 + .0716 + .0278 + .0068 + .0008$
   $= .2374$

   d. $P(x \leq 15) = 1 - P(x \geq 16) = 1 - .2374 = .7626$

   e. $E(x) = np = 20(.7) = 14$

   f. $\text{Var}(x) = np(1-p) = 20(.7)(.3) = 4.2$

   $\sigma = \sqrt{4.2} = 2.0494$

30. a. $n = 12, p = .10, x = 2$

    $f(2) = .2301$

    b. $P(x \geq 2) = 1 - f(0) - f(1) = 1 - .2824 - .3766 = .3410$

    c. $n = 20$ here

    $P(x \geq 1) = 1 - f(0) = 1 - .1216 = .8784$

31. i) sequence of 15 trials corresponding to 15 individuals taking the test

    ii) success is passing the exam; failure is not passing the exam

    iii) $p = .30$; this must remain the same for each trial

    iv) trials must be independent

32. a. Probability of a defective part being produced must be .03 for each trial; trails must be independent.

    b. Let: D = defective
             G = not defective

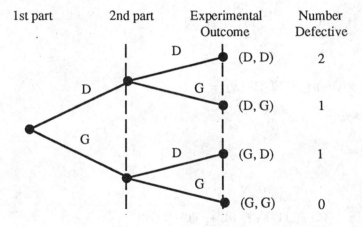

1st part	2nd part	Experimental Outcome	Number Defective
	D	(D, D)	2
D	G	(D, G)	1
G	D	(G, D)	1
	G	(G, G)	0

    c. 2 outcomes result in exactly one defect.

    d. P (no defects) = (.97) (.97) = .9409

       P (1 defect) = 2 (.03) (.97) = .0582

       p (2 defects) = (.03) (.03) = .0009

33. a. Yes; Since they are selected randomly, p is the same from trial to trial and the trials are independent.

    b. .0574 (from Table 5 in Appendix B)

c. .3487 (from Table 5 in Appendix B)

d. $P(x \geq 1) = 1 - f(0) = 1 - .3487 = .6513$

34. You must use a calculator since $p = .64$ is not in Table 5 of Appendix B.

a. $P(x \geq 8) = f(8) + f(9) + f(10)$

$$= \binom{10}{8}(.64)^8(.36)^2 + \binom{10}{9}(.64)^9(.36) + \binom{10}{10}(.64)^{10}(.36)^0$$

$$= 45(.0281)(.1296) + 10(.0180)(.36) + 1(.0115)(1)$$

$$= .1639 + .0648 + .0115$$

$$= .2402$$

b. $f(1) = \binom{3}{1}(.64)^1(.36)^2 = 3(.64)(.1296) = .2488$

35. a. $f(12) = \dfrac{12!}{12!\,0!}(.15)^{12}(.85)^0 = 0$

b. $f(12) = \dfrac{12!}{12!\,0!}(.85)^{12}(.15)^0$

$$= 1(.1422)(1) = .1422$$

c. $f(1) = \dfrac{12!}{1!\,11!}(.15)^1(.85)^{11}$

$$= 12(.15)(.16734) = .3012$$

d. P(at least 3) = 1 - P (2 or less)

P (2 or less) $= f(0) + f(1) + f(2)$

$f(0) = \dfrac{12!}{0!\,12!}(.15)^0(.85)^{12} = .1422$

$f(1) = .3012$ from (c)

$f(2) = \dfrac{12!}{2!\,10!}(.15)^2(.85)^{10} = .2924$

Therefore, P (2 or less) $= .1422 + .3012 + .2924 = .7358$

Hence, P (at least 3) $= 1 - .7358 = .2642$

36. a. .90

   b. P (at least 1) $= f(1) + f(2)$

   $$f(1) = \frac{2!}{1! \ 1!} (.9)^1 (.1)^1$$

   $$= 2 (.9) (.1) = .18$$

   $$f(2) = \frac{2!}{2! \ 0!} (.9)^2 (.1)^0$$

   $$= 1 (.81) (1) = .81$$

   $$\therefore \text{P (at least 1)} = .18 + .81 = .99$$

   Alternatively

   $$\text{P (at least 1)} = 1 - f(0)$$

   $$f(0) = \frac{2!}{0! \ 2!} (.9)^0 (.1)^2 = .01$$

   Therefore, P (at least 1) $= 1 - .01 = .99$

   c. P (at least 1) $= 1 - f(0)$

   $$f(0) = \frac{3!}{0! \ 3!} (.9)^0 (.1)^3 = .001$$

   Therefore, P (at least 1) $= 1 - .001 = .999$

   d. Yes; P (at least 1) becomes very close to 1 with multiple systems and the inability to detect an attack would be catastrophic.

37. a. $$f(0) = \frac{2!}{0! \ 2!} (.82)^0 (.18)^2 = .0324$$

   $$f(1) = \frac{2!}{1! \ 1!} (.82)^1 (.18)^1 = .2952$$

   $$f(2) = \frac{2!}{2! \ 0!} (.82)^2 (.18)^0 = .6724$$

   b. Similar to a except $p = .56; f(0) = .1936, f(1) = .4928, f(2) = .3136$

   c. Yes, foul the player with the worst free throw percentage.

38. a. $n = 5 \quad p = .10$

   Use binomial tables. $f(0) = .5905$

b. $n = 10$ $p = .10$

Use binomial tables. $f(2) = .1937$

c. $n = 20$ $p = .10$

$$1 - [f(0) + f(1)]$$
$$= 1 - [.1216 + .2702]$$

$$= 1 - .3918$$

$$= .6082$$

39. a. $f(0) + f(1) + f(2) = .0115 + .0576 + .1369 = .2060$

b. $f(4) = .2182$

c. $1 - [f(0) + f(1) + f(2) + f(3)] = 1 - .2060 - .2054$

$$= .5886$$

d. $\mu = np = 20(.20) = 4$

40.

x	$f(x)$	$x - \mu$	$(x - \mu)^2$	$(x - \mu)^2 f(x)$
0	.343	-.9	.81	.27783
1	.441	.1	.01	.00441
2	.189	1.1	1.21	.22869
3	.027	2.1	4.41	.11907
	1.000		$\sigma^2 =$	.63000

41. $E(x) = \mu = 25(.20) = 5$

$\text{Var}(x) = \sigma^2 = 25(.20)(.80) = 4$

$\sigma = \sqrt{4} = 2$

42. $E(x) = \mu = 250(.85) = 212.5$

$\text{Var}(x) = \sigma^2 = 250(.85)(.15) = 31.88$

43. $E(x) = \mu = 100(18/38) = 47.37$

$\text{Var}(x) = \sigma^2 = 100(18/38)(20/38) = 24.93$

44. a. $f(x) = \dfrac{3^x e^{-3}}{x!}$

b.
$$f(2) = \frac{3^2 e^{-3}}{2!} = \frac{9 (.0498)}{2} = .2241$$

c.
$$f(1) = \frac{3^1 e^{-3}}{1!} = 3 (.0498) = .1494$$

d. $P(x \geq 2) = 1 - f(0) - f(1) = 1 - .0498 - .1494 = .8008$

45. a.
$$f(x) = \frac{2^x e^{-2}}{x!}$$

b. $\mu = 6$ for 3 time periods

c.
$$f(x) = \frac{6^x e^{-6}}{x!}$$

d.
$$f(2) = \frac{2^2 e^{-2}}{2!} = \frac{4 (.1353)}{2} = .2706$$

e.
$$f(6) = \frac{6^6 e^{-6}}{6!} = .1606$$

f.
$$f(5) = \frac{4^5 e^{-4}}{5!} = .1563$$

46. a. $\mu = 48 (5 / 60) = 4$

$$f(3) = \frac{4^3 e^{-4}}{3!} = \frac{(64) (.0183)}{6} = .1952$$

b. $\mu = 48 (15 / 60) = 12$

$$f(10) = \frac{12^{10} e^{-12}}{10!} = .1048$$

c. $\mu = 48 (5 / 60) = 4$ I expect 4 callers to be waiting after 5 minutes.

$$f(0) = \frac{4^0 e^{-4}}{0!} = .0183$$

The probability none will be waiting after 5 minutes is .0183.

d. $\mu = 48 (3/60) = 2.4$

$$f(0) = \frac{2.4^0 e^{-2.4}}{0!} = .0907$$

The probability of no interruptions in 3 minutes is .0907.

47. a. 30 per hour

b. $\mu = 1(5/2) = 5/2$

$$f(3) = \frac{(5/2)^3 e^{-(5/2)}}{3!} = .2138$$

c. $f(0) = \dfrac{(5/2)^0 e^{-(5/2)}}{0!} = e^{-(5/2)} = .0821$

48. a. 5 minutes is $1/6$ of a half - hour. Use $\mu = 15/6$.

$$f(0) = \frac{(15/6)^0 e^{-15/6}}{0!} = e^{-2.5} = .0821$$

b. Use $\mu = 5$. $\quad f(8) = \dfrac{5^8 e^{-5}}{8!} = .0653$

c. $1 - [f(0) + f(1) + f(2) + f(3) + f(4) + f(5)]$

$= 1 - [.0067 + .0337 + .0842 + .1404 + .1755 + .1755]$

$= 1 - .6160$

$= .3840$

49. a. Set $\mu = (1.5)(2) = 3$ and $x = 0$

$f(0) = .0498$

b. Set $\mu = (2)(2) = 4$ and $x = 2$

$f(2) = .1465$

c. $1 - [f(0) + f(1) + f(2) + f(3)] = 1 - (.0498 + .1494 + .2240 + .2240)$

$= 1 - .6472$

$= .3528$

d. Set $\mu = 7$ and $x = 0$

$f(0) = .0009$

50. a. $f(0) = \dfrac{10^0 e^{-10}}{0!} = e^{-10} = .000045$

b. $f(0) + f(1) + f(2) + f(3)$

$f(0) = .000045$ (part a)

$f(1) = \dfrac{10^1 e^{-10}}{1!} = .00045$

Similarly, $f(2) = .00225, f(3) = .0075$

and $f(0) + f(1) + f(2) + f(3) = .010245$

c. 2.5 arrivals / 15 sec. period Use $\mu = 2.5$

$f(0) = \dfrac{2.5^0 e^{-2.5}}{0!} = .0821$

d. $1 - f(0) = 1 - .0821 = .9179$

51. a. $\mu = 3(1.2) = 3.6$ The expected number of failures is 3.6.

b. $\mu = 3(2) = 6$

P (at least 2) $= 1 - f(0) - f(1) = 1 - .0025 - .0149$

$= .9826$

c. $\mu = 3(.4) = 1.2$

$f(3) = .0867$

Probability of 3 failures in 10 days is .0867.

52. a. $f(1) = \dfrac{\binom{3}{1}\binom{10-3}{4-1}}{\binom{10}{4}} = \dfrac{\left(\dfrac{3!}{1!\,2!}\right)\left(\dfrac{7!}{3!\,4!}\right)}{\dfrac{10!}{4!\,6!}}$

$= \dfrac{(3)(35)}{210} = .50$

b.
$$f(2) = \frac{\binom{3}{2}\binom{10-3}{2-2}}{\binom{10}{2}} = \frac{(3)(1)}{45} = .067$$

c.
$$f(0) = \frac{\binom{3}{0}\binom{10-3}{2-0}}{\binom{10}{2}} = \frac{(1)(21)}{45} = .4667$$

d.
$$f(2) = \frac{\binom{3}{2}\binom{10-3}{4-2}}{\binom{10}{4}} = \frac{(3)(21)}{210} = .30$$

53.
$$f(3) = \frac{\binom{4}{3}\binom{15-4}{10-3}}{\binom{15}{10}} = \frac{(4)(330)}{3003} = .4396$$

54. Use the hypergeometric probability distribution. Think of the hand being a sample of size $n = 7$ from a population of $N = 52$. Thus,

$$N = 52 \qquad r = 4 \quad \text{(total number of aces)}$$

$$n = 7 \qquad x = 3 \quad \text{(number of aces in hand)}$$

$$f(3) = \frac{\binom{4}{3}\binom{52-4}{7-3}}{\binom{52}{7}} = .00582$$

So, the probability of any particular three of a kind (say, 3 aces) is .00582.

55. a.
$$f(2) = \frac{\binom{11}{2}\binom{14}{3}}{\binom{25}{5}} = \frac{(55)(364)}{53,130} = .3768$$

b.
$$f(2) = \frac{\binom{14}{2}\binom{11}{3}}{\binom{25}{5}} = \frac{(91)(165)}{53,130} = .2826$$

c.

$$f(5) = \frac{\binom{14}{5}\binom{11}{0}}{\binom{25}{5}} = \frac{(2002)\,(1)}{53{,}130} = .0377$$

d.

$$f(0) = \frac{\binom{14}{0}\binom{11}{5}}{\binom{25}{5}} = \frac{(1)\,(462)}{53{,}130} = .0087$$

56. $N = 60$ $n = 10$

a. $r = 20$ $x = 0$

$$f(0) \;=\; \frac{\binom{20}{0}\binom{40}{10}}{\binom{60}{10}} = \frac{(1)\left(\dfrac{40!}{10!\,30!}\right)}{\dfrac{60!}{10!\,50!}} = \left(\frac{40!}{10!\,30!}\right)\left(\frac{10!\,50!}{60!}\right)$$

$$= \frac{40 \cdot 39 \cdot 38 \cdot 37 \cdot 36 \cdot 35 \cdot 34 \cdot 33 \cdot 32 \cdot 31}{60 \cdot 59 \cdot 58 \cdot 57 \cdot 56 \cdot 55 \cdot 54 \cdot 53 \cdot 52 \cdot 51}$$

$$\approx .01$$

b. $r = 20$ $x = 1$

$$f(0) \;=\; \frac{\binom{20}{1}\binom{40}{9}}{\binom{60}{10}} = 20\left(\frac{40!}{9!\,31!}\right)\left(\frac{10!\,50!}{60!}\right)$$

$$\approx .07$$

c. $1 - f(0) - f(1) = 1 - .08 = .92$

d.   Same as the probability one will be from Hawaii. In part b that was found to equal approximately .07.

57.   Check to see if the probabilities are all greater than or equal to zero, and if they sum to one.

a.   No, $\Sigma f(x) = 1.1 \neq 1.0$

b.   yes

c.   no, $f(1) = -.10$ is an acceptable probability.

58. a. $E(x) = 0(.15) + 1(.30) + 2(.40) + 3(.10) + 4(.05) = 1.6$

    b. $75 $E(x) = $120.$

59. $E(x) = 2.4 \quad \sigma^2 = 1.94$

60. a. $E(x) = 2.2$

    b. $\sigma^2 = 1.16$

61. a.

x	$f(x)$
0	.10
1	.40
2	.30
3	.15
4	.05
	1.00

    b. $\mu = 1.65 \quad \sigma^2 = 1.0275$

    The training program has reduced the expected number of lost time injuries. The variability in the number of injuries is slightly smaller.

62. a. $f(x) \geq 0$

    $\Sigma f(x) = .35 + .25 + .25 + .10 + .05 = 1.0$

    b. $E(x) = \Sigma f(x)$

    $= 16(.35) + 17(.25) + 18(.25) + 19(.10) + 20(.05)$

    $= 17.25$

    c. $E(\text{GAIN}) = E(x) - 16 = 17.25 - 16 = 1.25$

    or $1.25 / 16.00 (100) = 7.8\%$

    d.

x	$f(x)$	$x - \mu$	$(x - \mu)^2$	$(x - \mu)^2 f(x)$
16	.35	-1.25	1.5625	.5469
17	.25	-.25	.0625	.1056
18	.25	.75	.5625	.1406
19	.10	+1.75	3.0625	.3063
20	.05	+2.75	7.5625	.3781
			$\sigma^2 =$	1.3875

    e. The first stock is preferred with the lower variance of 1.3875.

63. a.

x	$f(x)$
9	.30
10	.20
11	.25
12	.05
13	.20

b. $E(x) = \Sigma x f(x)$

   $= 9\,(.30) + 10\,(.20) + 11\,(.25) + 12\,(.05) + 13\,(.20)$

   $= 10.65$

   Expected value of expenses: $10.65 million

c. $Var(x) = \Sigma (x - \mu)^2 f(x)$

   $= (9 - 10.65)^2\,(.30) + (10 - 10.65)^2\,(.20) + (11 - 10.65)^2\,(.25)$
   $+ (12 - 10.65)^2\,(.05) + (13 - 10.65)^2\,(.20)$

   $= 2.1275$

d. Looks Good: $E\,(Profit) = 12 - 10.65 = 1.35$ million

   However, there is a .20 probability that expenses will equal $13 million and the college will run a deficit.

64. a. $E(x) = \Sigma x f(x)$
       $= 1\,(1/10) + 2\,(2/10) + 3\,(3/10) + 4\,(4/10) = 30/10 = 3$

   b. $Var(x) = \Sigma (x - \mu)^2 f(x)$
       $= (1 - 3)^2\,(1/10) + (2 - 3)^2\,(2/10) + (3 - 3)^2\,(3/10)$
       $+ (4 - 3)^2\,(4/10) = 10/10 = 1.0$

65. a. $E\,(total\ points) = E\,(midterm) + E\,(final)$

       $= 72 + 68$

       $= 140$

   b. $Var\,(total\ points) = Var\,(midterm) + Var\,(final)$

       $= 144 + 196$

       $= 340$

       Standard deviation $= \sqrt{340} = 18.44$

66. a.   Mean: $10 (2.28) = 22.80$

Variance: $10 (.75)^2 = 5.625$

Standard deviation: 2.37

b.   Mean: $100 (2.28) = 228$

Variance: $100 (.75)^2 = 56.25$

Standard deviation: 7.5

67.   Use the binomial probability distribution with $n = 12$ and $p = .42$.

a. $f(6) = \binom{12}{6}(.42)^6 (.58)^6 = 924 (.42)^6 (.58)^6 = .1931$

b. $f(3) = \binom{12}{3}(.42)^3 (.58)^9 = 220 (.42)^3 (.58)^9 = .1211$

c. $P(x \geq 3) = 1 - f(0) - f(1) - f(2) = 1 - .0014 - .0126 - .0502$

$= 1 - .0642 = .9358$

68. a.   Use binomial distribution with $n = 5$ and $p = .34$

$f(3) = \binom{5}{3}(.34)^3 (.66)^2 = .1712$

b. $f(2) = \binom{5}{2}(.24)^2 (.76)^3 = .2529$

c.   This would depend on whether or not we believed *Better Homes and Gardens* women readers are representative of the population of all women. If we believed they were the answers would be approximately the same. Otherwise, we would need to approximate p for the binomial probabilities some other way.

69. a.   Use binomial probability distribution with

$n = 4 \quad p = .65 \quad$ and $\quad x = 0$

$f(0) = \binom{4}{0}(.65)^0 (.35)^4 = .0150$

b. $f(0) = \binom{4}{0}(.01)^0 (.99)^4 = .9606$

c. $f(3) = \binom{4}{3}(.65)^3(.35)^1 = .3845$

$$f(4) = \binom{4}{4}(.65)^4(.35)^0 = .1785$$

P (3 or more) $= f(3) + f(4)$

$$= .3845 + .1785$$

$$= .563$$

d. $f(1) = \binom{4}{1}(.01)^1(.99)^3 = .0388$

70. a. $f(10) = \dfrac{10!}{10!\,0!}(.88)^{10}(.12)^0 = 1\,(.2785)\,(1) = .2785$

b. P (at least 2) $= 1 - $ P (0 or 1)

$$f(0) = \frac{10!}{10!\,0!}(.12)^0(.88)^{10}$$

$$= .2785$$

$$f(1) = \frac{10!}{1!\,9!}(.12)^1(.88)^9$$

$$= 10\,(.12)\,(.3165) = .3798$$

Therefore P (at least 2) $= 1 - (.2785 + .3798)$

$$= .3417$$

71. a. $f(1) = \dfrac{5!}{1!\,4!}(.03)^1(.97)^4 = .1328$

b. $1 - f(0) = 1 - .8587 = .1413$

72. Since the shipment is large we can assume that the probabilities do not change from trial to trial and use the binomial probability distribution.

a. $n = 5$

$$f(0) = \binom{5}{0}(.01)^0(.99)^5 = .9510$$

b. $f(1) = \binom{5}{1}(.01)^1(.99)^4 = .0480$

c. $1 - f(0) = 1 - .9510 = .0490$

d. No, the probability of finding one or more items in the sample defective when only 1% of the items in the population are defective is small (only .0490). I would consider it likely that more than 1% of the items are defective.

73. $\mu = 15$

prob of 20 or more arrivals $= f(20) + f(21) + \cdots$

$$= .0418 + .0299 + .0204 + .0133 + .0083 + .0050 + .0029$$
$$+ .0016 + .0009 + .0004 + .0002 + .0001 + .0001 = .1249$$

74. $\mu = 1.5$

prob of 3 or more breakdowns is $1 - [f(0) + f(1) + f(2)]$.

$1 - [f(0) + f(1) + f(2)]$

$= 1 - [.2231 + .3347 + .2510]$

$= 1 - .8088$

$= .1912$

75. $\mu = 10 \quad f(4) = .0189$

76. a. $f(3) = \dfrac{3^3 e^{-3}}{3!} = .2240$

b. $f(3) + f(4) + \cdots = 1 - [f(0) + f(1) + f(2)]$

$f(0) = \dfrac{3^0 e^{-3}}{0!} = e^{-3} = .0498$

Similarily, $f(1) = .1494, f(2) = .2240$

$\therefore 1 - [.0498 + .1494 + .2241] = .5767$

77. a. $f(8) = \dfrac{8^8 e^{-8}}{8!} = \dfrac{(16,777,216)(.000335)}{40,320} = .1394$

b. 1 / 2 hr, period: 4 / period   Use $\mu = 4$.

$$f(3) = \frac{4^3 e^{-4}}{3!} = .1954$$

Chapter 6
Continuous Probability Distributions

Learning Objectives

1. Understand the difference between how probabilities are computed for discrete and continuous random variables.

2. Know how to compute probability values for a continuous uniform probability distribution and be able to compute the expected value and variance for such a distribution.

3. Be able to compute probabilities using a normal probability distribution. Understand the role of the standard normal distribution in this process.

4. Know how and when the normal distribution can be used to approximate binomial probabilities.

5. Be able to compute probabilities using an exponential probability distribution.

6. Understand the relationship between the Poisson and exponential probability distributions.

Solutions:

1. a. $f(x)$

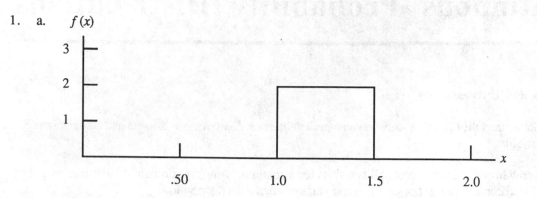

b. $P(x = 1.25) = 0$. The probability of any single point is zero since the area under the curve above any single point is zero.

c. $P(1.0 \leq x \leq 1.25) = 2(.25) = .50$

d. $P(1.20 < x < 1.5) = 2(.30) = .60$

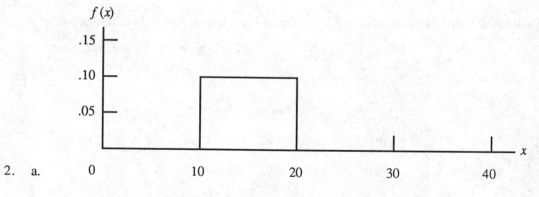

2. a.

b. $P(x < 15) = .10(5) = .50$

c. $P(12 \leq x \leq 18) = .10(6) = .60$

d. $E(x) = \dfrac{10 + 20}{2} = 15$

e. $\mathrm{Var}(x) = \dfrac{(20 - 10)^2}{12} = 8.33$

3. a.

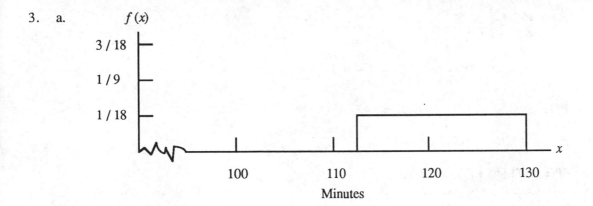

b. $P(x \leq 117) = (1/18)(117 - 112) = 5/18 = .2778$

c. $P(x > 122) = (1/18)(130 - 122)$
    $= 8/18 = .4444$

d. $E(x) = \dfrac{112 + 130}{2} = 121$ minutes

4. a.

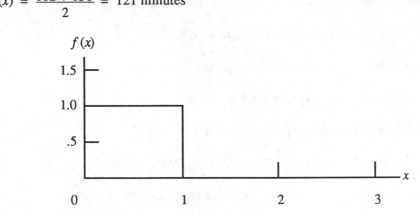

b. $P(.25 < x < .75) = 1(.50) = .50$

c. $P(x \leq .30) = 1(.30) = .30$

d. $P(x > .60) = 1(.40) = .40$

5. a.
$$f(x) = \begin{cases} \dfrac{1}{4} & \text{for } 3 \leq x \leq 7 \\ \\ 0 & \text{elsewhere} \end{cases}$$

b. $P(x < 3) = 0$

c. $P(x \leq 5) = 1/4(2) = .50$

d. $E(x) = \dfrac{3+7}{2} = 5$

$$Var(x) = \dfrac{(7-3)^2}{12} = \dfrac{16}{12} = 1.33$$

6. a. $P(12 \leq x \leq 12.05) = .05(8) = .40$

b. $P(x \geq 12.02) = .08(8) = .64$

c. $P(x < 11.98) + P(x > 12.02)$

$.005(8) = .04 \qquad .64 = .08(8)$

Therefore, the probability is $.04 + .64 = .68$

7. a. $P(10{,}000 \leq x < 12{,}000) = 2000(1/5000) = .40$

The probability your competitor will bid lower than you, and you get the bid, is .40.

b. $P(10{,}000 \leq x < 14{,}000) = 4000(1/5000) = .80$

c. A bid of $15,000 gives a probability of 1 of getting the property.

d. Yes, the bid that maximizes expected profit is $13,000.

The probability of getting the property with a bid of $13,000 is

$$P(10{,}000 \leq x < 13{,}000) = 3000(1/5000) = .60.$$

The probability of not getting the property with a bid of $13,000 is .40.

The profit you will make if you get the property with a bid of $13,000 is $3000 = $16,000 - 13,000. So your expected profit with a bid of $13,000 is

$$EP(\$13{,}000) = .6(\$3000) + .4(0) = \$1800.$$

If you bid $15,000 the probability of getting the bid is 1, but the profit if you do get the bid is only $1000 = $16,000 - 15,000. So your expected profit with a bid of $15,000 is

$$EP(\$15{,}000) = 1(\$1000) + 0(0) = \$1{,}000.$$

8.

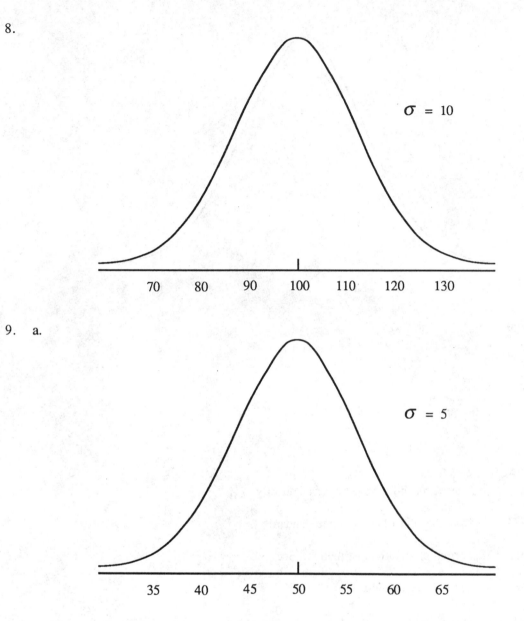

9. a.

$\sigma = 10$

70   80   90   100   110   120   130

$\sigma = 5$

35   40   45   50   55   60   65

b. .6826 since 45 and 55 are within plus or minus 1 standard deviation from the mean of 50.

c. .9544 since 40 and 60 are within plus or minus 2 standard deviations from the mean of 50.

10.

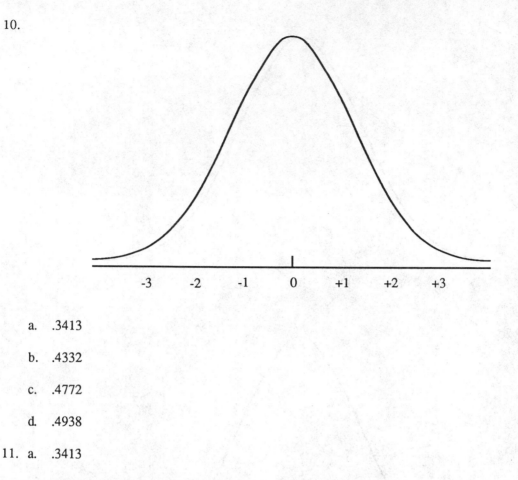

    a.   .3413

    b.   .4332

    c.   .4772

    d.   .4938

11. a.   .3413

    b.   .4332   These probability values are read directly

    c.   .4772   from the table of areas for the standard

    d.   .4938   normal probability distribution. See

    e.   .4986   Table 1 in Appendix B.

12. a.   .2967

    b.   .4418

    c. $.5000 - .1700 = .3300$

    d. $.0910 + .5000 = .5910$

    e. $.3849 + .5000 = .8849$

    f. $.5000 - .2612 = .2388$

13. a. .4761 + .1879 = .6640

    b. .3888 - .1985 = .1903

    c. .4599 - .3508 = .1091

14. a. Using the table of areas for the standard normal probability distribution, the area of .4750 corresponds to $z = 1.96$.

    b. Using the table, the area of .2291 corresponds to $z = .61$.

    c. Look in the table for an area of .5000 - .1314 = .3686. This provides $z = 1.12$.

    d. Look in the table for an area of .6700 - .5000 = .1700. This provides $z = .44$.

15. a. Look in the table for an area of .5000 - .2119 = .2881. Since the value we are seeking is below the mean, the z value must be negative. Thus, for an area of .2881, $z = -.80$.

    b. Look in the table for an area of .9030 / 2 = .4515; $z = 1.66$.

    c. Look in the table for an area of .2052 / 2 = .1026; $z = .26$.

    d. Look in the table for an area of .9948 - .5000 = .4948; $z = 2.56$.

    e. Look in the table for an area of .6915 - .5000 = .1915. Since the value we are seeking is below the mean, the z value must be negative. Thus, $z = -.50$.

16. a. Look in the table for an area of .5000 - .0100 = .4900. The area value in the table closest to .4900 provides the value $z = 2.33$.

    b. Look in the table for an area of .5000 - .0250 = .4750. This corresponds to $z = 1.96$.

    c. Look in the table for an area of .5000 - .0500 = .4500. Since .4500 is exactly halfway between .4495 ($z = 1.64$) and .4505 ($z = 1.65$), we select $z = 1.645$. However, $z = 1.64$ or $z = 1.65$ are also acceptable answers.

    d. Look in the table for an area of .5000 - .1000 = .4000. The area value in the table closest to .4000 provides the value $z = 1.28$.

17. a. At $x = 180$

$$z = \frac{180 - 200}{40} = -.50$$

At $x = 220$

$$z = \frac{220 - 200}{40} = +.50$$

Area
.1915
.1915

$$P(180 \leq x \leq 220) = .3830$$

b. At $x = 250$

$$z = \frac{250 - 200}{40} = 1.25$$

$$\text{Area} = .3944$$

$$P(x \geq 250) = .5000 - .3944 = .1056$$

c. At $x = 100$

$$z = \frac{100 - 200}{40} = -2.50$$

$$\text{Area} = .4938$$

$$P(x \leq 100) = .5000 - .4938 = .0062$$

d. At $x = 250$

$$z = 1.25$$

$$\text{Area} = .3944$$

At $x = 225$

$$z = \frac{225 - 200}{40} = .625$$

$$\text{Area} = .2341$$

$$P(225 \leq x \leq 250) = .3944 - .2341 = .1603$$

18. a. $z = \dfrac{12,000 - 10,000}{2200} = .91$

$P(x \leq 12,000) = P(z \leq .91) = .5000 + .3186 = .8186$

$P(x \geq 12,000) = 1 - P(x \leq 12,000) = 1 - .8186 = .1814$

So, the probability a rehabilitation program will cost at least $12,000 is .1814.

b. $z = \dfrac{6000 - 10,000}{2200} = -1.82$

$P(x \geq 6000) = P(z \geq -1.82) = .4656 + .5000 = .9656$

The probability a rehabilitation program will cost at least $6000 is .9656.

c. First, find the value of z that cuts off an area of .10 in the upper tail of the standard normal distribution. A value of $z = 1.28$ does this.

Now find the value of x corresponding to $z = 1.28$.

$$\frac{x - 10,000}{2200} = 1.28$$

$$x = 10,000 + 1.28\,(2200)$$

$$= 12,816$$

The cost range for the 10% most expensive programs is $12,816 or more.

19. a. At $x = 800$

$$z = \frac{800 - 550}{150} = \frac{250}{150} = 1.67$$

From tables, $P\,(x \geq 800) = .5000 - .4525 = .0475$

4.75% of customers carry average daily balances over $800.

b. At $x = 200$

$$z = \frac{200 - 550}{150} = \frac{-350}{150} = -2.33$$

From tables, $P(z \leq -2.33) = .5000 - .4901 = .0099$

.99% of customers carry average daily balances of less than $200.

c. $P(300 < x < 700) = P(-1.67 < z < 1)$

$$= .4525 + .3413$$

$$= .7938$$

79.38% of customers carry average daily balances between $300 and $700.

d. At $z = 1.645$ we have an area of .05 in the upper tail.

$$1.645 = \frac{x - 550}{150} \Rightarrow x = 550 + 1.645\,(150)$$

$$= 550 + 246.75$$

$$= 796.75$$

The bank should not pay interest on balances below $796.75. In practice this would probably be rounded off to $800.00.

20. a.   At $x = 500$

$$z = \frac{500 - 530}{70} = -\frac{3}{7} = -.43$$

At $x = 600$

$$z = \frac{600 - 530}{70} = 1$$

$$P(500 \leq x \leq 600) = P(-.43 \leq z \leq 1) = .1664 + .3413$$

$$= .5077$$

50.77% of students

b. $P(x \geq 600) = P(z \geq 1) = .5000 - .3413 = .1587$

15.87% of students

c.   At $x = 480$

$$z = \frac{480 - 530}{70} = -\frac{5}{7} = -.71$$

$$P(x \leq 480) = P(z \leq -.71) = .5000 - .2612 = .2388$$

23.88% of students

21.   At $x = 132$

$$z = \frac{132 - 100}{15} = 2.13$$

$$P(x \geq 132) = P(z \geq 2.13) = .5000 - .4834 = .0166$$

1.66% qualify

22. a.   At $x = 20$

$$z = \frac{20 - 28}{8} = -1$$

At $x = 40$

$$z = \frac{40 - 28}{8} = 1.5$$

$$\begin{array}{r} \underline{\text{Area}} \\ .3413 \\ \underline{.4332} \\ P(20 \leq x \leq 40) = .7745 \end{array}$$

b. At $z = 1.04$ we have an area of .1492 or approximately .15 in the upper tail.

$$1.04 = \frac{x - 28}{8}$$

Therefore $x = 8(1.04) + 28 = 36.32$. An account should be sent a reminder letter after 37 days.

c. $z = \frac{21 - 28}{8} = -.875 \approx -.88$ Area = .3106

Therefore $.5 - .3106 = .19$ or 19% of the accounts will receive the discount.

23. a. $z = \frac{60 - 80}{10} = -2$ Area = $.5 - .4772 = .0228$

b. At $x = 60$

$$z = \frac{60 - 80}{10} = -2$$

At $x = 75$

$$z = \frac{75 - 80}{10} = -.5$$

$$\begin{array}{r} \underline{\text{Area}} \\ .4772 \\ \underline{-.1915} \\ P(60 \leq x \leq 75) = .2857 \end{array}$$

c. $z = \frac{90 - 80}{10} = 1$ Area = $.5 - .3413 = .1587$

Therefore 15.87% of students will not complete on time.

$$(60)\,(.1587) = 9.522$$

We would expect 9.522 students to be unable to complete the exam in time.

24. a. At $z = -.77$ we have an area of .2206 or approximately .22 in the lower tail.

$$-.77 = \frac{x - 3.25}{.5}$$

Therefore $x = .5(-.77) + 3.25 = 2.865$

2.865 years is the manufacturer's advertised life.

b. At $x = 3$

$$z = \frac{3 - 3.25}{.5} = -.5$$

At $x = 4$

$$z = \frac{4 - 3.25}{.5} = 1.5$$

	Area
	.1915
	.4332
$P(3 \leq x \leq 4) =$	.6247

25. a. At $x = 4760$

$$z = \frac{4760 - 5000}{800} = -.3$$

At $x = 5800$

$$z = \frac{5800 - 5000}{800} = 1$$

	Area
	.1179
	.3413
$P(4760 \leq x \leq 5800) =$	.4592

b. $z = \frac{6500 - 5000}{800} = 1.875 \approx 1.88$

Area $= .5 - .4669 = .0331 =$ Probability of more than 6500 customers.

c. At z -1.28 we have an area of .1003 or approximately .10 in the lower tail.

$$-1.28 = \frac{x - 5000}{8000}$$

Therefore $x = 800(-1.28) + 5000 = 3,976$

The number of customers exceeds 3,976 90% of the time.

26. a. $\mu = np = 50(.22) = 11$

    b. $\sigma = \sqrt{np\,(1 - p)} = \sqrt{50\,(.22)\,(.78)} = 2.93$

    At $x = 7.5$

    $$z = \frac{7.5 - 11}{2.93} = -1.19$$

    At $x = 12.5$

    $$z = \frac{12.5 - 11}{2.93} = .51$$

	Area
	.3830
	.1950
$P(7.5 \le x \le 12.5) =$	.5780

    The probability 8 to 12 employees select early retirement is .5780.

    c. $z = \frac{14.5 - 11}{2.93} = 1.19$ Area $= .5 - .3830 = .1170$

    The probability of 15 or more is .1170

    d. $z = \frac{9.5 - 11}{2.93} = -.51$

    Area from $x = 9.5$ to $x = 11 = .1950$

    Area from $x = 11$ and beyond $= \underline{.5000}$

    Answer $= .6950$

    The probability the program is successful is .6950

27. a. $\mu = np = 100(.54) = 54$

    The expected number of voters who will favor the Democratic candidate is 54.

    b. $\sigma^2 = np\,(1 - p) = 100(.54)\,(.46) = 24.84$

    The variance in the number of voters who will favor the Democratic candidate is 24.84.

    c. Use the normal approximation to the binomial and compute $P(x \le 49.5)$.

    $$z = \frac{49.5 - 54}{\sqrt{24.84}} = -.90$$

$$P(z \leq -.90) \qquad = .5000 - .3159$$

$$= .1841$$

The probability 49 or fewer in the sample will express support the Democratic candidate is .1841.

28. a. At $x = 100$

$$z = \frac{100 - 70}{25} = 1.2$$

$$P(x \geq 100) = P(z \geq 1.2) = .5000 - .3849 = .1151$$

b. At $x = 31$

$$z = \frac{31 - 70}{25} = -1.56$$

At $x = 60$

$$z = \frac{60 - 70}{25} = -.40$$

$$P(31 \leq x \leq 60) = P(-1.56 \leq z \leq -.40) = .4406 - .1554$$
$$= .2852$$

c. $z = -.84$ cuts off approximately 20% in lower tail

$$-.84 = \frac{x - 70}{25}$$

$$x = 70 - .84\,(25)$$

$$= 49$$

The fastest selling 20% are on the market 49 days or less.

29. a. $\mu = np = 120(.75) = 90$

$$\sigma = \sqrt{np\,(1 - p)} = \sqrt{120\,(.75)\,(.25)} = 4.74$$

The probability at least half the rooms are occupied is the normal probability: $P(x \geq 59.5)$.

At $x = 59.5$

$$z = \frac{59.5 - 90}{4.74} = -6.43$$

Therefore, probability is approximately 1

b. Find the normal probability: $P(x \geq 99.5)$

At $x = 99.5$

$$z = \frac{99.5 - 90}{4.74} = 2.00$$

$P(x \geq 99.5) = P(z \geq 2.00) = .5000 - .4772 = .0228$

c. Find the normal probability: $P(x \leq 80.5)$

At $x = 80.5$

$$z = \frac{80.5 - 90}{4.74} = -2.00$$

$P(x \leq 80.5) = P(z \leq -2.00) = .5000 - .4772 = .0228$

30. a. $\mu = np = 150(.30) = 45$

$$\sigma = \sqrt{np\,(1-p)} = \sqrt{120\,(.30)\,(.70)} = 5.61$$

Find the normal probability: $P(39.5 \leq x \leq 60.5)$

At $x = 39.5$

$$z = \frac{39.5 - 45}{5.61} = -.98$$

At $x = 60.5$

$$z = \frac{60.5 - 45}{5.61} = 2.76$$

$P(39.5 \leq x \leq 60.5) = P(-.98 \leq z \leq 2.76) = .3365 + .4971 = .8336$

The probability that 40 to 60 pay before interest charges are incurred is .8336.

b. Find the normal probability: $P(x \leq 30.5)$.

At $x = 30.5$

$$z = \frac{30.5 - 45}{5.61} = -2.58$$

$P(x \leq 30.5) = P(z \leq -2.58) = .5000 - .4951 = .0049$

31. a. $P(x \leq 6) = 1 - e^{-6/8} = 1 - .4724 = .5276$

b. $P(x \leq 4) = 1 - e^{-4/8} = 1 - .6065 = .3935$

c. $P(x \geq 6) = 1 - P(x \leq 6) = 1 - .5276 = .4724$

d. $P(4 \leq x \leq 6) = P(x \leq 6) - P(x \leq 4) = .5276 - .3935 = .1341$

32. a. $P(x \leq x_0) = 1 - e^{-x_0/3}$

b. $P(x \leq 2) = 1 - e^{-2/3} = 1 - .5134 = .4866$

c. $P(x \geq 3) = 1 - P(x \leq 3) = 1 - (1 - e^{--3/3}) = e^{-1} = .3679$

d. $P(x \leq 5) = 1 - e^{-5/3} = 1 - .1889 = .8111$

e. $P(2 \leq x \leq 5) = P(x \leq 5) - P(x \leq 2) = .8111 - .4866$

$$= .3245$$

33. a. The mean time between fatalities is 1 / 34 year. So, for 1 month we have

$$\mu = \frac{12}{34}$$

$P(x \leq 1) = 1 - e^{-1/(12/34)} = 1 - e^{-34/12} = 1 - e^{-2.833}$

$$= 1 - .06$$

$$= .94$$

$P(\text{no fatalities in one month}) = P(x > 1) = 1 - .94 = .06$

b. $P(x \leq 1 \text{ week}) = 1 - e^{1/(52/34)} = 1 - e^{-34/52}$

$$= 1 - .52$$

$$= .48$$

Therefore, $P(x > 1 \text{ week}) = .52$

34. a.

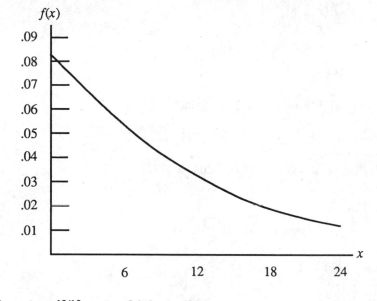

b. $P(x \leq 12) = 1 - e^{-12/12} = 1 - .3679 = .6321$

c. $P(x \leq 6) = 1 - e^{-6/12} = 1 - .6065 = .3935$

d. $P(x \geq 30) = 1 - P(x < 30)$

$$= 1 - (1 - e^{-30/12})$$

$$= .0821$$

35. a. 50 hours

b. $P(x \leq 25) = 1 - e^{-25/50} = 1 - .6065 = .3935$

c. $P(x \geq 100) = 1 - (1 - e^{-100/50})$

$$= .1353$$

36. a. 4 hours

b. $f(x) = (1/4) e^{-x/4}$ for $x \geq 0$

c. $P(x \geq 1) = 1 - P(x < 1)$

$$= 1 - (1 - e^{-1/4})$$

$$= .7788$$

d. $P(x > 8) \quad = 1 - P(x \leq 8)$

$$= e^{-8/4}$$

$$= .1353$$

37. a. $P(x \leq 15) = 1 - e^{-15/36} = 1 - .6592 = .3408$

b. $P(x \leq 45) = 1 - e^{-45/36} = 1 - .2865 = .7135$

Therefore $P(15 \leq x \leq 45) = .7135 - .3408 = .3727$

c. $P(x \geq 60) = 1 - P(x < 60)$

$$= 1 - (1 - e^{-60/36})$$

$$= .1889$$

38. a.

$$f(x) = \begin{cases} \dfrac{1}{5} & \text{for } 0 \leq x \leq 5 \\ \\ 0 & \text{elsewhere} \end{cases}$$

b. $P(x > 3.5) = 1.5 / 5 = .30$

c. $P(x \leq .75) = .75 / 5 = .15$

d. $P(1 < x < 3) = 2 / 5 = .40$

e. $E(x) = \dfrac{0 + 5}{2} = 2.50 \text{ minutes}$

39. a.

$$f(x) = \begin{cases} \dfrac{1}{10} & \text{for } 30 \leq x \leq 40 \\ \\ 0 & \text{elsewhere} \end{cases}$$

b. $P(x > 38) = 2 / 10 = .20$

c. $\dfrac{x - 30}{10} = .7 \Rightarrow x = 37$

The time standard should be set at 37 minutes.

d. $E(x) = \dfrac{30+40}{2} = 35$ $\qquad$ $Var(x) = \dfrac{(40-30)^2}{12} = 8.33$

Standard Deviation $= \sigma = 2.89$

40. a.
$$f(x) = \begin{cases} \dfrac{1}{200} & \text{for } 3900 \le x \le 4100 \\ \\ 0 & \text{elsewhere} \end{cases}$$

b. $P(x < 3950) = 50 / 200 = .25$

41. a. .2642

b. .1368 x 2 = .2736

c. .3078 - .0871 = .2207

d. .5000 - .3461 = .1539

42. a. .3106 + .5000 = .8106

b. .5000 - .4162 = .0838

c. .2054 + .4901 = .6955

d. .4750 x 2 = .9500

43. a. Look up an area value in the table of .90 / 2 = .45. This area is between $z = 1.64$ and $z = 1.65$. Use $z = 1.645$.

b. Look up an area closest to .5000 - .2000 = .3000; $z = .84$.

c. At $z = -1.66$, area = .4515. Moving .25 area toward the mean provides an area of .4515 - .2500 = .2015 remaining between the z value and the mean. Look up the area closest to .2015. The z value is -.53.

d. Look up an area closest to .5000 - .4000 = .1000; $z = -.25$.

e. At $z = 1.80$, the area is .4641. .4641 - .2000 = .2641. Look up an area closest to .2641; $z = .72$.

44. a. $P(\textit{defect}) = 1 - P(9.85 \leq x \leq 10.15)$

$= 1 - P(-1 \leq z \leq 1)$

$= 1 - .6826$

$= .3174$

Expected number of defects $= 1000(.3174) = 317.4$

b. $P(\textit{defect}) = 1 - P(9.85 \leq x \leq 10.15)$

$= 1 - P(-3 \leq z \leq 3)$

$= 1 - .9972$

$= .0028$

Expected number of defects $= 1000(.0028) = 2.8$

c. Reducing the process standard deviation causes a substantial reduction in the number of defects.

45. a. The area under the normal curve between 5000 and the mean of 23,618 is .5000 - .0770 = .4230. Therefore , the z value corresponding to an income level of $5,000 is approximately $z = -1.43$. And, hence

$$-1.43 = \frac{5000 - \mu}{\sigma}$$

Substituting $\mu = 23,618$, we get

$$-1.43\sigma = 5000 - 23,618 = -18,618$$
$$\sigma = 13,019$$

If household incomes are normally distributed, then $\sigma = \$13,019$.

b. With $\sigma = 13,019$, the z value at 50,000 is

$$z = \frac{50,000 - 23,618}{13,019}$$

$$= 2.03$$

The area under the curve to the right of $z = 2.03$ is .5000 - .4788 = .0212.

Given the standard deviation in part a, only 2.12% should have incomes in excess of $50,000.

c. The result of part b calls into question the assumption of normally distributed incomes. Incomes may be approximately normally distributed in the middle ranges, but none can be less than zero and some are very large.

46. $\mu = 10.75 \quad \sigma = .1$

At $x = 11$

$$z = \frac{11 - 10.75}{.1} = 2.50$$

Area = .4938

$$P(x > 11) = .5000 - .4938 = .0062$$

The overflow will occur .62% of the time.

47. $\mu = 10,000 \quad \sigma = 1500$

a. At $x = 12,000$

$$z = \frac{12,000 - 10,000}{1500} = 1.33$$

Area = .4082

$$P(x > 12,000) = .5000 - .4082 = .0918$$

b. At .95

$$z = 1.645 = \frac{x - 10,000}{1500}$$

Therefore, $x = 10,000 + 1.645(1500) = 12,468$.

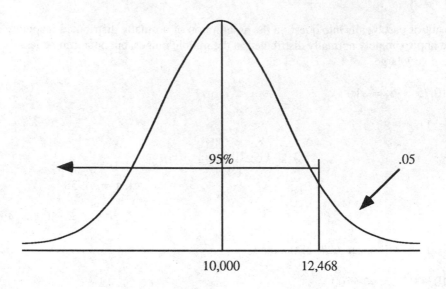

95%   .05

10,000   12,468

12,468 tubes should be produced.

48. a.   At $x = 20$

$$z = \frac{20 - 24}{6} = -.67$$

At $x = 30$

$$z = \frac{30 - 24}{6} = 1$$

Area
.2486
.3413

$$P(20 \leq x \leq 30) = .5899$$

The probability that the winning team scores between 20 and 30 points is .5899.

b.   At $z = .84$ the upper tail area is approximately .20

$$.84 = \frac{x - 24}{6}$$

$$x = 6\,(.84) + 24 = 29.04$$

If a team scores 30 points or more it will be in the top 20%.

49. a.   At $x = 200$

$$z = \frac{200 - 150}{25} = 2$$

Area $= .4772$

$$P(x > 200) = .5000 - .4772 = .0228$$

b. Expected Profit = Expected Revenue - Expected Cost

$$= 200 - 150 = \$50$$

50. $\mu = 45{,}000 \quad \sigma = 3000$

   a. At $x = 44{,}000$

$$z = \frac{44{,}000 - 45{,}000}{3000} = -.33$$

Area = .1293

At $x = 48{,}000$

$$z = \frac{48{,}000 - 45{,}000}{3000} = 1.00$$

Area = .3413

47.06% $P(44{,}000 \leq x \leq 48{,}000) = .4706$

b. At $x = 50{,}000$

$$z = \frac{50{,}000 - 45{,}000}{3000} = 1.67$$

Area = .4525

$P(x > 50{,}000) = .5000 - .4525 = .0475$

c. A z - value of -.84 cuts off an area of approximately .20 in the left tail.

$$-.84 = \frac{x - 45{,}000}{3000}$$

$$x = 45{,}000 - .84\,(3000)$$

$$= 42{,}480$$

Attendance will be greater than 42,480 approximately 80% of the time.

51. a. At 400,

$$z = \frac{400 - 450}{100} = -.500$$

Area = .1915

At 500,

$$z = \frac{500 - 450}{100} = +.500$$

Area = $\underline{.1915}$
.3830 or 38.3%

b. At 630,

$$z = \frac{630 - 450}{100} = 1.80$$

Area = .5000 - .4641
= .0359 or 3.59%

3.59% do better and 96.41% do worse.

c. At 480,

$$z = \frac{480 - 450}{100} = .30$$

Area = .5000 - .1179
= .3821 or 38.21%

38.21% are acceptable.

52. $\mu = 3.367$ $\sigma = .001$

a. $P(x < 3.365)$ is the probability of a defective card.

$$z = \frac{3.365 - 3.367}{.001} = \frac{-.002}{.001} = -2$$

Area to left of $z = -2$ is .0228.

The probability of obtaining a defective card is

$$P(x < 3.365) = .0228.$$

b. Do not use the die.

c. A z - value of -2.33 corresponds to an area in the left tail of approximately .01.

$$-2.33 = \frac{3.365 - \mu}{.001}$$

$$\mu = 3.365 + 2.33 \,(.001)$$

$$= 3.36733$$

The smallest permissible mean length is 3.36733 inches.

53. $\sigma = .6$

At 2%

$$z = -2.05 \quad x = 18$$

$$z = \frac{x - \mu}{\sigma} \qquad \therefore \; -2.05 = \frac{18 - \mu}{.6}$$

$$\mu = 18 + 2.05 \, (.6) = 19.23 \text{ oz.}$$

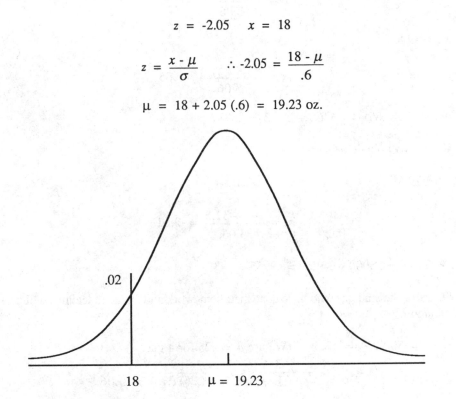

The mean filling weight must be 19.23 oz.

54.   Use normal approximation to binomial.

a. $\mu = np = 50 \, (.75) = 37.5$

$$\sigma = \sqrt{np \, (1 - p)} = \sqrt{50 \, (.75) \, (.25)} = 3.06$$

At $x = 42.5$

$$z = \frac{x - \mu}{\sigma} = \frac{42.5 - 37.5}{3.06} = 1.63$$

$$P(0 \leq z \leq 1.63) = .4484$$

Probability of an A grade $= .5000 - .4484 = .0516$

or 5.16% will obtain an A grade.

b. At $x = 34.5$

$$z = \frac{34.5 - 37.5}{3.06} = -.98$$

At $x = 39.5$

$$z = \frac{39.5 - 37.5}{3.06} = .65$$

$P(-.98 \leq z \leq .65) = .3365 + .2422 = .5787$

or 57.87% will obtain a C grade.

c. At $x = 29.5$

$$z = \frac{29.5 - 37.5}{3.06} = -2.61$$

$P(z \geq -2.61) = .5000 + .4955 = .9955$

or 99.55%of the students who have done their homework and attended lectures will pass the examination.

d. $\mu = np = 50\,(.25) = 12.5$ (We use $p = .25$ for a guess.)

$$\sigma = \sqrt{np\,(1 - p)} = \sqrt{50\,(.25)\,(.75)} = 3.06$$

At $x = 29.5$

$$z = \frac{29.5 - 12.5}{3.06} = 5.55$$

$P(z \geq 5.55) \approx 0$

Thus, essentially no one who simply guesses will pass the examination.

55.   Use normal approximation to binomial with

$\mu = np = 100\,(.64) = 64$

$$\sigma = \sqrt{np\,(1 - p)} = \sqrt{100\,(.64)\,(.36)} = 4.8$$

Find $P(59.5 \leq x \leq 70.5)$

At $x = 59.5$

$$z = \frac{59.5 - 64}{4.8} = -.94$$

At x = 70.5

$$z = \frac{70.5 - 64}{4.8} = 1.35$$

$$P(59.5 \leq x \leq 70.5) = P(-0.94 \leq x \leq 1.35) = .3264 + .4115$$

$$= .7379$$

The probability that at least 60 but no more than 70 will be living in the state they were born is .7379.

56. a. $\dfrac{1}{\mu} = .5$ therefore $\mu = 2$ minutes = mean time between telephone calls

   b. Note: 30 seconds = .5 minutes

   $$P(x \leq .5) = 1 - e^{-.5/2} = 1 - .7788 = .2212$$

   c. $P(x \leq 1) = 1 - e^{-1/2} = 1 - .6065 = .3935$

   d. $P(x \geq 5) = 1 - P(x < 5)$

   $$= 1 - (1 - e^{-5/2})$$

   $$= .0821$$

57. a. $f(x) = \dfrac{1}{1.2} e^{-x/1.2}$ for $x \geq 0$

   b. $P(.5 \leq x \leq 1.0) = P(x \leq 1.0) - P(x \leq .5)$

   $$= (1 - e^{-1/1.2}) - (1 - e^{-.5/1.2})$$

   $$= .5654 - .3408$$

   $$= .2246$$

   c. $P(x > 1) = 1 - P(x \leq 1)$

   $$= 1 - .5654$$

   $$= .4346$$

Chapter 7
Sampling and Sampling Distributions

Learning Objectives

1. Understand the importance of sampling and how results from samples can be used to provide estimates of population characteristics such as the population mean, the population standard deviation and / or the population proportion.

2. Know what simple random sampling is and how simple random samples are selected.

3. Understand the concept of a sampling distribution.

4. Know the central limit theorem and the important role it plays in sampling.

5. Specifically know the characteristics of the sampling distribution of the sample mean ($\bar{x}$) and the sampling distribution of the sample proportion ($\bar{p}$).

6. Become aware of the properties of point estimators including unbiasedness, consistency, and efficiency.

7. Know the definition of the following terms:

simple random sampling	finite population correction factor
sampling with replacement	standard error
sampling without replacement	unbiasedness
sampling distribution	consistency
point estimator	efficiency

Solutions:

1. a. AB, AC, AD, AE, BC, BD, BE, CD, CE, DE

    b. With 10 samples, each has a 1/10 probability.

    c. E and C because 8 and 0 do not apply.; 5 identifies E; 7 does not apply; 5 is skipped since E is already in the sample; 3 identifies C; 2 is not needed since the sample of size 2 is complete.

2. Using the last 3-digits of each 5-digit grouping provides the random numbers:

    601, 022, 448, 147, 229, 553, 147, 289, 209

    Numbers greater than 350 do not apply and the 147 can only be used once. Thus, the simple random sample of four includes 22, 147, 229, and 289.

3. 554, 459, 147, 385, 689, 640, 113, 340, 756, 953, 403, 827

4. a. 6   L.A. Gear
        8   New Balance
        5   Adidas
        4   Avia
        1   Reebok

    b. 0

    c. $$\frac{N!}{n! \, (N-n)!} = \frac{10!}{5! \, (10-5)!} = \frac{3,628,500}{(120)(120)} = 252$$

5. 283, 610, 39, 254, 568, 353, 602, 421, 638, 164

6. 2782, 493, 825, 1807, 289

7. 108, 290, 201, 292, 322, 9, 244, 249, 226, 125, (continuing at the top of column 9) 147, and 113.

8. 447, 348, 499, 568, 055, 392, 126, 036, 599, 294, 570, 159

9. 364, 702, 782, 263, 281, 243, 493, 337, 525, 825.

10. a. Using 3-digit random numbers, select a random number from 1 to 853 to identify a page in the directory. Then select a random number from 1 to 400 to identify a line on the page. The phone number on this line corresponds to a sampled household.

    b. Phone numbers that ate clearly business, restaurant, etc. phone numbers should be discarded on the basis that they a re not part of the household phone number population of interest in the study. Repeat the sampling method described in (a) above until 200 household phone numbers have been identified.

11. a. Yes, a population of consumer visits can be viewed as an infinite population. The consumers who

actually visit over a period of time are a portion of the infinite population of visits.

b. This sampling procedure satisfies the requirement of a simple random sample from an infinite population in that the customers are selected independently from the same population.

12. finite, infinite, infinite, infinite, finite

13. a. $\bar{x} = \sum x_i / n = 54/6 = 9$

b. $s = \sqrt{\dfrac{\sum (x_i - \bar{x})^2}{n-1}}$

$\sum (x_i - \bar{x})^2 = (-4)^2 + (-1)^2 + 1^2 (-2)^2 + 1^2 + 5^2 = 48$

$s = \sqrt{\dfrac{48}{6-1}} = 3.1$

14. a. $\bar{p} = 75/150 = .50$

b. $\bar{p} = 55/150 = .3667$

15. a. $\bar{x} = \sum x_i / n = 465/5 = 93$

b.

x_i	$(x_i - \bar{x})$	$(x_i - \bar{x})^2$
94	+1	1
100	+7	49
85	-8	64
94	+1	1
92	-1	1
Totals 465	0	116

$s = \sqrt{\dfrac{\sum (x_i - \bar{x})^2}{n-1}} = \sqrt{\dfrac{116}{4}} = 5.39$

16. a. $\bar{x} = \sum x_i / n = 142/16 = 8.875$

b. $s = \sqrt{\dfrac{\sum (x_i - \bar{x})^2}{n-1}} = \sqrt{\dfrac{25.75}{15}} = 1.31$

17. a. $\bar{x} = \sum x_i / n = 59.4/10 = 5.94$

b. $s = \sqrt{\dfrac{\sum (x_i - \bar{x})^2}{n-1}} = \sqrt{\dfrac{107.964}{9}} = 3.46$

18. $\bar{p} = 3/104 = .0288$

19. a. $\bar{p} = 310/400 = .775$

b. $\bar{p} = 225/400 = .5625$

c. $\bar{p} = 175/400 = .4375$

20. a. $E(\bar{x}) = \mu = 200$

b. $\sigma_{\bar{x}} = \sigma/\sqrt{n} = 50/\sqrt{100} = 5$

c. Normal with $E(\bar{x}) = 200$ and $\sigma_{\bar{x}} = 5$

d. It shows the probability distribution of all possible sample means that can be observed with random samples of size 100. This distribution can be used to compute the probability that $\bar{x}$ is within a specified ± from μ.

21.   The Central Limit Theorem provides the theoretical basis for using a normal probability distribution to approximate the sampling distribution of the sample mean. It is the basis for computing the probability of an $\bar{x}$ being within a certain plus or minus from population mean as was done in question 18.

22. a. The sampling distribution is normal with

$E(\bar{x}) = \mu = 200$

$\sigma_{\bar{x}} = \sigma/\sqrt{n} = 50/\sqrt{100} = 5$

For ±5, $(\bar{x} - \mu) = 5$

$$z = \frac{\bar{x} - \mu}{\sigma_{\bar{x}}} = \frac{5}{5} = 1$$

Area = .3413
       x2
      .6826

b. For ± 10, $(\bar{x} - \mu) = 10$

$$z = \frac{\bar{x} - \mu}{\sigma_{\bar{x}}} = \frac{10}{5} = 2$$

Area = .4772
x2
.9544

23. a. $E(\bar{x}) = \mu = 32$

b. Since $n / N = 30 / 1000 = .03$ is less than .05, use

$$\sigma_{\bar{x}} = \frac{\sigma}{\sqrt{n}} = \frac{5}{\sqrt{30}} = .91$$

24. $\sigma_{\bar{x}} = \sigma / \sqrt{n}$

$\sigma_{\bar{x}} = 25 / \sqrt{50} = 3.54$

$\sigma_{\bar{x}} = 25 / \sqrt{100} = 2.50$

$\sigma_{\bar{x}} = 25 / \sqrt{150} = 2.04$

$\sigma_{\bar{x}} = 25 / \sqrt{200} = 1.77$

The standard error of the mean decreases as the sample size increases.

25. a. $\sigma_{\bar{x}} = \frac{\sigma}{\sqrt{n}} = \frac{10}{\sqrt{50}} = 1.41$

b. $n / N = 50 / 50{,}000 = .001$

Use

$$\sigma_{\bar{x}} = \frac{\sigma}{\sqrt{n}} = \frac{10}{\sqrt{50}} = 1.41$$

c. $n / N = 50 / 5000 = .01$

Use

$$\sigma_{\bar{x}} = \frac{\sigma}{\sqrt{n}} = \frac{10}{\sqrt{50}} = 1.41$$

d. $n / N = 50 / 500 = .10$

Use

$$\sigma_{\bar{x}} = \sqrt{\frac{N - n}{N - 1}} \frac{\sigma}{\sqrt{n}}$$

$$= \sqrt{\frac{500 - 50}{500 - 1}} \frac{10}{\sqrt{50}} = 1.34$$

Note: Only case (d) where $n/N = .10$ requires the use of the finite population correction factor. Note that $\sigma_{\bar{x}}$ is approximately the same even though the population size varies from infinite to 500.

26. a. Using the central limit theorem, we can approximate the sampling distribution of $\bar{x}$ with a normal probability distribution provided $n \geq 30$.

   b. $n = 30$

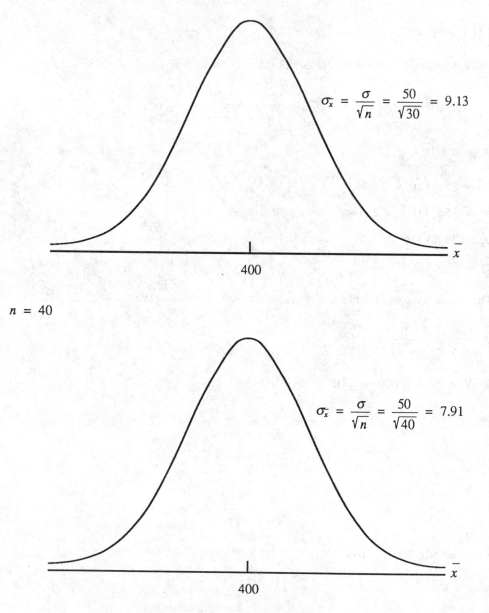

$$\sigma_{\bar{x}} = \frac{\sigma}{\sqrt{n}} = \frac{50}{\sqrt{30}} = 9.13$$

$n = 40$

$$\sigma_{\bar{x}} = \frac{\sigma}{\sqrt{n}} = \frac{50}{\sqrt{40}} = 7.91$$

27. a. $\sigma_{\bar{x}} = \frac{\sigma}{\sqrt{n}} = \frac{16}{\sqrt{50}} = 2.26$

For ± 2, $(\bar{x} - \mu) = 2$

$$z = \frac{\bar{x} - \mu}{\sigma_{\bar{x}}} = \frac{2}{2.26} = .88$$

Area = .3106
$$\underline{\quad x2}$$
.6212

b. $\sigma_{\bar{x}} = \dfrac{16}{\sqrt{100}} = 1.60$

$$z = \frac{\bar{x} - \mu}{\sigma_{\bar{x}}} = \frac{2}{1.60} = 1.25$$

Area = .3944
$$\underline{\quad x2}$$
.7888

c. $\sigma_{\bar{x}} = \dfrac{16}{\sqrt{200}} = 1.13$

$$z = \frac{\bar{x} - \mu}{\sigma_{\bar{x}}} = \frac{2}{1.13} = 1.77$$

Area = .4616
$$\underline{\quad x2}$$
.9232

d. $\sigma_{\bar{x}} = \dfrac{16}{\sqrt{400}} = 0.80$

$$z = \frac{\bar{x} - \mu}{\sigma_{\bar{x}}} = \frac{2}{.80} = 2.50$$

Area = .4938
$$\underline{\quad x2}$$
.9876

e. The larger sample provides a higher probability that the sample mean will be within ± 2 of μ.

28. a.

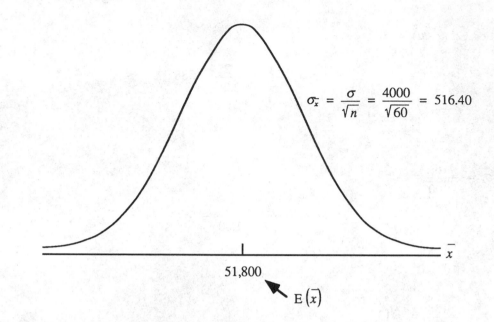

$$\sigma_{\bar{x}} = \frac{\sigma}{\sqrt{n}} = \frac{4000}{\sqrt{60}} = 516.40$$

51,800

$E\left(\bar{x}\right)$

The normal distribution is based on the Central Limit Theorem.

b. For $n = 120$, $E\left(\bar{x}\right)$ remains \$51,800 and the sampling distribution of $\bar{x}$ can still be approximates by a normal distribution. However, $\sigma_{\bar{x}}$ is reduced to $4000 / \sqrt{120} = 365.15$.

c. As the sample size is increased, the standard error of the mean, $\sigma_{\bar{x}}$, is reduced. This appears logical from the point of view that larger samples should tend to provide sample means that are closer to the population mean. Thus, the variability in the sample mean, measured in terms of $\sigma_{\bar{x}}$, should decrease as the sample size is increased.

29. a.

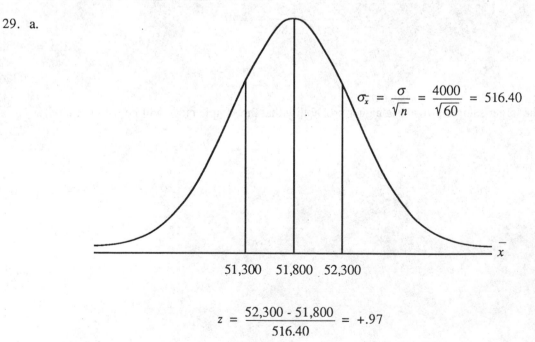

$$\sigma_{\bar{x}} = \frac{\sigma}{\sqrt{n}} = \frac{4000}{\sqrt{60}} = 516.40$$

51,300   51,800   52,300

$$z = \frac{52,300 - 51,800}{516.40} = +.97$$

Area = .3340
$$\underline{\quad \times 2}$$
.6680

b. $\sigma_{\bar{x}} = \dfrac{\sigma}{\sqrt{n}} = \dfrac{4000}{\sqrt{120}} = 365.15$

$$z = \dfrac{52,300 - 51,800}{365.15} = +1.37$$

Area
.4147
$$\underline{\quad \times 2}$$
.8294

30. a.

$$\sigma_{\bar{x}} = \dfrac{\sigma}{\sqrt{n}} = \dfrac{4}{\sqrt{40}} = .6325$$

12.55

b. $P(11.55 \leq \bar{x} \leq 13.55) = ?$

$$z = \dfrac{13.55 - 12.55}{.6325} = 1.58$$

Area
.4429
$$\underline{\quad \times 2}$$
.8858

c. $P(12.05 \leq \bar{x} \leq 13.05) = ?$

$$z = \dfrac{13.05 - 12.55}{.6325} = .79$$

Area
.2852
$$\underline{\quad \times 2}$$
.5704

31. $E(\bar{x}) = \mu = 72$

$$\sigma_{\bar{x}} = \sqrt{\frac{N-n}{N-1}} \frac{\sigma}{\sqrt{n}} = \sqrt{\frac{80-20}{80-1}} \frac{12}{\sqrt{20}} = 2.34$$

32. $E(\bar{x}) = \mu = 170$

$$\sigma_{\bar{x}} = \frac{\sigma}{\sqrt{n}} = \frac{28}{\sqrt{40}} = 4.43$$

33. a. $z = \dfrac{\bar{x} - 26{,}542}{\sigma / \sqrt{n}}$

Error = $\bar{x} - 26{,}542 = 250$

$n = 30 \qquad z = \dfrac{250}{2000 / \sqrt{30}} = .68 \qquad .2518 \; x2 = .5036$

$n = 50 \qquad z = \dfrac{250}{2000 / \sqrt{50}} = .88 \qquad .3106 \; x2 = .6212$

$n = 100 \qquad z = \dfrac{250}{2000 / \sqrt{100}} = 1.25 \qquad .3944 \; x2 = .7888$

$n = 200 \qquad z = \dfrac{250}{2000 / \sqrt{200}} = 1.77 \qquad .4616 \; x2 = .9232$

$n = 400 \qquad z = \dfrac{250}{2000 / \sqrt{400}} = 2.50 \qquad .4938 \; x2 = .9876$

b. A larger sample increases the probability that the sample mean will be within a specified distance from the population mean. In the salary example, the probability of being within ±250 of μ ranges from .5036 for a sample of size 30 to .9876 for a sample of size 400.

34. a. $\sigma_{\bar{x}} = \dfrac{\sigma}{\sqrt{n}} = \dfrac{1.5}{\sqrt{50}} = .2121$

$P(11.08 \leq \bar{x} \leq 11.48) = ?$

$$z = \frac{11.48 - 11.28}{.2121} = .94$$

$$\begin{array}{r} \underline{\text{Area}} \\ .3264 \\ \underline{\quad x2} \\ .6528 \end{array}$$

b. $P\ (11.18 \le \bar{x} \le 11.38)\ =\ ?$

$$z\ =\ \frac{11.38 - 11.28}{.2121}\ =\ .47$$

$$\begin{array}{r} \underline{\text{Area}} \\ .1808 \\ \underline{\text{x2}} \\ .3616 \end{array}$$

35. Current $\quad \sigma_{\bar{x}}\ =\ \dfrac{\sigma}{\sqrt{n}}\ =\ \dfrac{\sigma}{\sqrt{25}}\ =\ \dfrac{\sigma}{5}$

Desired $\quad \sigma_{\bar{x}}\ =\ \dfrac{1}{2}\ (\text{Current } \sigma_{\bar{x}})\ =\ \dfrac{1}{2}\left(\dfrac{\sigma}{5}\right)\ =\ \dfrac{\sigma}{10}$

Thus the new sample size n can be found by noting

Desired $\quad \sigma_{\bar{x}}\ =\ \dfrac{\sigma}{\sqrt{n}}\ =\ \dfrac{\sigma}{10}$

Thus, $\sqrt{n}\ =\ 10$ and $n\ =\ (10)^2\ =\ 100.$

36. a. Normal distribution,

$E\left(\bar{x}\right)\ =\ 16{,}012$

$\sigma_{\bar{x}}\ =\ \dfrac{\sigma}{\sqrt{n}}\ =\ \dfrac{4200}{\sqrt{100}}\ =\ 420$

b. $\quad z\ =\ \dfrac{\bar{x} - \mu}{\sigma / \sqrt{n}}\ =\ \dfrac{1000}{420}\ =\ 2.38 \quad (.4913\ \text{x2})\ =\ .9826$

c. $500 \quad z\ =\ 500/420\ =\ 1.19 \quad (.3830\ \text{x2})\ =\ .7660$

$250 \quad z\ =\ 250/420\ =\ .60 \quad (.2257\ \text{x2})\ =\ .4514$

$100 \quad z\ =\ 100/420\ =\ .24 \quad (.0948\ \text{x2})\ =\ .1896$

d. Increase sample size to improve precision of the estimate. Sample size of 100 has only a .4514 probability of being within $\pm$ $100.

37. a.

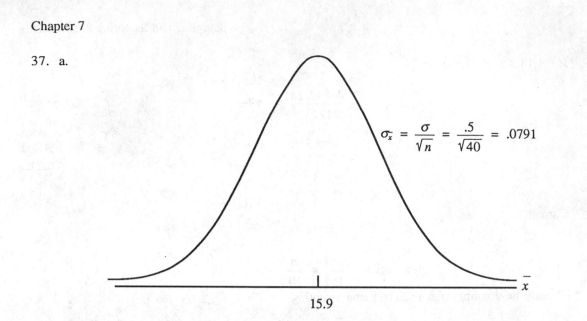

$$\sigma_{\bar{x}} = \frac{\sigma}{\sqrt{n}} = \frac{.5}{\sqrt{40}} = .0791$$

15.9

b. $P(\bar{x} > 16) = ?$

$$z = \frac{16 - 15.9}{.0791} = 1.26$$

Area
.3962

Thus, $P(15.9 \le \bar{x} \le 16) = .3962$ and $P(\bar{x} > 16) = .5000 - .3962 = .1038$

38. a.

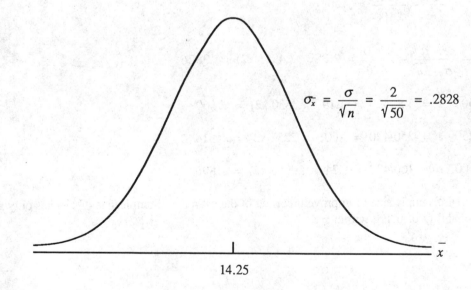

$$\sigma_{\bar{x}} = \frac{\sigma}{\sqrt{n}} = \frac{2}{\sqrt{50}} = .2828$$

14.25

b. $P(\bar{x} \ge 13.80) = ?$

$$z = \frac{13.80 - 14.25}{.2828} = -1.59$$

$$\begin{array}{r} \text{Area} \\ .4441 \\ +\underline{.5000} \\ .9441 \end{array}$$

c. $P\,(14.00 \leq \bar{x} \leq 14.50) = ?$

$$z = \frac{14.50 - 14.25}{.2828} = .88$$

$$\begin{array}{r} \text{Area} \\ .3106 \\ \underline{\times 2} \\ .6212 \end{array}$$

d. $\sigma_{\bar{x}} = \dfrac{\sigma}{\sqrt{n}} = \dfrac{2}{\sqrt{100}} = .20$

$P\,(\bar{x} \geq 13.80) = ?$

$$z = \frac{13.80 - 14.25}{.20} = -2.25$$

$$\begin{array}{r} \text{Area} \\ .4878 \\ +\underline{.5000} \\ .9878 \end{array}$$

$P\,(14.00 \leq \bar{x} \leq 14.50) = ?$

$$z = \frac{14.50 - 14.25}{.20} = 1.25$$

$$\begin{array}{r} \text{Area} \\ .3944 \\ \underline{\times 2} \\ .7888 \end{array}$$

39. a. $n/N = 40/4000 = .01 < .05$; therefore, the finite population correction factor is not necessary.

b. With the finite population correction factor

$$\sigma_{\bar{x}} = \sqrt{\frac{N-n}{N-1}}\,\frac{\sigma}{\sqrt{n}} = \sqrt{\frac{4000-40}{4000-1}}\,\frac{8.2}{\sqrt{40}} = 1.29$$

Without the finite population correction factor

$$\sigma_{\bar{x}} = \frac{\sigma}{\sqrt{n}} = \; = 1.30$$

Including the finite population correction factor provides only a slightly different value for $\sigma_{\bar{x}}$ than when the correction factor is not used.

$$\sigma_{\bar{x}} = \frac{\sigma}{\sqrt{n}} = \ = 1.30$$

$$z = \ = \frac{\bar{x} - \mu}{1.30} = \frac{2}{1.30} = 1.54$$

Area
.3944
x2
.7888

40. a.

$$\sigma_{\bar{x}} = \frac{\sigma}{\sqrt{n}} = \frac{75}{\sqrt{30}} = 13.69$$

320

b. $\sigma_{\bar{x}} = 13.69$

c. $P(300 \le \bar{x} \le 340) = ?$

$$z = \frac{340 - 320}{13.69} = 1.46$$

Area
.4279
x2
.8558

d. $P(\bar{x} > 325) = ?$

$$z = \frac{325 - 320}{13.69} = .37$$

Area
.1443

Thus, $P(320 \leq \bar{x} \leq 325) = .1443$ and $P(\bar{x} \geq 325) = .5000 - .1443 = .3557$

41. a. $E(\bar{p}) = p = .40$

b. $\sigma_{\bar{p}} = \sqrt{\dfrac{p(1-p)}{n}} = \sqrt{\dfrac{.40(.60)}{100}} = .0490$

c. Normal distribution with $E(\bar{p}) = .40$ and $\sigma_{\bar{p}} = .0490$

d. It shows the probability distribution for the sample proportion $\bar{p}$.

42. a. $E(\bar{p}) = .40$

$\sigma_{\bar{p}} = \sqrt{\dfrac{p(1-p)}{n}} = \sqrt{\dfrac{.40(.60)}{200}} = .0346$

$$z = \frac{\bar{p} - p}{\sigma_{\bar{p}}} = \frac{.03}{.0346} = .87$$

Area
.3078
  x2
.6156

b.

$$z = \frac{\bar{p} - p}{\sigma_{\bar{p}}} = \frac{.05}{.0346} = 1.45$$

Area
.4265
  x2
.8530

43.

$\sigma_{\bar{p}} = \sqrt{\dfrac{p(1-p)}{n}}$

$\sigma_{\bar{p}} = \sqrt{\dfrac{(.55)(.45)}{100}} = .0497$

$\sigma_{\bar{p}} = \sqrt{\dfrac{(.55)(.45)}{200}} = .0352$

$\sigma_{\bar{p}} = \sqrt{\dfrac{(.55)(.45)}{500}} = .0222$

$\sigma_{\bar{p}} = \sqrt{\dfrac{(.55)(.45)}{1000}} = .0157$

$\sigma_{\bar{p}}$ decreases as n increases

44. a.
$$\sigma_{\bar{p}} = \sqrt{\frac{(.30)\,(.70)}{100}} = .0458$$

$$z = \frac{\bar{p} - p}{\sigma_{\bar{p}}} = \frac{.04}{.0458} = .87$$

Area $= .3078 \times 2 = .6156$

b.
$$\sigma_{\bar{p}} = \sqrt{\frac{(.30)\,(.70)}{200}} = .0324$$

$$z = \frac{\bar{p} - p}{\sigma_{\bar{p}}} = \frac{.04}{.0324} = 1.23$$

Area $= .3907 \times 2 = .7814$

c.
$$\sigma_{\bar{p}} = \sqrt{\frac{(.30)\,(.70)}{500}} = .0205$$

$$z = \frac{\bar{p} - p}{\sigma_{\bar{p}}} = \frac{.04}{.0205} = 1.95$$

Area $= .4744 \times 2 = .9488$

d.
$$\sigma_{\bar{p}} = \sqrt{\frac{(.30)\,(.70)}{1000}} = .0145$$

$$z = \frac{\bar{p} - p}{\sigma_{\bar{p}}} = \frac{.04}{.0145} = 2.76$$

Area $= .4971 \times 2 = .9942$

e. With a larger sample, there is a higher probability $\bar{p}$ will be within $\pm .04$ of the population proportion p.

45. a.

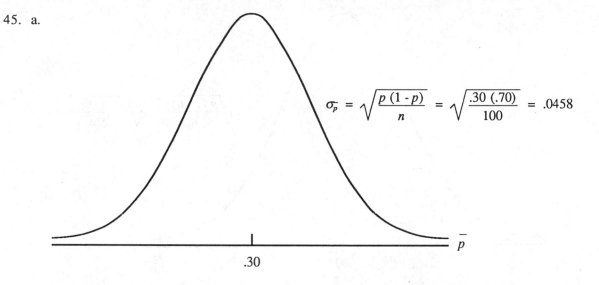

$$\sigma_{\bar{p}} = \sqrt{\frac{p\,(1-p)}{n}} = \sqrt{\frac{.30\,(.70)}{100}} = .0458$$

.30

The normal distribution is appropriate because $np = 100\,(.30) = 30$ and $n\,(1-p) = 100\,(.70) = 70$ are both greater than 5.

b. $P\,(.20 \le \bar{p} \le .40) = ?$

$$z = \frac{.40 - .30}{.0458} = 2.18$$

Area
.4854
x2
.9708

c. $P\,(.25 \le \bar{p} \le .35) = ?$

$$z = \frac{.35 - .30}{.0458} = 1.09$$

Area
.3621
x2
.7242

46. a.

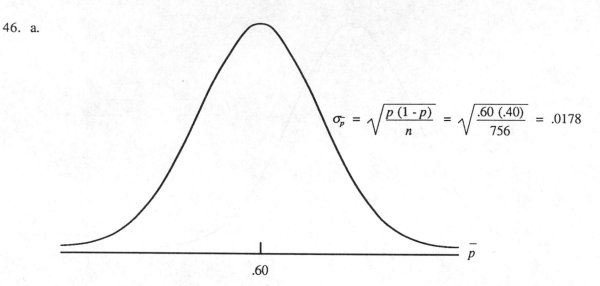

$$\sigma_{\bar{p}} = \sqrt{\frac{p(1-p)}{n}} = \sqrt{\frac{.60(.40)}{756}} = .0178$$

.60

$P(.56 \le \bar{p} \le .64) = ?$

$$z = \frac{.64 - .60}{.0178} = 2.25$$

Area
.4878
x2
.9756

b. $P(.58 \le \bar{p} \le .62) = ?$

$$z = \frac{.62 - .60}{.0178} = 1.12$$

Area
.3686
x2
.7372

c. Newsweek has a high probability or confidence (.9756) that the sample proportion $\bar{p}$ is within 4 percentage points of the population proportion. The probability or confidence is not high with a 2 percentage points error.

47. a. Normal with $E(\bar{p}) = .55$ and

$$\sigma_{\bar{p}} = \sqrt{\frac{(.55)(.45)}{1253}} = .0141$$

b.

$$z = \frac{\bar{p} - p}{\sigma_{\bar{p}}} = \frac{.02}{.0141} = 1.42$$

Area $= .4222 \times 2 = .8444$

c.

$$z = \frac{\bar{p} - p}{\sigma_{\bar{p}}} = \frac{.03}{.0141} = 2.13$$

Area $= .4834 \times 2 = .9668$

d. The Harris poll can be very confident $\bar{p}$ will be within $\pm .03$ of p as shown by the .9668 probability.

48. a.

$$\sigma_{\bar{p}} = \sqrt{\frac{(.42)(.58)}{300}} = .0285$$

$$z = \frac{\bar{p} - p}{\sigma_{\bar{p}}} = \frac{.03}{.0285} = 1.05$$

$$P(.39 \le \bar{p} \le .45) = (.3531) \times 2 = .7062$$

b. $P(\bar{p} \ge .45) = .5000 - .3531 = .1469$

c. $z = \dfrac{\bar{p} - p}{\sigma_{\bar{p}}} = \dfrac{.50 - .42}{.0285} = 2.81$

$$P(\bar{p} \ge .50) = .5000 - .4975 = .0025$$

49. a.

$$\sigma_{\bar{p}} = \sqrt{\frac{p(1-p)}{n}} = \sqrt{\frac{.09(.91)}{800}} = .0101$$

.09

$\bar{p}$

b. $P(\bar{p} \ge .08) = ?$

$$z = \frac{.08 - .09}{.0101} = -.99$$

Area
.3389

$P\ (.08 \leq \bar{p} \leq .09)\ =\ .3389$

Thus, $P\ (\bar{p} \geq .08)\ =\ .3389 + .5000\ =\ .8389$

50. a.

$$\sigma_{\bar{p}} = \sqrt{\frac{p\,(1-p)}{n}} = \sqrt{\frac{.80\,(.20)}{400}} = .02$$

.80

$\bar{p}$

b. $P\ (.77 \leq \bar{p} \leq .83)\ =\ ?$

$$z = \frac{.83 - .80}{.02} = 1.50$$

Area
.4332
x2
.8664

c. $\sigma_{\bar{p}} = \sqrt{\frac{p\,(1-p)}{n}} = \sqrt{\frac{.80\,(.20)}{750}} = .0146$

$$z = \frac{.83 - .80}{.0146} = 2.05$$

Area
.4798
x2
.9596

51. a. $P\ (.55 \leq \bar{p} \leq .65)\ =\ ?$

$$\sigma_{\bar{p}} = \sqrt{\frac{p\,(1-p)}{n}}$$

$n = 60$

$$\sigma_{\bar{p}} = \sqrt{\frac{.60\,(.40)}{60}} = .0632$$

$$z = \frac{.65 - .60}{.0632} = .79$$

Area
.2852
  x2
.5704

$n = 120$

$$\sigma_{\bar{p}} = \sqrt{\frac{.60\,(.40)}{120}} = .0477$$

$$z = \frac{.65 - .60}{.0447} = 1.12$$

Area
.3686
  x2
.7372

52. a.

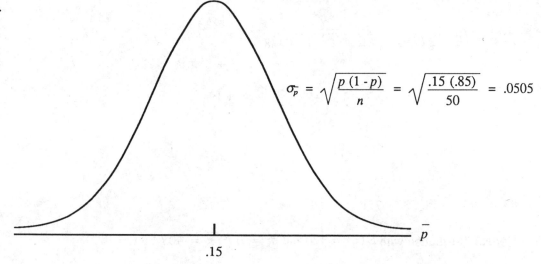

$$\sigma_{\bar{p}} = \sqrt{\frac{p\,(1-p)}{n}} = \sqrt{\frac{.15\,(.85)}{50}} = .0505$$

$\bar{p}$

.15

b. $P\,(.12 \le \bar{p} \le .18) = ?$

$$z = \frac{.18 - .15}{.0505} = .59$$

Area
.2224
x2
.4448

c. $P(\bar{p} \geq .10) = ?$

$$z = \frac{.10 - .15}{.0505} = -.99$$

Area
.3389
+.5000
.8389

53. a. $p = 900 / 2500 = .36$

b. $\sigma_{\bar{p}} = \sqrt{\frac{p(1-p)}{n}} = \sqrt{\frac{.36(.64)}{40}} = .0759$

$P(.31 \leq \bar{p} \leq .41) = ?$

$$z = \frac{.41 - .36}{.0759} = .66$$

Area
.2454
x2
.4908

c. $\sigma_{\bar{p}} = \sqrt{\frac{p(1-p)}{n}} = \sqrt{\frac{.36(.64)}{120}} = .0438$

$$z = \frac{.41 - .36}{.0438} = 1.14$$

Area
.3729
x2
.7458

54. 4324, 2875, 318, 538, 4771

55. a. Normal distribution with $E(\bar{x}) = 120$ and $\sigma_{\bar{x}} = \sigma / \sqrt{n} = 40 / \sqrt{30} = 7.30$

b. $P(\bar{x} < 100) = ?$

$$z = \frac{100 - 120}{7.30} = -2.74$$

Area
.4969

$P(\bar{x} < 100) = .5000 - .4969 = .0031$

$P(\bar{x} > 125) = ?$

$$z = \frac{125 - 120}{7.30} = +.68$$

Area
.2518

$P(\bar{x} > 125) = .5000 - .2518 = .2482$

56. a. Within 200 of \$28,085 is $P(27,885 \le \bar{p} \le 28,285)$.

$$\sigma_{\bar{x}} = \frac{\sigma}{\sqrt{n}} = \frac{3200}{\sqrt{100}} = 320$$

$$z = \frac{28,285 - 28,085}{320} = .63$$

Area
.2357
  x2
.4714

b. $\sigma_{\bar{x}} = \dfrac{\sigma}{\sqrt{n}} = \dfrac{3200}{\sqrt{300}} = 184.75$

$$z = \frac{28,285 - 28,085}{184.75} = 1.08$$

Area
.3599
  x2
.7198

c. For 90%

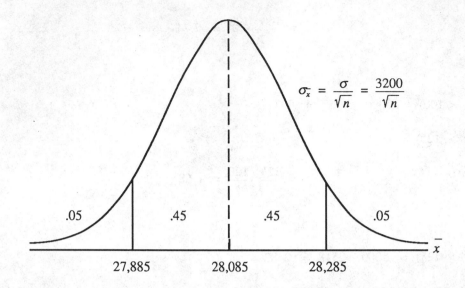

Using .45 area above 28,085, the standard normal table shows $z = 1.645$ occurs at \$28,285.

Thus

$$z = \frac{28,285 - 28,085}{3200 / \sqrt{n}} = 1.645$$

Solve for $\sqrt{n}$.

$$\sqrt{n} = \frac{(1.645)(3200)}{200} = 26.32$$

Thus $n = (26.32)^2 = 693$

57. $E(\bar{x}) = 3000$

$$\sigma_{\bar{x}} = \frac{\sigma}{\sqrt{n}} = \frac{800}{\sqrt{50}} = 113.14$$

$P(\bar{x} \geq 2750) = ?$

$$z = \frac{2750 - 3000}{113.14} = -2.21$$

Area
.4864
+.5000
.9864

$P(\bar{x} \geq 3200) = ?$

$$z = \frac{3200 - 3000}{113.14} = 1.77$$

Area
.4616

Thus, $P(\bar{p} \geq 3200) = .5000 - .4616 = .0384$

58. a. Normal,

$E(\bar{x}) = 49,000$

$\sigma_{\bar{x}} = \dfrac{\sigma}{\sqrt{n}} = \dfrac{12,000}{\sqrt{100}} = 1200$

b.

$$z = \frac{\bar{x} - \mu}{\sigma_{\bar{x}}} = \frac{1000}{1200} = .83$$

Area
.2967
x2
.5934

c.

$$z = \frac{\bar{x} - \mu}{\sigma / \sqrt{n}} = \frac{1000}{12,000 / \sqrt{200}} = 1.18$$

Area
.3810
x2
.7620

d.

$$z = \frac{\bar{x} - \mu}{\sigma / \sqrt{n}} = \frac{1000}{12,000 / \sqrt{400}} = 1.67$$

Area
.4525
x2
.9050

e. For 95%, $z = 1.96$

$$\frac{1000}{12000 / \sqrt{n}} = 1.96$$

$$1000 \sqrt{n} = 1.96 (12000)$$

$$\sqrt{n} = \frac{1.96 (12000)}{1000} = 23.52$$

$$n = 553$$

59. a.

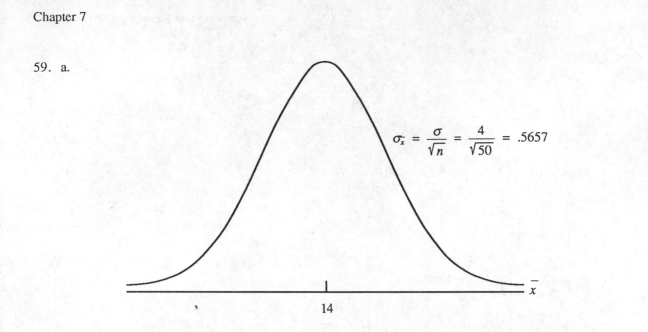

$$\sigma_{\bar{x}} = \frac{\sigma}{\sqrt{n}} = \frac{4}{\sqrt{50}} = .5657$$

14

b. Since $n \geq 30$, the central limit theorem enables us to use the normal probability distribution in part a.

c.
$$z = \frac{15 - 14}{.5657} = 1.77$$

Area
.4616

$P(\bar{x} \leq 15) = .5000 - .4616 = .9616$

d. $P(13.5 \leq \bar{x} \leq 14.5) = ?$

$$z = \frac{14.5 - 14}{.5657} = .88$$

Area
.3106
x2
.6212

60. a. $E(\bar{x}) = \mu = 67$

b. $\sigma_{\bar{x}} = \frac{\sigma}{\sqrt{n}} = \frac{6}{\sqrt{16}} = 1.5$

c. Normal with $E(\bar{x}) = 67$ and $\sigma_{\bar{x}} = 1.5$

d.
$$z = \frac{65 - 67}{1.5} = 1.33$$

Area
.4082

$$P(\bar{x} \geq 65) = .4082 \pm .5000 = .9082$$

e. $P(66 \leq \bar{x} \leq 68) = ?$

$$z = \frac{68 - 67}{1.5} = .67$$

Area
.2486
x2
.4972

61. a. $n / N = 100 / 500 = .20$. Yes, use the finite population correction factor.

b. $\sigma_{\bar{x}} = \sqrt{\frac{N - n}{N - 1}} \frac{\sigma}{\sqrt{n}} = \sqrt{\frac{500 - 100}{500 - 1}} \frac{40}{\sqrt{100}} = 3.58$

c.
$$z = \frac{\bar{x} - \mu}{3.58} = \frac{5}{3.58} = 1.40$$

Area
.4192
x2
.8384

62. a. $n / N = 50 / 5000 = .01$. Do not use the finite population correction factor since $n / N \leq .05$.

b. $\sigma_{\bar{x}} = \sqrt{\frac{N - n}{N - 1}} \frac{\sigma}{\sqrt{n}} = \sqrt{\frac{5000 - 50}{5000 - 1}} \frac{.40}{\sqrt{50}} = .0562$

$\sigma_{\bar{x}} = \frac{\sigma}{\sqrt{n}} = \frac{.40}{\sqrt{50}} = .0566$

Ignore the finite population correction factor because the difference between the two results is negligible.

c.
$$z = \frac{\bar{x} - \mu}{3.58} = \frac{5}{3.58} = 1.40$$

Area
.4616
x2
.9232

63. a. Different simple random samples will provide different sets of 50 billings and thus, different values for the sample mean. As a result $\bar{x}$ ill have a sampling distribution.

b. Normal distribution with $E(\bar{x}) = 22$ and $\sigma_{\bar{x}} = \sigma / \sqrt{n} = 7 / \sqrt{50} = .99$

c. $\sigma_{\bar{x}} = .99$

d. $\sigma_{\bar{x}} = \sigma / \sqrt{n} = 7 / \sqrt{100} = .70$ is the only change.

64. For a .95 probability, we have

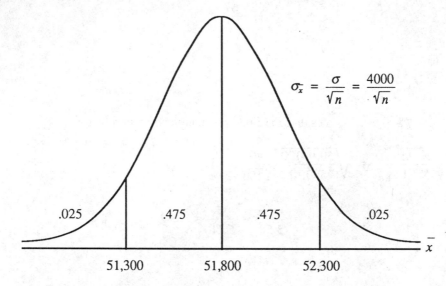

$$\sigma_{\bar{x}} = \frac{\sigma}{\sqrt{n}} = \frac{4000}{\sqrt{n}}$$

.025   .475   .475   .025

51,300   51,800   52,300

Using an area of .475, the standard normal distribution table shows 52,300 occurs at $z = 1.96$.

Thus,

$$z = \frac{52,300 - 51,800}{4000 / \sqrt{n}} = 1.96$$

Solve for $\sqrt{n}$.

$$\sqrt{n} = \frac{1.96\,(4000)}{500} = 15.68$$

Thus $n = (15.68)^2 = 246$

65. a. $\sigma_{\bar{x}} = \sqrt{\dfrac{N - n}{N - 1}} \dfrac{\sigma}{\sqrt{n}}$

$N = 2000$

$$\sigma_{\bar{x}} = \sqrt{\frac{2000 - 50}{2000 - 1}} \frac{144}{\sqrt{50}} = 20.11$$

$N = 5000$

$$\sigma_{\bar{x}} = \sqrt{\frac{5000 - 50}{5000 - 1}} \; \frac{144}{\sqrt{50}} = 20.26$$

$N = 10,000$

$$\sigma_{\bar{x}} = \sqrt{\frac{10,000 - 50}{10,000 - 1}} \; \frac{144}{\sqrt{50}} = 20.31$$

Note: With $n / N \leq .05$ for all three cases, common statistical practice would be to ignore the finite population correction factor and use

$$\sigma_{\bar{x}} = 144 / \sqrt{50} = 20.36$$

for each case.

b. $N = 2000$

$$z = \frac{25}{20.11} = 1.24$$

Area
.3925
x2
.7850

$N = 5000$

$$z = \frac{25}{20.26} = 1.23$$

Area
.3907
x2
.7814

$N = 10,000$

$$z = \frac{25}{20.31} = 1.23$$

Area
.3907
x2
.7814

All probabilities are approximately .78

66. a. $\sigma_{\bar{x}} = \dfrac{\sigma}{\sqrt{n}} = \dfrac{500}{\sqrt{n}} = 20$

$$\sqrt{n} \; 500 / 20 = 25 \quad \text{and} \quad n = (25)^2 = 625$$

b. For ± 25,

$$z = \frac{25}{20} = 1.25$$

Area
.3944
x2
.7888

67.   Sampling distribution of $\bar{x}$

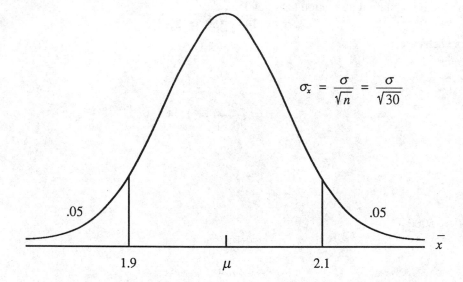

$$\sigma_{\bar{x}} = \frac{\sigma}{\sqrt{n}} = \frac{\sigma}{\sqrt{30}}$$

.05   .05

1.9 μ 2.1 $\bar{x}$

$$\mu = \frac{1.9 + 2.1}{2} = 2$$

The area between $\mu = 2$ and 2.1 must be .45. An area of .45 in the standard normal table shows $z = 1.645$.

Thus,

$$\mu = \frac{2.1 + 2.0}{\sigma / \sqrt{30}} = 1.645$$

Solve for σ.

$$\sigma = \frac{(.1) \sqrt{30}}{1.645} = .33$$

68. a.   Assume that the population of grade point averages has a normal distribution.

  b. $\sigma_{\bar{x}} = \frac{\sigma}{\sqrt{n}} = \frac{.50}{\sqrt{20}} = .11$

$$z = \frac{\bar{x} - \mu}{.11} = \frac{.2}{.11} = 1.79$$

Area
.4633
 x2
.9266

c. Take a larger sample with $n \geq 30$.

69. a. Many different samples of 80 are possible and provide different vales for $\bar{p}$.

b. Normal distribution with $E(\bar{p}) = .35$ and

$$\sigma_{\bar{p}} = \sqrt{\frac{p(1-p)}{n}} = \sqrt{\frac{.35(.65)}{80}} = .0533$$

c. $\sigma_{\bar{p}}$ decreases to

$$\sigma_{\bar{p}} = \sqrt{\frac{.35(.65)}{200}} = .0337$$

70. a. $\sigma_{\bar{p}} = \sqrt{\frac{p(1-p)}{n}} = \sqrt{\frac{.65(.35)}{100}} = .0477$

$P(.61 < \bar{p} < .69) = ?$

$$z = \frac{.69 - .65}{.0477} = .84$$

Area
.2995
 x2
.5990

b. $\sigma_{\bar{p}} = \sqrt{\frac{p(1-p)}{n}} = \sqrt{\frac{.65(.35)}{200}} = .0337$

$$z = \frac{.69 - .65}{.0337} = 1.19$$

Area
.3830
 x2
.7660

c.

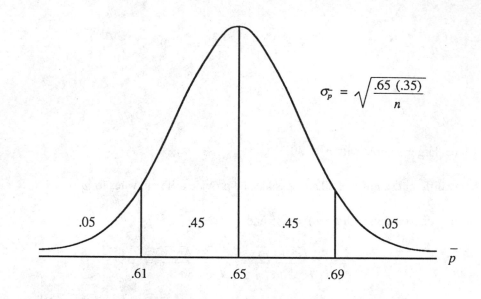

$$\sigma_{\bar{p}} = \sqrt{\frac{.65 \, (.35)}{n}}$$

.05   .45   .45   .05

.61   .65   .69 $\bar{p}$

Using an area of .45 and the standard normal distribution table, $z = 1.645$ at .69.

Thus,

$$z = \frac{.69 - .65}{\sqrt{\dfrac{.65 \, (.35)}{n}}} = 1.645$$

Solve for n.

$$n = \frac{(1.645)^2 \, (.65) \, (.35)}{(.04)^2} = 385$$

71. $\sigma_{\bar{p}} = \sqrt{\dfrac{p \, (1 - p)}{n}} = \sqrt{\dfrac{.40 \, (.60)}{400}} = .0245$

$P \, (\bar{p} \geq .375) = ?$

$$z = \frac{.375 - .40}{.0245} = -1.02$$

Area
.3461

$P \, (\bar{p} \geq .375) = .3461 + .5000 = .8461$

72. $\sigma_{\bar{p}} = \sqrt{\dfrac{p \, (1 - p)}{n}} = \sqrt{\dfrac{.40 \, (.60)}{400}} = .0245$

$P (\bar{p} \geq .05) = ?$

$$z = \frac{.05 - .10}{.03} = -1.67$$

$P (\bar{p} \geq .05) = .4525 + .5000 = .9525$

73. a. Normal distribution with $E (\bar{p}) = .15$ and

$$\sigma_{\bar{p}} = \sqrt{\frac{p (1 - p)}{n}} = \sqrt{\frac{.15 (.85)}{150}} = .0292$$

b. $P (.12 \leq \bar{p} \leq .18) = ?$

$$z = \frac{.18 - .15}{.0292} = 1.03$$

Area
.3485
x2
.6970

74. $\quad \sigma_{\bar{p}} = \sqrt{\frac{p (1 - p)}{n}} = \sqrt{\frac{.50 (.50)}{40}} = .0791$

$P (.45 \leq \bar{p} \leq .55) = ?$

$$z = \frac{.55 - .50}{.0791} = .63$$

Area
.2357
x2
.4714

75. a. $\quad \sigma_{\bar{p}} = \sqrt{\frac{p (1 - p)}{n}} = \sqrt{\frac{.25 (.75)}{n}} = .0625$

Solve for n

$$n = \frac{.25 (.75)}{(.0625)^2} = 48$$

b. Normal distribution with $E (\bar{p}) = .25$ and $\sigma_{\bar{x}} = .0625$

c. $P (\bar{p} \geq .30) = ?$

$$z = \frac{.375 - .40}{.0245} = -1.02$$

Area
.2881

Thus $P\ (.25 \leq \bar{p} \leq .30) = .2881$ and $P\ (\bar{p} \geq .30) = .5000 - .2881 = .2119$

Chapter 8
Interval Estimation

Learning Objectives

1. Know how to construct and interpret an interval estimate of a population mean and / or a population proportion.

2. Understand the concept of a sampling error.

3. Be able to use knowledge of a sampling distribution to make probability statements about the sampling error.

4. Learn about the t distribution and its use in constructing an interval estimate for a population mean.

5. Be able to determine the size of a simple random sample necessary to estimate a population mean and/or a population proportion with a specified level of precision.

6. Know the definition of the following terms:

    confidence interval   precision
    confidence coefficient   sampling error
    confidence level   degrees of freedom

Solutions:

1. a. $\sigma_{\bar{x}} = \sigma/\sqrt{n} = 5/\sqrt{40} = .79$

    b. At 95%, $z\,\sigma/\sqrt{n} = 1.96\,(5/\sqrt{40}) = 1.55$

        Sampling error 1.55 or less

2. a. $32 \pm 1.645\ \ (6/\sqrt{50})$

        32 ± 1.4 (30.6 to 33.4)

    b. $32 \pm 1.96\ \ \ (6/\sqrt{50})$

        32 ± 1.66 (30.34 to 33.66)

    c. $32 \pm 2.575\ \ (6/\sqrt{50})$

        32 ± 2.18 (29.82 to 34.18)

3. a. $80 \pm 1.96\ \ \ 15/\sqrt{60}$

        80 ± 3.8 (76.2 to 83.8)

    b. $80 \pm 1.96\ \ \ 15/\sqrt{120}$

        80 ± 2.68 (77.32 to 82.68)

    c. Larger sample provides a smaller sampling error at a fixed confidence level.

4. $126 \pm 1.96\ \ \sigma/\sqrt{n}$

    $$1.96\,\frac{16}{\sqrt{n}} = 4$$

    $$\sqrt{n} = \frac{1.96\,(16.07)}{4} = 7.874$$

    $$n = 62$$

5. a. $\sigma_{\bar{x}} = \sigma/\sqrt{n} = 2.50/\sqrt{49} = .3571$

    b. Sampling error less than or equal to $1.96\,\sigma_{\bar{x}} = .70$

    c. $12.60 \pm .70$ or (11.90 to 13.30)

6. $\bar{x} \pm 1.96 \ \sigma/\sqrt{n}$

    $310 \pm 1.96 \ 100/\sqrt{250}$

    310 ± 12.40 (297.60 to 322.40)

7. $10.2 \pm 1.96 \ 3/\sqrt{75}$

    $10.2 \pm .68$ (9.52 to 10.88)

8. a. $\bar{x} \pm z_{\alpha/2} \dfrac{\sigma}{\sqrt{n}}$

    $24{,}000 \pm 1.645 \ (5000/\sqrt{250})$

    $24{,}000 \pm 520$ (23,480 to 24,520)

    b. $24{,}000 \pm 1.96 \ (5000/\sqrt{250})$

    $24{,}000 \pm 620$ (23,380 to 24,620)

    c. $24{,}000 \pm 2.575 \ (5000/\sqrt{250})$

    $24{,}000 \pm 814$ (23,186 to 24,814)

    d.   The width of the confidence interval increases as the confidence level increases. The wider intervals increase the confidence that the interval contains the population mean.

9. a. $\sigma_{\bar{x}} = \sigma/\sqrt{n} = 5.5/\sqrt{36} = .9166$

    b.   Sampling error less than or equal to:

    At .75

    $$z_{.125} \ \sigma_{\bar{x}} = 1.15 \ (.9166) = 1.05$$

    At .90

    $$z_{.05} \ \sigma_{\bar{x}} = 1.645 \ (.9166) = 1.51$$

    At .99

    $$z_{.005} \ \sigma_{\bar{x}} = 2.575 \ (.9166) = 2.36$$

    For a higher confidence , a larger sampling error is shown to account for the higher probability or confidence requested.

    c. 48.6 ± 2.36 (46.24 to 50.96)

Chapter 8

10. a. $\bar{x} \pm z_{\alpha/2} \dfrac{\sigma}{\sqrt{n}}$

$47 \pm 1.96 \quad (8 / \sqrt{340})$

$47 \pm .85 \qquad\qquad$ (46.15 to 47.85)

b. $44 \pm 1.96 \quad (8 / \sqrt{114})$

$44 \pm 1.47 \qquad\qquad$ (42.53 to 45.47)

c. The interval for men had the better precision due to the larger sample size.

11. a. $\sigma_{\bar{x}} = \sigma / \sqrt{n} = 100 / \sqrt{36} = 16.67$

b.

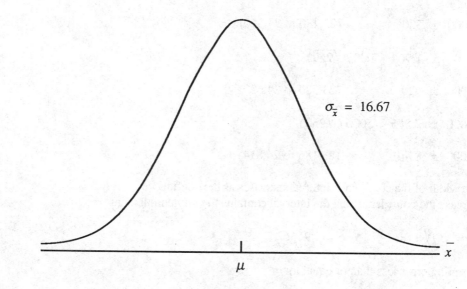

$\sigma_{\bar{x}} = 16.67$

μ

$\bar{x}$

c. For 80%,

$$z_{.10} = 1.28.$$

Sampling error less than or equal to $z\,\sigma_{\bar{x}} = 1.28\,(16.67) = 21.34$

d. $\bar{x} \pm z_{.01}\,\sigma_{\bar{x}} \qquad 196.50 \pm 2.33 \quad (16.67)$

$196.50 \pm 38.84 \qquad\qquad$ (157.66 to 235.34)

12. a. $\bar{x} = \dfrac{5.6 + 6.4}{2} = 6$ hours

b. Results show interval of $6 \pm .4$

Thus, at 95% confidence

$$1.96 \frac{\sigma}{\sqrt{n}} = 1.96 \frac{2}{\sqrt{n}} = .4$$

Solve for

$$\sqrt{n} = \frac{1.96 \, (2)}{.4} = 9.8$$

$$n = (9.8)^2 = 96$$

13. $\bar{x} \pm z_{.025} \, s / \sqrt{n}$

$250 \pm 1.96 \ (10 / \sqrt{30})$

$250 \pm 3.58 \qquad\qquad$ (246.42 to 253.58)

14. a. $\bar{x} \pm z_{\alpha/2} \, \sigma / \sqrt{n}$

$25.23 \pm 1.96 \ (3.21 / \sqrt{47})$

$25.23 \pm .92 \qquad\qquad$ (24.31 to 26.15)

b. $25.23 \pm 2.33 \ (3.21 / \sqrt{47})$

$25.23 \pm 1.09 \qquad\qquad$ (24.14 to 26.32)

15. a. .95

b. .90

c. .01

d. .05

e. .95

f. .85

16. a. 1.734

b. -1.321

c. 3.365

d. -1.761 and +1.761

e. -2.048 and +2.048

17. a. $\bar{x} = \sum x_i / n = 80 / 8 = 10$

b. $s = \sqrt{\dfrac{\sum (x_i - \bar{x})^2}{n - 1}} = \sqrt{\dfrac{84}{8 - 1}} = 3.464$

c. With 7 degrees of freedom, $t_{.025} = 2.365$

$\bar{x} = t_{.025}\, s / \sqrt{n}$

$10 \pm 2.365\left(3.464 / \sqrt{8}\right)$

10 ± 2.90 (7.10 to 12.90)

18. a. $17.25 \pm 1.729 \; 3.3 / \sqrt{20}$

17.25 ± 1.28 (15.97 to 18.53)

b. $17.25 \pm 2.093 \; 3.3 / \sqrt{20}$

17.25 ± 1.54 (15.71 to 18.79)

c. $17.25 \pm 2.861 \; 3.3 / \sqrt{20}$

17.25 ± 2.11 (15.14 to 19.36)

19.   At 90% $80 \pm t_{.05}\left(s / \sqrt{n}\right)$ with df = 17 $t_{.05} = 1.740$

$80 \pm 1.740 \; (10 / \sqrt{18})$

80 ± 4.10 (75.90 to 84.10)

At 95% $80 \pm 2.11\left(10 / \sqrt{18}\right)$ with df = 17 $t_{.05} = 2.110$

80 ± 4.97 (75.03 to 84.97)

20. a. $\bar{x} = \sum x_i / n = 132 / 10 = 13.2$

b. $s = \sqrt{\dfrac{\sum (x_i - \bar{x})^2}{n - 1}} = \sqrt{\dfrac{547.6}{9}} = 7.8$

c. With $df = 9, t_{.025} = 2.262$

$\bar{x} = t_{.025}\, s / \sqrt{n}$

$13.2 \pm 2.262 \quad (7.8 / \sqrt{10})$

$13.2 \pm 5.58 \qquad (7.62 \text{ to } 18.78)$

d.   The $\pm$ 5.58 shows poor precision. A larger sample size is desired.

21. $\bar{x} = 3.25 \quad s = 1.29$

With $df = 11, t_{.025} = 2.201$

$3.25 \pm 2.201 \quad (1.29 / \sqrt{12})$

$3.25 \pm .82 \qquad (2.43 \text{ to } 4.07)$

22. $\bar{x} = \sum x_i / n = 6.53 \text{ minutes}$

$s = \sqrt{\dfrac{\sum (x_i - \bar{x})^2}{n - 1}} = .54 \text{ minutes}$

$\bar{x} = t_{.025} \, s / \sqrt{n}$

$6.53 \pm 2.093 \quad (.54 / \sqrt{20})$

$6.53 \pm .25 \qquad (6.28 \text{ to } 6.78)$

23. a. $\bar{x} = \sum x / n = \$53$

   b. $\bar{x} = t_{.025} \, s / \sqrt{n} \qquad s = \sqrt{\dfrac{\sum (x_i - \bar{x})^2}{n - 1}} = 11.04$

$53 \pm 2.201 \quad (11.04 / \sqrt{12})$

$53 \pm 7.01 \qquad (45.99 \text{ to } 60.01)$

24. a. $22.4 \pm 1.96 \quad (5 / \sqrt{61})$

$22.4 \pm 1.25 \qquad (21.15 \text{ to } 23.65)$

   b.   With $df = 60, \; t_{.025} = 2.000$

$22.4 \pm 2 \quad (5 / \sqrt{61})$

$22.4 \pm 1.28 \qquad (21.12 \text{ to } 23.68)$

   c.   Confidence intervals are essentially the same regardless of whether z or t is used.

Chapter 8

25. a. $\bar{x} = t_{.025}\, s / \sqrt{n}$

With $df = 15$, $t_{.025} = 2.131$

$51 \pm 2.131 \quad (10.18 / \sqrt{16})$

$51 \pm 5.42 \qquad\qquad (45.58 \text{ to } 56.42)$

b. Population is assumed normal in order to use the t distribution.

c. Sampling error of error at $\pm\ 5.42$ is too large. A larger sample size is desired.

26. $\bar{x} = 5.55 \qquad s = 2.22$

With $df = 19$, $t_{.025} = 2.093$

$5.55 \pm 2.093 \quad (2.22 / \sqrt{20})$

$5.55 \pm 1.04 \qquad\qquad (4.51 \text{ to } 6.59)$

27. $n = \dfrac{z_{.025}^2\, \sigma^2}{E^2} = \dfrac{(1.96)^2\,(25)^2}{5^2} = 96$

28. a. Planning value of σ = Range $/ 4 = 36 / 4 = 9$

b. $n = \dfrac{z_{.025}^2\, \sigma^2}{E^2} = \dfrac{(1.96)^2\,(9)^2}{3^2} = 34.6 \approx 35$

c. $n = \dfrac{(1.96)^2\,(9)^2}{2^2} = 77.8 \approx 78$

29. $n = \dfrac{(1.96)^2\,(6.82)^2}{(1.5)^2} = 79.4 \approx 80$

$n = \dfrac{(1.645)^2\,(6.82)^2}{(2)^2} = 31.5 \approx 32$

30. a. $n = \dfrac{(1.96)^2\,(7.2)^2}{(2)^2} = 49.8 \approx 50$

$n = \dfrac{(1.96)^2\,(7.2)^2}{(1.5)^2} = 88.5 \approx 89$

$$n = \frac{(1.96)^2 (7.2)^2}{(1)^2} = 199.2 \approx 200$$

b.   The sample of 200 appears large given the information sought. Recommend going with $n = 200$ only if $E = 1$ is essential.

31. a. $n = \dfrac{(1.96)^2 (2,000)^2}{(500)^2} = 61.5$ or 62

    b. $n = \dfrac{(1.96)^2 (2,000)^2}{(200)^2} = 384.2$ or 385

    c. $n = \dfrac{(1.96)^2 (2,000)^2}{(100)^2} = 1536.6$ or 1537

32. $n = \dfrac{z_{.025}^2 \, \sigma^2}{E^2} = \dfrac{(1.96)^2 (20)^2}{2^2} = 384$

33. $n = \dfrac{(1.96)^2 (5000)^2}{(500)^2} = 384.2$ or 385

34.   From problem 14, $s = 7.8$.

$$n = \frac{(1.96)^2 (7.8)^2}{(2)^2} = 58.4 \text{ or } 59$$

35. $n = \dfrac{(1.96)^2 (6.25)^2}{(1)^2} = 150$

36. a. $n = \dfrac{(2.33)^2 (6)^2}{(2)^2} = 48.9$ or 49

    b. 32 ± 2 (30 to 34)

37. a. $\bar{p} = \dfrac{100}{400} = .25$

    b. $\sqrt{\dfrac{\bar{p}(1-\bar{p})}{n}} = \sqrt{\dfrac{.25\,(.75)}{400}} = .0217$

c. $\bar{p} \pm z_{.025} \sqrt{\dfrac{p(1-p)}{n}}$

$.25 \pm 1.96 \,(.0217)$

$.25 \pm .0425 \qquad\qquad (.2075 \text{ to } .2925)$

38. a. $.70 \pm 1.645 \sqrt{\dfrac{.70\,(.30)}{800}}$

$.70 \pm .0267 \qquad\qquad (.6733 \text{ to } .7267)$

b. $.70 \pm 1.96 \sqrt{\dfrac{.70\,(.30)}{800}}$

$.70 \pm .0318 \qquad\qquad (.6682 \text{ to } .7318)$

39. $n = \dfrac{z_{.025}^2 \, p\,(1-p)}{E^2} = \dfrac{(1.96)^2\,(.35)\,(.65)}{(.05)^2} = 350$

40. Use planning value $p = .50$

$n = \dfrac{(1.96)^2\,(.50)\,(.50)}{(.03)^2} = 1067$

41. a. $\bar{p} = \dfrac{248}{400} = .62$

$\bar{p} \pm 1.645 \sqrt{\dfrac{.62\,(.38)}{400}}$

$.62 \pm .04 \qquad\qquad (.58 \text{ to } .66)$

42. $\bar{p} \pm z_{\alpha/2} \sqrt{\dfrac{p(1-p)}{n}}$

$\bar{p} = 429 / 1227 = .35$

$.35 \pm 1.96 \sqrt{\dfrac{.35\,(.65)}{1277}}$

$.35 \pm .0267 \qquad\qquad (.3233 \text{ to } .3767)$

We can be 95% confident that .3233 to .3767 of the population of adults in the twelve southern states favor the U.S. Supreme Court ruling.

43. $\sigma_{\bar{p}} = \sqrt{\dfrac{.79\,(.21)}{305}} = .0233$

At 95%, $.79 \pm 1.96$ $(.0233)$

$.79 \pm .0457$ $(.7443 \text{ to } .8357)$

44. $.67 \pm 2.33 \sqrt{\dfrac{.67\,(.33)}{250}}$

$.67 \pm .0693$ $(.6007 \text{ to } .7393)$

45. a. $\bar{p} = \dfrac{64}{120} = .5333$

    b. $.5333 \pm 1.96 \sqrt{\dfrac{.5333\,(.4667)}{120}}$

$.5333 \pm .0893$ $(.4440 \text{ to } .6226)$

    c.   No; since the true proportion is believed to be from .4440 to .6226, a voter support of less than .50 may be present.

    d. $n = \dfrac{(1.96)^2\,(.5333)\,(.4667)}{(.05)^2} = 382.5 \text{ or } 383$

46. a. $.29 \pm 1.96 \sqrt{\dfrac{.29\,(.71)}{200}}$

$.29 \pm .0629$ $(.2271 \text{ to } .3529)$

    b. $.29 \pm 1.96 \sqrt{\dfrac{.29\,(.71)}{600}}$

$.29 \pm .0363$ $(.2537 \text{ to } .3263)$

    c. $.29 \pm 1.96 \sqrt{\dfrac{.29\,(.71)}{1000}}$

$.29 \pm .0281$ $(.2619 \text{ to } .3181)$

    d.   As the sample size increases, the width of the interval becomes smaller indicating a better precision.

47. a. $n = \dfrac{z_{.025}^2\, p\,(1-p)}{E^2} = \dfrac{(1.96)^2\,(.55)\,(.45)}{(.03)^2} = 1056.4 \text{ or } 1057$

Chapter 8

b. $n = \dfrac{(1.96)^2 (.55)(.45)}{(.06)^2} = 264.1$ or 265

48. a. $.47 \pm 1.96 \sqrt{\dfrac{.47(.53)}{250}}$

$.47 \pm .0619 \qquad (.4081$ to $.5319)$

b. $n = \dfrac{(1.96)^2 (.47)(.53)}{(.05)^2} = 382.8$ or 383

49. $n = \dfrac{(1.96)^2 (.50)(.50)}{E^2}$

a. $E = .03 \qquad n = 1068$

b. $E = .02 \qquad n = 2401$

c. $E = .01 \qquad n = 9604$

50. a. $n = \dfrac{(1.96)^2 (.75)(.25)}{(.10)^2} = 72$

b. $n = \dfrac{(1.96)^2 (.75)(.25)}{(.075)^2} = 128.1$ or 129

c. $n = \dfrac{(1.96)^2 (.75)(.25)}{(.05)^2} = 288.1$ or 289

d. $n = \dfrac{(1.96)^2 (.75)(.25)}{(.03)^2} = 800.3$ or 801

e. The sample size must be larger in order to decrease the margin of error.

51. a. $n = \dfrac{z^2 p(1-p)}{E^2} = \dfrac{(1.96)^2 (.25)(.75)}{(.025)^2} = 1153$

b. $\bar{p} = \dfrac{357}{1153} = .31$

$$.31 \pm 1.96 \ \sqrt{\frac{.31\,(.69)}{1153}}$$

$.31 \pm .0267$ (.2833 to .3367)

c.   A larger proportion of automobiles are being used 10 years or more in 1991 than in 1980.

52. $\bar{x} \pm z_{.025}\, \sigma / \sqrt{n}$

2.25 ± 1.96 $(1.2 / \sqrt{300})$

$2.25 \pm .14$ (2.11 to 2.39)

53. 3400 ± 2.33 $(650 / \sqrt{100})$

3400 ± 151.45 (3248.55 to 3551.45)

54. $\bar{x} \pm z_{.025}\, s / \sqrt{n}$

55.6 ± 1.96 $(7.37 / \sqrt{1033})$

$55.6 \pm .45$ (55.15 to 56.05)

55. a. $\bar{x} = \sum x_i / n = 440 / 8 = 55$

     b. $s = 6.78$

         With $df = 7$, $t_{.025} = 2.365$

         55 ± 2.365 $(6.78 / \sqrt{8})$

         55 ± 5.67 (49.33 to 60.67)

     c.   With $df = 7$, $t_{.005} = 3.499$

         55 ± 3.499 $(6.78 / \sqrt{8})$

         55 ± 8.39 (46.61 to 63.39)

56. a. $\bar{x} = 1483.1$

     b. $s = \sqrt{\dfrac{\sum (x_i - \bar{x})^2}{n - 1}} = 374.9$

c. With $df = 6,$ $t_{.025} = 2.447$

1483.1 ± 2.447 $(374.9 / \sqrt{7})$

1483.1 ± 346.7 $(1136.4 \text{ to } 1829.8)$

57. $\bar{x} = 20$ $s = 2.28$

With $df = 5,$ $t_{.025} = 2.571$

20 ± 2.571 $(2.28 / \sqrt{6})$

20 ± 2.39 $(17.61 \text{ to } 22.39)$

58. $\bar{x} = 12$ $s = 3.41$

With $5df$ $t_{.05} = 2.015$

12 ± 2.015 $(3.41 / \sqrt{6})$

12 ± 2.80 $(9.20 \text{ to } 14.80)$

59. 131.44 ± 1.645 $(16.19 / \sqrt{100})$

131.44 ± 2.66 $(128.78 \text{ to } 134.10)$

60. $n = \dfrac{(1.645)^2 (16.19)^2}{1^2} = 709.3 \text{ or } 710$

61. $n = \dfrac{(2.575)^2 (2.28)^2}{1^2} = 34.5 \text{ or } 35$

62. $n = \dfrac{(2.33)^2 (2.6)^2}{1^2} = 36.7 \text{ or } 37$

63. $n = \dfrac{(1.96)^2 (8)^2}{2^2} = 61.5 \text{ or } 62$

$n = \dfrac{(2.575)^2 (8)^2}{2^2} = 106.1 \text{ or } 107$

64. $n = \dfrac{(1.96)^2 (375)^2}{(100)^2} = 54$

65. $\bar{p} = 18 / 400 = .045$

$.045 \pm 1.645 \sqrt{\dfrac{.045\,(.955)}{400}}$

$.045 \pm .0171$ (.0279 to .0621)

66. $\bar{p} = 7 / 50 = .14$

$.14 \pm 1.96 \sqrt{\dfrac{.14\,(.86)}{50}}$

$.14 \pm .0962$ (.0438 to .2362)

67. $\bar{p} \pm 1.96 \sqrt{\dfrac{\bar{p}\,(1 - \bar{p})}{n}}$ $\bar{p} = \dfrac{602}{1400} = .43$

$.43 \pm 1.96 \sqrt{\dfrac{.43\,(.57)}{1400}}$

$.43 \pm .0259$ (.4041 to .4559)

68. Recognition:

$.56 \pm 1.96 \sqrt{\dfrac{.56\,(.44)}{500}}$

$.56 \pm .0435$ (.5165 to .6035)

Cash / Stock Rewards:

$.26 \pm 1.96 \sqrt{\dfrac{.26\,(.74)}{500}}$

$.26 \pm .0384$ (.2216 to .2984)

A greater proportion, approximately 2 times as large, uses recognition to encourage quality.

69. a. $\bar{p} = 504 / 1400 = .36$

 b. $1.96 \sqrt{\dfrac{(.36)\,(.64)}{1400}} = .0251$

70. a. $n = \dfrac{(2.33)^2\,(.70)\,(.30)}{(.03)^2} = 1266.7 \text{ or } 1267$

b. $n = \dfrac{(2.33)^2 (.50)(.50)}{(.03)^2} = 1508$

71. a. $\bar{p} = 110/200 = .55$

$.55 \pm 1.96 \sqrt{\dfrac{.55(.45)}{200}}$

$.55 \pm .0689$ (.4811 to .6189)

b. $n = \dfrac{(1.96)^2 (.55)(.45)}{(.05)^2} = 380.3 \text{ or } 381$

72. $.55 \pm 1.645 \sqrt{\dfrac{.55(.45)}{500}}$

$.55 \pm .0366$ (.5134 to .5866)

73. a. $n = \dfrac{z^2 p(1-p)}{E^2} = \dfrac{(1.96)^2 (.30)(.70)}{(.02)^2} = 2017$

b. $\bar{p} = 555/2017 = .2752$

$.2752 \pm 1.96 \sqrt{\dfrac{.2752(.7248)}{2017}}$

$.2752 \pm .0195$ (.2557 to .2947)

74. a. $n = \dfrac{(1.645)^2 (.60)(.40)}{(.04)^2} = 405.9 \text{ or } 406$

b. $\bar{p} = 313/406 = .77$

$.77 \pm 1.645 \sqrt{\dfrac{.77(.23)}{406}}$

$.77 \pm .0344$ (.7356 to .8044)

c. $\bar{p} = 260/406 = .64$

$.64 \pm 1.645 \sqrt{\dfrac{.64(.36)}{406}}$

$.64 \pm .0392$ (.6008 to .6792)

d.   Yes; the margin of errors of .0344 and .0392 are both within the desired .04.

Solution to Computer Case

Descriptive statistics including a frequency distribution and a histogram are shown below.

```
                    Histogram of C1  N = 50
                Midpoint       Count
                  25000          1    *
                  35000          6    * * * * * *
                  45000          1    *
                  55000          5    * * * * *
                  65000         11    * * * * * * * * * * *
                  75000          8    * * * * * * * *
                  85000          9    * * * * * * * * *
                  95000          3    * * *
                 105000          1    *
                 115000          3    * * *
                 125000          1    *
                 135000          1    *
```

	N	MEAN	MEDIAN	TRMEAN	STDEV	SEMEAN
MILES	50	73340	72705	72705	24899	3521

	MIN	MAX	Q1	Q3
MILES	25066	138114	59881	87309

	N	MEAN	STDEV	SE MEAN	95.0 PERCENT C. I.
MILES	50	73340.3	24898.7	3521.3	(66428.9, 80251.7)

The 95% confidence interval for the population mean is 66,429 to 80,252 indicating that there is a 95% confidence that this interval contains the population mean. Note that the Data Analyst software provides a 95% confidence interval of 66,439 to 80,242 due to the fact that it uses $z = 1.96$ in the computation of the interval estimate. Software packages can differ slightly in interval estimates due to the number of decimal places used in the z values. Minitab uses additional decimal places with $z = 1.9623$.

The mean is 73,340 and median is 72,705. The first quartile of 59,881 shows 25% of the repairs occurred with less than 60,000 miles on the vehicle. Also, the histogram shows seven (14%) repairs occurred with less than 40,000 miles. These data tend to support the conclusion of early transmission failures for this automobile manufacturer.

In order to bring the precision for the population mean to within ± 5,000 miles a sample size of 96 automobile transmission repair records would be needed as shown below.

$$n = \frac{z^2_{.025}\, \sigma^2}{E^2} = \frac{(1.96)^2\,(24,899)^2}{(5,000)^2} = 95.3 \text{ or } 96$$

Additional information that would be helpful in more fully evaluating the transmission problem include

1. transmission failure data for other automobile manufacturers

2. the proportion of all automobiles that experience the transmission failures

3. industry standards for transmission failures

With this information we could make comparative statements about how the manufacturer in question compares to other manufacturers as well as to industry standards. However, with the data available, the manufacturer in question appears to have problems with early transmission failures.

Chapter 9
Hypothesis Testing

Learning Objectives

1. Learn how to formulate and test hypotheses about a population mean and/or a population proportion.

2. Understand the types of errors possible when conducting a hypothesis test.

3. Be able to determine the probability of making various errors in hypothesis tests.

4. Know how to compute and interpret p-values.

5. Be able to determine the size of a simple random sample necessary to keep the probability of hypothesis testing errors within acceptable limits.

6. Know the definition of the following terms:

null hypothesis	one-tailed test
alternative hypothesis	two-tailed test
type I error	p-value
type II error	operating characteristic curve
critical value	power curve
level of significance	

Solutions:

1. a. $H_0: \mu \leq 400$ Manager's claim.

   $H_a: \mu > 400$

   b. We are not able to conclude that the manager's claim is wrong.

   c. The manager's claim can be rejected. We can conclude that $\mu > 400$.

2. a. $H_0: \mu \leq 14$

   $H_a: \mu > 14$ Research hypothesis

   b. There is no statistical evidence that the new bonus plan increases sales volume.

   c. The research hypothesis that $\mu > 14$ is supported. We can conclude that the new bonus plan increases the mean sales volume.

3. a. $H_0: \mu = 32$ Specified filling weight

   $H_a: \mu \neq 32$ Overfilling or underfilling exists

   b. There is no evidence that the production line is not operating properly. Allow the production process to continue.

   c. Conclude $\mu \neq 32$ and that overfilling or underfilling exists. Shut down and adjust the production line.

4. a. $H_0: \mu \geq 220$

   $H_a: \mu < 220$ Research hypothesis to see if mean cost is less than $220.

   b. We are unable to conclude that the new method reduces costs.

   c. Conclude $\mu < 220$. Consider implementing the new method based on the conclusion that it lowers the mean cost per hour.

5. a. Claiming $\mu > 6.08$ when it is not. The researcher would claim an annual rate higher than the national average when this is not the case.

   b. Concluding $\mu \leq 6.08$ when it is not. The researcher would not detect the fact that adults in Des Moines have a higher annual rate.

6. a. $H_0: \mu \leq 1$ The label claim or assumption.

   $H_a: \mu > 1$

b. Claiming $\mu > 1$ when it is not. This is the error of rejecting the product's claim when the claim is true.

c. Concluding $\mu \leq 1$ when it is not. In this case, we miss the fact that the product is not meeting its label specification.

7. a. $H_0: \mu \leq 8000$

$H_a: \mu > 8000$ Research hypothesis to see if the plan increases average sales.

b. Claiming $\mu > 8000$ when the plan does not increase sales. A mistake could be implementing the plan when it does not help.

c. Concluding $\mu \leq 8000$ when the plan really would increase sales. This could lead to not implementing a plan that would increase sales.

8. a. $H_0: \mu \geq 220$

$H_a: \mu < 220$

b. Claiming $\mu < 220$ when the new method does not lower costs. A mistake could be implementing the method when it does not help.

c. Concluding $\mu \geq 220$ when the method really would lower costs. This could lead to not implementing a method that would lower costs.

9. a. $z = -1.645$

Reject H_0 if $z < -1.645$

b. $z = \dfrac{\bar{x} - \mu}{\sigma / \sqrt{n}} = \dfrac{9.46 - 10}{2 / \sqrt{50}} = -1.91$

Reject H_0; conclude H_a is true.

10. a. $z = 2.05$

Reject H_0 if $z > 2.05$

b. $z = \dfrac{\bar{x} - \mu}{\sigma / \sqrt{n}} = \dfrac{16.5 - 15}{7 / \sqrt{40}} = 1.36$

c. Area at $z = 1.36 = .4131$

p-value $= .5000 - .4131 = .0869$

d. Do not reject H_0

11.   Reject H_0 if $z < -1.645$

a. $z = \dfrac{\bar{x} - \mu}{\sigma / \sqrt{n}} = \dfrac{22 - 25}{12 / \sqrt{100}} = -2.50$ Reject H_0

b. $z = \dfrac{24 - 25}{12 / \sqrt{100}} = -.83$ Do not reject H_0

c. $z = \dfrac{23.5 - 25}{12 / \sqrt{100}} = -1.25$ Do not reject H_0

d. $z = \dfrac{22.8 - 25}{12 / \sqrt{100}} = -1.83$ Reject H_0

12. a. p-value $= .5000 - .4656 = .0344$ Reject H_0

b. p-value $= .5000 - .1736 = .3264$ Do not reject H_0

c. p-value $= .5000 - .4332 = .0668$ Do not reject H_0

d. $z = 3.09$ is the largest table value with $.5000 - .4990 = .001$ area in tail. For $z = 3.30$, the p-value is less than .001 or approximately 0. Reject H_0.

e. Since z is to the left of the mean and the rejection region is in the upper tail, p-value $= .5000 + .3413 = .8413$. Do not reject H_0.

13. a. H_0: $\mu \geq 26,100$

H_a: $\mu < 26,100$ Research hypothesis.

b. Reject H_0 if $z < -1.645$

$$z = \frac{\bar{x} - \mu_0}{\sigma / \sqrt{n}} = \frac{25,000 - 26,100}{2400 / \sqrt{36}} = -2.75$$

Reject H_0 and conclude that the mean cost is less than $26,100.

c. p-value $= .5000 - .4970 = .0030$

14. a. H_0: $\mu \leq 6.5$

H_a: $\mu > 6.5$

b. Reject H_0 if $z > 2.33$

$$z = \frac{\bar{x} - \mu}{\sigma / \sqrt{n}} = \frac{7.8 - 6.5}{2.2 / \sqrt{100}} = 5.91$$

Reject H_0; conclude individuals are driving cars longer in 1990.

c. Less new car sales as individuals are driving their current cars longer.

15. $H_0: \mu \leq 19{,}780$

      $H_a: \mu > 19{,}780$

$$z = \frac{\bar{x} - \mu}{\sigma / \sqrt{n}} = \frac{21{,}040 - 19{,}780}{6000 / \sqrt{150}} = 2.57$$

Reject H_0 if $z > 1.645$. Therefore, reject H_0. The mean annual income in Japan is greater than the mean annual income in the U.S..

p-value $= .5000 - .4949 = .0051$

16. $H_0: \mu \leq 40$

      $H_a: \mu > 40$

      Reject H_0 if $z > 2.05$

$$z = \frac{\bar{x} - \mu_0}{\sigma / \sqrt{n}} = \frac{45 - 40}{20 / \sqrt{50}} = 1.77$$

Do not reject H_0. Thus the president's claim cannot be rejected.

17. $H_0: \mu \leq 15$

      $H_a: \mu > 15$

      Reject H_0 if $z > 2.33$

$$z = \frac{\bar{x} - \mu_0}{\sigma / \sqrt{n}} = \frac{17 - 15}{4 / \sqrt{35}} = 2.96$$

Reject H_0; the premium rate should be charged.

Chapter 9

18. H_0: $\mu \geq 28{,}000$

    H_a: $\mu < 28{,}000$

    Reject H_0 if $z < -1.645$

$$z = \frac{\bar{x} - \mu_0}{\sigma / \sqrt{n}} = \frac{27{,}500 - 28{,}000}{1000 / \sqrt{30}} = -2.74$$

    Reject H_0; Tires are not meeting the at least 28,000 design specification.

    p-value $= .5000 - .4969 = .0031$

19. a. H_0: $\mu \geq 15$

    H_a: $\mu < 15$

    Reject H_0 if $z < -1.28$

$$z = \frac{\bar{x} - \mu_0}{\sigma / \sqrt{n}} = \frac{14 - 15}{2.40 / \sqrt{40}} = -2.64$$

    Reject H_0; the mean wage rate at this location is less than $15.00 per hour.

   b. p-value $= .5000 - .4959 = .0041$

20. H_0: $\mu \geq 8$

    H_a: $\mu < 8$

   a. Reject H_0 if $z < -1.645$

   b. $z = \dfrac{\bar{x} - \mu_0}{\sigma / \sqrt{n}} = \dfrac{7 - 8}{3.2 / \sqrt{40}} = -1.98$

    Reject H_0; the average loss is less than 8 pounds.

   c. p-value $= .5000 - .4761 = .0239$

21. a. Reject H_0 if $z < -1.96$ or $z > 1.96$

   b. $z = \dfrac{\bar{x} - \mu}{\sigma / \sqrt{n}} = \dfrac{10.8 - 10}{2.5 / \sqrt{36}} = 2.40$ Reject H_0; conclude H_a is true.

22. a. Reject H_0 if $z < -2.33$ or $z > 2.33$

    b. $z = \dfrac{\bar{x} - \mu}{\sigma / \sqrt{n}} = \dfrac{14.2 - 15}{5 / \sqrt{50}} = -1.13$

    c. p-value $= (2)(.5000 - .3708) = .2584$

    d. Do not reject H_0

23.   Reject H_0 if $z < -1.96$ or $z > 1.96$

    a. $z = \dfrac{22 - 25}{10 / \sqrt{80}} = -2.68$ Reject H_0

    b. $z = \dfrac{27 - 25}{10 / \sqrt{80}} = 1.79$ Do not reject H_0

    c. $z = \dfrac{23.5 - 25}{10 / \sqrt{80}} = -1.34$ Do not reject H_0

    d. $z = \dfrac{28 - 25}{10 / \sqrt{80}} = 2.68$ Reject H_0

24. a. p-value $= 2(.5000 - .4641) = .0718$ D not reject H_0

    b. p-value $= 2(.5000 - .1736) = .6528$ Do not reject H_0

    c. p-value $= 2(.5000 - .4798) = .0404$ Reject H_0

    d. approximately 0   Reject H_0

    e. p-value $= 2(.5000 - .3413) = .3174$ Do not reject H_0

25. a. $H_0: \mu = 9.70$

    $H_a: \mu \neq 9.70$

    Reject H_0 if $z < -1.96$ or if $z > 1.96$

    $$z = \dfrac{\bar{x} - \mu_0}{\sigma / \sqrt{n}} = \dfrac{9.30 - 9.70}{1.05 / \sqrt{49}} = -2.67$$

    Reject H_0; conclude that wage rates in the city are not $\mu = 9.70$.

    b. p-value $= 2(.5000 - .4962) = .0076$

26. a.   Reject H_0 if $z < -1.96$ or if $z > 1.96$

$$z = \frac{\bar{x} - \mu_0}{\sigma / \sqrt{n}} = \frac{208 - 220}{80 / \sqrt{50}} = -1.06$$

Do not reject H_0; there is no justification for concluding that the mean parking time has changed.

b. p-value $= 2 (.5000 - .3554) = .2892$

27. a. $H_0: \mu = 16$ Continue production

$H_a: \mu \neq 16$ Shut down

Reject H_0 if $z < -1.96$ or if $z > 1.96$

b. $z = \dfrac{\bar{x} - \mu_0}{\sigma / \sqrt{n}} = \dfrac{16.32 - 16}{.8 / \sqrt{30}} = 2.19$

Reject H_0 and shut down for adjustment.

c. $z = \dfrac{\bar{x} - \mu_0}{\sigma / \sqrt{n}} = \dfrac{15.82 - 16}{.8 / \sqrt{30}} = -1.23$

Do not reject H_0; continue to run.

d.   For $\bar{x} = 16.32, p$-value $= 2 (.5000 - .4857) = .0286$

For $\bar{x} = 15.82, p$-value $= 2 (.5000 - .3907) = .2186$

28. $H_0: \mu = 2.2$

$H_a: \mu \neq 2.2$

Reject H_0 if $z < -2.33$ or if $z > 2.33$

$$z = \frac{\bar{x} - \mu_0}{\sigma / \sqrt{n}} = \frac{2.39 - 2.20}{.20 / \sqrt{45}} = 6.37$$

Reject H_0 and conclude 2.2 - minute standard is not being met.

29. $H_0: \mu = 15.20$

$H_a: \mu \neq 15.20$

Reject H_0 if $z < -1.96$ or if $z > 1.96$

$$z = \frac{\bar{x} - \mu_0}{\sigma / \sqrt{n}} = \frac{14.30 - 15.20}{5 / \sqrt{35}} = -1.06$$

Do not reject H_0; the sample does not provide evidence to conclude that there has been a change.

p-value $= 2 (.5000 - .3554) = .2892$

30. a. $\bar{x} \pm z_{.025} \dfrac{\sigma}{\sqrt{n}}$

$52,000 \pm 1.96 \dfrac{5000}{\sqrt{36}}$

$52,000 \pm 1633$

$\$50,367$ to $\$53,633$

b. Since the interval does not include $\$45,300$, we can reject H_0. Conclude that the mean salary of full professors at business colleges differs from the reported $\$45,300$.

31. a. $\bar{x} \pm z_{.025} \dfrac{\sigma}{\sqrt{n}}$

$935 \pm 1.96 \left(\dfrac{180}{\sqrt{200}} \right)$

935 ± 25 or 910 to 960

Since 900 is not in the interval, reject H_0 and conclude $\mu \neq 900$.

b. Reject H_0 if $z < -1.96$ or if $z > 1.96$

$$z = \frac{\bar{x} - \mu_0}{\sigma / \sqrt{n}} = \frac{935 - 900}{180 / \sqrt{200}} = 2.75$$

Reject H_0

c. p-value $= 2 (.5000 - .4970) = .0060$

32. a. The upper 95% confidence limit is computed as follows:

$$\bar{x} + z_{.05} (\sigma / \sqrt{n})$$

$$8.50 + 1.645 (.60 / \sqrt{36}) = 8.66$$

Thus, we are 95% confident that μ is $\$8.66$ per hour or less.

Chapter 9

b. Since \$9.00 is not in the interval \$8.66 per hour or less, we reject H_0.

Conclude that the mean wage rate is less than \$9.00.

33. a. With 15 degrees of freedom, $t_{.05} = 1.753$

Reject H_0 if $t > 1.753$

b. $t = \dfrac{\bar{x} - \mu}{s / \sqrt{n}} = \dfrac{11 - 10}{3 / \sqrt{16}} = 1.33$ Do not reject H_0

34. a. $\bar{x} = \Sigma x_i / n = 108 / 6 = 18$

b. $s = \sqrt{\dfrac{\Sigma (x_i - \bar{x})}{n - 1}} = \sqrt{\dfrac{10}{6 - 1}} = 1.414$

c. Reject H_0 if $t < -2.571$ or $t > 2.571$

d. $t = \dfrac{\bar{x} - \mu}{s / \sqrt{n}} = \dfrac{18 - 20}{1.414 / \sqrt{6}} = -3.46$

e. Reject H_0; conclude H_a is true.

35.   Reject H_0 if $t < -1.721$

a. $t = \dfrac{13 - 15}{8 / \sqrt{22}} = -1.17$ Do not reject H_0

b. $t = \dfrac{11.5 - 15}{8 / \sqrt{22}} = -2.05$ Reject H_0

c. $t = \dfrac{15 - 15}{8 / \sqrt{22}} = 0$ Do not reject H_0

d. $t = \dfrac{19 - 15}{8 / \sqrt{22}} = +2.35$ Do not reject H_0

36.   Use the t distribution with 15 degrees of freedom

a. p-value $= .01$ Reject H_0

b. p-value $= .10$ Do not reject H_0

c. p-value is between .025 and .05   Reject H_0

d. *p*-value is greater than .10   Do not reject H_0

e. *p*-value is approximately 0   Reject H_0

37. a. H_0: $\mu \leq 200$

   H_a: $\mu > 200$

   With 9 degrees of freedom, reject H_0 if $t > 1.833$

$$\bar{x} = \frac{\sum x_i}{n} = 218$$

$$s = \sqrt{\frac{\sum (x_i - \bar{x})^2}{n - 1}} = \sqrt{\frac{6210}{9}} = 26.27$$

$$t = \frac{\bar{x} - \mu_0}{s / \sqrt{n}} = \frac{218 - 200}{26.27 / \sqrt{10}} = 2.17$$

   Reject H_0; conclude the population mean rental rate exceeds the $200 per month rate in Baltimore.

   b. Using the *t* distribution table with 9 degrees of freedom, we find

$$t_{.05} = 1.833 \quad \text{and} \quad t_{.025} = 2.262$$

   Thus the *p*-value is between .05 and .025. Actual *p*-value = .029.

38. H_0: $\mu = 10.05$

   H_a: $\mu \neq 10.05$

   Degrees of freedom = 24

   Reject H_0 if $t \leq -2.064$ or if $t > 2.064$

$$t = \frac{10.83 - 10.05}{3.25 / \sqrt{25}} = 1.20$$

   Cannot reject H_0. The sample does not indicate Phoenix differs from the national average. A larger sample of wages in Phoenix is recommended.

39. a. H_0: $\mu \leq 55$

   H_a: $\mu > 55$

With 7 degrees of freedom, reject H_0 if $t < 1.895$.

$$\bar{x} = \frac{\sum x_i}{n} = \frac{475}{8} = 59.38$$

$$s = \sqrt{\frac{\sum (x_i - \bar{x})^2}{n-1}} = \sqrt{\frac{123.87}{7}} = 4.21$$

$$t = \frac{\bar{x} - \mu_0}{s / \sqrt{n}} = \frac{59.38 - 55}{4.21 / \sqrt{8}} = 2.94$$

Reject H_0; the mean number of hours worked per week exceeds 55.

b. Using 7 degrees of freedom, $t = 2.94$ is bewteen $t_{.025} = 2.365$ and $t_{.01} = 2.998$.

Thus the p-value is between .025 and .01.

40. a. $H_0: \mu \geq 0$

$H_a: \mu < 0$

With 24 degrees of freedom, reject H_0 if $t < -1.711$

$$t = \frac{\bar{x} - \mu_0}{s / \sqrt{n}} = \frac{-10 - 0}{15 / \sqrt{25}} = -3.33$$

Reject H_0; conclude that the drug lowers the mean blood pressure.

b. Using 24 degrees of freedom, $t_{.025} = -2.797$. Thus, p-value $< .005$.

41. $H_0: \mu \geq 300$

$H_a: \mu < 300$

With 5 degrees of freedom, reject H_0 if $t < -2.015$

$$\bar{x} = \frac{\sum x_i}{n} = \frac{1680}{6} = 280$$

$$s = \sqrt{\frac{\sum (x_i - \bar{x})^2}{n-1}} = \sqrt{\frac{1550}{5}} = 17.61$$

$$t = \frac{\bar{x} - \mu_0}{s / \sqrt{n}} = \frac{280 - 300}{17.61 / \sqrt{6}} = -2.78$$

Reject H_0; conclude that the mean number of lunches per day is less than 300.

42. $H_0: \mu \le 2$

        $H_a: \mu > 2$

With 9 degrees of freedom, reject H_0 if $t > 1.833$

$$\bar{x} = \frac{\sum x_i}{n} = \frac{24}{10} = 2.4$$

$$s = \sqrt{\frac{\sum (x_i - \bar{x})^2}{n-1}} = \sqrt{\frac{2.40}{9}} = .516$$

$$t = \frac{\bar{x} - \mu_0}{s / \sqrt{n}} = \frac{2.4 - 2}{.516 / \sqrt{10}} = 2.45$$

Reject H_0 and claim μ is greater than 2 hours. For cost estimating purposes, consider using more than 2 hours of labor time.

43. a. Reject H_0 if $z > 1.645$

$$\sigma_{\bar{p}} = \sqrt{\frac{.50(.50)}{200}} = .0354$$

b. $z = \frac{\bar{p} - p}{\sigma_{\bar{p}}} = \frac{.57 - .50}{.0354} = 1.69 \quad$ Reject H_0

44. a. Reject H_0 if $z < -1.96$ or $z > 1.96$

b. $\sigma_{\bar{p}} = \sqrt{\frac{.20(.80)}{400}} = .02$

        $z = \frac{\bar{p} - p}{\sigma_{\bar{p}}} = \frac{.175 - .20}{.02} = -1.25$

c. p-value $= 2(.5000 - .3944) = .2122$

d.   Do not reject H_0.

45.   Reject H_0 if $z < -1.645$

$$\sigma_{\bar{p}} = \sqrt{\frac{.75(.25)}{300}} = .0250$$

a. $z = \frac{.68 - .75}{.025} = -2.80$

p-value = .5000 - .4974 = .0026

Reject H_0.

b. $z = \dfrac{.72 - .75}{.025} = -1.20$

p-value = .5000 - .3849 = .1151

Do not reject H_0.

c. $z = \dfrac{.70 - .75}{.025} = -2.00$

p-value = .5000 - .4772 = .0228

Reject H_0.

d. $z = \dfrac{.77 - .75}{.025} = .80$

p-value = .5000 + .2881 = .7881

Do not reject H_0.

46. $H_0: p = .30$

$H_a: p \neq .30$

$\sigma_{\bar{p}} = \sqrt{\dfrac{.30\,(.70)}{480}} = .0209$

Reject H_0 if $z < -1.96$ or if $z > 1.96$

$\bar{p} = \dfrac{128}{480} = .2667$

$z = \dfrac{.2667 - .30}{.0209} = -1.59$

p-value = .0559 (2) = .1118

H_0 cannot be rejected.

47. H_0: $p \leq .113$

H_a: $p > .113$

Reject H_0 if $z > 1.645$.

$$\sigma_{\bar{p}} = \sqrt{\frac{p\,(1-p)}{n}} = \sqrt{\frac{.113\,(.887)}{200}} = .0224$$

$$\bar{p} = \frac{29}{200} = .145$$

$$z = \frac{\bar{p} - p_0}{\sigma_{\bar{p}}} = \frac{.145 - .113}{.0224} = 1.43$$

Do not reject H_0. There is no statistical evidence to justify concluding $p > .113$.

48. H_0: $p \geq .80$

H_a: $p < .80$

Reject H_0 if $z < 1.645$.

$$\sigma_{\bar{p}} = \sqrt{\frac{.80\,(.20)}{100}} = .04$$

$$z = \frac{\bar{p} - p_0}{\sigma_{\bar{p}}} = \frac{.75 - .80}{.04} = -1.25$$

Do not reject H_0; the manager's claim of at least 80% cannot be rejected.

p-value $= .5000 - .3944 = .1056$

49. H_0: $p = .25$

H_a: $p \neq .25$

Reject H_0 if $z < -1.645$ or if $z > 1.645$

$$\sigma_{\bar{p}} = \sqrt{\frac{.25\,(.75)}{200}} = .0306 \qquad \bar{p} = \frac{42}{200} = .21$$

$$z = \frac{\bar{p} - p_0}{\sigma_{\bar{p}}} = \frac{.21 - .25}{.0306} = -1.31$$

Do not reject H_0; the magazine's claim of 25% cannot be rejected.

p-value $= 2\,(.5000 - .4049) = .1902$

50. a. $H_0: p \leq .25$

   $H_a: p > .25$

   Reject H_0 if $z > 1.28$

$$\sigma_{\bar{p}} = \sqrt{\frac{.25\,(.75)}{400}} = .0217 \qquad \bar{p} = \frac{112}{400} = .28$$

$$z = \frac{\bar{p} - p_0}{\sigma_{\bar{p}}} = \frac{.28 - .25}{.0217} = 1.38$$

Reject H_0; the series can be judged successful.

b. p-value $= .5000 - .4162 = .0838$

   Since p-value $< .10$, reject H_0

51. $H_0: p \geq .70$

   $H_a: p < .70$

   Reject H_0 if $z < -1.645$

$$\bar{p} = \frac{78}{120} = .65 \qquad \sigma_{\bar{p}} = \sqrt{\frac{.70\,(.30)}{120}} = .0418$$

$$z = \frac{\bar{p} - p_0}{\sigma_{\bar{p}}} = \frac{.65 - .70}{.0418} = -1.20$$

Do not reject H_0; The accountant's claim of at least 70% cannot be rejected.

52. $H_0: p \geq .268$

   $H_a: p < .268$

$$\sigma_{\bar{p}} = \sqrt{\frac{.268\,(.732)}{100}} = .0140$$

$$z = \frac{\bar{p} - p_0}{\sigma_{\bar{p}}} = \frac{.222 - .268}{.0140} = -3.29$$

Reject H$_0$ if $z < -2.33$.

Thus, reject H$_0$; conclude that the proportion of smokers in 1991 is less than the proportion of smokers in 1987.

53. a. Claiming $p > .50$ when the proportion voting for the candidate is .50 or less. This would lead to the mistake of declaring a winner when the candidate did not win.

   b. Concluding $p \leq .50$ when the proportion voting for the candidate is greater than .50. This would mean withholding the declaration of a winner for a candidate who would eventually win.

   c. The Type I error is embarrassing to the television station. Use $\alpha = .01$ to make the probability of this error small.

54.   H$_0$: $p \leq .15$

   H$_a$: $p > .15$

   Reject H$_0$ if $z > 2.33$

$$\sigma_{\bar{p}} = \sqrt{\frac{p(1-p)}{n}} = \sqrt{\frac{.15(.85)}{500}} = .0160$$

$$\bar{p} = \frac{88}{500} = .176$$

$$z = \frac{\bar{p} - p_0}{\sigma_{\bar{p}}} = \frac{.176 - .15}{.0160} = 1.63$$

Do not reject H$_0$; $p \leq .15$ cannot be rejected. Thus the special offer should not be initiated.

p-value $= .5000 - .4484 = .0516$

55.   H$_0$: $p = .05$

   H$_a$: $p \neq .05$

   Reject H$_0$ if $z < -1.96$ or if $z > 1.96$

$$\sigma_{\bar{p}} = \sqrt{\frac{p(1-p)}{n}} = \sqrt{\frac{.05(.95)}{250}} = .0138$$

$$\bar{p} = \frac{10}{250} = .04$$

$$z = \frac{.04 - .05}{.0138} = -.72$$

Do not reject H_0; the claim of 5% cannot be rejected.

p-value $= 2\,(.5000 - .2642) = .4716$

56. $$\sigma_{\bar{x}} = \frac{\sigma}{\sqrt{n}} = \frac{5}{\sqrt{120}} = .46$$

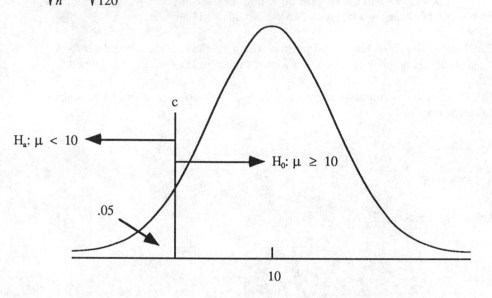

$$c = 10 - 1.645\,(5 / \sqrt{120}) = 9.25$$

Reject H_0 if $\bar{x} < 9.25$

a. When $\mu = 9$,

$$z = \frac{9.25 - 9}{5 / \sqrt{120}} = .55$$

Prob $(H_0) = (.5000 - .2088) = .2912$

b. Type II error

c. When $\mu = 8$,

$$z = \frac{9.25 - 8}{5 / \sqrt{120}} = 2.74$$

$\beta = (.5000 - .4969) = .0031$

57. Reject H_0 if $z < -1.96$ or if $z > 1.96$

$$\sigma_{\bar{x}} = \frac{\sigma}{\sqrt{n}} = \frac{10}{\sqrt{200}} = .71$$

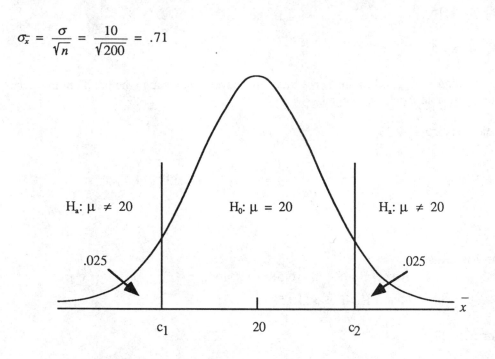

$H_a: \mu \neq 20$ $H_0: \mu = 20$ $H_a: \mu \neq 20$

.025   .025

c_1 20 c_2

$c_1 = 20 - 1.96 \, (10 / \sqrt{200}) = 18.61$

$c_2 = 20 + 1.96 \, (10 / \sqrt{200}) = 21.39$

a. $\mu = 18$

$$z = \frac{18.61 - 18}{10 / \sqrt{200}} = .86$$

$\beta = .5000 - .3051 = .1949$

b. $\mu = 22.5$

$$z = \frac{21.39 - 22.5}{10 / \sqrt{200}} = -1.57$$

$\beta = .5000 - .4418 = .0582$

c. $\mu = 21$

$$z = \frac{21.39 - 21}{10 / \sqrt{200}} = .55$$

$\beta = .5000 + .2088 = .7088$

58. a. $H_0: \mu \leq 15$

   $H_a: \mu > 15$

   Concluding $\mu \leq 15$ when this is not true. Fowle would not charge the premium rate even though the rate should be charged.

   b. Reject H_0 if $z > 2.33$

   $$z = \frac{\bar{x} - \mu_0}{\sigma / \sqrt{n}} = \frac{\bar{x} - 15}{4 / \sqrt{35}} = 2.33$$

   Solve for $\bar{x} = 16.58$

   Decision Rule:

   Accept H_0 if $\bar{x} \leq 16.58$

   Reject H_0 if $\bar{x} > 16.58$

   For $\mu = 17$,

   $$z = \frac{16.58 - 17}{4 / \sqrt{35}} = -.62$$

   $$\beta = .5000 - .2324 = .2676$$

   c. For $\mu = 18$,

   $$z = \frac{16.58 - 18}{4 / \sqrt{35}} = -2.10$$

   $$\beta = .5000 - .4821 = .0179$$

59. a. $H_0: \mu \geq 25$

   $H_a: \mu < 25$

   Reject H_0 if $z < -2.05$

   $$z = \frac{\bar{x} - \mu_0}{\sigma / \sqrt{n}} = \frac{\bar{x} - 25}{3 / \sqrt{30}} = -2.05$$

   Solve for $\bar{x} = 23.88$

Decision Rule:

$$\text{Accept } H_0 \text{ if } \bar{x} \geq 23.88$$

$$\text{Reject } H_0 \text{ if } \bar{x} < 23.88$$

b.   For $\mu = 23$,

$$z = \frac{23.88 - 23}{3 / \sqrt{30}} = 1.61$$

$$\beta = .5000 - .4463 = .0537$$

c.   For $\mu = 24$,

$$z = \frac{23.88 - 24}{3 / \sqrt{30}} = -.22$$

$$\beta = .5000 + .0871 = .5871$$

d.   The Type II error cannot be made in this case. Note that when $\mu = 25.5$ H_0 is true. The Type II error can only be made when H_0 is false.

60. a.   Accepting H_0 and concluding the mean average age was 28 years when it was not.

b.   Reject H_0 if $z < -1.96$ or if $z > 1.96$

$$z = \frac{\bar{x} - \mu_0}{\sigma / \sqrt{n}} = \frac{\bar{x} - 28}{6 / \sqrt{100}}$$

Solving for $\bar{x}$, we find

at $z = -1.96$, $\bar{x} = 26.82$

at $z = +1.96$, $\bar{x} = 29.18$

Decision Rule:

$$\text{Accept } H_0 \text{ if } 26.82 \leq \bar{x} \leq 29.18$$
$$\text{Reject } H_0 \text{ if } \bar{x} < 26.82 \text{ or if } \bar{x} > 29.18$$

At $\mu = 26$,

$$z = \frac{26.82 - 26}{6 / \sqrt{100}} = 1.37$$

$$\beta = .5000 - .4147 = .0853$$

At $\mu = 27$,

$$z = \frac{26.82 - 27}{6 / \sqrt{100}} = -.30$$

$$\beta = .5000 + .1179 = .6179$$

At $\mu = 29$,

$$z = \frac{29.18 - 29}{6 / \sqrt{100}} = .30$$

$$\beta = .5000 + .1179 = .6179$$

At $\mu = 30$,

$$z = \frac{29.18 - 30}{6 / \sqrt{100}} = -1.37$$

$$\beta = .5000 - .4147 = .0853$$

c. Power $= 1 - \beta$

at $\mu = 26$, Power $= 1 - .0853 = .9147$

When $\mu = 26$, there is a .9147 probability that the test will correctly reject the null hypothesis that $\mu = 28$.

61. a. Accepting H_0 and letting the process continue to run when actually over - filling or under - filling exists.

b. Decision Rule: Reject H_0 if $z < -1.96$ or if $z > 1.96$ indicates

Accept H_0 if $15.71 \leq \bar{x} \leq 16.29$

Reject H_0 if $\bar{x} < 15.71$ or if $\bar{x} > 16.29$

For $\mu = 16.5$

$$z = \frac{16.29 - 16.5}{.8 / \sqrt{30}} = -1.44$$

$$\beta = .5000 - .4251 = .0749$$

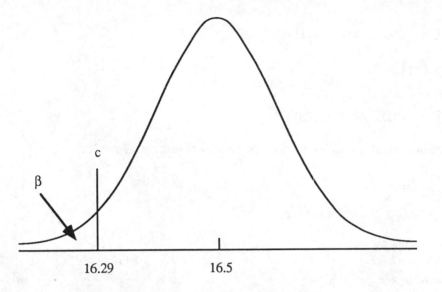

c. Power = 1 - .0749 = .9251

d. The power curve shows the probability of rejecting H_0 for various possible values of μ. In particular, it shows the probability of stopping and adjusting the machine under a variety of underfilling and overfilling situations. The general shape of the power curve for this case is

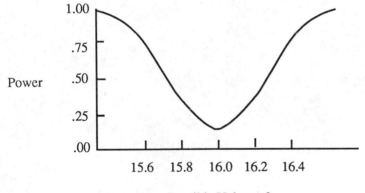

Possible Values of u

62.

$$c = \mu_0 + z_{.01}\, \sigma / \sqrt{n}$$

$$= 15 + 2.33\, (4 / \sqrt{50})$$

$$= 16.32$$

At $\mu = 17$ $z = \dfrac{16.32 - 17}{4 / \sqrt{50}} = -1.20$

$$\beta = .5000 - .3849 = .1151$$

At $\mu = 18$ $\qquad z = \dfrac{16.32 - 18}{4 / \sqrt{50}} = -2.97$

$$\beta = .5000 - .4985 = .0015$$

Increasing the sample size reduces the probability of making a Type II error.

63. a. Accept $\mu \le 100$ when it is false.

   b. Critical value for test:

   $$c = \mu_0 + z_{.05}\, \sigma / \sqrt{n}$$

   $$= 100 + 1.645\, (75 / \sqrt{40})$$

   $$= 119.51$$

   At $\mu = 120$ $\qquad z = \dfrac{119.51 - 120}{75 / \sqrt{40}} = -.04$

   $$\beta = .5000 - .0160 = .4840$$

   c. At $\mu = 130$ $\qquad z = \dfrac{119.51 - 130}{75 / \sqrt{40}} = -.88$

   $$\beta = .5000 - .3106 = .1894$$

   d. Critical value for test:

   $$c = \mu_0 + z_{.05}\, \sigma / \sqrt{n}$$

   $$= 100 + 1.645\, (75 / \sqrt{80})$$

   $$= 113.79$$

   At $\mu = 120$ $\qquad z = \dfrac{113.79 - 120}{75 / \sqrt{80}} = -.74$

   $$\beta = .5000 - .2704 = .2296$$

   At $\mu = 130$ $\qquad z = \dfrac{113.79 - 130}{75 / \sqrt{80}} = -1.93$

   $$\beta = .5000 - .4732 = .0268$$

Increasing the sample size from 40 to 80 reduces the probability of making a Type II error.

64. $n = \dfrac{(z_\alpha + z_\beta)^2 \sigma^2}{(\mu_0 - \mu_a)^2} = \dfrac{(1.645 + 1.28)^2 (5)^2}{(10 - 9)^2} = 214$

65. $n = \dfrac{(z_{\alpha/2} + z_\beta)^2 \sigma^2}{(\mu_0 - \mu_a)^2} = \dfrac{(1.96 + 1.645)^2 (10)^2}{(20 - 22)^2} = 325$

66. At $\mu_0 = 3$, $\quad \alpha = .01$. $\quad z_{.01} = 2.33$

   At $\mu_a = 2.9375$, $\beta = .10$. $\quad z_{.10} = 1.28$

   $\sigma = .18$

   $n = \dfrac{(z_\alpha + z_\beta)^2 \sigma^2}{(\mu_0 - \mu_a)^2} = \dfrac{(2.33 + 1.28)^2 (.18)^2}{(3 - 2.9375)^2} = 108$

67. At $\mu_0 = 400$, $\quad \alpha = .02$. $\quad z_{.02} = 2.05$

   At $\mu_a = 385$, $\quad \beta = .10$. $\quad z_{.10} = 1.28$

   $\sigma = 30$

   $n = \dfrac{(z_\alpha + z_\beta)^2 \sigma^2}{(\mu_0 - \mu_a)^2} = \dfrac{(2.05 + 1.28)^2 (30)^2}{(400 - 385)^2} = 44.4 \quad \text{or} \quad 45$

68. At $\mu_0 = 28$, $\quad \alpha = .05$. Note however for this two - tailed test, $z_{\alpha/2} = z_{.025} = 1.96$

   At $\mu_a = 29$, $\quad \beta = .15$. $\quad z_{.15} = 1.04$

   $\sigma = 6$

   $n = \dfrac{(z_{\alpha/2} + z_\beta)^2 \sigma^2}{(\mu_0 - \mu_a)^2} = \dfrac{(1.96 + 1.04)^2 (6)^2}{(28 - 29)^2} = 324$

69. At $\mu_0 = 25$, $\quad \alpha = .02$. $\quad z_{.02} = 2.05$

   At $\mu_a = 24$, $\quad \beta = .20$. $\quad z_{.20} = .84$

$$\sigma = 3$$

$$n = \frac{(z_\alpha + z_\beta)^2 \sigma^2}{(\mu_0 - \mu_a)^2} = \frac{(2.05 + .84)^2 (3)^2}{(25 - 24)^2} = 75.2 \quad \text{or} \quad 76$$

70. a. $H_0: \mu \le 27$

   $H_a: \mu > 27$

   Reject H_0 if $z > 2.33$

$$z = \frac{\bar{x} - \mu_0}{\sigma / \sqrt{n}} = \frac{27.6 - 27}{1.5 / \sqrt{45}} = 2.68$$

   Reject H_0; conclude that the mean age at the Eastern school is greater than 27.

   b. p-values $= .5000 - .4963 = .0037$

   c. $\bar{x} \pm z_{.05} \sigma / \sqrt{n}$

   $27.6 \pm 1.96 (1.5 / \sqrt{45})$

   $27.6 \pm .44 \quad (27.16 \text{ to } 28.04)$

71. $H_0: \mu \ge 28{,}000$

   $H_a: \mu < 28{,}000$

   Reject H_0 if $z < -1.645$

$$z = \frac{\bar{x} - \mu_0}{\sigma / \sqrt{n}} = \frac{27{,}200 - 28{,}000}{3000 / \sqrt{58}} = -2.03$$

   Reject H_0; the manager's claim should be rejected

   p-values $= .5000 - .4788 = .0212$

72. $H_0: \mu \le 25{,}000$

   $H_a: \mu > 25{,}000$

   Reject H_0 if $z > 1.645$

$$z = \frac{\bar{x} - \mu_0}{\sigma / \sqrt{n}} = \frac{26{,}000 - 25{,}000}{2{,}500 / \sqrt{32}} = 2.26$$

Reject H$_0$; the claim should be rejected. The mean cost is greater than $25,000.

73.　　H$_0$: $\mu = 120$

　　　　H$_a$: $\mu \neq 120$

With $n = 10$, use a t distribution with 9 degrees of freedom.

Reject H$_0$ if $t < -2.262$ or of $t > 2.262$

$$\bar{x} = \sum x_i / n = 118.9$$

$$s = \sqrt{\frac{\sum (x_i - \bar{x})^2}{n-1}} = 4.93$$

$$t = \frac{\bar{x} - \mu_0}{s/\sqrt{n}} = \frac{118.9 - 120}{4.93/\sqrt{10}} = -.71$$

Do not reject H$_0$; the results do not permit rejection of the assumption that $\mu = 120$.

74. a.　H$_0$: $\mu = 350$

　　　　H$_a$: $\mu \neq 350$

Reject H$_0$ if $z < -1.96$ or if $z > 1.96$

$$z = \frac{\bar{x} - \mu_0}{\sigma/\sqrt{n}} = \frac{362 - 350}{40/\sqrt{36}} = 1.80$$

Do not reject H$_0$; the claim of $350 per month cannot be rejected.

b.　p-values $= 2(.5000 - .4641) = .0718$

c.　$\bar{x} \pm z_{.025}(\sigma/\sqrt{n})$

$362 \pm 1.96(40/\sqrt{36})$

362 ± 13　　(349 to 375)

Do not reject H$_0$ since 350 is in the above interval.

75. a.　H$_0$: $\mu \leq 75$

　　　　H$_a$: $\mu > 75$

Reject H_0 if $z > 1.645$

b.
$$z = \frac{\bar{x} - \mu_0}{\sigma / \sqrt{n}} = \frac{82.50 - 75.00}{30 / \sqrt{40}} = 1.58$$

Do not reject H_0; there is no evidence to conclude an increase in maintenance cost exists.

c. p-value $= .5000 - .4429 = .0571$

Since $.0571 > .05$, do not reject H_0.

76. a. $H_0: \mu \leq 72$

$H_a: \mu > 72$

$$z = \frac{\bar{x} - 72}{\sigma / \sqrt{n}} = \frac{80 - 72}{20 / \sqrt{30}} = 2.19$$

p-value $= .5000 - .4857 = .0143$

b. Since p-value $< .05$, reject H_0; the mean idle time exceeds 72 minutes per day.

77. a. $H_0: p \leq .60$

$H_a: p > .60$

Reject H_0 if $z > 1.645$

$$\sigma_{\bar{p}} = \sqrt{\frac{p(1-p)}{n}} = \sqrt{\frac{.60(.40)}{40}} = .0775$$

$$\bar{p} = \frac{27}{40} = .675$$

$$z = \frac{\bar{p} - p}{\sigma_{\bar{p}}} = \frac{.675 - .60}{.0775} = .97$$

Do not reject H_0; the sample results do not justify the conclusion that $p > .60$ for Midwesterners.

b. p-value $= .5000 - .3340 = .1660$

78. H_0: $p = .72$

        H_a: $p \neq .72$

        Reject H_0 if $z < -1.96$ or if $z > 1.96$

$$\sigma_{\bar{p}} = \sqrt{\frac{.72\,(.28)}{200}} = .0317$$

$$\bar{p} = \frac{160}{200} = .80$$

$$z = \frac{\bar{p} - p_0}{\sigma_{\bar{p}}} = \frac{.80 - .72}{.0317} = 2.52$$

Reject H_0; a change in paying practice exists.

p-value $= .5000 - .4941 = .0059$

79. H_0: $p \geq .30$

        H_a: $p < .30$

        Reject H_0 if $z < -1.645$

$$\sigma_{\bar{p}} = \sqrt{\frac{.30\,(.70)}{250}} = .0290$$

$$\bar{p} = \frac{60}{250} = .24$$

$$z = \frac{\bar{p} - p_0}{\sigma_{\bar{p}}} = \frac{.24 - .30}{.0290} = -2.07$$

Reject H_0; the manager's claim is rejected.

80. a. The research is attempting to see if it can be concluded that less than 50% of the working population hold jobs that they planned to hold.

     b. $$\sigma_{\bar{p}} = \sqrt{\frac{.50\,(.50)}{1350}} = .0136$$

$$z = \frac{.41 - .50}{.0136} = -6.62$$

Reject H_0 if $z < -2.33$

Reject H_0; it can be concluded that less than 50% of the working population hold jobs that they planned to hold. The majority hold jobs due to chance, lack of choice, or some other unplanned reason.

81.

$$\sigma_{\bar{p}} = \sqrt{\frac{.75\,(.25)}{356}} = .0229$$

$$\bar{p} = \frac{313}{356} = .88$$

$$z = \frac{.88 - .75}{.0229} = +5.68$$

Reject H_0; conclude $p \neq .75$. Data suggests near 88% of women wear shoes that are at least a size too small.

82. $H_0: p \leq .08$

$H_a: p > .08$

Reject H_0 if $z > 2.05$

$$\sigma_{\bar{p}} = \sqrt{\frac{.08\,(.92)}{80}} = .0303$$

$$\bar{p} = \frac{9}{80} = .1125$$

$$z = \frac{\bar{p} - p}{\sigma_{\bar{p}}} = \frac{.1125 - .08}{.0303} = 1.07$$

Do not reject H_0; there is no evidence to indicate that the machine should be adjusted.

p-value $= .5000 - .3577 = .1423$

83. $H_0: p \geq .90$

$H_a: p < .90$

Reject H_0 if $z < -1.645$

$$\sigma_{\bar{p}} = \sqrt{\frac{.90\,(.10)}{58}} = .0394$$

$$\bar{p} = \frac{49}{58} = .845$$

$$z = \frac{\bar{p} - p}{\sigma_{\bar{p}}} = \frac{.845 - .90}{.0394} = -1.40$$

Do not reject H$_0$; the station's claim cannot be rejected

p-value $= .5000 - .4192 = .0808$

84.   H$_0$: $p \geq .90$

H$_a$: $p < .90$

Reject H$_0$ if $z < -2.05$

$$\sigma_{\bar{p}} = \sqrt{\frac{.90\,(.10)}{92}} = .0313$$

$$\bar{p} = \frac{78}{92} = .848$$

$$z = \frac{\bar{p} - p}{\sigma_{\bar{p}}} = \frac{.848 - .90}{.0313} = -1.66$$

Do not reject H$_0$.

p-value $= .5000 - .4515 = .0485$

85. a.   H$_0$: $\mu \leq 72$

H$_a$: $\mu > 72$

Reject H$_0$ if $z > 1.645$

$$z = \frac{\bar{x} - \mu_0}{\sigma / \sqrt{n}} = \frac{\bar{x} - 72}{20 / \sqrt{30}} = 1.645$$

Solve for $\bar{x} = 78$

Decision Rule:
> Accept H$_0$ *if* $\bar{x} \leq 78$

$$\text{Reject } H_0 \text{ if } \bar{x} > 78$$

For $\mu = 80$,

$$z = \frac{78 - 80}{20 / \sqrt{30}} = -.55$$

$$\beta = .5000 - .2088 = .2912$$

b. For $\mu = 75$,

$$z = \frac{78 - 75}{20 / \sqrt{30}} = .82$$

$$\beta = .5000 + .2939 = .7939$$

c. For $\mu = 70$, H_0 is true. In this case the Type II error cannot be made.

d. Power $= 1 - \beta$

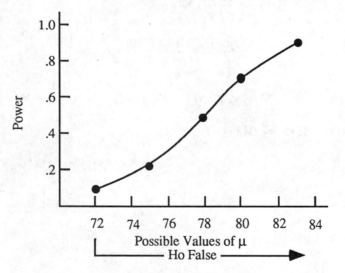

86. $H_0: \mu \geq 7000$

        $H_a: \mu < 7000$

        At $\mu_0 = 7000$, $\alpha = .02$. $z_{.02} = 2.05$

        At $\mu_a = 6500$, $\beta = .05$. $z_{.10} = 1.645$

$$n = \frac{(z_\alpha + z_\beta)^2 \sigma^2}{(\mu_0 - \mu_a)^2} = \frac{(2.05 + 1.645)^2 (2000)^2}{(7000 - 6500)^2} = 218.5 \quad \text{or} \quad 219$$

87. H_0: $\mu = 120$

H_a: $\mu \neq 120$

At $\mu_0 = 120$, $\alpha = .05$. With a two - tailed test, $z_{\alpha/2} = z_{.025} = 1.96$

At $\mu_a = 117$, $\beta = .02$. $z_{.02} = 2.05$

$$n = \frac{(z_{\alpha/2} + z_\beta)^2 \sigma^2}{(\mu_0 - \mu_a)^2} = \frac{(1.96 + 2.05)^2 (5)^2}{(120 - 117)^2} = 44.7 \quad \text{or} \quad 45$$

b. Example calculation for $\mu = 118$.

Reject H_0 if $z < -1.96$ or if $z > 1.96$

$$z = \frac{\bar{x} - \mu_0}{\sigma / \sqrt{n}} = \frac{\bar{x} - 120}{5 / \sqrt{45}}$$

Solve for $\bar{x}$.   At $z = -1.96$, $\bar{x} = 118.54$

At $z = +1.96$, $\bar{x} = 121.46$

Decision Rule:

Accept H_0 if $118.54 \leq \bar{x} \leq 121.46$

Reject H_0 if $\bar{x} < 118.54$ or if $\bar{x} > 121.46$

For $\mu = 118$,

$$z = \frac{118.54 - 118}{5 / \sqrt{45}} = .72$$

$$\beta = .5000 - .2642 = .2358$$

Other Results:

If μ is	z	β
117	2.07	.0192
118	.72	.2358
119	-.62	.7291
121	+.62	.7291
122	+.72	.2358
123	-2.07	.0192

Solution to Computer Case

Note to Instructor:

Some computer packages, such as Minitab, provide the hypothesis test results including p-values automatically. Other packages such as the Data Analyst do not have a hypothesis testing option. In this case, the students should run the basic descriptive statistics option to obtain the sample mean for each sample. With the sample mean, the z value of

$$z = \frac{\bar{x} - \mu}{\sigma / \sqrt{n}}$$

can be easily computed. Corresponding p-values can be obtained from the standard normal probability distribution as discussed in the text.

Solution

The hypothesis testing results for each test are shown below.

	N	MEAN	STDEV	SE MEAN	Z	P VALUE
SAMPLE 1	30	11.9587	0.2204	0.0383	-1.08	0.28
SAMPLE 2	30	12.0287	0.2204	0.0383	0.75	0.45
SAMPLE 3	30	11.8890	0.2072	0.0383	-2.90	0.0039
SAMPLE 4	30	12.0813	0.2061	0.0383	2.12	0.034

Only sample 3 leads to the rejection of the hypothesis Ho: $\mu = 12$. Thus, corrective action is warranted for sample 3. The other samples indicate Ho cannot be rejected and thus from all we can tell, the process is operating satisfactorily. Sample 3 with $\bar{x} = 11.889$ shows the process is operating below the desired mean. Sample 4 with $\bar{x} = 12.0813$ is on the high side, but the p-value of .034 is not sufficient to reject Ho.

The sample standard deviations for all four samples are in the .20 to .22 range. It appears that the process population standard deviation assumption of .21 is good.

With $\alpha = .01$, $z_{.005} = 2.575$. Using the standard error of the mean

$$\sigma_{\bar{x}} = \sigma / \sqrt{n} = .0383$$

the upper and lower control limits are computed as follows:

Upper Control Limit $= 12 + 2.575 (0.0383) = 12.0986$

Lower Control Limit $= 12 - 2.575 \, (0.0383) = 11.9014$

As long as a sample mean $\bar{x}$ is between these two limits, the process is in control and no corrective action is required. Note that sample 3 with a mean of 11.889 shows corrective action is necessary when the sample mean is outside the control limits.

Increasing the level of significance will cause the null hypothesis to be rejected more often. While this may mean quicker corrective action when the process is out of control, it also means that there will be a higher error probability of stopping the process and attempting corrective action when the process is operating satisfactorily. This would be an increase in the probability of a making a Type I error.

Chapter 10
Statistical Inference about Means and Proportions with Two Populations

Learning Objectives

1. Be able to develop interval estimates and conduct hypothesis tests about the difference between the means of two populations.

2. Know the properties of the sampling distribution of the difference between two means $(\bar{x}_1 - \bar{x}_2)$.

3. Be able to use the t distribution to conduct statistical inferences about the difference between the means of two normal populations with equal variances.

4. Understand the concept and use of a pooled variance estimate.

5. Learn how to analyze the difference between the means of two populations when the samples are independent and when the samples are matched.

6. Be able to develop interval estimates and conduct hypothesis tests about the difference between the proportions of two populations.

7. Know the properties of the sampling distribution of the difference between two proportions $(\bar{p}_1 - \bar{p}_2)$.

Chapter 10

Solutions:

1. a. $\bar{x}_1 - \bar{x}_2 = 13.6 - 11.6 = 2$

    b. $s_{\bar{x}_1 - \bar{x}_2} = \sqrt{\dfrac{s_1^2}{n_1} + \dfrac{s_2^2}{n_2}} = \sqrt{\dfrac{(2.2)^2}{50} + \dfrac{3^2}{35}} = .595$

    $2 \pm 1.645\,(.595)$

    $2 \pm .98 \qquad (1.02 \text{ to } 2.98)$

    c. $2 \pm 1.96\,(.595)$

    $2 \pm 1.17 \qquad (0.83 \text{ to } 3.17)$

2. a. $\bar{x}_1 - \bar{x}_2 = 22.5 - 20.1 = 2.4$

    b. $s^2 = \dfrac{(n_1 - 1)\,s_1^2 + (n_2 - 1)\,s_2^2}{n_1 + n_2 - 2} = \dfrac{9\,(2.5)^2 + 7\,(2)^2}{10 + 8 - 2} = 5.27$

    c. $s_{\bar{x}_1 - \bar{x}_2} = \sqrt{s^2 \left(\dfrac{1}{n_1} + \dfrac{1}{n_2} \right)} = \sqrt{5.27 \left(\dfrac{1}{10} + \dfrac{1}{8} \right)} = 1.09$

    16 degrees of freedom, $t_{.025} = 2.12$

    $2.4 \pm 2.12\,(1.09)$

    $2.4 \pm 2.31 \qquad (.09 \text{ to } 4.71)$

3. a. $\bar{x}_1 = \dfrac{\sum x_i}{n} = \dfrac{54}{6} = 9$

    $\bar{x}_2 = \dfrac{\sum x_i}{n} = \dfrac{42}{6} = 7$

    b. $s_1 = \sqrt{\dfrac{\sum (x_i - \bar{x}_1)^2}{n_1 - 1}} = \sqrt{\dfrac{18}{6 - 1}} = 1.90$

    $s_2 = \sqrt{\dfrac{\sum (x_i - \bar{x}_2)^2}{n_2 - 1}} = \sqrt{\dfrac{16}{6 - 1}} = 1.79$

    c. $\bar{x}_1 - \bar{x}_2 = 9 - 7 = 2$

    d. $s^2 = \dfrac{(n_1 - 1)\,s_1^2 + (n_2 - 1)\,s_2^2}{n_1 + n_2 - 2} = \dfrac{5\,(1.90)^2 + 5\,(1.79)^2}{6 + 6 - 2} = 3.41$

e. With 10 degrees of freedom, $t_{.025} = 2.228$

$$s_{\bar{x}_1 - \bar{x}_2} = \sqrt{s^2 \left(\frac{1}{n_1} + \frac{1}{n_2} \right)} = \sqrt{3.41 \left(\frac{1}{6} + \frac{1}{6} \right)} = 1.07$$

$2 \pm 2.228\,(1.07)$

2 ± 2.37 (-0.37 to 4.37)

4. a. $\bar{x}_1 - \bar{x}_2 = \$40{,}800 - \$36{,}000 = \$4{,}800$

b. $$s_{\bar{x}_1 - \bar{x}_2} = \sqrt{\frac{s_1^2}{n_1} + \frac{s_2^2}{n_2}} = \sqrt{\frac{(3{,}600)^2}{41} + \frac{(1{,}400)^2}{71}} = 586$$

$4{,}800 \pm 1.96\,(586)$

$4{,}800 \pm 1149$ ($3{,}651 to $5{,}949)

5. a. $\bar{x}_1 - \bar{x}_2 = 3.02 - 2.72 = .30$

b. $$s_{\bar{x}_1 - \bar{x}_2} = \sqrt{\frac{(.38)^2}{46} + \frac{(.45)^2}{33}} = .0963$$

$.30 \pm 1.645\,(.0963)$

$.30 \pm .16$ (.14 to .46)

c. $.30 \pm 1.96\,(.0963)$

$.30 \pm .19$ (.11 to .49)

6. $\bar{x}_1 - \bar{x}_2 = 23{,}750 - 21{,}000 = 2750$

$$s_{\bar{x}_1 - \bar{x}_2} = \sqrt{\frac{(1200)^2}{220} + \frac{(1000)^2}{250}} = 102.69$$

$2750 \pm 1.96\,(102.69)$

2750 ± 201.27 (2548.73 to 2951.27)

7. a. $\bar{x}_1 - \bar{x}_2 = 500 - 375 = 125$

b. $s_{\bar{x}_1 - \bar{x}_2} = \sqrt{\dfrac{(150)^2}{32} + \dfrac{(130)^2}{36}} = 34.24$

$125 \pm 2.575 \, (34.24)$

$125 \pm 88.18 \quad (36.82 \text{ to } 213.18)$

8. a. $\bar{x}_1 - \bar{x}_2 = 15{,}700 - 14{,}500 = 1{,}200$

b. Pooled variance

$$s^2 = \frac{7\,(700)^2 + 11\,(850)^2}{18} = 632{,}083$$

$$s_{\bar{x}_1 - \bar{x}_2} = \sqrt{632{,}083 \left(\frac{1}{8} + \frac{1}{12}\right)} = 362.88$$

With 18 degrees of freedom $t_{.025} = 2.101$

$1200 \pm 2.101 \, (362.88)$

$1200 \pm 762 \quad (438 \text{ to } 1962)$

c. Populations are normally distributed with equal variances.

9. $n_1 = 5 \qquad n_2 = 5$

$\bar{x}_1 = 20.2 \qquad \bar{x}_2 = 21.4$

$s_1 = 1.48 \qquad s_2 = 2.41$

$\bar{x}_1 - \bar{x}_2 = 20.2 - 21.4 = -1.2$ (Worker 2 has the higher rate.)

b. Degrees of freedom $= n_1 + n_2 - 2 = 8$

$t_{.05} = 1.860$

$$s^2 = \frac{4\,(1.48)^2 + 4\,(2.41)^2}{8} = 4$$

$$s_{\bar{x}_1 - \bar{x}_2} = \sqrt{4 \left(\frac{1}{5} + \frac{1}{5}\right)} = 1.265$$

For worker 2 - worker 1

$1.2 \pm 1.86 (1.265)$

$1.2 \pm 2.35 \quad (-1.15 \text{ to } 3.55)$

No; the difference $\mu_1 - \mu_2$ could be positive indicating worker 1 as the higher rate worker.

10. $n_1 = 15 \qquad n_2 = 12$

      $\bar{x}_1 = 5.2 \qquad \bar{x}_2 = 2.7$

      $s_1 = 1.4 \qquad s_2 = 1.1$

   a. $s^2 = \dfrac{(n_1 - 1) s_1^2 + (n_2 - 1) s_2^2}{n_1 + n_2 - 2} = \dfrac{14 (1.4)^2 + 11 (1.1)^2}{15 + 12 - 2} = 1.63$

   b. $\bar{x}_1 - \bar{x}_2 \pm t_{.025} \sqrt{s^2 \left(\dfrac{1}{n_1} + \dfrac{1}{n_2}\right)} \qquad df = 25$

      $(5.2 - 2.7) \pm 2.060 \sqrt{1.63 \left(\dfrac{1}{15} + \dfrac{1}{12}\right)}$

      $2.5 \pm 1.02 \qquad (1.48 \text{ to } 3.52)$

11. a. $s_{\bar{x}_1 - \bar{x}_2} = \sqrt{\dfrac{s_1^2}{n_1} + \dfrac{s_2^2}{n_2}} = \sqrt{\dfrac{(5.2)^2}{40} + \dfrac{6^2}{50}} = 1.18$

      $z = \dfrac{(\bar{x}_1 - \bar{x}_2) - (\mu_1 - \mu_2)}{s_{\bar{x}_1 - \bar{x}_2}} = \dfrac{(25.2 - 22.8)}{1.18} = 2.03$

      Reject H_0 if $z > 1.645$

      Reject H_0; conclude H_a is true and $\mu_1 - \mu_2 > 0$.

   b. p - value $= .5000 - .4788 = .0212$

12. a. $s_{\bar{x}_1 - \bar{x}_2} = \sqrt{\dfrac{s_1^2}{n_1} + \dfrac{s_2^2}{n_2}} = \sqrt{\dfrac{(8.4)^2}{80} + \dfrac{(7.6)^2}{70}} = 1.31$

      $z = \dfrac{(104 - 106) - 0}{1.31} = -1.53$

      Reject H_0 if $z < -1.96$ or $z > 1.96$

Do not reject H_0

b. p - value $= 2(.5000 - .4370) = .1260$

13. $\bar{x}_1 - \bar{x}_2 = 1.4 - 1.0 = 0.4$

$$s^2 = \frac{(n_1 - 1) s_1^2 + (n_2 - 1) s_2^2}{n_1 + n_2 - 2} = \frac{7 (.4)^2 + 6 (.6)^2}{8 + 7 - 2} = 0.2523$$

$$s_{\bar{x}_1 - \bar{x}_2} = \sqrt{0.2523 \left(\frac{1}{8} + \frac{1}{7}\right)} = 0.26$$

With 13 degrees of freedom. $t_{.025} = 2.16$

Reject H_0 if $t < -2.16$ or $t > 2.16$

$$t = \frac{(\bar{x}_1 - \bar{x}_2) - (\mu_1 - \mu_2)}{s_{\bar{x}_1 - \bar{x}_2}} = \frac{0.4}{0.26} = 1.54$$

Do not reject H_0

14. H_0: $\mu_1 - \mu_2 \leq 0$

H_a: $\mu_1 - \mu_2 > 0$

Reject H_0 if $z > 1.645$

$$s_{\bar{x}_1 - \bar{x}_2} = \sqrt{\frac{s_1^2}{n_1} + \frac{s_2^2}{n_2}} = \sqrt{\frac{(2000)^2}{30} + \frac{(1800)^2}{36}} = 472.58$$

$\bar{x}_1 - \bar{x}_2 = \$500$

$$z = \frac{500 - 0}{472.58} = 1.06$$

p - value $= .5000 - .3554 = .1446$

Cannot reject H_0; the data does not support the conclusion that a difference between means exists for male and female graduates.

15. H_0: $\mu_1 - \mu_2 = 0$

H_a: $\mu_1 - \mu_2 \neq 0$

Reject H_0 if $z < -1.96$ or if $z > 1.96$

$$z = \frac{(\bar{x}_1 - \bar{x}_2) - 0}{\sqrt{\sigma_1^2 / n_1 + \sigma_2^2 / n_2}} = \frac{40 - 35}{\sqrt{(9)^2 / 36 + (10)^2 / 49}} = 2.41$$

Reject H_0; customers at the two stores differ in terms of mean ages.

16. H_0: $\mu_1 - \mu_2 \leq 0$

H_a: $\mu_1 - \mu_2 > 0$

Reject H_0 if $z > 2.05$

$$z = \frac{(\bar{x}_1 - \bar{x}_2) - (\mu_1 - \mu_2)}{\sqrt{\sigma_1^2 / n_1 + \sigma_2^2 / n_2}} = \frac{(547 - 525) - 0}{\sqrt{(83)^2 / 562 + (78)^2 / 852}} = 4.99$$

Reject H_0; conclude that the females have a higher mean verbal score.

17. Population 1 is supplier A.

Population 2 is supplier B.

H_0: $\mu_1 - \mu_2 \leq 0$ Stay with supplier A

H_a: $\mu_1 - \mu_2 > 0$ Change to supplier B

Reject H_0 if $z > 1.645$

$$z = \frac{(\bar{x}_1 - \bar{x}_2) - (\mu_1 - \mu_2)}{\sqrt{\sigma_1^2 / n_1 + \sigma_2^2 / n_2}} = \frac{(14 - 12.5) - 0}{\sqrt{(3)^2 / 50 + (2)^2 / 30}} = 2.68$$

Reject H_0; change to supplier B.

18. H_0: $\mu_1 - \mu_2 \leq 0$

H_a: $\mu_1 - \mu_2 > 0$

Reject H_0 if $z > 2.33$

$$z = \frac{(\bar{x}_1 - \bar{x}_2) - (\mu_1 - \mu_2)}{\sqrt{\sigma_1^2 / n_1 + \sigma_2^2 / n_2}} = \frac{(6.25 - 5.70) - 0}{\sqrt{(1)^2 / 44 + (.80)^2 / 32}} = 2.66$$

Reject H_0; wage discrimination appears to exist.

19. H_0: $\mu_1 - \mu_2 = 5$

H_a: $\mu_1 - \mu_2 \neq 5$

Reject H_0 if $z < -2.33$ or if $z > 2.33$

$$z = \frac{(\bar{x}_1 - \bar{x}_2) - (\mu_1 - \mu_2)}{\sqrt{\sigma_1^2 / n_1 + \sigma_2^2 / n_2}} = \frac{(14.8 - 10.4) - 5}{\sqrt{(.8)^2 / 100 + (.6)^2 / 50}} = -5.14$$

Reject H_0; the difference between means is not 5 minutes.

20. a. H_0: $\mu_1 - \mu_2 = 0$

H_a: $\mu_1 - \mu_2 \neq 0$

Reject H_0 if $t < 2.074$ or if $t > 2.074$

$\bar{x}_1 = 27.30$ $\bar{x}_2 = 25.61$

$s_1 = 1.766$ $s_1 = 1.952$

$$s^2 = \frac{(n_1 - 1) s_1^2 + (n_2 - 1) s_2^2}{n_1 + n_2 - 2} = 3.47$$

$$t = \frac{(27.30 - 25.61) - 0}{\sqrt{3.47 \left(\frac{1}{12} + \frac{1}{12}\right)}} = \frac{1.69}{.76} = 2.22$$

Reject H_0; conclude that there is a difference between the mean annual starting salaries for the two majors.

b. $27.30 - 25.61 = 1.69$ or $1,690 more per year for accounting majors

$1.69 \pm 2.074\ (.76)$

1.69 ± 1.58 (.11 to 3.27) or $110 to $3,270

21. a.   1, 2, 0, 0, 2

b. $\bar{d} = \dfrac{\sum d_i}{n} = \dfrac{5}{5} = 1$

c. $s_d = \sqrt{\dfrac{\sum (d_i - \bar{d})^2}{n - 1}} = \sqrt{\dfrac{4}{5 - 1}} = 1$

d. With 4 degrees of freedom, $t_{.05} = 2.132$

Reject H_0 if $t > 2.132$

$t = \dfrac{\bar{d} - \mu_d}{s_d / \sqrt{n}} = \dfrac{1 - 0}{1 / \sqrt{5}} = 2.24$

Reject H_0; conclude $\mu_d > 0$.

22. a. 3, -1, 3, 5, 3, 0, 1

b. $\bar{d} = \dfrac{\sum d_i}{n} = \dfrac{14}{7} = 2$

c. $s_d = \dfrac{\sqrt{\sum (d_i - \bar{d})^2}}{n - 1} = \sqrt{\dfrac{26}{7 - 1}} = 2.082$

d. $\bar{d} = 2$

e. With 6 degrees of freedom $t_{.025} = 2.447$

$2 \pm 2.447\left(2.082 / \sqrt{7}\right)$

2 ± 1.93 (.07 to 3.93)

23.   Difference = rating after - rating before

H_0: $\mu_d \leq 0$

H_a: $\mu_d > 0$

With 7 degrees of freedom, reject H_0 if $t > 1.895$

$\bar{d} = .625$ $s_d = 1.302$

$t = \dfrac{\bar{d} - \mu_d}{s_d / \sqrt{n}} = \dfrac{.625 - 0}{1.302 / \sqrt{8}} = 1.36$

Do not reject H_0; we cannot conclude that seeing the commercial improves the mean potential to purchase.

24. a.   Difference = 1988 - 1987

Data (d): .55, -1.63, 1.52, .95, 1.11, .54, .41, .70, 1.91, 1.04

H_0: $\mu_d \leq 0$

H_a: $\mu_d > 0$

With 9 degrees of freedom, reject H_0 if $t > 1.833$

$\bar{d} = .71$ $s_d = .945$

$$t = \frac{\bar{d} - \mu_d}{s_d / \sqrt{n}} = \frac{.71}{.945 / \sqrt{10}} = 2.38$$

Reject H_0; conclude mean earnings per share were significantly higher in 1988.

d. $\bar{d} \pm t_{.025} \, s_d / \sqrt{n}$

.71 ± 2.262 (.945 / $\sqrt{10}$)

.71 ± .68   (.03 to 1.39)

25.   Differences: 8, 9.5, 6, 10.5, 15, 9, 11, 7.5, 12, 5

$\bar{d} = 93.5 / 10 = 9.35$ $s_d = 2.954$

$t_{.025} = 2.262$

9.35 ± 2.262 (2.954 / $\sqrt{10}$)

9.35 ± 2.11   (7.24 to 11.46)

26.   Using matched samples, the differences are as follows 4, -2, 8, 8, 5, 6, -4, -2, -3, 0, 11, -5, 5, 9, 5.

H_0: $\mu_d \leq 0$

H_a: $\mu_d > 0$

$\bar{d} = 3$ $s_d = 5.21$

$$t = \frac{\bar{d} - \mu_d}{s_d / \sqrt{n}} = \frac{3 - 0}{5.21 / \sqrt{15}} = 2.23$$

With 14 degrees of freedom, reject H_0 if $t > 1.761$

Reject H_0. Conclude that the population of readers spends more time, on average, watching television than reading.

27. a. Difference = Price deluxe - Price Standard

H_0: $\mu_d = 10$

H_a: $\mu_d \neq 10$

With 6 degrees of freedom, reject H_0 if $t < -2.447$ or if $t > 2.447$

$\bar{d} = 8.86$ $s_d = 2.61$

$$t = \frac{\bar{d} - \mu_d}{s_d / \sqrt{n}} = \frac{8.86 - 10}{2.61 / \sqrt{7}} = -1.16$$

Do not reject H_0; we cannot reject the hypothesis that a $10 price differential exists.

b. $\bar{d} \pm t_{\alpha/2} s_d / \sqrt{n}$

$8.86 \pm 2.447 \, (2.61 / \sqrt{7})$

8.86 ± 2.41 (6.45 to 11.27)

28. a. Difference = after - before

H_0: $\mu_d \leq 0$

H_a: $\mu_d > 0$

With 4 degrees of freedom, reject H_0 if $t > 2.132$

$\bar{d} = 2.2$ $s_d = .837$

$$t = \frac{\bar{d} - \mu_d}{s_d / \sqrt{n}} = \frac{2.2 - 0}{.837 / \sqrt{5}} = 5.88$$

Reject H_0; the bonus plan appears to increase sales.

b. $\bar{d} \pm t_{\alpha/2} s_d / \sqrt{n}$ $t_{.05} = 2.132$

$2.2 \pm 2.132 \, (.837 / \sqrt{5})$

$2.2 \pm .8$ (1.4 to 3.0)

29.   Difference = Word Processor - Typewriter

H_0: $\mu_d \leq 0$

H_a: $\mu_d > 0$

With 6 degrees of freedom, reject H_0 if $t > 1.943$

$\bar{d} = 2.43$ $s_d = 2.76$

$$t = \frac{\bar{d} - \mu_d}{s_d / \sqrt{n}} = \frac{2.43 - 0}{2.76 / \sqrt{7}} = 2.33$$

Reject H_0; the word processor has a greater mean typing rate.

30. a. $\bar{p}_1 - \bar{p}_2 = .48 - .36 = .12$

b. $s_{\bar{p}_1 - \bar{p}_2} = \sqrt{\frac{\bar{p}_1 (1 - \bar{p}_1)}{n_1} + \frac{\bar{p}_2 (1 - \bar{p}_2)}{n_2}} = \sqrt{\frac{.48 (.52)}{400} + \frac{.36 (.64)}{300}} = .0373$

0.12 $\pm$ 1.645 (0.0373)

0.12 $\pm$ 0.0614 (0.0586 to 0.1814)

c. 0.12 $\pm$ 1.96 (0.0373)

0.12 $\pm$ 0.0731   (0.0469 to 0.1931)

31. a. $\bar{p} = \frac{n_1 \bar{p}_1 + n_2 \bar{p}_2}{n_1 + n_2} = \frac{200 (.22) + 300 (.16)}{200 + 300} = 0.184$

$s_{\bar{p}_1 - \bar{p}_2} = \sqrt{(0.184)(0.816)\left(\frac{1}{200} + \frac{1}{300}\right)} = 0.0354$

Reject H_0 if $z > 1.645$

$$z = \frac{(.22 - .16) - 0}{.0354} = 1.69$$

Reject H_0

b. p - value = (.5000 - .4545) = .0455

32. $$s_{\bar{p}_1 - \bar{p}_2} = \sqrt{\frac{.59\,(.41)}{1250} + \frac{.34\,(.66)}{1250}} = 0.0193$$

$$\bar{p}_1 - \bar{p}_2 \pm z_{.025}\, \sigma_{\bar{p}_1 - \bar{p}_2}$$

$$(.59 - .34) \pm 1.96\,(0.0193)$$

$$.25 \pm .0379 \qquad\qquad (.2121 \text{ to } .2879)$$

We can be 95% confident that between 21.21% and 28.79% of adults felt their children's future was better in 1989 compared to 1992.

33. $$\bar{p}_1 = 270\,/\,500 = .54 \qquad\qquad \bar{p}_2 = 162\,/\,360 = .45$$

$$\bar{p}_1 - \bar{p}_2 = .54 - .45 = .09$$

$$.09 \pm 1.96 \sqrt{\frac{.54\,(.46)}{500} + \frac{.45\,(.55)}{360}}$$

$$.09 \pm .0675 \qquad (.0225 \text{ to } .1575)$$

34. a. Population 1 is 1988; Population 2 is 1987.

$$H_0\!: \ p_1 - p_2 \le 0$$

$$H_a\!: \ p_1 - p_2 > 0$$

Reject H_0 if $z > 1.645$

$$\bar{p}_1 = .36 \qquad \bar{p}_2 = .28$$

$$\bar{p} = \frac{n_1\,\bar{p}_1 + n_2\,\bar{p}_2}{n_1 + n_2} = \frac{400\,(.36) + 400\,(.28)}{400 + 400} = .32$$

$$s_{\bar{p}_1 - \bar{p}_2} = \sqrt{\bar{p}\,(1 - \bar{p})\left(\frac{1}{n_1} + \frac{1}{n_2}\right)} = \sqrt{.32\,(.68)\left(\frac{1}{400} + \frac{1}{400}\right)} = .0330$$

$$z = \frac{(\bar{p}_1 - \bar{p}_2) - (p_1 - p_2)}{s_{\bar{p}_1 - \bar{p}_2}} = \frac{(.36 - .28) - 0}{.0330} = 2.42$$

Reject H_0; conclude the proportion spending less is greater in 1988.

p - value $= .5000 - .4922 = .0078$

b. The retailer should be aware of the potential for less spending in 1988.

Chapter 10

c.

$$\bar{p}_1 - \bar{p}_2 \pm z_{.025} \sqrt{\frac{\bar{p}_1(1-\bar{p}_1)}{n_1} + \frac{\bar{p}_2(1-\bar{p}_2)}{n_2}}$$

$$(.36 - .28) \pm 1.96 \sqrt{\frac{.36(.64)}{400} + \frac{.28(.72)}{400}}$$

$.08 \pm .0644$ $(.0156$ to $.1444)$

35. $H_0: p_1 - p_2 = 0$

$H_a: p_1 - p_2 \neq 0$

Reject H_0 if $z < -1.96$ or if $z > 1.96$

$$\bar{p} = \frac{9+6}{60+80} = .1071$$

$$s_{\bar{p}_1 - \bar{p}_2} = \sqrt{(.1071)(.8929)\left(\frac{1}{60} + \frac{1}{80}\right)} = .0528$$

$$z = \frac{(\bar{p}_1 - \bar{p}_2) - (p_1 - p_2)}{s_{\bar{p}_1 - \bar{p}_2}} = \frac{(.15 - .075) - 0}{.0528} = 1.42$$

Do not reject H_0; we cannot detect a difference between the default rates of the two loan officers.

36. $H_0: p_1 - p_2 = 0$

$H_a: p_1 - p_2 \neq 0$

Reject H_0 if $z < -1.96$ or if $z > 1.96$

$$\bar{p} = \frac{n_1 \bar{p}_1 + n_2 \bar{p}_2}{n_1 + n_2} = \frac{500(.16) + 500(.05)}{500 + 500} = .105$$

$$s_{\bar{p}_1 - \bar{p}_2} = \sqrt{\bar{p}(1-\bar{p})\left(\frac{1}{n_1} + \frac{1}{n_2}\right)} = \sqrt{.105(.895)\left(\frac{1}{500} + \frac{1}{500}\right)} = .0194$$

$$z = \frac{(\bar{p}_1 - \bar{p}_2) - (p_1 - p_2)}{s_{\bar{p}_1 - \bar{p}_2}} = \frac{(.16 - .05) - 0}{.0194} = 5.67$$

Reject H_0; the proportions differ significantly. A greater percentage of men would want to be president.

37. H_0: $p_1 - p_2 = 0$

H_a: $p_1 - p_2 \neq 0$

Reject H_0 if $z < -1.96$ or if $z > 1.96$

$$\bar{p} = \frac{110 + 210}{200 + 300} = .64$$

$$s_{\bar{p}_1 - \bar{p}_2} = \sqrt{(.64)(.36)\left(\frac{1}{200} + \frac{1}{300}\right)} = .0438$$

$$\bar{p}_1 = 110 / 200 = .55 \quad \bar{p}_2 = 210 / 300 = .70$$

$$z = \frac{(\bar{p}_1 - \bar{p}_2) - (p_1 - p_2)}{s_{\bar{p}_1 - \bar{p}_2}} = \frac{(.55 - .70) - 0}{.0438} = -3.42$$

Reject H_0; there is a difference between response rates for men and women.

b. $.15 \pm 1.96 \sqrt{\dfrac{.55(.45)}{200} + \dfrac{.70(.30)}{300}}$

$.15 \pm .0863$ (.0637 to .2363)   Greater response rate for women.

38. H_0: $p_1 - p_2 = 0$

H_a: $p_1 - p_2 \neq 0$

Reject H_0 if $z < -1.96$ or if $z > 1.96$

$$\bar{p} = \frac{63 + 60}{150 + 200} = .3514$$

$$s_{\bar{p}_1 - \bar{p}_2} = \sqrt{(.3514)(.6486)\left(\frac{1}{150} + \frac{1}{200}\right)} = .0516$$

$$\bar{p}_1 = 63 / 150 = .42 \quad \bar{p}_2 = 60 / 200 = .30$$

$$z = \frac{(\bar{p}_1 - \bar{p}_2) - (p_1 - p_2)}{s_{\bar{p}_1 - \bar{p}_2}} = \frac{(.42 - .30) - 0}{.0516} = 2.33$$

Reject H_0; there is a difference between the recall rates for the two commercials.

b. $(.42 - .30) \pm 1.96 \sqrt{\dfrac{.42(58)}{150} + \dfrac{.30(.70)}{200}}$

$.12 \pm .10$ (.02 to .22)

39. a. $\bar{p}_1 = 520 / 1679 = .31$ $\bar{p}_2 = 293 / 1629 = .18$

$$\bar{p} = \frac{520 + 293}{1679 + 1629} = \frac{813}{3308} = 0.2458$$

$$s_{\bar{p}_1 - \bar{p}_2} = \sqrt{(.2458)(.7542)\left(\frac{1}{1679} + \frac{1}{1629}\right)} = .0150$$

H_0: $p_1 - p_2 = 0$

H_a: $p_1 - p_2 \neq 0$

Reject H_0 if $z < -2.575$ or if $z > 2.575$

$$\bar{z} = \frac{.31 - .18 - 0}{.0150} = 8.67$$

Reject H_0

Conclude that there has been a shift in the proportion who felt California was on the right track.

b. $$\bar{p}_1 - \bar{p}_2 \pm z_{.025} \sqrt{\frac{\bar{p}_1(1 - \bar{p}_1)}{n_1} + \frac{\bar{p}_2(1 - \bar{p}_2)}{n_2}}$$

$$.31 - .18 \pm 1.96 \sqrt{\frac{.31(.69)}{1679} + \frac{.18(.82)}{1629}}$$

$.31 - .18 \pm .029$ $(.101 \text{ to } .159)$

From 10.1% to 15.9% decrease in percentage who felt California was on the right track.

40. $$(\bar{x}_1 - \bar{x}_2) \pm z_{.05} \sqrt{\frac{s_1^2}{n_1} + \frac{s_2^2}{n_2}}$$

$$(23{,}000 - 21{,}000) \pm 1.645 \sqrt{\frac{(2500)^2}{60} + \frac{(2000)^2}{80}}$$

2000 ± 646 $(1354 \text{ to } 2646)$

41. H_0: $\mu_1 - \mu_2 = 0$

H_a: $\mu_1 - \mu_2 \neq 0$

Reject H_0 if $z < -1.96$ or if $z > 1.96$

$$z = \frac{(\bar{x}_1 - \bar{x}_2) - (\mu_1 - \mu_2)}{\sqrt{\sigma_1^2 / n_1 + \sigma_2^2 / n_2}} = \frac{(4.1 - 3.3) - 0}{\sqrt{\frac{(2.2)^2}{120} + \frac{(1.5)^2}{100}}} = 3.19$$

Reject H_0; a difference exists with system B having the lower mean checkout time.

42. $H_0: \ \mu_1 - \mu_2 \ = \ 0$

$H_a: \ \mu_1 - \mu_2 \ \neq \ 0$

Use 25 degrees of freedom. Reject H_0 if $t < -2.06$ or if $t > 2.06$

$$s^2 = \frac{11 \, (8)^2 + 14 \, (10)^2}{25} = 84.16$$

$$t = \frac{(\bar{x}_1 - \bar{x}_2) - (\mu_1 - \mu_2)}{\sqrt{s^2 \left(\frac{1}{n_1} + \frac{1}{n_2} \right)}} = \frac{(72 - 78) - 0}{\sqrt{84.16 \left(\frac{1}{12} + \frac{1}{15} \right)}} = -1.69$$

Do not reject H_0; cannot conclude a difference exists.

43. $H_0: \ \mu_1 - \mu_2 \ = \ 0$

$H_a: \ \mu_1 - \mu_2 \ \neq \ 0$

Reject H_0 if $z < -1.96$ or if $z > 1.96$

$$z = \frac{(\bar{x}_1 - \bar{x}_2) - (\mu_1 - \mu_2)}{\sqrt{\sigma_1^2 / n_1 + \sigma_2^2 / n_2}} = \frac{(7.2 - 6.4) - 0}{\sqrt{\frac{(1.7)^2}{50} + \frac{(1.4)^2}{50}}} = 2.57$$

Reject H_0; conclude that men and women do not have the same level of job satisfaction.

44.   Difference = before - after

$H_0: \ \mu_d \ \leq \ 0$

$H_a: \ \mu_d \ > \ 0$

With 5 degrees of freedom, reject H_0 if $t > 2.015$

$$\bar{d} = 6.167 \qquad s_d = 6.585$$

$$t = \frac{\bar{d} - \mu_d}{s_d / \sqrt{n}} = \frac{6.167 - 0}{6.585 / \sqrt{6}} = 2.29$$

Reject H_0; conclude that the program provides weight loss.

45. $\bar{p}_1 = 175 / 500 = .35 \qquad \bar{p}_2 = 360 / 800 = .45$

$$s_{\bar{p}_1 - \bar{p}_2} = \sqrt{\frac{.35\,(.65)}{500} + \frac{(.45)\,(.55)}{800}} = .0276$$

$.10 \pm 2.575\,(.0276)$

$.10 \pm .071 \qquad (.029 \text{ to } .171)$

46.   Population 1 - nicotine chewing gum

Population 2 - regular chewing gum

a. $H_0: p_1 - p_2 \leq 0$

$H_a: p_1 - p_2 > 0$

Reject H_0 if $z > 1.645$

b. $\bar{p} = \frac{23 + 12}{60 + 53} = .3097 \qquad \bar{p}_1 = 23 / 60 = .3833 \qquad \bar{p}_2 = 12 / 53 = .2264$

$$s_{\bar{p}_1 - \bar{p}_2} = \sqrt{\bar{p}\,(1 - \bar{p})\left(\frac{1}{n_1} + \frac{1}{n_2}\right)} = \sqrt{.3097\,(.6903)\left(\frac{1}{60} + \frac{1}{53}\right)} = .0872$$

$$z = \frac{(\bar{p}_1 - \bar{p}_2) - (p_1 - p_2)}{s_{\bar{p}_1 - \bar{p}_2}} = \frac{(.3833 - .2264) - 0}{.0872} = 1.80$$

Reject H_0; conclude that the nicotine gum provided a larger proportion of nonsmokers.

p - value $= .5000 - .4641 = .0359$

47. a. $H_0: p_1 - p_2 = 0$

$H_a: p_1 - p_2 \neq 0$

Reject H_0 if $z < -1.96$ or if $z > 1.96$

$$\bar{p} = \frac{76 + 90}{400 + 900} = .1277$$

$$s_{\bar{p}_1 - \bar{p}_2} = \sqrt{.1277\,(.8723)\left(\frac{1}{400} + \frac{1}{900}\right)} = .02$$

$$\bar{p}_1 = 76 / 400 = .19 \qquad \bar{p}_2 = 90 / 900 = .10$$

$$z = \frac{(\bar{p}_1 - \bar{p}_2) - (p_1 - p_2)}{s_{\bar{p}_1 - \bar{p}_2}} = \frac{(.19 - .10) - 0}{.02} = 4.50$$

Reject H_0; there is a difference between claim rates.

b. $.09 \pm 1.96 \sqrt{\dfrac{.19\,(.81)}{400} + \dfrac{.10\,(.90)}{900}}$

$.09 \pm .0432 \qquad (.0468 \text{ to } .1332)$

48.
$$\bar{p} = \frac{9 + 5}{142 + 268} = \frac{14}{410} = .0341$$

$$s_{\bar{p}_1 - \bar{p}_2} = \sqrt{.0341\,(.9659)\left(\frac{1}{142} + \frac{1}{268}\right)} = .0188$$

$$\bar{p}_1 = 9 / 142 = .0634 \qquad \bar{p}_2 = 5 / 268 = .0187$$

$$\bar{p}_1 - \bar{p}_2 = .0634 - .0187 = .0447$$

$$z = \frac{.0447 - 0}{.0188} = 2.38$$

p - value $= 2(.5000 - .4913) = .0174$

Reject H_0; There is a significant difference in drug resistance between the two states. New Jersey has the higher drug resistance rate.

Solution to Computer Case

This case can provide discussion and differing opinions as to what hypothesis test should be conducted. Students should begin to see that logical arguments exist for structuring the hypotheses differently. In some interpretations of the problem, a two - tailed test can be appropriate for Par, Inc. In other interpretations of the same problem, a one - tailed test may be preferred. We suggest accepting different formulations of the Par, Inc. hypothesis test provided convincing rationale is provided.

Letting μ_1 = the population mean for the current golf ball
μ_2 = the population mean for the new golf ball,

We suggest the following hypothesis test:

H_0: $\mu_1 - \mu_2 \leq 0$

H_a: $\mu_1 - \mu_2 > 0$

This formulation is based on the information that the new golf balls is being designed to "resist cuts and yet still offer good driving distances." The research hypothesis is not to prove the new golf ball out distances the current golf ball. In fact, Par could claim an improved quality with the cut resistance improvement provided the new golf ball has the same or better driving distance. In fact, Par should be concerned about the new golf ball if the statistical evidence shows the mean driving distance of the current golf ball. The hypotheses have been structured so that rejection of H_0 will show the new golf ball has the lower mean driving distances, indicating the cut resistance advantage may be offset by the loss of distance.

Minitab's TWOSAMPLE routine provides the following results:

TWOSAMPLE	T FOR CURRENT	VS	NEW		
	N	MEAN	STDEV	SE	MEAN
CURRENT	40	270.27	8.75		1.4
NEW	40	267.50	9.90		1.6

95 PCT CI FOR MU CURRENT - MU NEW: (-1.4, 6.9)

TTEST MU CURRENT = MU NEW (VS GT) : T = 1.33 P = 0.094 DF = 76

The interval estimation procedure shows

$$\bar{x}_1 - \bar{x}_2 = 2.77$$

and a standard error of the difference of

$$s_{\bar{x}_1} - s_{\bar{x}_2} = 2.089.$$

The test statistic would be

$$z = (2.77 - 0) / 2.089 = 1.33$$

From the standard normal distribution table, the p-value is .0918.

Using the .05 level of significance, H_0 cannot be rejected. The data does not provide statistical evidence to conclude that the new golf ball has a lower mean driving distance than the current golf ball.

95% confidence intervals are as follows:

Current Golf Ball:	267.56 to 272.99
New Golf Ball:	264.43 to 270.57
Difference:	-1.32 to +6.87

The sample mean for the current golf ball was 270.27 and the sample mean for the new golf ball was 267.50. On average, the current golf ball had a 2.77 yard average. A variety of descriptive statistics including histograms would be helpful is summarizing the data.

The argument should be made that in failing to reject H_0, the research findings are inconclusive. While the data do not show the new golf ball with a significantly lower mean driving distance, the researcher should not be ready to conclude the mean distance for the new golf ball is equal to or better than the current golf ball. A potential for a Type II error exists with this conclusion. This is a case where continued study with more data should be relatively easy. With the mechanical hitting machine, samples of several hundred golf balls should be taken without much trouble. With more data, Par should have a good idea of the difference between the means for the two golf balls.

Additional Descriptive Statistics:

	N	MEAN	MEDIAN	TRMEAN	STDEV	SEMEAN
CURRENT	40	270.27	270.00	270.06	8.75	1.38
NEW	40	267.50	265.00	267.36	9.90	1.56

	MIN	MAX	Q1	Q3
CURRENT	255.00	289.00	263.00	275.75
NEW	250.00	289.00	262.00	275.50

Chapter 11
Inferences About Population Variances

Learning Objectives

1. Understand the importance of variance in a decision-making situation.

2. Understand the role of statistical inference in developing conclusions about the variance of a single population.

3. Know the sampling distribution of $(n - 1) s^2 / \sigma^2$ has a chi - square distribution and be able to use this result to develop a confidence interval estimate of σ^2.

4. Know how to test hypotheses involving σ^2.

5. Understand the role of statistical inference in developing conclusions about the variances of two populations.

6. Know that the sampling distribution of s_1^2 / s_2^2 has an F distribution and be able to use this result to test hypotheses involving the variances of two populations.

Chapter 11

Solutions:

1. a. 11.0705

   b. 24.4884

   c. 9.59083

   d. 23.2093

   e. 9.39046

2. $s^2 = 25$

   a. With 19 degrees of freedom $\chi^2_{.05} = 30.1435$ and $\chi^2_{.95} = 10.1170$

   $$\frac{19\,(25)}{30.1435} \leq \sigma^2 \leq \frac{19\,(25)}{10.1170}$$

   $$15.76 \leq \sigma^2 \leq 46.95$$

   b. With 19 degrees of freedom $\chi^2_{.025} = 32.8523$ and $\chi^2_{.975} = 8.90655$

   $$\frac{19\,(25)}{32.8523} \leq \sigma^2 \leq \frac{19\,(25)}{8.90655}$$

   $$14.46 \leq \sigma^2 \leq 53.33$$

   c. $\qquad\qquad 3.8 \leq \sigma^2 \leq 7.3$

3. With 15 degrees of freedom $\chi^2_{.05} = 24.9958$

   Reject H_0 if $\chi^2 > 24.9958$

   $$\chi^2 = \frac{(n-1)\,s^2}{\sigma^2} = \frac{(16-1)\,(8)^2}{50} = 19.2$$

   Do not reject H_0

4.   a. $n = 18$

$$s^2 = .36$$

$$\chi^2_{.05} = 27.5871 \qquad \chi^2_{.95} = 8.67176 \ \text{(17 degrees of freedom)}$$

$$\frac{(17)\,(.36)}{27.5871} \leq \sigma^2 \leq \frac{(17)\,(.36)}{8.67176}$$

$$.22 \leq \sigma^2 \leq .71$$

b. $.47 \leq \sigma \leq .84$

5. $n = 12$

$$s^2 = .0442$$

$$\chi^2_{.025} = 21.92 \qquad \chi^2_{.975} = 3.81575 \ \text{(11 degrees of freedom)}$$

$$\frac{(11)\,(.0442)}{21.92} \leq \sigma^2 \leq \frac{(11)\,(.0442)}{3.81575}$$

$$.0222 \leq \sigma^2 \leq .1274$$

$$.1489 \leq \sigma \leq .3570$$

6.   a.   Degrees of freedom = 29

$$\chi^2_{.025} = 45.7222 \qquad \chi^2_{.975} = 16.0471$$

$$\frac{29\,(9.5)^2}{45.7222} \leq \sigma^2 \leq \frac{29\,(9.5)^2}{16.0471}$$

$$57.24 \leq \sigma^2 \leq 163.10$$

$$7.57 \leq \sigma \leq 12.77$$

b.   Degrees of freedom = 50

$$\chi^2_{.025} = 71.4202 \qquad \chi^2_{.975} = 32.3574$$

$$\frac{50\,(9.5)^2}{71.4202} \leq \sigma^2 \leq \frac{50\,(9.5)^2}{32.3574}$$

$$63.18 \leq \sigma^2 \leq 139.46$$

$$7.95 \leq \sigma \leq 11.81$$

c. Degrees of freedom $= 100$

$$\chi^2_{.025} = 129.561 \qquad \chi^2_{.975} = 74.2219$$

$$\frac{100\,(9.5)^2}{129.561} \leq \sigma^2 \leq \frac{100\,(9.5)^2}{74.2219}$$

$$69.66 \leq \sigma^2 \leq 121.59$$

$$8.35 \leq \sigma \leq 11.03$$

d. The larger the sample size the smaller width and greater precision for the interval estimate.

7. $\quad n = 10$

$\quad s^2 = 4.8$

a. $\quad \dfrac{(n-1)\,s^2}{\chi^2_{\alpha/2}} \leq \sigma^2 \leq \dfrac{(n-1)\,s^2}{\chi^2_{1-\alpha/2}}$

$$\chi^2_{.025} = 19.0228 \ \text{(9 degrees of freedom)}$$

$$\chi^2_{.975} = 2.70039$$

$$\frac{(9)\,(4.8)}{19.0228} \leq \sigma^2 \leq \frac{(9)\,(4.8)}{2.70039}$$

$$2.27 \leq \sigma^2 \leq 16.00$$

b. $\chi^2_{.025} = 39.3641 \quad \chi^2_{.975} = 12.4011 \ \text{(24 degrees of freedom)}$

$$\frac{(24)\,(4.8)}{39.3641} \leq \sigma^2 \leq \frac{(24)\,(4.8)}{12.4011}$$

$$2.93 \leq \sigma^2 \leq 9.29$$

c. A larger sample size results in an interval with smaller width which shows larger samples provide better precision.

8. a. $H_0: \ \sigma^2 \leq 48$

$\quad H_a: \ \sigma^2 > 48$

At $\alpha = .05$, reject H_0 if $\chi^2 > 35.1725$

$$\chi^2 = \frac{(n-1)s^2}{\sigma^2} = \frac{23\,(67.6)}{48} = 32.39$$

Do not reject H_0. However, it will a good idea to continue to monitor the variance in percent returns. A variance increase and associated higher risk may be in the future.

b.
$$\frac{(23)\,(67.6)}{38.0757} \le \sigma^2 \le \frac{(23)\,(67.6)}{11.6885}$$

$$40.83 \le \sigma^2 \le 133.02$$

c.
$$6.39 \le \sigma \le 11.53$$

9. $H_0 : \sigma^2 \le .0004$

$H_a : \sigma^2 > .0004$

$n = 30$

$$\chi^2_{.05} = 42.5569 \ (29 \text{ degrees of freedom})$$

$$\chi^2 = \frac{(29)\,(.0005)}{.0004} = 36.25$$

Do not reject H_0 ; the product specification does not appear to be violated.

10. $n = 22$

$s^2 = 1.5$

$H_0 : \sigma^2 \le 1$

$H_a : \sigma^2 > 1$

$$\chi^2_{.10} = 29.6151 \ (21 \text{ degrees of freedom})$$

$$\chi^2 = \frac{(n-1)s^2}{\sigma^2_0} = \frac{(21)\,(1.5)}{1} = 31.5$$

Reject H_0; the conclusion $\sigma^2 > 1$ can be made.

11. a. $H_0:$ $\sigma^2 \leq .25$

$H_a:$ $\sigma^2 > .25$

$$n = 18$$
$$s^2 = .40$$

$$\chi^2 = \frac{(n-1)\,s^2}{\sigma^2} = \frac{17\,(.40)}{.25} = 27.2$$

$$\chi^2_{.05} = 27.5871$$

We cannot reject the hypotheses that the machine provides an acceptable variance.

b. $$\frac{(n-1)\,s^2}{\chi^2_{.05}} \leq \sigma^2 \leq \frac{(n-1)\,s^2}{\chi^2_{.95}}$$

$$\frac{17\,(.40)}{27.5871} \leq \sigma^2 \leq \frac{17\,(.40)}{8.67176}$$

$$.246 \leq \sigma^2 \leq .784$$

12. $$s^2 = \frac{101.56}{8} = 12.69$$

$H_0:$ $\sigma^2 = 10$

$H_a:$ $\sigma^2 \neq 10$

With 8 degrees of freedom

$$\chi^2_{.95} = 2.73264, \qquad \chi^2_{.05} = 15.5073$$

$$\chi^2 = \frac{(n-1)\,s^2}{\sigma^2} = \frac{8\,(12.69)}{10} = 10.16$$

We cannot reject the hypothesis that the variance in the number of patients seen per day is 10.

13. a. $F_{.05} = 2.91$

b. $F_{.025} = 2.76$

c. $F_{.01} = 4.50$

d. $F_{.975} = \dfrac{1}{F_{.025,20,10}} = \dfrac{1}{3.42} = .29$

Remember to reverse the degrees of freedom in the $F_{.025}$ above.

14. $F_{.05,15,19} = 2.23$

Reject H_0 if $F > 2.23$

$F = \dfrac{s_1^2}{s_2^2} = \dfrac{5.8}{2.4} = 2.42$

Reject H_0 ; conclude $\sigma_1^2 > \sigma_2^2$

15.   We recommend placing the larger sample variance in the numerator. With $\alpha = .05$,

$F_{.025,20,24} = 2.33$.   Reject if $F > 2.33$.

$F = 8.2 / 4.0 = 2.05$ Do not reject H_0

Or if we had the lower tail F value,

$F_{.025,20,24} = \dfrac{1}{F_{.025,24,20}} = \dfrac{1}{2.41} = .41$

$F = 4.0 / 8.2 = .49$ $\therefore F > .41$ Do not reject H_0

16. $H_0: \sigma_{92}^2 \leq \sigma_{91}^2$

$H_2: \sigma_{92}^2 > \sigma_{91}^2$

$F = \dfrac{s_{92}^2}{s_{91}^2} = \dfrac{(4200)^2}{(3850)^2} = 1.19$

Reject H_0 if $F > 1.35$

Do not reject H_0. The mean price has increased in 1991; however, the sample data do not support the conclusion that the variance in price has also increased.

17.   Let σ_1^2 = variance in repair costs (4 year old automobiles)

σ_2^2 = variance in repair costs (2 year old automobiles)

H_0: $\sigma_1^2 \le \sigma_2^2$

H_a: $\sigma_1^2 > \sigma_2^2$

b. $s_1^2 = (170)^2 = 28{,}900$

$s_2^2 = (100)^2 = 10{,}000$

$$F = \frac{s_1^2}{s_2^2} = \frac{28{,}900}{10{,}000} = 2.89$$

$F_{.01,24,24} = 2.66$

Reject H_0; conclude that 4 year old automobiles have a larger variance in annual repair costs compared to 2 year old automobiles. This is expected due to the fact that older automobiles are more likely to have some very expensive repairs which lead to greater variance in the annual repair costs.

18. H_0 : $\sigma_1^2 = \sigma_2^2$

H_a : $\sigma_1^2 \ne \sigma_2^2$

$F_{.025} = 1.43$

$$F = \frac{s_1^2}{s_2^2} = \frac{83^2}{78^2} = 1.13$$

Do not reject H_0; we cannot conclude the variances differ for females and males.

19. H_0 : $\sigma_1^2 \le \sigma_2^2$

H_a : $\sigma_1^2 > \sigma_2^2$

$F_{.05} = 1.79$ (Degrees of freedom are 40 numerator, 30 denominator)

$$F = \frac{s_1^2}{s_2^2} = \frac{38}{2.0} = 1.9$$

Reject H_0; Durham Electric has a larger population variance. Therefore, recommend Raleigh Electronics.

20. Let B = population 1 (Large sample variance)

   A = population 2

   $F_{.05}$ = 2.03 (Degrees of freedom are 20 numerator, 24 denominator)

   F = 11 / 5 = 2.20

   Reject H_0; the population variances are not equal.

21. $H_0 : \sigma_1^2 = \sigma_2^2$

   $H_a : \sigma_1^2 \neq \sigma_2^2$

   $s_1^2 = (5.2)^2 = 27.04 \qquad n_1 = 8$

   $s_2^2 = (3.8)^2 = 14.44 \qquad n_2 = 8$

   Using larger variance in the numerator,

   F = 27.04 / 14.44 = 1.87

   $F_{.05}$ = 3.79

   Do not reject H_0; the variances in typing speeds so not appear to differ.

22. $H_0 : \sigma_{wet}^2 \leq \sigma_{dry}^2$

   $H_a : \sigma_{wet}^2 > \sigma_{dry}^2$

   $s_{wet}^2 = 32^2 = 1024 \qquad s_{dry}^2 = 16^2 = 256$

   $F_{.05} = 2.40 \qquad F = \dfrac{s_{wet}^2}{s_{dry}^2} = \dfrac{1024}{256} = 4$

   Since F = 4 > 2.40, reject H_0 and conclude that there is greater variability in stopping distances on wet pavement.

   b. Drive carefully on wet pavement because of the uncertainty in stopping distances.

23. a. $s^2 = (30)^2 = 900$

   b. $\chi_{.05}^2 = 30.1435$ and $\chi_{.95}^2 = 10.1170$ (19 degrees of freedom)

$$\frac{(19)\,(900)}{30.1435} \le \sigma^2 \le \frac{(19)\,(900)}{10.1170}$$

$$567.29 \le \sigma^2 \le 1690.22$$

c. $23.82 \le \sigma \le 41.11$

24.   With 12 degrees of freedom,

$$\chi^2_{.025} = 23.3367$$

$$\chi^2_{.975} = 4.40379$$

$$\frac{12\,(14.95)^2}{23.3367} \le \sigma^2 \le \frac{12\,(14.95)^2}{4.40379}$$

$$114.93 \le \sigma^2 \le 609.03$$

$$10.72 \le \sigma \le 24.68$$

25. a. $H_0 : \sigma^2 = .25$

$H_a : \sigma^2 \ne .25$

$\chi^2_{.025} = 35.4789$ (21 degrees of freedom)

$$\chi^2 = \frac{(n-1)\,s^2}{\sigma_0^2} = \frac{(21)\,(.75)^2}{.25} = 47.25$$

Reject H_0; conclude that the variance is not the same.

b. $\chi^2_{.025} = 35.4789$ and $\chi^2_{.975} = 10.28293$ (21 degrees of freedom)

$$\frac{(21)\,(.75)^2}{35.4789} \le \sigma^2 \le \frac{(21)\,(.75)^2}{10.28293}$$

$$.33 \le \sigma^2 \le 1.15$$

$$.58 \le \sigma \le 1.07$$

26. a. $H_0: \sigma^2 \leq .0001$

    $H_a: \sigma^2 > .0001$

    $\chi^2_{.10} = 21.0642$ (14 degrees of freedom)

    $$\chi^2 = \frac{(14)(.014)^2}{.0001} = 27.44$$

    Reject H_0; σ^2 exceeds maximum variance requirement.

    b. $\chi^2_{.05} = 23.6848$ and $\chi^2_{.95} = 6.57063$ (14 degrees of freedom)

    $$\frac{(14)(.014)^2}{23.6848} \leq \sigma^2 \leq \frac{(14)(.014)^2}{6.57063}$$

    $$.00012 \leq \sigma^2 \leq .00042$$

27. $H_0: \sigma^2 \leq .02$

    $H_a: \sigma^2 > .02$

    $\chi^2_{.05} = 55.7585$ (40 degrees of freedom)

    $$\chi^2 = \frac{40(.16)^2}{.02} = 51.2$$

    Do not reject H_0; the variance does not appear to be exceeding the standard.

28. a. Try $n = 15$

    $\chi^2_{.025} = 26.1190$ $\chi^2_{.975} = 5.62872$ (14 degrees of freedom)

    $$\frac{(14)(64)}{26.1190} \leq \sigma^2 \leq \frac{(14)(64)}{5.62872}$$

    $$34.30 \leq \sigma^2 \leq 159.18$$

    $$5.86 \leq \sigma \leq 12.62$$

    $\therefore$ A sample size of 15 was used.

    b. $n = 25$; expected the width of the interval to be e smaller.

    $\chi^2_{.05} = 39.3641$ $\chi^2_{.975} = 12.4011$ (24 degrees of freedom)

$$\frac{(24)\,(8)^2}{39.3641} \;\le\; \sigma^2 \;\le\; \frac{(24)\,(8)^2}{12.4011}$$

$$39.02 \le \sigma^2 \le 123.86$$

$$6.25 \le \sigma \le 11.13$$

29.   Population 1 female; population 2 male

$H_0 : \sigma_1^2 = \sigma_2^2$

$H_a : \sigma_1^2 \ne \sigma_2^2$

$F_{.025} = 2.62$ (15 numerator and 19 denominator degrees of freedom)

$$F = \frac{s_1^2}{s_2^2} = \frac{220}{80} = 2.75$$

Reject H_0; conclude the variances are not equal. Female applicants show the greater variance in test scores.

30. $H_0 : \sigma_1^2 = \sigma_2^2$

$H_a : \sigma_1^2 \ne \sigma_2^2$

$F_{.025} = 1.45$

$$F = \frac{s_1^2}{s_2^2} = \frac{(.940)^2}{(.797)^2} = 1.39$$

Do not reject H_0. We are not able to conclude students who complete the course and students who drop out have different variances of grade point averages.

31. $n_1 = 16 \qquad s_1^2 = 5.4$

$n_2 = 16 \qquad s_2^2 = 2.3$

$H_0 : \sigma_1^2 = \sigma_2^2$

$H_a : \sigma_1^2 \ne \sigma_2^2$

$F_{.05} = 2.40$ (Degrees of freedom are 15 numerator, 15 denominator)

$$F = \frac{s_1^2}{s_2^2} = \frac{5.4}{2.3} = 2.35$$

Do not reject H_0; data does not indicate a difference between the population variances.

32. $H_0 : \sigma_1^2 = \sigma_2^2$

$H_a : \sigma_1^2 \neq \sigma_2^2$

$F_{.05} = 1.94$ (30 numerator and 24 denominator degrees of freedom)

$$F = \frac{s_1^2}{s_2^2} = \frac{25}{12} = 2.08$$

Reject H_0; conlude that the variances of assembly times are not equal.

Solution To Computer Case

Some descriptive statistics about the current and proposed methods are as follows:

	N	MEAN	MEDIAN	TRMEAN	STDEV	SEMEAN
CURRENT	61	75.066	76.000	75.109	3.945	0.505
PROPOSED	61	75.426	76.000	75.455	2.506	0.321

	MIN	MAX	Q1	Q3
CURRENT	65.000	84.000	72.000	78.000
PROPOSED	69.000	82.000	74.000	77.000

Histograms

Midpoint	Current Count		Proposed Count	
66	2	* *	0	
68	0		0	
70	7	* * * * * * *	2	* *
72	7	* * * * * * *	7	* * * * * * *
74	11	* * * * * * * * * * *	9	* * * * * * * * *
76	11	* * * * * * * * * * *	22	* *
78	11	* * * * * * * * * * *	17	* * * * * * * * * * * * * * * * *
80	7	* * * * * * *	3	* * *
82	4	* * * *	1	*
84	1	*	0	

The sample mean of 75.066 and 75.426 hours show that both methods have approximately the same mean completion time. The standard deviations of 3.945 hours for the current method and 2.506 hours for the proposed method show the proposed method has less variation.

A test of the difference between population means with $H_0: \mu_1 - \mu_2 = 0$ has a z value of -.60 and a corresponding p - value of .55. Thus, the null hypothesis cannot be rejected. The sample evidence does not indicate the methods differ in terms of mean completion times. The 95% confidence interval estimate of the difference between two population means is -1.55 to .83 hours.

The standard deviations and variances of the two methods are as follows:

	Current	Proposed
Standard Deviations	3.94	2.51
Variance	15.52	6.30

For the hypothesis test $H_0: \sigma_1^2 = \sigma_2^2$, we find $F = s_1^2 / s_2^2 = 15.52 / 6.30 = 2.46$. Using the F tables, we find $F_{.025} = 1.67$. Thus, with $\alpha = .05$, H_0 is rejected; we can conclude that the two methods differ in terms of variance. The data show the proposed method has the smaller variance indicating that students trained under this method are more consistent in terms of completion time.

Based on the data available, the proposed method is preferred. The two methods are very close in terms of mean completion times with the 95% confidence interval of the difference being -1.55 to 0.83 hours. However, the proposed method has a significantly lower variance. Under the proposed method, students are more likely to complete the training in approximately the same amount of time. There should be less chances of faster students waiting for slower students to complete training.

Before making a final decision, we recommend that data be collected on the amount of learning under the two methods. The time data favors switching to the proposed method. However, is the quality of the training with the proposed method the same or better than the quality of the training with the current method? Both groups could be given an examination at the end of the training program. Analysis of the examination scores would determine if the programs were similar or different in terms of the amount of learning provided by the programs. This analysis should be made prior to the final decision to switch to the proposed method.

Chapter 12
Tests of Goodness of Fit and Independence

Learning Objectives

1.   Know how to conduct a goodness of fit test.

2.   Know how to use sample data to test for independence of two variables.

3.   Understand the role of the chi-square distribution in conducting tests of goodness of fit and independence.

4.   Be able to conduct a goodness of fit test for cases where the population is hypothesized to have either a multinomial, a Poisson, or a normal probability distribution.

5.   For a test of independence, be able to set up a contingency table, determine the observed and expected frequencies, and determine if the two variables are independent.

Solutions:

1.   Expected frequencies: $e_1 = 200\,(.40) = 80,\, e_2 = 200\,(.40) = 80$

$e_3 = 200\,(.20) = 40$

Actual frequencies: $f_1 = 60,\, f_2 = 120,\, f_3 = 20$

$$x^2 = \frac{(60 - 80)^2}{80} + \frac{(120 - 80)^2}{80} + \frac{(20 - 40)^2}{20}$$

$$= \frac{400}{80} + \frac{1600}{80} + \frac{400}{20}$$

$$= 5 + 20 + 20$$

$$= 45$$

$\chi^2_{.01} = 9.21034$ with $k - 1 = 3 - 1 = 2$ degrees of freedom

Since $\chi^2 = 45 > 9.21034$ reject the null hypothesis. The population proportions are not as stated in the null hypothesis.

2.   Expected frequencies: $e_1 = 300\,(.25) = 75,\, e_2 = 300\,(.25) = 75$

$e_3 = 300\,(.25) = 75,\, e_4 = 300\,(.25) = 75$

Actual frequencies: $f_1 = 85,\, f_2 = 95,\, f_3 = 50,\, f_4 = 70$

$$x^2 = \frac{(85 - 75)^2}{75} + \frac{(95 - 75)^2}{75} + \frac{(50 - 75)^2}{75} + \frac{(70 - 75)^2}{75}$$

$$= \frac{100}{75} + \frac{400}{75} + \frac{625}{75} + \frac{25}{75}$$

$$= \frac{1150}{75}$$

$$= 15.33$$

$\chi^2_{.05} = 7.81473$ with $k - 1 = 4 - 1 = 3$ degrees of freedom

Since $\chi^2 = 15.33 > 7.81473$ reject H_0

We conclude that the proportions are not all equal.

3.   Expected frequencies: $300\,(.29) = 87,\, 300\,(.28) = 84$

$300\,(.25) = 75,\, 300\,(.18) = 54$

$e_1 = 87,\, e_2 = 84,\, e_3 = 75,\, e_4 = 54$

Actual frequencies: $\qquad f_1 = 95, f_2 = 70, f_3 = 89, f_4 = 46$

$\chi^2_{.05} = 7.81$ (3 degrees of freedom)

$$\chi^2 = \frac{(95 - 87)^2}{87} + \frac{(70 - 84)^2}{84} + \frac{(89 - 75)^2}{75} + \frac{(46 - 54)^2}{54}$$

$$= 6.87$$

Do not reject H_0; there is no significant change in the viewing audience proportions.

4.   Expected frequencies: $\qquad e_i = .25 (300) = 75$

$$\chi^2 = \frac{(63 - 75)^2}{75} + \frac{(62 - 75)^2}{75} + \frac{(100 - 75)^2}{75} + \frac{(75 - 75)^2}{75} = 12.51$$

With 3 degrees of freedom, $\chi^2_{.05} = 7.81$

Reject H_0; conclude that the proportion of millionaires is not the same for all regions of the country.

5. $H_0 = p_S = .290, p_H = .188, p_I = .160, p_D = .116,$ and $p_O = .246$

H_a = The population proportions are not as in H_0

Expected frequencies: $\qquad e_s = 400 (.290) = 116, e_H = 400 (.188) = 75.2,$

$e_I = 400 (.160) = 64, e_D = 400 (.116) = 46.4, e_O = 400 (.246) = 98.4$

Actual frequencies: $\qquad f_S = 106, f_H = 72, f_I = 80, f_D = 48, f_O = 94$

$$\chi^2 = \frac{(106 - 116)^2}{116} + \frac{(72 - 75.2)^2}{75.2} + \frac{(80 - 64)^2}{64} + \frac{(48 - 46.4)^2}{46.4} + \frac{(94 - 98.4)^2}{98.4}$$

$$= \frac{100}{116} + \frac{10.24}{75.2} + \frac{256}{64} + \frac{2.56}{46.4} + \frac{19.36}{98.4}$$

$$= 5.25$$

$\chi^2_{.05} = 9.48773$ with $k - 1 = 5 - 1 = 4$ degrees of freedom

Since $\chi^2 = 5.25 \leq 9.48773$ we cannot conclude that market share has changed

6.   Expected frequencies: $\qquad e_i = 1 / 3 (150) = 50$

$$\chi^2 = \frac{(40 - 50)^2}{50} + \frac{(64 - 50)^2}{50} + \frac{(46 - 50)^2}{50} = 6.24$$

With 2 degrees of freedom, $\chi^2_{.10} = 4.60517$

Reject H_0; conclude that preference is not the same for all colors.

7.   Expected frequencies: $e_i = 1/3 (135) = 45$

$$\chi^2 = \frac{(43 - 45)^2}{45} + \frac{(53 - 45)^2}{45} + \frac{(39 - 45)^2}{45} = 2.31$$

With 2 degrees of freedom, $\chi^2_{.05} = 5.99$

Do not reject H_0; there is no justification for concluding a difference in preference exists.

8.

Observed (f_i)	18	30	40	22	10
Expected (e_i)	12	36	48	18	6

$\chi^2_{.05} = 9.48773$ (4 degrees of freedom)

$\chi^2 = 8.89$

Do not reject H_0; there is no evidence that the grade distribution guidelines are not being satisfied.

9. H_0 = The column factor is independent of the row factor

H_a = The column factor is not independent of the row factor

Expected Frequencies:

	A	B	C
P	27.5	38.5	44
Q	22.5	31.5	36

$$\chi^2 = \frac{(20 - 27.5)^2}{27.5} + \frac{(44 - 38.5)^2}{38.5} + \frac{(50 - 44)^2}{44} + \frac{(30 - 22.5)^2}{22.5} + \frac{(26 - 31.5)^2}{31.5} + \frac{(30 - 36)^2}{36}$$
$$= 8.1097$$

$\chi^2_{.025} = 7.37776$ with $(2 - 1)(3 - 1) = 2$ degrees of freedom

Since $\chi^2 = 8.1097 > 7.37776$ Reject H_0

Conclude that column factor is not independent of the row factor.

10. H_0 = The column factor is independent of the row factor

H_a = The column factor is not independent of the row factor

Expected Frequencies:

	A	B	C
P	17.5000	30.6250	21.8750
Q	28.7500	50.3125	35.9375
R	13.7500	24.0625	17.1875

$$\chi^2 = \frac{(20 - 17.5000)^2}{17.5000} + \frac{(30 - 30.6250)^2}{30.6250} + \cdots + \frac{(30 - 17.1875)^2}{17.1875}$$

$$= 19.78$$

$\chi^2_{.05} = 9.48773$ with $(3 - 1)(3 - 1) = 4$ degrees of freedom

Since $\chi^2 = 19.78 > 9.48773$ Reject H_0 Conclude that the column factor is not independent of the row factor.

11. H_0 : There is no difference in shooting percentage among the teams

H_a: There is a difference in shooting percentage among the teams.

Row 1 Total = 629   Row 2 Total = 988

Column 1 Total = 374 Column 2 Total = 341

Column 3 Total = 369 Column 4 Total = 533

Overall Total = 1617

Using these totals we compute the expected frequencies.

Expected Frequencies:

	Duke	Michigan	Indiana	Cincinnati
Made	145.4830	132.6463	143.5380	207.3327
Missed	228.5170	208.3537	225.4620	325.6673

$$\chi^2 = \frac{(160 - 145.4830)^2}{145.4830} + \frac{(113 - 132.6463)^2}{132.6463} + \cdots + \frac{(331 - 325.6673)^2}{325.6673}$$

$$= 1.4486 + 2.9098 + .7625 + .1372 + .9222 + 1.8525 + .4855 + .0873$$

$$= 8.6056$$

$\chi^2_{.05} = 7.81473$ with 3 degrees of freedom

Since $\chi^2 = 8.6056 > 7.81473$ Reject H_0 . Conclude that there is a difference in 3-point shooting ability for the teams.

12.

		Product	
Salesperson	A	B	C
Troutman	14.29	9.43	6.23
Kempton	21.43	14.14	9.43
McChristian	14.29	9.43	6.29

Note: Values above are the expected frequencies.

$\chi^2_{.05} = 9.48773$ (4 degrees of freedom: 2 x 2 = 4)

$\chi^2 = 6.31$

Do not reject H_0; conclude that the assumption of independence of salesperson and product cannot be rejected.

13.

		Industry		
Major	Oil	Chemical	Electrical	Computer
Business	30	22.5	17.5	30
Engineering	30	22.5	17.5	30

Note: Values shown above are the expected frequencies.

$\chi^2_{.01} = 11.3449$ (3 degrees of freedom: 1 x 3 = 3)

$\chi^2 = 12.39$

Reject H_0; conclude that major and industry not independent.

14. H_0 = There is no difference of opinion between men and women

H_a = There is a difference of opinion between men and women

Expected Frequencies:

	Men	Women
Right Thing	225	225
Waited Longer	57	57
Not Sure	18	18

$$\chi^2 = \frac{(243 - 225)^2}{225} + \frac{(207 - 225)^2}{225} + \frac{(48 - 57)^2}{57} + \frac{(66 - 57)^2}{57} + \frac{(9 - 18)^2}{18} + \frac{(27 - 18)^2}{18}$$

$$= 14.72$$

$\chi^2_{.05} = 5.99147$ with 2 degrees of freedom

Since $\chi^2 = 14.72 > 5.99147$ Reject H_0

Conclude that there is a difference of opinion between men and women.

15. $H_0 =$ There is no difference in the programs

$H_a =$ There is a difference in the programs

Expected Frequencies:

	Hospital	AA Only	Choice
Sober	17.7445	17.7445	17.5110
Not Sober	58.2555	58.2555	57.4890

$$\chi^2 = \frac{(28 - 17.7445)^2}{17.7445} + \frac{(13 - 17.7445)^2}{17.7445} + \frac{(12 - 17.5110)^2}{17.5110}$$
$$+ \frac{(48 - 58.2555)^2}{58.2555} + \frac{(63 - 58.2555)^2}{58.2555} + \frac{(63 - 57.4890)^2}{57.4890}$$
$$= 11.6503$$

$\chi^2_{.01} = 9.21034$ with 2 degrees of freedom

Since $\chi^2 = 11.6503 > 9.21034$ Reject H_0

Conclude that there is a difference in the programs.

16. Expected Frequencies:

	Program Quality	Convenience Cost	Other	Totals
Full-time	378.8	454.9	56.3	890
Part-time	442.2	531.1	65.7	1039
Totals	821	986	122	1929

$$\chi^2 = \sum \sum \frac{(f_{ij} - e_{ij})^2}{e_{ij}} = 37.17$$

With 2 degrees of freedom, $\chi^2_{.01} = 9.21034$

Reject H_0; conclude that the primary reason for application is not independent of choice to be a full-time or part-time student.

17.   Expected Frequencies:

	Baseball	Basketball	Football
Men	18.80	17.72	21.48
Women	16.20	15.28	18.52

$$\chi^2 = \frac{(19 - 18.80)^2}{18.80} + \frac{(15 - 17.72)^2}{17.72} + \cdots + \frac{(16 - 18.52)^2}{18.52}$$

$$= 1.54$$

$\chi^2_{.05} = 5.99147$ with 2 degrees of freedom

Do not reject H_0. The assumption of independence cannot be rejected.

18.   Expected Frequencies:

		Part Quality	
Supplier	Good	Minor Defect	Major Defect
A	88.76	6.07	5.14
B	173.09	11.83	10.08
C	133.15	9.10	7.75

$\chi^2 = 7.96$

$\chi^2_{.05} = 9.48773$ (4 degrees of freedom: 2 x 2 = 4)

Do not reject H_0; conclude that the assumption of independence cannot be rejected

19.   Expected Frequencies:

	Party Affiliation		
Education Level	Democratic	Republican	Independent
Did not complete high school	28	28	14
High school degree	32	32	16
College degree	40	40	20

$\chi^2 = 13.42$

$\chi^2_{.01} = 13.2767$ (4 degrees of freedom: 2 x 2 = 4)

Reject H_0; conclude that party affiliation is not independent of education level.

20. a.   Expected Frequencies:

$$e_{ij} = \frac{(\text{row } i)(\text{column } j)}{\text{total}}$$

Expected Frequencies:

	Selected	Not Selected	Total
Male	6	34	40
Female	6	34	40
Total	12	68	80

$\chi^2 = .39$. With 1 degree of freedom, $\chi^2_{.10} = 2.70554$

Do not reject H_0; the assumption of independence cannot be rejected. There is no evidence of selection bias.

b. Observed frequencies would be

	Selected	Not Selected	Total
Male	8	32	40
Female	4	36	40
Total	12	68	80

$\chi^2 = 1.57 \qquad \chi^2_{.10} = 2.70554$

Do not reject H_0.

c. With 9 males and 3 females, $\chi^2 = 3.53$. In this case H_0 would be rejected indicating a selection bias may exist.

21. First estimate μ from the sample data. Sample size $= 120$.

$$\mu = \frac{0\,(39) + 1\,(30) + 2\,(30) + 3\,(18) + 4\,(3)}{120} = \frac{156}{120} = 1.3$$

Therefore, we use Poisson probabilities with $\mu = 1.3$ to compute expected frequencies.

x	Observed Frequency	Poisson Probability	Expected Frequency	Difference $(f_i - e_i)$
0	39	.2725	32.700	6.300
1	30	.3543	42.516	-12.516
2	30	.2303	27.636	2.364
3	18	.0998	11.976	6.024
4 or more	3	.0430	5.160	- 2.160

$$\chi^2 = \frac{(6.300)^2}{32.700} + \frac{(-12.516)^2}{42.516} + \frac{(2.364)^2}{27.636} + \frac{(6.024)^2}{11.976} + \frac{(-2.160)^2}{5.160}$$

$$= 9.0348$$

$\chi^2_{.05} = 7.81473$ with $5 - 1 - 1 = 3$ degrees of freedom

Since $\chi^2 = 9.0348 > 7.81473$ Reject H_0

Conclude that the data do not follow a Poisson probability distribution.

22. With $N = 30$ we will use six classes with $16\,^2/_3\%$ of the probability associated with each class.

$\bar{x} = 22.80 \quad s = 6.2665$

The z values that create 6 intervals, each with probability .1667 are -.98, -.43, 0, .43, .98

z	Cut off value of x
-.98	$22.8 - .98\,(6.2665) = 16.66$
-.43	$22.8 - .43\,(6.2665) = 20.11$
0	$22.8 + 0\,(6.2665) = 22.80$
.43	$22.8 + .43\,(6.2665) = 25.49$
.98	$22.8 + .98\,(6.2665) = 28.94$

Interval	Observed Frequency	Expected Frequency	Difference
less than 16.66	3	5	-2
16.66 - 20.11	7	5	2
20.11 - 22.80	5	5	0
22.80 - 25.49	7	5	2
25.49- 28.94	3	5	-2
28.94 and up	5	5	0

$$\chi^2 = \frac{(-2)^2}{5} + \frac{(2)^2}{5} + \frac{(0)^2}{5} + \frac{(2)^2}{5} + \frac{(-2)^2}{5} + \frac{(0)^2}{5}$$

$$= \frac{16}{5} = 3.20$$

$\chi^2_{.025} = 9.34840$ with $6 - 2 - 1 = 3$ degrees of freedom

Since $\chi^2 = 3.20 \leq 9.34840$ Do not reject H_0

The claim that the data comes from a normal distribution cannot be rejected.

23. $\mu = \dfrac{0\,(34) + 1\,(25) + 2\,(11) + 3\,(7) + 4\,(3)}{80} = 1$

Use Poisson probabilities with $\mu = 1$.

x	Observed	Poisson Probabilities	Expected	
0	34	.3679	29.432	
1	25	.3679	29.432	
2	11	.1839	14.712	
3	7	.0613	4.904	combine into 1
4	3	.0153	1.224	category of 3 or more to make
5 or more	-	.0037	.296	$e_i \geq 5$.

$\chi^2 = 4.30$

$\chi^2_{.05} = 5.99147$ (2 degrees of freedom)

Do not reject H_0; the assumption of a Poisson distribution cannot be rejected.

24.
$$\mu = \frac{0\,(15) + 1\,(31) + 2\,(20) + 3\,(15) + 4\,(13) + 5\,(4) + 6\,(2)}{100} = 2$$

x	Observed	Poisson Probabilities	Expected
0	15	.1353	13.53
1	31	.2707	27.07
2	20	.2707	27.07
3	15	.1804	18.04
4	13	.0902	9.02
5 or more	6	.0527	5.27

$\chi^2 = 4.98$

$\chi^2_{.10} = 7.77944$ (4 degrees of freedom)

Do not reject H_0; the assumption of a Poisson distribution cannot be rejected.

25. $\bar{x} = 24.5 \quad s = 3 \quad n = 30$ Use 6 classes

Interval	Observed Frequency	Expected Frequency
less than 21.56	5	5
21.56 - 23.21	4	5
23.21 - 24.50	3	5
24.50 - 25.79	7	5
25.79 - 27.44	7	5
27.41 up	4	5

$\chi^2 = 2.8$

$\chi^2_{.10} = 6.25139$ (3 degrees of freedom: 6 - 2 - 1 = 3)

Do not reject H_0; the assumption of a normal distribution cannot be rejected.

26. $\bar{x} = 71 \quad s = 17 \quad n = 25$ Use 5 classes

Interval	Observed Frequency	Expected Frequency
less than 56.7	7	5
56.7 - 66.5	7	5
66.5 - 74.6	1	5
74.6 - 84.5	1	5
84.5 up	9	5

$\chi^2 = 11.2$

$\chi^2_{.01} = 9.21034$ (2 degrees of freedom)

Reject H_0; conclude the distribution is not a normal distribution.

27.

Observed	60	45	59	36
Expected	50	50	50	50

$\chi^2 = 8.04$

$\chi^2_{.05} = 7.81473$ (3 degrees of freedom)

Reject H_0; conclude that the order potentials are not the same in each sales territory.

28.

Observed Frequency	Expected Frequency
135	.20 (606) = 121.2
234	.40 (606) = 242.4
139	.25 (606) = 151.5
98	.15 (606) = 90.9
606	606

$\chi^2 = 3.55$

$\chi^2_{.05} = 7.81473$ (3 degrees of freedom)

Do not reject H_0; the administrator's hypothesized percentages cannot be rejected.

29.

Observed Frequency	Expected Frequency
68	.15 (500) = 75
110	.20 (500) = 100
140	.30 (500) = 150
122	.25 (500) = 125
60	.10 (500) = 50
500	500

$\chi^2 = 4.39$

$\chi^2_{.10} = 7.77944$

Do not reject H_0; there is no evidence that the historical percentages have changed.

30.

Observed	13	16	28	17	16
Expected	18	18	18	18	18

$\chi^2 = 7.44$

$\chi^2_{.05} = 9.48773$

Do not reject H_0; the assumption that the number of riders is uniformly distributed cannot be rejected.

31.   Expected Frequencies:

	Quality	
Shift	Good	Defective
1st	368.44	31.56
2nd	276.33	23.67
3rd	184.22	15.78

$\chi^2 = 8.11$

$\chi^2_{.05} = 5.99147$ (2 degrees of freedom)

Reject H_0; conclude that shift and quality are not independent.

32.   Expected Frequencies:

	Program Quality	Convenience Cost	Other	Totals
Male	510.20	617.61	76.19	1204
Female	306.80	371.39	45.81	724
Totals	817	989	122	1928

$\chi^2 = 5.26$

$\chi^2_{.05} = 5.99147$

Do not reject H_0; cannot conclude that males and females differ in the reason for application to MBA programs.

33.   Expected frequencies:

Loan Offices	Loan Approval Decision	
	Approved	Rejected
Miller	24.86	15.14
McMahon	18.64	11.36
Games	31.07	18.93
Runk	12.43	7.57

$\chi^2 = 2.21$

$\chi^2_{.05} = 7.81473$ (3 degrees of freedom)

Do not reject H_0; the loan decision does not appear to be dependent on the officer.

34.   Expected Frequencies:

	80 or above	70's	Below 70	Totals
0	12.25	11.20	11.55	35
1 - 5	11.55	10.56	10.89	33
More than 5	11.20	10.24	10.56	32
Totals	35	32	33	100

$\chi^2 = 22.87$

$\chi^2_{.05} = 9.48773$

Reject H_0; conclude that the grade on final is not independent of the number of classes missed.

35. Expected Frequencies:

Reason for Taking the Course	Poor	Rating Good	Excellent	Totals
Required	14	33.6	22.4	70
Elective	6	14.4	9.6	30
Totals	20	48	32	100

$\chi^2 = 8.97$

$\chi^2_{.01} = 9.21034$

Do not reject H_0; conclude that the assumption of independence of reason and rating cannot be rejected at $\alpha = .01$.

36. Expected Frequencies:

County	Sun	Mon	Tues	Days of the Week Wed	Thur	Fri	Sat	Total
Urban	56.7	47.6	55.1	56.7	60.1	72.6	44.2	393
Rural	11.3	9.4	10.9	11.3	11.9	14.4	8.8	78
Total	68	57	66	68	72	87	53	471

$\chi^2 = 6.20$

$\chi^2_{.05} = 12.5916$ (6 degrees of freedom)

Do not reject H_0; the assumption of independence cannot be rejected.

37. $\bar{x} = 76.83 \quad s = 12.43$

Interval	Observed Frequency	Expected Frequency
less than 62.54	5	5
62.54 - 68.50	3	5
68.50 - 72.85	6	5
72.85 - 76.83	5	5
76.83 - 80.81	5	5
80.81 - 85.16	7	5
85.16 - 91.12	4	5
91.12 up	5	5

$\chi^2 = 2$

$\chi^2_{.05} = 11.0705$ (5 degrees of freedom)

Do not reject H_0; the assumption of a normal distribution cannot be rejected.

38.   Expected Frequencies:

	Los Angeles	San Diego	San Francisco	San Jose	Total
Occupied	165.7	124.3	186.4	165.7	642
Vacant	34.3	25.7	38.6	34.3	133
Total	200.0	150.0	225.0	200.0	775

$$\chi^2 = \frac{(160 - 165.7)^2}{165.7} + \frac{(116 - 124.3)^2}{124.3} + \cdots + \frac{(26 - 34.3)^2}{34.3}$$

$$= 7.78$$

$\chi^2_{.05} = 7.81473$ with 3 degrees of freedom

Since $\chi^2 = 7.88 \leq 7.81473$ Do not reject H_0.

We cannot conclude that office vacancies are dependent on metropolitan area, but it is close: the p-value is slightly larger than .05.

39. a

	Observed	Binomial Prob.	Expected
x	Frequencies	$n = 4, p = .30$	Frequencies
0	30	.2401	24.01
1	32	.4116	41.16
2	25	.2646	26.46
3	10	.0756	7.56
4	3	.0081	.81
	100		100.00

The expected frequency of $x = 4$ is .81. Combine $x = 3$ and $x = 4$ into one category so that all expected frequencies are 5 or more.

	Observed	Expected
x	Frequencies	Frequencies
0	30	24.01
1	32	41.16
2	25	26.46
3 or 4	13	8.37
	100	100.00

    b.   With 3 degrees of freedom, $\chi^2_{.05} = 7.81473$. Reject H_0 if $\chi^2 > 7.81473$.

$$\chi^2 = \sum \frac{(f_i - e_i)^2}{e_i} = 6.17$$

Do not reject H_0; conclude that the assumption of a binomial distribution cannot be rejected.

Chapter 13
Experimental Design and Analysis of Variance

Learning Objectives

1.   Understand how the analysis of variance procedure can be used to determine if the means of more than two populations are equal.

2.   Know the assumptions necessary to use the analysis of variance procedure.

3.   Understand the use of the F distribution in performing the analysis of variance procedure.

4.   Know how to set up an ANOVA table and interpret the entries in the table.

5.   Be able to use output from computer software packages to solve analysis of variance problems.

6.   Know how to use Fisher's least significant difference (LSD) procedure, Fisher's LSD with the Bonferroni adjustment, and Turkey's procedure to conduct statistical comparisons between pairs of populations means.

7.   Understand the difference between a completely randomized design, a randomized block design, and factorial experiments.

8.   Know the definition of the following terms:

comparisonwise Type I error rate   partitioning
experimentwise Type I error rate   blocking
factor   main effect
level   interaction
treatment
replication

Solutions:

1. a.

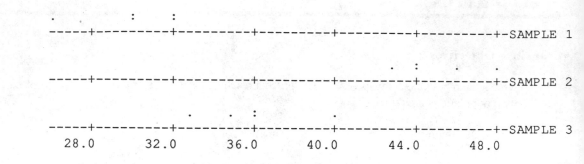

b. $\bar{\bar{x}} = (30 + 45 + 36) / 3 = 37$

$$SSB = \sum_{j=1}^{k} n_j (\bar{x}_j - \bar{\bar{x}})^2$$

$$= 5(30 - 37)^2 + 5(45 - 37)^2 + 5(36 - 37)^2 = 570$$

$MSB = SSB / (k - 1) = 570 / 2 = 285$

c. $$SSW = \sum_{j=1}^{k} (n_j - 1) s_j^2$$

$$= 4(6) + 4(4) + 4(6.5) = 66$$

$MSW = SSW / (n_T - k) = 66 / (15 - 3) = 5.5$

d. $F = MSB / MSW = 285 / 5.5 = 51.82$

$F_{.05} = 3.89$ (2 degrees of freedom numerator and 12 denominator)

Since $F = 51.82 > F_{.05} = 3.89$, we reject the null hypothesis that the means of the three populations are equal.

e.

Source of Variation	Sum of Squares	Degrees of Freedom	Mean Square	F
Between	570	2	285	51.82
Within	66	12	5.5	
Total	636	14		

2. a. $\bar{\bar{x}} = (153 + 169 + 158) / 3 = 160$

$$SSB = \sum_{j=1}^{k} n_j (\bar{x}_j - \bar{\bar{x}})^2$$

$$= 4(153 - 160)^2 + 4(169 - 160)^2 + 4(158 - 160)^2 = 536$$

$MSB = SSB / (k - 1) = 536 / 2 = 268$

b. $$SSW = \sum_{j=1}^{k} (n_j - 1) s_j^2$$

$$= 3(96.67) + 3(97.33) + 3(82.00) = 828.00$$

$MSW = SSW / (n_T - k) = 828.00 / (12 - 3) = 92.00$

c. $F = MSB / MSW = 268 / 92 = 2.91$

$F_{.05} = 4.26$ (2 degrees of freedom numerator and 9 denominator)

Since $F = 2.91 < F_{.05} = 4.26$, we can not reject the null hypothesis.

d.

Source of Variation	Sum of Squares	Degrees of Freedom	Mean Square	F
Between	536	2	268	2.91
Within	828	9	92	
Total	1,364	11		

3. a. $\bar{\bar{x}} = \dfrac{4(100) + 6(85) + 5(79)}{15} = 87$

$$SSB = \sum_{j=1}^{k} n_j (\bar{x}_j - \bar{\bar{x}})^2$$

$$= 4(100 - 87)^2 + 6(85 - 87)^2 + 5(79 - 87)^2 = 1,020$$

$MSB = SSB / (k - 1) = 1,020 / 2 = 510$

b. $$SSW = \sum_{j=1}^{k} (n_j - 1) s_j^2$$

$$= 3(35.33) + 5(35.60) + 4(43.50) = 458$$

$$MSW = SSW / (n_T - k) = 458 / (15 - 3) = 38.17$$

c. $F = MSB / MSW = 510 / 38.17 = 13.36$

$F_{.05} = 3.89$ (2 degrees of freedom numerator and 12 denominator)

Since $F = 13.36 > F_{.05} = 3.89$ we reject the null hypothesis that the means of the three populations are equal.

d.

Source of Variation	Sum of Squares	Degrees of Freedom	Mean Square	F
Between	1,020	2	510	13.36
Within	458	12	38.17	
Total	1,478	14		

4. a.

Source of Variation	Sum of Squares	Degrees of Freedom	Mean Square	F
Between	1200	3	400	80
Within	300	60	5	
Total	1500	63		

b. $F_{.05} = 2.76$ (3 degrees of freedom numerator and 60 denominator)

Since $F = 80 > F_{.05} = 2.76$ we reject the null hypothesis that the means of the 4 populations are equal.

5. a.

Source of Variation	Sum of Squares	Degrees of Freedom	Mean Square	F
Between	120	2	60	20
Within	216	72	3	
Total	336	74		

b. $F_{.05} = 3.15$ (2 numerator degrees of freedom and 60 denominator)

$F_{.05} = 3.07$ (2 numerator degrees of freedom and 120 denominator)

The critical value is between 3.07 and 3.15

Since $F = 20$ must exceed the critical value, no matter what its actual value, we reject the null hypothesis that the 3 population means are equal.

6.

	Manufacturer 1	Manufacturer 2	Manufacturer 3
Sample Mean	23	28	21
Sample Variance	6.67	4.67	3.33

$\bar{\bar{x}} = (23 + 28 + 21) / 3 = 24$

$$SSB = \sum_{j=1}^{k} n_j (\bar{x}_j - \bar{\bar{x}})^2$$

$= 4(23 - 24)^2 + 4(28 - 24)^2 + 4(21 - 24)^2 = 104$

$MSB = SSB / (k - 1) = 104 / 2 = 52$

$$SSW = \sum_{j=1}^{k} (n_j - 1) s_j^2$$

$= 3(6.67) + 3(4.67) + 3(3.33) = 44.01$

$MSW = SSW / (n_T - k) = 44.01 / (12 - 3) = 4.89$

$F = MSB / MSW = 52 / 4.89 = 10.63$

$F_{.05} = 4.26$ (2 degrees of freedom numerator and 9 denominator)

Since $F = 10.63 > F_{.05} = 4.26$ we reject the null hypothesis that the mean time needed to mix a batch of material is the same for each manufacturer.

7.

	South Korea	Soviet Union	United States
Sample Mean	78	71	67
Sample Variance	53.6	32.8	27.6

$\bar{\bar{x}} = (78 + 71 + 67) / 3 = 72$

$$SSB = \sum_{j=1}^{k} n_j (\bar{x}_j - \bar{\bar{x}})^2$$

$= 6(78 - 72)^2 + 6(71 - 72)^2 + 6(67 - 72)^2 = 372$

$MSB = SSB / (k - 1) = 372 / 2 = 186$

$$SSW = \sum_{j=1}^{k} (n_j - 1) s_j^2$$

$= 5(53.6) + 5(32.8) + 5(27.6) = 570$

$$MSW = SSW / (n_T - k) = 570 / (18 - 3) = 38$$

$$F = MSB / MSW = 186 / 38 = 4.89$$

$F_{.05} = 3.68$ (2 degrees of freedom numerator and 15 denominator)

Since $F = 4.89 > F_{.05} = 3.68$ we reject the null hypothesis that the mean test score is the same for each country.

8.

	Superior	Peer	Subordinate
Sample Mean	5.75	5.5	5.25
Sample Variance	1.64	2.00	1.93

$$\overline{\overline{x}} = (5.75 + 5.5 + 5.25) / 3 = 5.5$$

$$SSB = \sum_{j=1}^{k} n_j (\overline{x}_j - \overline{\overline{x}})^2$$

$$= 8(5.75 - 5.5)^2 + 8(5.5 - 5.5)^2 + 8(5.25 - 5.5)^2 = 1$$

$$MSB = SSB / (k - 1) = 1 / 2 = .5$$

$$SSW = \sum_{j=1}^{k} (n_j - 1) s_j^2$$

$$= 7(1.64) + 7(2.00) + 7(1.93) = 38.99$$

$$MSW = SSW / (n_T - k) = 38.99 / 21 = 1.86$$

$$F = MSB / MSW = 0.5 / 1.86 = 0.27$$

$F_{.05} = 3.47$ (2 degrees of freedom numerator and 21 denominator)

Since $F = 0.27 < F_{.05} = 3.47$, we cannot reject the null hypothesis that the means of the three populations are equal; thus, the source of information does not significantly affect the dissemination of the information.

9.

	Marketing Managers	Marketing Research	Advertising
Sample Mean	5	4.5	6
Sample Variance	.8	.3	.4

$$\overline{\overline{x}} = (5 + 4.5 + 6) / 3 = 5.17$$

$$SSB = \sum_{j=1}^{k} n_j (\bar{x}_j - \bar{\bar{x}})^2$$

$$= 6(5 - 5.17)^2 + 6(4.5 - 5.17)^2 + 6(6 - 5.17)^2 = 7.00$$

$$MSB = SSB / (k - 1) = 7.00 / 2 = 3.5$$

$$SSW = \sum_{j=1}^{k} (n_j - 1) s_j^2$$

$$= 5(.8) + 5(.3) + 5(.4) = 7.50$$

$$MSW = SSW / (n_T - k) = 7.50 / (18 - 3) = .5$$

$$F = MSB / MSW = 3.5 / .50 = 7.00$$

$F_{.05} = 3.68$ (2 degrees of freedom numerator and 15 denominator)

Since $F = 7.00 > F_{.05} = 3.68$, we reject the null hypothesis that the mean perception score is the same for the three groups of specialists.

10.

	Machine 1	Machine 2	Machine 3	Machine 4
Sample Mean	7.1	9.1	9.9	11.4
Sample Variance	1.21	.93	.70	1.02

$$\bar{\bar{x}} = (7.1 + 9.1 + 9.9 + 11.4) / 4 = 9.38$$

$$SSB = \sum_{j=1}^{k} n_j (\bar{x}_j - \bar{\bar{x}})^2$$

$$= 6(7.1 - 9.38)^2 + 6(9.1 - 9.38)^2 + 6(9.9 - 9.38)^2 + 6(11.4 - 9.38)^2 = 57.77$$

$$MSB = SSB / (k - 1) = 57.77 / 3 = 19.26$$

$$SSW = \sum_{j=1}^{k} (n_j - 1) s_j^2$$

$$= 5(1.21) + 5(.93) + 5(.70) + 5(1.02) = 19.30$$

$$MSW = SSW / (n_T - k) = 19.30 / (24 - 4) = .97$$

$$F = MSB / MSW = 19.26 / .97 = 19.86$$

$F_{.05} = 3.10$ (3 degrees of freedom numerator and 20 denominator)

Since $F = 19.86 > F_{.05} = 3.10$, we reject the null hypothesis that the mean time between breakdowns is the same for the four machines.

11. a

$$LSD = t_{\alpha/2} \sqrt{MSW\left(\frac{1}{n_i} + \frac{1}{n_j}\right)}$$

$$= t_{.025} \sqrt{5.5\left(\frac{1}{5} + \frac{1}{5}\right)}$$

$$= 2.776 \sqrt{2.2} = 4.12$$

$|\bar{x}_1 - \bar{x}_2| = |30 - 45| = 15 > LSD$; significant difference

$|\bar{x}_1 - \bar{x}_3| = |30 - 36| = 6 > LSD$; significant difference

$|\bar{x}_2 - \bar{x}_3| = |45 - 36| = 9 > LSD$; significant difference

b.

$$\bar{x}_1 - \bar{x}_2 \pm t_{\alpha/2} \sqrt{MSW\left(\frac{1}{n_1} + \frac{1}{n_2}\right)}$$

$$(30 - 45) \pm 2.776 \sqrt{5.5\left(\frac{1}{n_1} + \frac{1}{n_2}\right)}$$

$-15 \pm 4.12 = -19.12$ to -10.88

c. $\alpha = .05/3 = .017$

$t_{.017/2} = t_{.0085}$ which is approximately $t_{.01} = 3.747$

$$BSD = 3.747 \sqrt{5.5\left(\frac{1}{5} + \frac{1}{5}\right)} = 5.56$$

Thus, if the absolute value of the difference between any two sample means exceeds 5.56, there is sufficient evidence to reject the hypothesis that the corresponding population means are equal. Since the differences in absolute value are each greater than 5.56, all three means appear to be different.

d.

$$TSD = q \sqrt{\frac{MSW}{n}}$$

$$= 5.04 \sqrt{\frac{5.5}{5}} = 5.29$$

Since the absolute value of the differences between any two sample means exceeds 5.29, there is sufficient evidence to conclude that the three population means are different.

e. $$\bar{x}_i - \bar{x}_j = q \sqrt{\frac{MSW}{n}}$$

$$\bar{x}_i - \bar{x}_j = 5.04 \sqrt{\frac{5.5}{5}} = \bar{x}_i - \bar{x}_j \pm 5.29$$

Populations 1 and 2

$$30 - 45 \pm 5.29 = -20.29 \text{ to } -9.71$$

Populations 1 and 3

$$30 - 36 \pm 5.29 = -11.29 \text{ to } -.71$$

Populations 2 and 3

$$45 - 36 \pm 5.29 = 3.71 \text{ to } 14.29$$

12. a.

	Sample 1	Sample 2	Sample 3
Sample Mean	51	77	58
Sample Variance	96.67	97.34	81.99

$$\bar{\bar{x}} = (51 + 77 + 58) / 3 = 62$$

$$SSB = \sum_{j=1}^{k} n_j (\bar{x}_j - \bar{\bar{x}})^2$$

$$= 4(51 - 62)^2 + 4(77 - 62)^2 + 4(58 - 62)^2 = 1{,}448$$

$$MSB = SSB / (k - 1) = 1{,}448 / 2 = 724$$

$$SSW = \sum_{j=1}^{k} (n_j - 1) s_j^2$$

$$= 3(96.67) + 3(97.34) + 3(81.99) = 828$$

$$MSW = SSW / (n_T - k) = 828 / (12 - 3) = 92$$

$$F = MSB / MSW = 724 / 92 = 7.87$$

$F_{.05} = 4.26$ (2 degrees of freedom numerator and 9 denominator)

Since $F = 7.87 > F_{.05} = 4.26$, we reject the null hypothesis that the means of the three populations are equal.

b.
$$LSD = t_{\alpha/2} \sqrt{MSW\left(\frac{1}{n_i} + \frac{1}{n_j}\right)}$$

$$= t_{.025} \sqrt{92\left(\frac{1}{4} + \frac{1}{4}\right)}$$

$$= 2.262 \sqrt{46} = 15.34$$

$|\bar{x}_1 - \bar{x}_2| = |51 - 77| = 26 > $ LSD; significant difference

$|\bar{x}_1 - \bar{x}_3| = |51 - 58| = 7 < $ LSD; no significant difference

$|\bar{x}_2 - \bar{x}_3| = |77 - 58| = 19 > $ LSD; significant difference

c. $\alpha = .05/3 = .017$

$t_{.017/2} = t_{.0085}$ which is approximately $t_{.01} = 2.821$

$$BSD = 2.821 \sqrt{92\left(\frac{1}{4} + \frac{1}{4}\right)} = 19.13$$

The absolute value of the difference between 1 and 2 exceeds BSD = 19.13; therefore the means for populations 1 and 2 appear to be different.

d. $$TSD = q \sqrt{\frac{MSW}{n}}$$

$$= 3.95 \sqrt{\frac{92}{4}} = 18.94$$

The means for populations 1 and 2 appear to be different and the means for populations 2 and 3 appear to be different.

13.
$$LSD = t_{\alpha/2} \sqrt{MSW\left(\frac{1}{n_1} + \frac{1}{n_3}\right)}$$

$$= t_{.025} \sqrt{4.89\left(\frac{1}{4} + \frac{1}{4}\right)}$$

$$= 2.262 \sqrt{2.45} = 3.54$$

Since $|\bar{x}_1 - \bar{x}_3| = |23 - 21| = 2 < 3.54$, there does not appear to be any significant difference between the means of population 1 and population 2.

14.
$$\bar{x}_1 - \bar{x}_2 \pm q \sqrt{\frac{MSW}{n}}$$

$$23 - 28 = 3.95 \sqrt{\frac{4.89}{4}}$$

$-5 \pm 4.37 = -9.37$ to $-.63$

15.
$$TSD = q \sqrt{\frac{MSW}{n}}$$

$$= 3.67 \sqrt{\frac{38}{6}}$$

$$= 3.67 \sqrt{6.33} = 9.24$$

The absolute value of the difference between the sample means is $|78 - 67| = 11$; Since the difference exceeds TSD = 9.24, we reject the hypothesis that the means for South Korea and the United States are equal.

Note: even though we only compared the means of South Korea and the United States, Tukey's procedure is designed to enable us to perform tests of all 3 possible pairwise comparisons and still maintain an overall experimentwise Type I error rate of $\alpha_{EW} = .05$.

16.   Note: we assume that the decision to test for the equality of the means for South Korea and the United States was made after observing the sample data. Thus, the appropriate number of comparisons is 3.

$$\alpha = .05 / 3 = .017$$

$t_{.017/2} = t_{.0085}$ which is approximately $t_{.01} = 2.602$

$$BSD = 2.602 \sqrt{38 \left(\frac{1}{6} + \frac{1}{6} \right)} = 9.26$$

Since the absolute value of the difference is $|78 - 67| = 11$; , we reject the hypothesis that the means for South Korea and the United States are equal.

17.   <u>Hypothesis Test:</u>

$$TSD = q \sqrt{\frac{MSW}{n}}$$

$$= 3.67 \sqrt{\frac{38}{6}} = 9.24$$

Since the absolute value of the difference is 11, we reject the hypothesis that the means are equal.

<u>Confidence Interval:</u>

$$|78 - 67| \pm q \sqrt{\frac{MSW}{n}}$$

$$11 \pm 9.24 = 1.76 \text{ to } 20.24$$

18.   Since there are only 3 possible pairwise comparisons we will use the Bonferroni adjustment.

$\alpha = .05 / 3 = .017$

$t_{.017/2} = t_{.0085}$ which is approximately $t_{.01} = 2.602$

$$BSD = 2.602 \sqrt{MSW \left(\frac{1}{n_i} + \frac{1}{n_j} \right)}$$

$$= 2.602 \sqrt{.5 \left(\frac{1}{6} + \frac{1}{6} \right)} = 1.06$$

$|\bar{x}_1 - \bar{x}_2| = |5 - 4.5| = .5 < 1.06;$ no significant difference

$|\bar{x}_1 - \bar{x}_3| = |5 - 6| = 1 < 1.06;$ no significant difference

$|\bar{x}_2 - \bar{x}_3| = |4.5 - 6| = 1.5 > 1.06;$ significant difference

19. a. $\bar{\bar{x}} = (156 + 142 + 134) / 3 = 144$

$$SSTR = \sum_{j=1}^{k} n_j (\bar{x}_j - \bar{\bar{x}})^2$$

$$= 6(156 - 144)^2 + 6(142 - 144)^2 + 6(134 - 144)^2 = 1,488$$

  b.   MSTR = SSTR / $(k - 1)$ = 1488 / 2 = 744

  c. $s_1^2 = 164.4$ $s_2^2 = 131.2$ $s_3^2 = 110.4$

$$SSE = \sum_{j=1}^{k} (n_j - 1) s_j^2$$

$$= 5(164.4) + 5(131.2) + 5(110.4) = 2030$$

  d.   MSE = SSE / $(n_T - k)$ = 2030 / (12 - 3) = 135.3

  e. F = MSTR / MSE = 744 / 135.3 = 5.50

$F_{.05} = 3.68$ (2 degrees of freedom numerator and 15 denominator)

Since $F = 5.50 > F_{.05} = 3.68$, we reject the hypothesis that the means for the three treatments are equal.

20. a.

Source of Variation	Sum of Squares	Degrees of Freedom	Mean Square	F
Treatments	1488	2	744	5.50
Error	2030	15	135.3	
Total	3518	17		

b.
$$\text{TSD} = q \sqrt{\frac{\text{MSW}}{n}}$$

$$= 3.67 \sqrt{\frac{135.3}{6}} = 17.43$$

$|156 - 142| = 14 < 17.43$; no significant difference

$|156 - 134| = 22 > 17.43$; significant difference

$|142 - 134| = 8 < 17.43$; no significant difference

21.

Source of Variation	Sum of Squares	Degrees of Freedom	Mean Square	F
Treatments	300	4	75	14.07
Error	160	30	5.33	
Total	480	34		

22. a. $H_0: u_1 = u_2 = u_3 = u_4 = u_5$

H_a: Not all the population means are equal

b. $F_{.05} = 2.69$ (4 degrees of freedom numerator and 30 denominator)

Since $F = 14.07 > 2.69$ we reject H_0

23.

Source of Variation	Sum of Squares	Degrees of Freedom	Mean Square	F
Treatments	150	2	75	4.80
Error	250	16	15.63	
Total	400	18		

$F_{.05} = 3.63$ (2 degrees of freedom numerator and 16 denominator)

Since $F = 4.80 > F_{.05} = 3.63$, we reject the null hypothesis that the means of the three treatments are equal.

24.

Source of Variation	Sum of Squares	Degrees of Freedom	Mean Square	F
Treatments	1200	2	600	43.99
Error	600	44	13.64	
Total	1800	46		

$F_{.05} = 3.23$ (2 degrees of freedom numerator and 40 denominator)

$F_{.05} = 3.15$ (2 degrees of freedom numerator and 60 denominator)

The critical F value is between 3.15 and 3.23.

Since $F = 43.99$ exceeds the critical value, whatever it is, we reject the hypothesis that the treatment means are equal.

25.

| | Treatment | | |
	A	B	C
Sample Mean	119	107	100
Sample Variance	146.89	96.43	173.78

$$\overline{\overline{x}} = \frac{8(119) + 10(107) + 10(100)}{28} = 107.93$$

$$SSTR = \sum_{j=1}^{k} n_j (\overline{x}_j - \overline{\overline{x}})^2$$

$$= 8(119 - 107.93)^2 + 10(107 - 107.93)^2 + 10(100 - 107.93)^2 = 1617.9$$

$$MSTR = SSTR / (k - 1) = 1617.9 / 2 = 809.95$$

$$SSE = \sum_{j=1}^{k} (n_j - 1) s_j^2$$

$$= 7(146.86) + 9(96.44) + 9(173.78) = 3,460$$

$$MSE = SSE / (n_T - k) = 3,460 / (28 - 3) = 138.4$$

$$F = MSTR / MSE = 809.95 / 138.4 = 5.85$$

$F_{.05} = 3.39$ (2 degrees of freedom numerator and 25 denominator)

Since $F = 5.85 > F_{.05} = 3.39$, we reject the null hypothesis that the means of the three treatments are equal.

26. a.

Source of Variation	Sum of Squares	Degrees of Freedom	Mean Square	F
Treatments	4,560	2	2,280	9.87
Error	6,240	27	231.11	
Total	10,800	29		

b. $F_{.05} = 3.35$ (2 degrees of freedom numerator and 27 denominator)

Since $F = 9.87 > F_{.05} = 3.35$, we reject the null hypothesis that the means of the three assembly methods are equal.

27.

Source of Variation	Sum of Squares	Degrees of Freedom	Mean Square	F
Between	61.64	3	20.55	17.56
Error	23.41	20	1.17	
Total	85.05	23		

$F_{.05} = 3.10$ (3 degrees of freedom numerator and 20 denominator)

Since $F = 17.56 > F_{.05} = 3.10$, we reject the null hypothesis that the mean breaking strength of the four cables is the same.

28.

	50°	60°	70°
Sample Mean	33	29	28
Sample Variance	32	17.5	9.5

$\bar{\bar{x}} = (33 + 29 + 28) / 3 = 30$

$$SSTR = \sum_{j=1}^{k} n_j (\bar{x}_j - \bar{\bar{x}})^2$$

$$= 5(33 - 30)^2 + 5(29 - 30)^2 + 5(28 - 30)^2 = 70$$

$MSTR = SSTR / (k - 1) = 70 / 2 = 35$

$$SSE = \sum_{j=1}^{k} (n_j - 1) s_j^2$$

$$= 4(32) + 4(17.5) + 4(9.5) = 236$$

$MSE = SSE / (n_T - k) = 236 / (15 - 3) = 19.67$

$F = MSTR / MSE = 35 / 19.67 = 1.78$

$F_{.05} = 3.89$ (2 degrees of freedom numerator and 12 denominator)

Since $F = 1.78 < F_{.05} = 3.89$, we can not reject the null hypothesis that the mean yields for the three temperatures are equal.

29.

	Direct Experience	Indirect Experience	Combination
Sample Mean	17.0	20.4	25.0
Sample Variance	5.01	6.26	4.01

$\bar{\bar{x}} = (17 + 20.4 + 25) / 3 = 20.8$

$$SSTR = \sum_{j=1}^{k} n_j (\bar{x}_j - \bar{\bar{x}})^2$$

$$= 7(17 - 20.8)^2 + 7(20.4 - 20.8)^2 + 7(25 - 20.8)^2 = 225.68$$

$MSTR = SSTR / (k - 1) = 225.68 / 2 = 112.84$

$$SSE = \sum_{j=1}^{k} (n_j - 1) s_j^2$$

$$= 6(5.01) + 6(6.26) + 6(4.01) = 91.68$$

$MSE = SSW / (n_T - k) = 91.68 / (21 - 3) = 5.09$

$F = MSTR / MSE = 112.84 / 5.09 = 22.17$

$F_{.05} = 3.55$ (2 degrees of freedom numerator and 18 denominator)

Since $F = 22.17 > F_{.05} = 3.55$, we reject the null hypothesis that the means for the three groups are equal.

30.

	Paint 1	Paint 2	Paint 3	Paint 4
Sample Mean	13.3	139	136	144
Sample Variance	47.5	.50	21	54.5

$\bar{\bar{x}} = (133 + 139 + 136 + 144) / 3 = 138$

$$SSTR = \sum_{j=1}^{k} n_j (\bar{x}_j - \bar{\bar{x}})^2$$

$$= 5(133 - 138)^2 + 5(139 - 138)^2 + 5(136 - 138)^2 + 5(144 - 138)^2 = 330$$

$MSTR = SSTR / (k - 1) = 330 / 3 = 110$

$$SSE = \sum_{j=1}^{k} (n_j - 1) s_j^2$$

$= 4(47.5) + 4(50) + 4(21) + 4(54.5) = 692$

$MSE = SSE / (n_T - k) = 692 / (20 - 4) = 43.25$

$F = MSTR / MSE = 110 / 43.25 = 2.54$

$F_{.05} = 3.24$ (3 degrees of freedom numerator and 16 denominator)

Since $F = 2.54 < F_{.05} = 3.24$, we can not reject the null hypothesis that the mean drying times for the four paints are equal.

31.

	A	B	C
Sample Mean	20	21	25
Sample Variance	1	25	2.5

$\bar{\bar{x}} = (20 + 21 + 25) / 3 = 22$

$$SSTR = \sum_{j=1}^{k} n_j (\bar{x}_j - \bar{\bar{x}})^2$$

$= 5(20 - 22)^2 + 5(21 - 22)^2 + 5(25 - 22)^2 = 70$

$MSTR = SSTR / (k - 1) = 70 / 2 = 35$

$$SSE = \sum_{j=1}^{k} (n_j - 1) s_j^2$$

$= 4(1) + 4(2.5) + 4(2.5) = 24$

$MSE = SSE / (n_T - k) = 24 / (15 - 3) = 2$

$F = MSTR / MSE = 35 / 2 = 17.5$

$F_{.05} = 3.89$ (2 degrees of freedom numerator and 12 denominator)

Since $F = 17.5 > F_{.05} = 3.89$, we reject the null hypothesis that the mean miles per gallon ratings are the same for the three automobiles.

32.

$$TSD = q \sqrt{\frac{MSE}{n}}$$

$$= 3.61 \sqrt{\frac{5.09}{7}} = 3.08$$

$|\bar{x}_1 - \bar{x}_2| = |17.0 - 20.4| = 3.4 > 3.08$; significant difference

$|\bar{x}_1 - \bar{x}_3| = |17.0 - 25.0| = 8 > 3.08$; significant difference

$|\bar{x}_2 - \bar{x}_3| = |20.4 - 25| = 4.6 > 3.08$; significant difference

$$TSD = q \sqrt{\frac{MSE}{n}}$$

33.

$$= 3.77 \sqrt{\frac{2}{5}} = 2.38$$

$|\bar{x}_1 - \bar{x}_2| = |20 - 21| = 1 < 2.38$; no significant difference

$|\bar{x}_1 - \bar{x}_3| = |20 - 25| = 5 > 2.38$; significant difference

$|\bar{x}_2 - \bar{x}_3| = |21 - 25| = 4 > 2.38$; significant difference

34.   Treatment Means:

$$\bar{x}_{.1} = 13.6 \quad \bar{x}_{.2} = 11.0 \quad \bar{x}_{.3} = 10.6$$

Block Means:

$$\bar{x}_{1.} = 9 \quad \bar{x}_{2.} = 7.67 \quad \bar{x}_{3.} = 15.67 \quad \bar{x}_{4.} = 18.67 \quad \bar{x}_{5.} = 7.67$$

Overall Mean:

$$\bar{\bar{x}} = 176 / 15 = 11.73$$

Step 1

$$SST = \sum_i \sum_j (x_{ij} - \bar{\bar{x}})^2$$

$$= (10 - 11.73)^2 + (9 - 11.73)^2 + \cdots + (8 - 11.73)^2 = 354.93$$

Step 2

$$SSTR = b \sum_j (\bar{x}_{.j} - \bar{\bar{x}})^2$$

$$= 5 [(13.6 - 11.73)^2 + (11.0 - 11.73)^2 + (10.6 - 11.73)^2] = 26.53$$

Step 3

$$SSBL = k \sum_i (\bar{x}_{i.} - \bar{\bar{x}})^2$$

$$= 3 [(9 - 11.73)^2 + (7.67 - 11.73)^2 + (15.67 - 11.73)^2 + (18.67 - 11.73)^2$$
$$+ (7.67 - 11.73)^2] = 312.32$$

Step 4

$$SSE = SST - SSTR - SSBL$$

$$= 354.93 - 26.53 - 312.32 = 16.08$$

Source of Variation	Sum of Squares	Degrees of Freedom	Mean Square	F
Treatments	26.53	2	13.27	6.60
Blocks	312.32	4	78.08	
Error	16.08	8	2.01	
Total	354.93	14		

$F_{.05} = 4.46$ (2 degrees of freedom numerator and 8 denominator)

Since $F = 6.60 > F_{.05} = 4.46$, we reject the null hypothesis that the means of the three treatments are equal.

35.

Source of Variation	Sum of Squares	Degrees of Freedom	Mean Square	F
Treatments	310	4	77.5	17.69
Blocks	85	2	42.5	
Error	35	8	4.38	
Total	430	14		

$F_{.05} = 3.84$ (4 degrees of freedom numerator and 8 denominator)

Since $F = 17.69 > F_{.05} = 3.84$, we reject the null hypothesis that the means of the treatments are equal.

36.

Source of Variation	Sum of Squares	Degrees of Freedom	Mean Square	F
Treatments	900	3	300	12.60
Blocks	400	7	57.14	
Error	500	21	23.81	
Total	1800	31		

$F_{.05} = 3.07$ (3 degrees of freedom numerator and 21 denominator)

Since $F = 12.60 > F_{.05} = 3.07$, we reject the null hypothesis that the means of the treatments are equal.

37.   <u>Treatment Means:</u>

$\bar{x}_{.1} = 56 \quad \bar{x}_{.2} = 44$

<u>Block Means:</u>

$\bar{x}_{1.} = 46 \quad \bar{x}_{2.} = 49.5 \quad \bar{x}_{3.} = 54.5$

<u>Overall Mean:</u>

$\bar{\bar{x}} = 300 / 6 = 50$

<u>Step 1</u>

$$SST = \sum_i \sum_j (x_{ij} - \bar{\bar{x}})^2$$

$$= (50 - 50)^2 + (42 - 50)^2 + \cdots + (46 - 50)^2 = 310$$

<u>Step 2</u>

$$SSTR = b \sum_j (\bar{x}_{.j} - \bar{\bar{x}})^2$$

$$= 3 [(56 - 50)^2 + (44 - 50)^2] = 216$$

<u>Step 3</u>

$$SSBL = k \sum_i (\bar{x}_{i.} - \bar{\bar{x}})^2$$

$$= 2 [(46 - 50)^2 + (49.5 - 50)^2 + (54.5 - 50)^2] = 73$$

<u>Step 4</u>

$$SSE = SST - SSTR - SSBL$$

$$= 310 - 216 - 73 = 21$$

Source of Variation	Sum of Squares	Degrees of Freedom	Mean Square	F
Treatments	216	1	216	20.57
Blocks	73	2	36.5	
Error	21	2	10.5	
Total	310	5		

$F_{.05} = 18.51$ (1 degree of freedom numerator and 2 denominator)

Since $F = 20.57 > F_{.05} = 18.51$, we reject the null hypothesis that the mean tuneup times are the same for both analyzers.

38.

Source of Variation	Sum of Squares	Degrees of Freedom	Mean Square	F
Treatments	45	4	11.25	7.12
Blocks	36	3	12	
Error	19	12	1.58	
Total	100	19		

$F_{.05} = 3.26$ (4 degrees of freedom numerator and 12 denominator)

Since $F = 7.12 > F_{.05} = 3.26$, we reject the null hypothesis that the mean total audit times for the five auditing procedures are equal.

39. <u>Treatment Means:</u>

$\bar{x}_{.1} = 16 \quad \bar{x}_{.2} = 15 \quad \bar{x}_{.3} = 21$

<u>Block Means:</u>

$\bar{x}_{1.} = 18.67 \quad \bar{x}_{2.} = 19.33 \quad \bar{x}_{3.} = 15.33 \quad \bar{x}_{4.} = 14.33 \quad \bar{x}_{5.} = 19$

<u>Overall Mean:</u>

$\bar{\bar{x}} = 260 / 15 = 17.33$

<u>Step 1</u>

$SST = \sum_i \sum_j (x_{ij} - \bar{\bar{x}})^2$

$= (16 - 17.33)^2 + (16 - 17.33)^2 + \cdots + (22 - 17.33)^2 = 175.33$

<u>Step 2</u>

$$SSTR = b \sum_j (\bar{x}_{.j} - \bar{\bar{x}})^2$$

$$= 5\,[\,(16 - 17.33)^2 + (15 - 17.33)^2 + (21 - 17.33)^2\,] = 103.33$$

Step 3

$$SSBL = k \sum_i (\bar{x}_{i.} - \bar{\bar{x}})^2$$

$$= 3\,[\,(18.67 - 17.33)^2 + (19.33 - 17.33)^2 + \cdots + (19 - 17.33)^2\,] = 64.75$$

Step 4

$$SSE = SST - SSTR - SSBL$$

$$= 175.33 - 103.33 - 64.75 = 7.25$$

Source of Variation	Sum of Squares	Degrees of Freedom	Mean Square	F
Treatments	100.33	2	51.67	56.78
Blocks	64.75	4	16.19	
Error	7.25	8	.91	
Total	175.33	14		

$F_{.05} = 4.46$ (2 degrees of freedom numerator and 8 denominator)

Since $F = 56.78 > F_{.05} = 4.46$, we reject the null hypothesis that the mean times for the three systems are equal.

40.

		Factor B			Factor A
		Level 1	Level 2	Level 3	Means
Factor A	Level 1	$\bar{x}_{11} = 150$	$\bar{x}_{12} = 78$	$\bar{x}_{13} = 84$	$\bar{x}_{1.} = 104$
	Level 2	$\bar{x}_{21} = 110$	$\bar{x}_{22} = 116$	$\bar{x}_{23} = 128$	$\bar{x}_{2.} = 118$
Factor B Means		$\bar{x}_{.1} = 130$	$\bar{x}_{.2} = 97$	$\bar{x}_{.3} = 106$	$\bar{\bar{x}} = 111$

Step 1

$$SST = \sum_i \sum_j \sum_k (x_{ijk} - \bar{\bar{x}})^2$$

$$= (135 - 111)^2 + (165 - 111)^2 + \cdots + (136 - 111)^2 = 9{,}028$$

Step 2

$$SSA = br \sum_i (x_i. - \bar{\bar{x}})^2$$

$$= 3(2)[(104 - 111)^2 + (118 - 111)^2] = 588$$

Step 3

$$SSB = ar \sum_j (x._j - \bar{\bar{x}})^2$$

$$= 2(2)[(130 - 111)^2 + (97 - 111)^2 + (106 - 111)^2] = 2{,}328$$

Step 4

$$SSAB = r \sum_i \sum_j (\bar{x}_{ij} - \bar{x}_i. - \bar{x}._j + \bar{\bar{x}})^2$$

$$= 2[(150 - 104 - 130 + 111)^2 + (78 - 104 - 97 + 111)^2 +$$
$$\cdots + (128 - 118 - 106 + 111)^2] = 4{,}392$$

Step 5

$$SSE = SST - SSA - SSB - SSAB$$

$$= 9{,}028 - 588 - 2{,}328 - 4{,}392 = 1{,}720$$

Source of Variation	Sum of Squares	Degrees of Freedom	Mean Square	F
Factor A	588	1	588	2.05
Factor B	2,328	2	1,164	4.06
Interaction	4,392	2	2,196	7.66
Error	1,720	6	286.67	
Total	9,028	11		

$F_{.05} = 5.99$ (1 degree of freedom numerator and 6 denominator)

$F_{.05} = 5.14$ (2 degrees of freedom numerator and 6 denominator)

Since $F = 2.05 < F_{.05} = 5.99$, Factor A is not significant.

Since $F = 4.06 < F_{.05} = 5.14$, Factor B is not significant.

Since $F = 7.66 > F_{.05} = 5.14$, Interaction is significant.

41.

Source of Variation	Sum of Squares	Degrees of Freedom	Mean Square	F
Factor A	26	3	8.67	3.72
Factor B	23	2	11.50	4.94
Interaction	175	6	29.17	12.52
Error	56	24	2.33	
Total	280	35		

$F_{.05} = 3.01$ (3 degrees of freedom numerator and 24 denominator)

Since $F = 3.72 > F_{.05} = 3.01$, Factor A is significant.

$F_{.05} = 3.40$ (2 degrees of freedom numerator and 24 denominator)

Since $F = 4.94 > F_{.05} = 3.40$, Factor B is significant.

$F_{.05} = 2.51$ (6 degrees of freedom numerator and 24 denominator)

Since $F = 12.52 > F_{.05} = 2.51$, Interaction is significant

42.

Factor A		Factor B Small	Factor B Large	Factor B Means
	A	$\bar{x}_{11} = 10$	$\bar{x}_{12} = 10$	$\bar{x}_{1.} = 10$
Factor A	B	$\bar{x}_{21} = 18$	$\bar{x}_{22} = 28$	$\bar{x}_{2.} = 23$
	C	$\bar{x}_{31} = 14$	$\bar{x}_{32} = 16$	$\bar{x}_{3.} = 15$
Factor B	Means	$\bar{x}_{.1} = 14$	$\bar{x}_{.2} = 18$	$\bar{\bar{x}} = 16$

Step 1

$$SST = \sum_i \sum_j \sum_k (x_{ijk} - \bar{\bar{x}})^2$$

$$= (8 - 16)^2 + (12 - 16)^2 + (12 - 16)^2 + \cdots + (14 - 16)^2 = 544$$

Step 2

$$SSA = br \sum_i (x_{i.} - \bar{\bar{x}})^2$$

$$= 2(2)[(10 - 16)^2 + (23 - 16)^2 + (15 - 16)^2] = 344$$

Step 3

$$SSB = ar \sum_j (x_{.j} - \bar{\bar{x}})^2$$

$$= 3(2)[(14 - 16)^2 + (18 - 16)^2] = 48$$

Step 4

$$SSAB = r \sum_i \sum_j (\bar{x}_{ij} - \bar{x}_{i.} - \bar{x}_{.j} + \bar{\bar{x}})^2$$

$$= 2[(10 - 10 - 14 + 16)^2 + \cdots + (16 - 15 - 18 + 16)^2] = 56$$

Step 5

$$SSE = SST - SSA - SSB - SSAB$$

$$= 544 - 344 - 48 - 56 = 96$$

Source of Variation	Sum of Squares	Degrees of Freedom	Mean Square	F
Factor A	344	2	172	172/16 = 10.75
Factor B	48	1	48	48/16 = 3.00
Interaction	56	2	28	28/16 = 1.75
Error	96	6	6	
Total	544	11		

$F_{.05} = 5.14$ (2 degrees of freedom numerator and 6 denominator)

Since $F = 10.75 > F_{.05} = 5.14$, Factor A is significant, there is a difference due to the type of advertisement design.

$F_{.05} = 5.99$ (1 degree of freedom numerator and 6 denominator)

Since $F = 3 < F_{.05} = 5.99$, Factor B is not significant; there is not a significant difference due to size of advertisement.

Since $F = 1.75 < F_{.05} = 5.14$, Interaction is not significant.

43.

| | Factor B | | | Factor A |
	Roller Coaster	Screaming Demon	Log Flume	Means
Factor A Method 1	$\bar{x}_{11} = 42$	$\bar{x}_{12} = 48$	$\bar{x}_{13} = 48$	$\bar{x}_{1.} = 46$
Method 2	$\bar{x}_{21} = 50$	$\bar{x}_{22} = 48$	$\bar{x}_{23} = 46$	$\bar{x}_{2.} = 48$
Factor B Means	$\bar{x}_{.1} = 46$	$\bar{x}_{.2} = 48$	$\bar{x}_{.3} = 47$	$\bar{\bar{x}} = 47$

<u>Step 1</u>

$$SST = \sum_i \sum_j \sum_k (x_{ijk} - \bar{\bar{x}})^2$$

$$= (41 - 47)^2 + (43 - 47)^2 + \cdots + (44 - 47)^2 = 136$$

<u>Step 2</u>

$$SSA = br \sum_i (x_{i.} - \bar{\bar{x}})^2$$

$$= 3(2)[(46 - 47)^2 + (48 - 47)^2] = 12$$

<u>Step 3</u>

$$SSB = ar \sum_j (x_{.j} - \bar{\bar{x}})^2$$

$$= 2(2)[(46 - 47)^2 + (48 - 47)^2 + (47 - 47)^2] = 8$$

<u>Step 4</u>

$$SSAB = r \sum_i \sum_j (\bar{x}_{ij} - \bar{x}_{i.} - \bar{x}_{.j} + \bar{\bar{x}})^2$$

$$= 2[(41 - 46 - 46 + 47)^2 + \cdots + (44 - 48 - 47 + 47)^2] = 56$$

<u>Step 5</u>

$$SSE = SST - SSA - SSB - SSAB$$

$$= 136 - 12 - 8 - 56 = 60$$

Source of Variation	Sum of Squares	Degrees of Freedom	Mean Square	F
Factor A	12	1	12	12/10 = 1.2
Factor B	8	2	4	4/10 = .4
Interaction	56	2	28	28/10 = 2.8
Error	60	6	10	
Total	136	11		

$F_{.05} = 5.99$ (1 numerator degree of freedom and 6 denominator)

$F_{.05} = 5.14$ (2 numerator degrees of freedom and 6 denominator)

Since none of the F values exceed the corresponding critical values, there is no significant effect due to the loading and unloading method, the type of ride, or interaction.

44.

		Factor B			Factor A
		$1.49	$1.79	$1.99	Means
Factor A	1/4 Pound	$\bar{x}_{11} = 970$	$\bar{x}_{12} = 852.5$	$\bar{x}_{13} = 832.5$	$\bar{x}_{1.} = 885$
	1/3 Pound	$\bar{x}_{21} = 910$	$\bar{x}_{22} = 907.5$	$\bar{x}_{23} = 897.5$	$\bar{x}_{2.} = 905$
Factor B		$\bar{x}_{.1} = 940$	$\bar{x}_{.2} = 880$	$\bar{x}_{.3} = 865$	$\bar{\bar{x}} = 895$

Step 1

$$SST = \sum_i \sum_j \sum_k (x_{ijk} - \bar{\bar{x}})^2$$

$$= (955 - 895)^2 + (985 - 895)^2 + \cdots + (935 - 895)^2 = 29,600$$

Step 2

$$SSA = br \sum_i (x_{i.} - \bar{\bar{x}})^2$$

$$= 3 (2) [(885 - 895)^2 + (905 - 895)^2] = 1,200$$

Step 3

$$SSB = ar \sum_j (x_{.j} - \bar{\bar{x}})^2$$

$$= 2 (2) [(940 - 895)^2 + (880 - 895)^2 + (865 - 895)^2] = 12,600$$

Step 4

$$SSAB = r \sum_i \sum_j (\bar{x}_{ij} - \bar{x}_{i\cdot} - \bar{x}_{\cdot j} + \bar{\bar{x}})^2$$

$$= 2 \left[(970 - 885 - 940 - 895)^2 + (8525 - 885 - 880 + 895)^2 + \cdots + (897.5 - 90.5 - 865 + 895)^2 \right] = 9,650$$

Step 5

$$SSE = SST - SSA - SSB - SSAB$$

$$= 29,000 - 1,200 - 12,600 - 9,650 = 6,150$$

Source of Variation	Sum of Squares	Degrees of Freedom	Mean Square	F
Factor A	1,200	1	1,200	1.17
Factor B	12,600	2	6,300	6.15
Interaction	9,650	2	4,825	4.71
Error	6,150	6	1,025	
Total	29,600	11		

$F_{.05} = 5.99$ (1 degree of freedom numerator and 6 denominator)

$F_{.05} = 5.14$ (2 degrees of freedom numerator and 6 denominator)

Since $F = 1.17 < F_{.05} = 5.99$, Factor A (size) is not significant.

Since $F = 6.15 > F_{.05} = 5.14$, Factor B (price) is significant.

Since $F = 4.71 < F_{.05} = 5.14$, Interaction is not significant.

45.   The ANOVA procedure is used to test whether the means of k populations are equal.

46.   The means of the k populations have to be equal.

47.   In order for the ANOVA procedure to work correctly, the population variances must be equal.

48.   MSB is based upon the variation between sample means whereas MSW is computed based upon the variation within each sample.

49.   MSB is an unbiased estimate of σ^2 when all the population means are the same. When they are not, the squared deviations will be larger causing MSTR to be larger.

50. a.

	Area 1	Area 2
Sample Mean	96	94
Sample Variance	50	40

$$\text{pooled estimate} = \frac{s_1^2 + s_2^2}{2} = \frac{50 + 40}{2} = 45$$

$$\text{estimate of standard deviation of } \bar{x}_1 - \bar{x}_2 = \sqrt{45\left(\frac{1}{4} + \frac{1}{4}\right)} = 4.74$$

$$t = \frac{\bar{x}_1 - \bar{x}_2}{4.74} = \frac{96 - 94}{4.74} = .42$$

$t_{.025} = 2.447$ (6 degrees of freedom)

Since $t = .42 < t_{.025} = 2.477$, the means are not significantly different.

b. $\bar{\bar{x}} = (96 + 94) / 2 = 95$

$$SSB = \sum_{j=1}^{k} n_j (\bar{x}_j - \bar{\bar{x}})^2$$

$$= 4(96 - 95)^2 + 4(94 - 95)^2 = 8$$

$$MSB = SSB / (k - 1) = 8 / 1 = 8$$

$$SSW = \sum_{j=1}^{k} (n_j - 1) s_j^2$$

$$= 3(50) + 3(40) = 270$$

$$MSW = SSW / (n_T - k) = 270 / (8 - 2) = 45$$

$$F = MSB / MSW = 8 / 45 = .18$$

$F_{.05} = 5.99$ (1 degree of freedom numerator and 6 denominator)

Since $F = .18 < F_{.05} = 5.99$ the means are not significantly different.

51.

	Area 1	Area 2	Area 3
Sample Mean	96	94	83
Sample Variance	50	40	42

$\bar{\bar{x}} = (96 + 94 + 83) / 3 = 91$

$SSB = \sum_{j=1}^{k} n_j (\bar{x}_j - \bar{\bar{x}})^2$

$= 4(96 - 91)^2 + 4(94 - 91)^2 + 4(83 - 91)^2 = 392$

$MSB = SSB / (k - 1) = 392 / 2 = 196$

$SSW = \sum_{j=1}^{k} (n_j - 1) s_j^2$

$= 3(50) + 3(40) + 3(42) = 396$

$MSW = SSW / (n_T - k) = 396 / (12 - 3) = 44$

$F = MSB / MSW = 196 / 44 = 4.45$

$F_{.05} = 4.26$ (2 degrees of freedom numerator and 6 denominator)

Since $F = 4.45 > F_{.05} = 4.26$ we reject the null hypothesis that the mean asking prices for all three areas are equal.

52. $\bar{\bar{x}} = (130 + 120 + 132 + 114) / 4 = 124$

$SSB = \sum_{j=1}^{k} n_j (\bar{x}_j - \bar{\bar{x}})^2$

$= 10(130 - 124)^2 + 10(120 - 124)^2 + 10(132 - 124)^2 + 10(114 - 124)^2 = 2,160$

$MSB = SSB / (k - 1) = 2160 / 3 = 720$

$SSW = \sum_{j=1}^{k} (n_j - 1) s_j^2$

$= 9(72) + 9(64) + 9(69) + 9 (67) = 2,448$

$MSW = SSW / (n_T - k) = 2,448 / (40 - 4) = 68$

$F = MSB / MSW = 720 / 68 = 10.59$

$F_{.05} = 2.92$ (3 degrees of freedom numerator and 30 denominator)

$F_{.05} = 2.84$ (3 degrees of freedom numerator and 40 denominator)

Thus, the critical F value is between 2.84 and 2.92

Since $F = 10.59$ exceeds the critical F value, we reject the null hypothesis that the mean number of units sold in the four sales territories are equal.

53. $\bar{\bar{x}} = \dfrac{10(130) + 12(120) + 10(132) + 15(114)}{47} = 122.77$

$SSB = \displaystyle\sum_{j=1}^{k} n_j (\bar{x}_j - \bar{\bar{x}})^2$

$= 10(130 - 122.77)^2 + 12(120 - 122.77)^2 + 10(132 - 122.77)^2 + 15(114 - 122.77)^2$

$= 2620.43$

$MSB = SSB / (k - 1) = 2620.43 / 3 = 873.48$

$SSW = \displaystyle\sum_{j=1}^{k} (n_j - 1) s_j^2$

$= 9(72) + 11(64) + 9(69) + 14(67) = 2{,}911$

$MSW = SSW / (n_T - k) = 2{,}911 / (47 - 4) = 67.70$

$F = MSB / MSW = 873.48 / 67.70 = 12.90$

$F_{.05} = 2.84$ (3 degrees of numerator and 40 denominator)

$F_{.05} = 2.76$ (3 degrees of freedom numerator and 60 denominator)

Thus, the critical F value is between 2.76 and 2.84.

Since $F = 12.90$ exceeds the critical F value, we reject the null hypothesis that the mean number of units sold in the four sales territories are equal.

54.

	Airlines	Retail	Hotel	Automotive
Sample Mean	52.14	56.17	65.6	50.20
Sample Variance	25.81	23.77	23.30	7.70

$$\bar{\bar{x}} = \frac{7(52.14) + 6(56.17) + 5(65.6) + 5(50.20)}{23} = 55.70$$

$$SSB = \sum_{j=1}^{k} n_j (\bar{x}_j - \bar{\bar{x}})^2$$

$$= 7(52.14 - 55.70)^2 + 6(56.17 - 55.70)^2 + 5(65.6 - 55.70)^2 \div 5(50.20 - 55.70)^2$$

$$= 731.34$$

$$MSB = SSB / (k - 1) = 731.34 / 3 = 243.78$$

$$SSW = \sum_{j=1}^{k} (n_j - 1) s_j^2$$

$$= 6(25.81) + 5(23.77) + 4(23.30) + 4(7.70) = 397.71$$

$$MSW = SSW / (n_T - k) = 397.71 / (23 - 4) = 20.93$$

$$F = MSB / MSW = 243.78 / 20.93 = 11.65$$

$F_{.05} = 3.13$ (3 degrees of freedom numerator and 19 denominator

Since $F = 11.65 > F_{.05} = 3.13$, we reject the null hypothesis that the mean quality ratings for the three industries are equal.

55.

	Method A	Method B	Method C
Sample Mean	90	84	81
Sample Variance	98.00	168.44	159.78

$$\bar{\bar{x}} = (90 + 84 + 81) / 3 = 85$$

$$SSTR = \sum_{j=1}^{k} n_j (\bar{x}_j - \bar{\bar{x}})^2$$

$$= 10(90 - 85)^2 + 10(84 - 85)^2 + 10(81 - 85)^2 = 420$$

$$MSTR = SSTR / (k - 1) = 420 / 2 = 210$$

$$SSE = \sum_{j=1}^{k} (n_j - 1) s_j^2$$

$$= 9(98.00) + 9(168.44) + 9(159.78) = 3,836$$

$$\text{MSE} = \text{SSE} / (n_T - k) = 3,836 / (30 - 3) = 142.07$$

$$F = \text{MSTR} / \text{MSE} = 210 / 142.07 = 1.48$$

$F_{.05} = 3.35$ (2 degrees of freedom numerator and 27 denominator)

Since $F = 1.48 < F_{.05} = 3.35$, we can not reject the null hypothesis that the means are equal.

56.

	X	Y	Z
Sample Mean	92	97	84
Sample Variance	30	6	35.33

$$\bar{\bar{x}} = (92 + 97 + 44) / 3 = 91$$

$$\text{SSTR} = \sum_{j=1}^{k} n_j (\bar{x}_j - \bar{\bar{x}})^2$$

$$= 4(92 - 91)^2 + 4(97 - 91)^2 + 4(84 - 91)^2 = 344$$

$$\text{MSTR} = \text{SSTR} / (k - 1) = 344 / 2 = 172$$

$$\text{SSE} = \sum_{j=1}^{k} (n_j - 1) s_j^2$$

$$= 3(30) + 3(6) + 3(35.33) = 213.99$$

$$\text{MSE} = \text{SSE} / (n_T - k) = 213.99 / (12 - 3) = 23.78$$

$$F = \text{MSTR} / \text{MSE} = 172 / 23.78 = 7.23$$

$F_{.05} = 4.26$ (2 degrees of freedom numerator and 9 denominator)

Since $F = 7.23 > F_{.05} = 4.26$, we reject the null hypothesis that the mean absorbency ratings for the three brands are equal.

57.

	Method 1	Method 2	Method 3
Sample Mean	62	60	52
Sample Variance	27.5	26.5	31

$\bar{\bar{x}} = (62 + 60 + 52) / 3 = 58$

$$SSTR = \sum_{j=1}^{k} n_j (\bar{x}_j - \bar{\bar{x}})^2$$

$$= 5(62 - 58)^2 + 5(60 - 58)^2 + 5(52 - 58)^2 = 280$$

$MSTR = SSTR / (k - 1) = 280 / 2 = 140$

$$SSE = \sum_{j=1}^{k} (n_j - 1) s_j^2$$

$$= 4(27.5) + 4(26.5) + 4(31) = 340$$

$MSE = SSE / (n_T - k) = 340 / (15 - 3) = 28.33$

$F = MSTR / MSE = 140 / 28.33 = 4.94$

$F_{.05} = 3.89$ (2 degrees of freedom numerator and 12 denominator)

Since $F = 4.94 > F_{.05} = 3.89$, we reject the null hypothesis that the mean number of units produced each week by each of the three methods is equal.

58.

	First Year	Second Year	Third Year	Fourth Year
Sample Mean	1.03	-0.99	15.24	9.81
Sample Variance	416.93	343.04	159.31	55.43

$\bar{\bar{x}} = (1.03 - .99 + 15.24 + 9.81) / 4 = 6.27$

$$SSTR = \sum_{j=1}^{k} n_j (\bar{x}_j - \bar{\bar{x}})^2$$

$$= 7(1.03 - 6.27)^2 + 7(-.99 - 6.27)^2 + 7(15.24 - 6.27)^2 + (9.81 - 6.27)^2 = 1,212.10$$

$MSTR = SSTR / (k - 1) = 1,212.10 / 3 = 404.03$

$$SSE = \sum_{j=1}^{k} (n_j - 1) s_j^2$$

$$= 6(416.93) + 6(343.04) + 6(159.31) + 6(55.43) = 5,848.26$$

$$\text{MSE} = \text{SSE} / (n_T - k) = 5,848.26 / (28 - 4) = 243.68$$

$$F = \text{MSTR} / \text{MSE} = 404.03 / 243.68 = 1.66$$

$F_{.05} = 3.01$ (3 degrees of freedom numerator and 24 denominator)

Since $F = 1.66 < F_{.05} = 3.01$, we can not reject the null hypothesis that the mean percent changes in each of the four years are equal.

59.

	Type A	Type B	Type C	Type D
Sample Mean	32,000	27,500	34,200	30,300
Sample Variance	2,102,500	2,325,625	2,722,500	1,960,000

$$\bar{\bar{x}} = (32,000 + 27,500 + 34,200 + 30,000) / 4 = 31,000$$

$$\text{SSTR} = \sum_{j=1}^{k} n_j (\bar{x}_j - \bar{\bar{x}})^2$$

$$= 30(32,000 - 31,000)^2 + 30(27,500 - 31,000)^2 + 30(34,200 - 31,000)^2 +$$
$$30(30,300 - 31,000)^2 = 719,400,000$$

$$\text{MSTR} = \text{SSTR} / (k - 1) = 719,400,000 / 3 = 239,800,000$$

$$\text{SSE} = \sum_{j=1}^{k} (n_j - 1) s_j^2$$

$$= 29(2,102,500) + 29(2,325,625) + 29(2,722,500) + 29(1,960,000) = 264,208,125$$

$$\text{MSE} = \text{SSE} / (n_T - k) = 264,208,125 / (120 - 4) = 2,277,656.25$$

$$F = \text{MSTR} / \text{MSE} = 239,800,000 / 2,277,656.25 = 105.28$$

$F_{.05}$ is approximately 2.68, the table value for 3 degrees of freedom numerator and 120 denominator; the value we would look up, if it were available, would correspond to 116 denominator degrees of freedom.

Since $F = 105.28$ exceeds $F_{.05}$, whatever its value actually is, we reject the null hypothesis that the population means are equal.

60.

	Design A	Design B	Design C
Sample Mean	90	107	109
Sample Variance	82.67	68.67	100.67

$$\bar{\bar{x}} = (90 + 107 + 109) / 3 = 102$$

$$SSTR = \sum_{j=1}^{k} n_j (\bar{x}_j - \bar{\bar{x}})^2$$

$$= 4(90 - 102)^2 + 4(107 - 102)^2 + (109 - 102)^2 = 872$$

$$MSTR = SSTR / (k - 1) = 872 / 2 = 436$$

$$SSE = \sum_{j=1}^{k} (n_j - 1) s_j^2$$

$$= 3(82.67) + 3(68.67) + 3(100.67) = 756.03$$

$$MSE = SSE / (n_T - k) = 756.03 / (12 - 3) = 84$$

$$F = MSTR / MSE = 436 / 84 = 5.19$$

$$F_{.05} = 4.26 \quad \text{(2 degrees of freedom numerator and 9 denominator)}$$

Since $F = 5.19 > F_{.05} = 4.26$, we reject the null hypothesis that the mean lifetime in hours is the same for the three designs.

61. a.

	Non - Browser	Light Browser	Heavy Browser
Sample Survey	4.25	5.25	5.75
Sample Variance	1.07	1.07	1.36

$$\bar{\bar{x}} = (4.25 + 5.25 + 5.75) / 3 = 5.08$$

$$SSB = \sum_{j=1}^{k} n_j (\bar{x}_j - \bar{\bar{x}})^2$$

$$= 8(4.25 - 5.08)^2 + 8(5.25 - 5.08)^2 + 8(5.75 - 5.08)^2 = 9.33$$

$$MSB = SSB / (k - 1) = 9.33 / 2 = 4.67$$

$$SSW = \sum_{j=1}^{k} (n_j - 1) s_j^2$$

$$= 7(1.07) + 7(1.07) + 7(1.36) = 24.5$$

$$MSW = SSW / (n_T - k) = 24.5 / (24 - 3) = 1.17$$

$F = $ MSB / MSW $= 4.67 / 1.17 = 3.99$

$F_{.05} = 3.47$ (2 degrees of freedom numerator and 21 denominator)

Since $F = 3.99 > F_{.05} = 3.47$, we reject the null hypothesis that the mean comfort scores are the same for the three groups.

b. $\text{TSD} = q \sqrt{\dfrac{\text{MSW}}{n}}$

$= 3.58 \sqrt{\dfrac{1.17}{8}} = 1.37$

Note: q is approximately 3.58, the value for 20 degrees of freedom; the value we really need is for 21 degrees of freedom, but this is not shown in the table.

Since the absolute value of the difference between the sample means for non-browsers and light browsers is $\left| 4.25 - 5.25 \right| = 1$, we cannot reject the null hypothesis that the two population means are equal.

62.   Treatment Means:

$\bar{x}_{.1} = 22.8 \quad \bar{x}_{.2} = 24.8 \quad \bar{x}_{.3} = 25.80$

Block Means:

$\bar{x}_{1.} = 19.67 \quad \bar{x}_{2.} = 25.67 \quad \bar{x}_{3.} = 31 \quad \bar{x}_{4.} = 23.67 \quad \bar{x}_{5.} = 22.33$

Overall Mean:

$\bar{\bar{x}} = 367 / 15 = 24.47$

Step 1

$$\text{SST} = \sum_i \sum_j (x_{ij} - \bar{\bar{x}})^2$$

$= (18 - 24.47)^2 + (21 - 24.47)^2 + \cdots + (24 - 24.47)^2 = 253.73$

Step 2

$$\text{SSTR} = b \sum_j (\bar{x}_{.j} - \bar{\bar{x}})^2$$

$= 5 [(22.8 - 24.47)^2 + (24.8 - 24.47)^2 + (25.8 - 24.47)^2] = 23.33$

Step 3

$$SSBL = k \sum_i (\bar{x}_{i.} - \bar{\bar{x}})^2$$

$$= 3\,[\,(19.67 - 24.47)^2 + (25.67 - 24.47)^2 + \cdots + (22.33 - 24.47)^2\,] = 217.02$$

Step 4

$$SSE = SST - SSTR - SSBL$$

$$= 253.73 - 23.33 - 217.02 = 13.38$$

Source of Variation	Sum of Squares	Degrees of Freedom	Mean Square	F
Treatments	23.33	2	11.67	6.99
Blocks	217.02	4	54.26	32.49
Error	13.38	8	1.67	
Total	253.73	14		

$F_{.05} = 4.46$ (2 degrees of freedom numerator and 8 denominator)

Since $F = 6.99 > F_{.05} = 4.46$ we reject the null hypothesis that the mean miles per gallon ratings for the three brands of gasoline are equal.

63.

	I	II	III
Sample Mean	22.8	24.8	25.8
Sample Variance	21.2	9.2	27.2

$$\bar{\bar{x}} = (22.8 + 24.8 + 25.8)\,/\,3 = 24.47$$

$$SSTR = \sum_{j=1}^{k} n_j\,(\bar{x}_j - \bar{\bar{x}})^2$$

$$= 5(22.8 - 24.47)^2 + 5(24.8 - 24.47)^2 + 5(25.8 - 24.47)^2 = 23.33$$

$$MSTR = SSTR\,/\,(k-1) = 23.33\,/\,2 = 11.67$$

$$SSE = \sum_{j=1}^{k} (n_j - 1)\,s_j^2$$

$$= 4(21.2) + 4(9.2) + 4(27.2) = 230.4$$

$$MSE = SSE\,/\,(n_T - k) = 230.4\,/\,(15 - 3) = 19.2$$

$$F = MSTR\,/\,MSE = 11.67\,/\,19.2 = .61$$

$F_{.05} = 3.89$ (2 degrees of freedom numerator and 12 denominator)

Since $F = .61 < F_{.05} = 3.89$, we can not reject the null hypothesis that the mean miles per gallon ratings for the three brands of gasoline are equal.

Thus, we must remove the block effect in order to detect a significant difference due to the brand of gasoline. The following table illustrates the relationship between the randomized block design and the completely randomized design.

Sum of Squares	Randomized Block Design	Completely Randomized Design
SST	253.73	253.73
SSTR	23.33	23.33
SSBL	217.02	does not exist
SSE	13.38	230.4

Note that SSE for the completely randomized design is the sum of SSBL (217.02) and SSE (13.38) for the randomized block design. This illustrates that the effect of blocking is to remove the block effect from the error sum of squares; thus, the estimate of σ^2 for the randomized block design is substantially smaller than it is for the completely randomized design.

64.   Block means: 90, 84, 82

Treatment means: 87.333, 74.667, 84, 95.333

Overall mean: 85.333

Step 1: SST $= (99 - 85.333)^2 + (73 - 85.333)^2 + \cdots + (86 - 85.333)^2 = 1046.667$

Step 2: SSTR $= 4[(90 - 85.333)^2 + (84 - 85.333)^2 + (82 - 85.333)^2] = 138.667$

Step 3: SSB $= 3[(87.333 - 85.333)^2 + \cdots + (95.333 - 85.333)^2] = 658.667$

Step 4:

SSE $= 1046.667 - 138.667 - 658.667 = 249.333$

MSTR $= 138.667 / 2 = 69.333$ MSE $= 249.333 / (2)(3) = 41.556$
$F = 69.333 / 41.556 = 1.67$

$F_{.01} = 10.92$ (2 degrees of freedom numerator and 6 denominator)

Since $1.67 < 10.92$ we cannot reject H_0; there is no significant difference between the road repair compounds.

65.

		Factor B			Factor B
		Spanish	French	German	Means
Factor A	System 1	$\bar{x}_{11} = 10$	$\bar{x}_{12} = 12$	$\bar{x}_{13} = 14$	$\bar{x}_{1.} = 12$
	System 2	$\bar{x}_{21} = 8$	$\bar{x}_{22} = 15$	$\bar{x}_{23} = 19$	$\bar{x}_{2.} = 14$
Factor B Means		$\bar{x}_{.1} = 9$	$\bar{x}_{.2} = 13.5$	$\bar{x}_{.3} = 16.5$	$\bar{\bar{x}} = 13$

Step 1

$$SST = \sum_i \sum_j \sum_k (x_{ijk} - \bar{\bar{x}})^2$$

$$= (8 - 13)^2 + (12 - 13)^2 + \cdots + (22 - 13)^2 = 204$$

Step 2

$$SSA = br \sum_i (x_{i.} - \bar{\bar{x}})^2$$

$$= 3(2)[(12 - 13)^2 + (14 - 13)^2] = 12$$

Step 3

$$SSB = ar \sum_j (x_{.j} - \bar{\bar{x}})^2$$

$$= 2(2)[(9 - 13)^2 + (13.5 - 13)^2 + (16.5 - 13)^2] = 114$$

Step 4

$$SSAB = r \sum_i \sum_j (\bar{x}_{ij} - \bar{x}_{i.} - \bar{x}_{.j} + \bar{\bar{x}})^2$$

$$= 2[(8 - 12 - 9 + 13)^2 + \cdots + (22 - 14 - 16.5 + 13)^2] = 26$$

Step 5

$$SSE = SST - SSA - SSB - SSAB$$

$$= 204 - 12 - 114 - 26 = 52$$

Source of Variation	Sum of Squares	Degrees of Freedom	Mean Square	F
Factor A	12	1	12	1.38
Factor B	114	2	57	6.57
Interaction	26	2	12	1.50
Error	52	6	8.67	
Total	204	11		

$F_{.05} = 5.99$ (1 degree of freedom numerator and 6 denominator)

$F_{.05} = 5.14$ (2 degrees of freedom numerator and 6 denominator)

Since $F = 6.57 > F_{.05} = 5.14$, Factor B is significant; that is, there is a significant difference due to the language translated.

Type of system and interaction are not significant since both F values are less than the constant order.

66.

		Factor B	Factor B	Factor B
		Manual	Automatic	Means
Factor A	Machine 1	$\bar{x}_{11} = 32$	$\bar{x}_{12} = 28$	$\bar{x}_{1.} = 36$
	Machine 2	$\bar{x}_{21} = 21$	$\bar{x}_{22} = 26$	$\bar{x}_{2.} = 23.5$
Factor B Means		$\bar{x}_{.1} = 26.5$	$\bar{x}_{.2} = 27$	$\bar{\bar{x}} = 26.75$

Step 1

$$SST = \sum_i \sum_j \sum_k (x_{ijk} - \bar{\bar{x}})^2$$

$$= (30 - 26.75)^2 + (34 - 26.75)^2 + \cdots + (28 - 26.75)^2 = 151.5$$

Step 2

$$SSA = br \sum_i (x_{i.} - \bar{\bar{x}})^2$$

$$= 2 (2) [(30 - 26.75)^2 + (23.5 - 26.75)^2] = 84.5$$

13 - 41

Step 3

$$SSB = ar \sum_j (x_{.j} - \bar{\bar{x}})^2$$

$$= 2(2)[(26.5 - 26.75)^2 + (27 - 26.75)^2] = 0.5$$

Step 4

$$SSAB = r \sum_i \sum_j (\bar{x}_{ij} - \bar{x}_{i.} - \bar{x}_{.j} + \bar{\bar{x}})^2$$

$$= 2[(30 - 30 - 26.5 + 26.75)^2 + \cdots + (28 - 23.5 - 27 + 26.75)^2] = 40.5$$

Step 5

$$SSE = SST - SSA - SSB - SSAB$$

$$= 151.5 - 84.5 - 0.5 - 40.5 = 26$$

Source of Variation	Sum of Squares	Degrees of Freedom	Mean Square	F
Factor A	84.5	1	84.5	13
Factor B	.5	1	.5	.08
Interaction	40.5	1	40.5	6.23
Error	26	4	6.5	
Total	151.5	7		

$F_{.05} = 7.71$ (1 degree of freedom numerator and 4 denominator)

Since $F = 13 > F_{.05} = 7.71$, Factor A (Type of Machine) is significant.

Type of Loading System and Interaction are not significant since both F values are less than the critical value.

Solution To Computer Case

Descriptive statistics for the individuals in reasonably good health (MEDICAL1) are shown below:

	N	MEAN	MEDIAN	TRMEAN	STDEV	SEMEAN
FLA	20	5.550	6.000	5.556	2.139	0.478
NY	20	8.000	8.000	7.944	2.200	0.492
NC	20	7.050	7.500	7.000	2.837	0.634

	MIN	MAX	Q1	Q3
FLA	2.000	9.000	3.250	7.000
NY	4.000	13.000	7.000	8.750
NC	3.000	12.000	4.250	8.750

Descriptive statistics for the individuals who had a chronic health condition (MEDICAL2) are shown below:

	N	MEAN	MEDIAN	TRMEAN	STDEV	SEMEAN
FLA	20	14.500	14.500	14.444	3.171	0.709
NY	20	15.250	14.500	15.111	4.128	0.923
NC	20	13.950	14.000	14.000	2.946	0.659

	MIN	MAX	Q1	Q3
FLA	9.000	21.000	12.000	17.000
NY	9.000	24.000	12.250	17.750
NC	8.000	19.000	12.000	16.750

The depression levels for the individuals who had a chronic health condition are, on average, much higher than the depression levels of individuals in reasonably good health.

The analysis of variance results for the individuals in reasonably good health (MEDICAL1) are shown below:

```
ANALYSIS OF VARIANCE
SOURCE      DF        SS         MS        F        p
FACTOR       2      61.03      30.52     5.24    0.008
ERROR       57     331.90       5.82
TOTAL       59     392.93
                                    INDIVIDUAL 95 PCT CI'S FOR MEAN
                                    BASED ON POOLED STDEV
 LEVEL      N       MEAN     STDEV   -+---------+---------+---------+-----
FLA        20      5.550     2.139   (------*------)
NY         20      8.000     2.200                   (------*-------)
NC         20      7.050     2.837              (------*------)
                                    -+---------+---------+---------+-----
POOLED STDEV =    2.413            4.5       6.0       7.5       9.0
```

The *p*-value of .008 supports the conclusion that the mean depression scores are not the same for the three states. The observed differences appear to be due to the difference between the mean depression score for residents of Florida and New York.

The analysis of variance results for the individuals who had a chronic health condition (MEDICAL2) are shown below:

```
ANALYSIS OF VARIANCE
SOURCE      DF        SS        MS        F          p
FACTOR       2      17.0       8.5     0.71      0.494
ERROR       57     679.7      11.9
TOTAL       59     696.7
                                     INDIVIDUAL 95 PCT CI'S FOR MEAN
                                     BASED ON POOLED STDEV
  LEVEL      N      MEAN     STDEV   -------+---------+---------+---------
FLA         20    14.500     3.171        (-------------*------------)
NY          20    15.250     4.128            (------------*------------)
NC          20    13.950     2.946   (------------*------------)
                                     -------+---------+---------+---------
POOLED STDEV =     3.453             13.2      14.4       15.6
```

At the 5% level of significance there does not appear to be any significant difference in the mean depression scores among the three states.

Chapter 14
Simple Linear Regression and Correlation

Learning Objectives

1. Understand how regression analysis can be used to develop an equation that estimates mathematically how two variables are related.

2. Understand how correlation analysis can be used to determine the strength of the linear relationship between two variables.

3. Specifically, know how to fit an estimates regression equation to a set of sample data based upon the least-squares method.

4. Be able to test for a significant relationship and determine how good a fit is provided by the estimated regression equation.

5. Understand the assumptions necessary for statistical inference.

6. Learn how to use a residual plot to make a judgement as to the validity of the regression assumptions, recognize outliers, and identify influential observations.

7. Know how to develop confidence interval estimates of y given a specific value of x in both the case of a mean value of y and an individual value of y.

8. Be able to compute the sample correlation coefficient from the regression analysis output as well as without performing a regression analysis.

9. Know the definition of the following terms:

   independent and dependent variable
   simple linear regression
   scatter diagram
   coefficient of determination
   regression model
   regression equation and estimated regression equation
   standard error of the estimate
   confidence interval
   prediction interval
   residual plot
   standardized residual plot
   influential observation
   leverage
   covariance
   correlation coefficient

Solutions:

1. a.

```
Y         -                                                          *
          -
          -
          -
   12.0+
          -                                                   *
          -
          -
          -
    8.0+
          -                           *
          -
          -
          -                                        *
    4.0+
          -                 *
          -
          -
          -
          +---------+---------+---------+---------+---------+------X
        0.0       1.0       2.0       3.0       4.0       5.0
```

b. There appears to be a linear relationship between x and y.

c. Many different straight lines can be drawn to provide a linear approximation of the relationship between x *and* y; in part d we will determine the equation of a straight line that "best" represents the relationship according to the least squares criterion.

d. Summations needed to compute the slope and y-intercept are:

$$\sum x_i = 15 \quad \sum y_i = 40 \quad \sum x_i y_i = 146 \quad \sum x_i^2 = 55$$

$$b_1 = \frac{\sum x_i y_i - \left(\sum x_i \sum y_i\right)/n}{\sum x_i^2 - \left(\sum x_i\right)^2/n} = \frac{146 - (15)(40)/5}{55 - (15)^2/5} = 2.6$$

$$b_0 = \bar{y} - b_1 \bar{x} = 8 - (2.6)(3) = .2$$

$$\hat{y} = .2 + 2.6\, x$$

e. $\hat{y} = .2 + 2.6\, x = .2 + 2.6\,(4) = 10.6$

2. a.

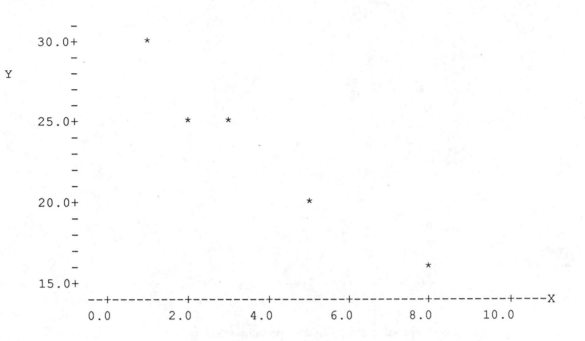

b. There appears to be a linear relationship between x and y.

c. Many different straight lines can be drawn to provide a linear approximation of the relationship between x and y; in part d we will determine the equation of a straight line that "best" represents the relationship according to the least squares criterion.

d. Summations needed to compute the slope and y-intercept are:

$$\sum x_i = 19 \quad \sum y_i = 116 \quad \sum x_i y_i = 383 \quad \sum x_i^2 = 103$$

$$b_1 = \frac{\sum x_i y_i - \left(\sum x_i \sum y_i\right)/n}{\sum x_i^2 - \left(\sum x_i\right)^2/n} = \frac{383 - (19)\,(116)/5}{103 - (19)^2/5} = -1.8766$$

$$b_0 = \bar{y} - b_1\bar{x} = 23.2 - (-1.8766)(3.8) = 30.3311$$

$$\hat{y} = 30.33 - 1.88\,x$$

e. $\hat{y} = 30.33 - 1.88(6) = 19.05$

3. a.

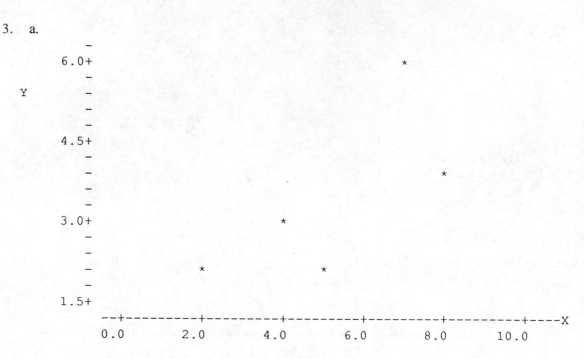

b. Summations needed to compute the slope and y-intercept are:

$$\sum x_i = 26 \quad \sum y_i = 17 \quad \sum x_i y_i = 100 \quad \sum x_i^2 = 158$$

$$b_1 = \frac{\sum x_i y_i - \left(\sum x_i \sum y_i\right)/n}{\sum x_i^2 - \left(\sum x_i\right)^2/n} = \frac{100 - (26)\,(17)\,/\,5}{158 - (26)^2\,/\,5} = .5088$$

$$b_0 = \bar{y} - b_1\bar{x} = 3.4 - (.5088)(5.2) = .7542$$

$$\hat{y} = .75 + .51\,x$$

e. $\hat{y} = .75 + .51(4) = 2.79$

4 a.

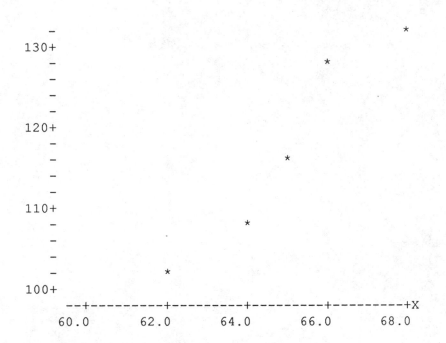

b. There appears to be a linear relationship between x and y.

c. Many different straight lines can be drawn to provide a linear approximation of the
    relationship between x *and* y; in part d we will determine the equation of a straight line that
    "best" represents the relationship according to the least squares criterion.

d. Summations needed to compute the slope and y-intercept are:

$$\sum x_i = 325 \quad \sum y_i = 585 \quad \sum x_i y_i = 38,135 \quad \sum x_i^2 = 21,145$$

$$b_1 = \frac{\sum x_i y_i - \left(\sum x_i \sum y_i\right)/n}{\sum x_i^2 - \left(\sum x_i\right)^2/n} = \frac{38,135 - (325)(585)/5}{21,145 - (325)^2/5} = 5.5$$

$$b_0 = \bar{y} - b_1\bar{x} = 117 - (5.5)(65) = -240.5$$

$$\hat{y} = -240.5 + 5.5\,x$$

e. $\hat{y} = -240.5 + 5.5(63) = 106$ pounds

5   a.

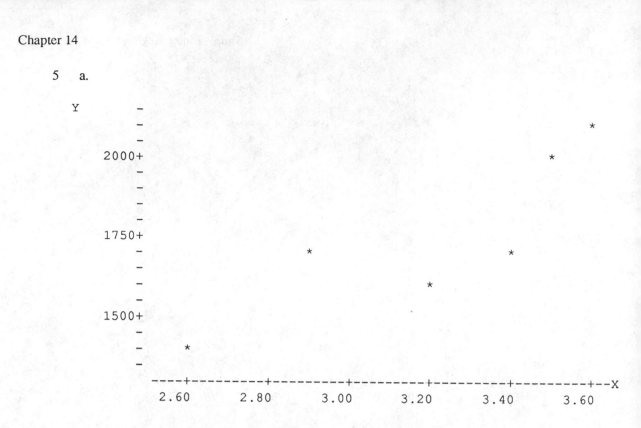

```
Y        -
         -
         -                                                              *
 2000+                                                         *
         -
         -
         -
         -
 1750+
         -                         *                    *
         -
         -                                    *
         -
 1500+
         -
         -             *
         -
       ----+---------+---------+---------+---------+---------+--X
         2.60      2.80      3.00      3.20      3.40      3.60
```

b. There appears to be a linear relationship between x and y.

c. Many different straight lines can be drawn to provide a linear approximation of the relationship between x and y; in part d we will determine the equation of a straight line that "best" represents the relationship according to the least squares criterion.

d. Summations needed to compute the slope and y-intercept are:

$$\sum x_i = 19.2 \quad \sum y_i = 10,500 \quad \sum x_i y_i = 34,030 \quad \sum x_i^2 = 62.18$$

$$b_1 = \frac{\sum x_i y_i - \left(\sum x_i \sum y_i\right)/n}{\sum x_i^2 - \left(\sum x_i\right)^2/n} = \frac{34,030 - (19.2)\,(10,500)\,/\,6}{62.18 - \left(19.2\right)^2/6} = 581.0811$$

$$b_0 = \bar{y} - b_1\bar{x} = 1,750 - (581.0811)(3.2) = -109.4595$$

$$\hat{y} = -109.46 + 581.08\,x$$

e. $\hat{y} = -109.46 + 581.08(3) = 1,633.78$

$$\hat{y} = -109.46 + 581.08(3.5) = 1,924.32$$

6   a.

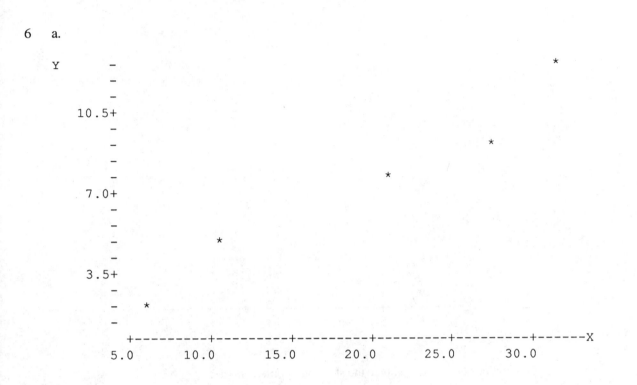

b.   There appears to be a linear relationship between x and y.

c.   Summations needed to compute the slope and y-intercept are:

$$\sum x_i = 96.7 \quad \sum y_i = 36.2 \quad \sum x_i y_i = 865.74 \quad \sum x_i^2 = 2337$$

$$b_1 = \frac{\sum x_i y_i - \left(\sum x_i \sum y_i\right)/n}{\sum x_i^2 - \left(\sum x_i\right)^2/n} = \frac{865.74 - (96.7)\,(36.2)/5}{2337 - (96.7)^2/5} = .3548$$

$$b_0 = \bar{y} - b_1 \bar{x} = 7.24 - (.3548)(19.34) = .3782$$

$$\hat{y} = .38 + .35\,x$$

d $\hat{y} = .38 + .35(25) = 9.13$

7.

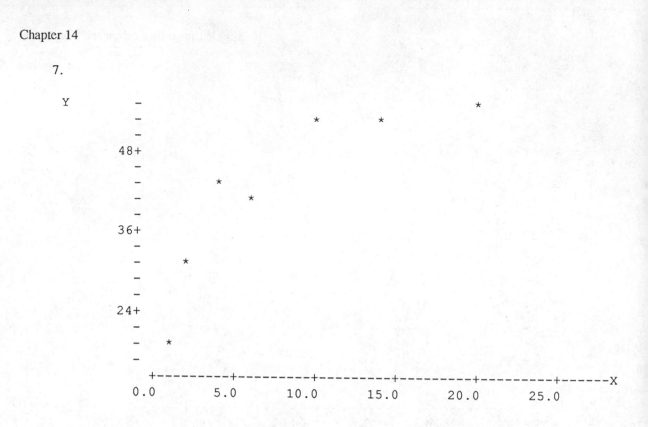

8.   a.   Summations needed to compute the slope and y-intercept are:

$$\sum x_i = 15 \quad \sum y_i = 1380 \quad \sum x_i y_i = 4895 \quad \sum x_i^2 = 55$$

$$b_1 = \frac{\sum x_i y_i - \left(\sum x_i \sum y_i\right)/n}{\sum x_i^2 - \left(\sum x_i\right)^2/n} = \frac{4895 - (15)(1380)/5}{55 - (15)^2/5} = 75.5$$

$$b_0 = \bar{y} - b_1\bar{x} = 276 - (75.5)(3) = 49.5$$

$$\hat{y} = 49.5 + 75.5\,x$$

   b $\hat{y} = 49.5 + 75.5(3) = 276$

9.   a.

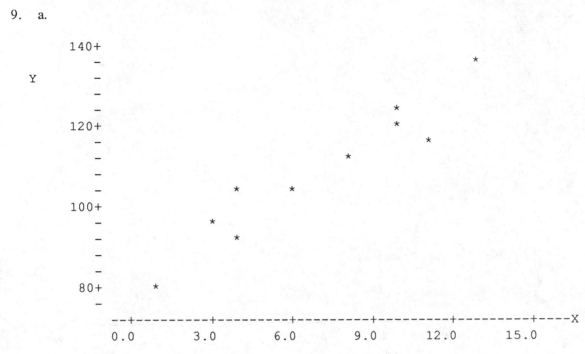

b.   Summations needed to compute the slope and y-intercept are:

$$\sum x_i = 70 \quad \sum y_i = 1080 \quad \sum x_i y_i = 8128 \quad \sum x_i^2 = 632$$

$$b_1 = \frac{\sum x_i y_i - \left(\sum x_i \sum y_i\right) / n}{\sum x_i^2 - \left(\sum x_i\right)^2 / n} = \frac{8128 - (70)(1080)/10}{632 - (70)^2/10} = 4$$

$$b_0 = \bar{y} - b_1\bar{x} = 108 - (4)(7) = 80$$

$$\hat{y} = 80 + 4\,x$$

c $\hat{y} = 80 + 4(9) = 116$

10. a.

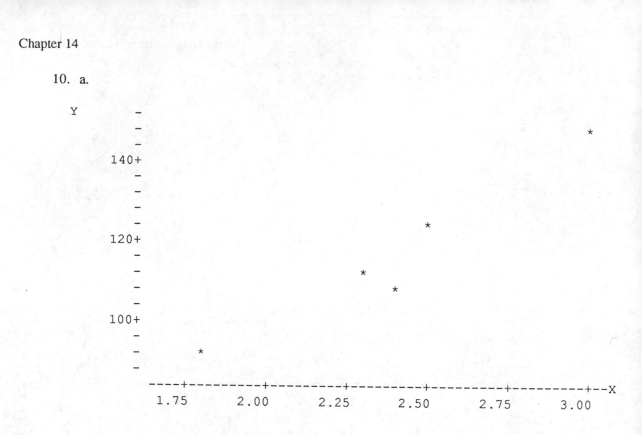

b. Many different straight lines can be drawn to provide a linear approximation of the relationship between x *and* y; in part d we will determine the equation of a straight line that "best" represents the relationship according to the least squares criterion.

c. There does appear to be a linear relationship between x and y.

d. To simplify the calculations we will work with square footagae measured in 1000s and price measured in 1000s. The summations needed to compute the slope and the y-intercept are:

$$\sum x_i = 12 \quad \sum y_i = 580 \quad \sum x_i y_i = 1425.8 \quad \sum x_i^2 = 29.54$$

$$b_1 = \frac{\sum x_i y_i - \left(\sum x_i \sum y_i\right)/n}{\sum x_i^2 - \left(\sum x_i\right)^2/n} = \frac{1425.8 - (12)\,(580)/5}{29.54 - \left(12\right)^2/5} = 45.6757$$

$$b_0 = \bar{y} - b_1\bar{x} = 116 - (45.6757)(2.4) = 6.3783$$

$$\hat{y} = 6.38 + 45.68\,x$$

c $\hat{y} = 6.38 + 45.68(2.7) = 129.716$
For a house with 2700 square feet the predicted selling price is $129,716

11. a.

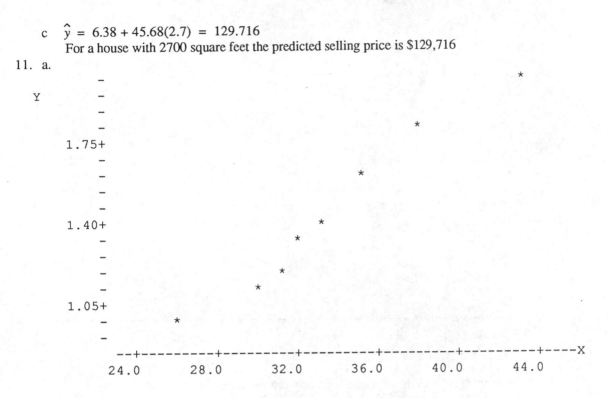

b. There appears to be a linear relationship between the variables.

c. The summations needed to compute the slope and the y-intercept are:

$$\sum x_i = 268 \quad \sum y_i = 11.4 \quad \sum x_i y_i = 394.4 \quad \sum x_i^2 = 9168$$

$$b_1 = \frac{\sum x_i y_i - \left(\sum x_i \sum y_i\right)/n}{\sum x_i^2 - \left(\sum x_i\right)^2/n} = \frac{394.4 - (268)(11.4)/8}{9168 - (268)^2/8} = .0658$$

$$b_0 = \bar{y} - b_1\bar{x} = 1.425 - (.0658)(33.5) = -.7793$$

$$\hat{y} = -.78 + .07x$$

c $\hat{y} = -.78 + .07(57) = 3.21$

The data provided ranges from $x = 26$ to $x = 43$; thus, the estimated regression equation is only applicable for predictions over this range. If we want to make a prediction outside this range we must keep in mind that the relationship between x and y may be considerable different.

12. a.

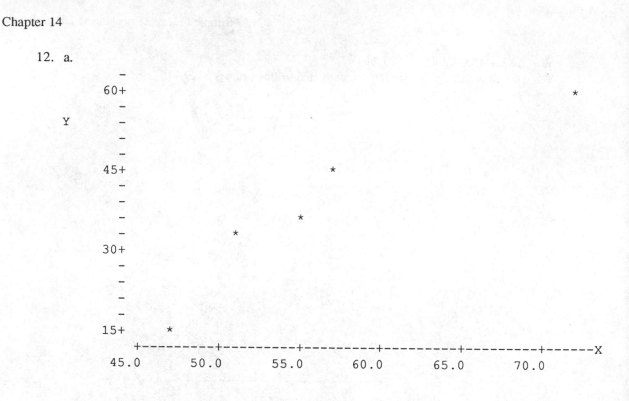

b. There appears to be a linear relationship between the variables.

c. The summations needed to compute the slope and the y-intercept are:

$$\sum x_i = 282 \quad \sum y_i = 191 \quad \sum x_i\, y_i = 11378 \quad \sum x_i^2 = 16268$$

$$b_1 = \frac{\sum x_i\, y_i - \left(\sum x_i \sum y_i\right)/n}{\sum x_i^2 - \left(\sum x_i\right)^2 / n} = \frac{11378 - (282)\,(191)/5}{16268 - (282)^2/5} = 1.6674$$

$$b_0 = \bar{y} - b_1 \bar{x} = 38.2 - (1.6674)(56.4) = -55.8414$$

d. $\hat{y} = -55.84 + 1.67\, x$

e. $\hat{y} = -55.84 + 1.67(55) = 44.36;\ 44.36\%$

The predicted value is almost identical to the observed value.

13. a.

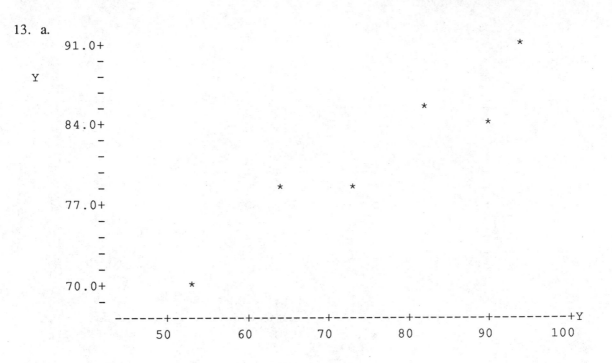

```
     91.0+                                                    *
        -
  Y     -
        -
        -                                             *
     84.0+                                                *
        -
        -
        -
        -                         *           *
     77.0+
        -
        -
        -
        -
     70.0+              *
        -
          ------+---------+---------+---------+---------+---------+---------+Y
              50        60        70        80        90       100
```

b. The summations needed to compute the slope and the y-intercept are:

$$\sum x_i = 456 \quad \sum y_i = 486 \quad \sum x_i y_i = 37480 \quad \sum x_i^2 = 35894$$

$$b_1 = \frac{\sum x_i y_i - \left(\sum x_i \sum y_i\right)/n}{\sum x_i^2 - \left(\sum x_i\right)^2/n} = \frac{37480 - (456)(486)/6}{35894 - (456)^2/6} = .4394$$

$$b_0 = \bar{y} - b_1\bar{x} = 81 - (.4394)(76) = 47.6056$$

$$\hat{y} = 47.61 + .44x$$

c $\hat{y} = 47.61 + .44(85) = 85.01$

A blood pressure of 85.01 is predicted.

14. a.

```
         _
 1400+                                                         *

Y        _

         _

         _
 1050+                                   *                              *
         _                           *     *         *
         _
         _
         _
  700+

         _

         _
                                              *
         _       *            *
  350+
         ----+---------+---------+---------+---------+---------+---------+--Y
            3.0       6.0       9.0      12.0      15.0      18.0
```

The two variables may be linearly related.

b. The summations needed to compute the slope and the y-intercept are:

$$\sum x_i = 102 \quad \sum y_i = 7760 \quad \sum x_i y_i = 97634 \quad \sum x_i^2 = 1320$$

$$b_1 = \frac{\sum x_i y_i - \left(\sum x_i \sum y_i\right)/n}{\sum x_i^2 - \left(\sum x_i\right)^2/n} = \frac{97,634 - (102)\,(7760)\,/\,9}{1320 - (102)^2\,/\,9} = 59.0691$$

$$b_0 = \bar{y} - b_1\bar{x} = 862.2222 - (59.0691)(11.3333) = 192.7744$$

$$\hat{y} = 192.77 + 59.07\,x$$

c $\hat{y} = 192.77 + 59.07(10) = 783.47$

The estimated cash flow is much greater than the observed value for Upjohn.

15. a. The estimated regression equation and the mean for the dependent variable are:

$$\hat{y}_i = .2 + 2.6\, x_i \text{ and } \bar{y} = 8$$

The sum of squares due to error and the total sum of squares are

$$SSE = \sum \left(y_i - \hat{y}_i \right)^2 = 12.40 \quad SST = \sum \left(y_i - \bar{y} \right)^2 = 80$$

Thus, SSR = SST - SSE = 80 - 12.4 = 67.6

b. r^2 = SSR/SST = 67.6/80 = .845

The least squares line provided a very good fit; 84.5% of the variability in y has been explained by the least squares line.

c. The summations needed to compute SSR and SST are:

$$\sum x_i = 15 \quad \sum y_i = 40 \quad \sum x_i y_i = 146 \quad \sum x_i^2 = 55 \quad \sum y_i^2 = 400$$

$$SSR = \frac{\left[\sum x_i y_i - \left(\sum x_i \sum y_i \right) / n \right]^2}{\sum x_i^2 - \left(\sum x_i \right)^2 / n} = \frac{\left[146 - (15)(40)/5 \right]^2}{55 - (15)^2 / 5} = 67.6$$

$$SST = \sum y_i^2 - \frac{\left(\sum y_i \right)^2}{n} = 400 - \frac{(40)^2}{5} = 80$$

16. a. The estimated regression equation and the mean for the dependent variable are:

$$\hat{y}_i = 30.33 - 1.88\, x_i \text{ and } \bar{y} = 23.2$$

The sum of squares due to error and the total sum of squares are

$$SSE = \sum \left(y_i - \hat{y}_i \right)^2 = 6.3325 \quad SST = \sum \left(y_i - \bar{y} \right)^2 = 114.80$$

Thus, SSR = SST - SSE = 114.80 - 6.33 = 108.47

b. r^2 = SSR/SST = 108.47/114.80 = .945

The least squares line provided an excellent fit; 94.5% of the variability in y has been explained by the least squares line.

c. The summations needed to compute SSR and SST are:

$$\sum x_i = 19 \quad \sum y_i = 116 \quad \sum x_i y_i = 383 \quad \sum x_i^2 = 103 \quad \sum y_i^2 = 2806$$

$$SSR = \frac{\left[\sum x_i y_i - \left(\sum x_i \sum y_i\right)/n\right]^2}{\sum x_i^2 - \left(\sum x_i\right)^2/n} = \frac{\left[383 - (19)(116)/5\right]^2}{103 - (19)^2/5} = 108.47$$

$$SST = \sum y_i^2 - \frac{\left(\sum y_i\right)^2}{n} = 2806 - \frac{(116)^2}{5} = 114.80$$

17. a. The estimated regression equation and the mean for the dependent variable are:

$$\hat{y}_i = .75 + .51 \, x_i \text{ and } \bar{y} = 3.4$$

The sum of squares due to error and the total sum of squares are

$$SSE = \sum \left(y_i - \hat{y}_i\right)^2 = 5.2983 \quad SST = \sum \left(y_i - \bar{y}\right)^2 = 11.20$$

Thus, SSR = SST - SSE = 11.20 - 5.30 = 5.90

b. r^2 = SSR/SST = 5.90/11.20 = .527

We see that 52.7% of the variability in y has been explained by the least squares line.

c. The summations needed to compute SSR and SST are:

$$\sum x_i = 26 \quad \sum y_i = 17 \quad \sum x_i y_i = 100 \quad \sum x_i^2 = 158 \quad \sum y_i^2 = 69$$

$$SSR = \frac{\left[\sum x_i y_i - \left(\sum x_i \sum y_i\right)/n\right]^2}{\sum x_i^2 - \left(\sum x_i\right)^2/n} = \frac{\left[100 - (26)(17)/5\right]^2}{158 - (17)^2/5} = 5.90$$

$$SST = \sum y_i^2 - \frac{\left(\sum y_i\right)^2}{n} = 69 - \frac{(17)^2}{5} = 11.20$$

18. a. The summations needed to compute SSR and SST are:

$$\sum x_i = 19.2 \quad \sum y_i = 10,500 \quad \sum x_i y_i = 34,030 \quad \sum x_i^2 = 62.18 \quad \sum y_i^2 = 18,710,000$$

$$SSR = \frac{\left[\sum x_i y_i - \left(\sum x_i \sum y_i\right)/n\right]^2}{\sum x_i^2 - \left(\sum x_i\right)^2/n} = \frac{[34{,}030 - (19.2)(10{,}500)/6]^2}{62.18 - (19.2)^2/6} = 249{,}864.86$$

$$SST = \sum y_i^2 - \frac{\left(\sum y_i\right)^2}{n} = 18{,}710{,}000 - \frac{(10{,}500)^2}{6} = 335{,}000$$

$SSE = SST - SSR = 335{,}000 - 249{,}864.86 = 85{,}135.14$

b. $r^2 = SSR/SST = 249{,}864.86/335{,}000 = .746$

We see that 74.6% of the variability in y has been explained by the least squares line.

19. The summations needed to compute SSR and SST are:

$$\sum x_i = 57 \quad \sum y_i = 294 \quad \sum x_i y_i = 2841 \quad \sum x_i^2 = 753 \quad \sum y_i^2 = 13{,}350$$

$$SSR = \frac{\left[\sum x_i y_i - \left(\sum x_i \sum y_i\right)/n\right]^2}{\sum x_i^2 - \left(\sum x_i\right)^2/n} = \frac{[2841 - (57)(294)/7]^2}{753 - (57)^2/7} = 691.72$$

$$SST = \sum y_i^2 - \frac{\left(\sum y_i\right)^2}{n} = 13{,}350 - \frac{(294)^2}{7} = 1002$$

$r^2 = SSR/SST = 691.72/1002 = .69$

We see that 69% of the variability in y has been explained by the least squares line. However, the curvature in the scatter diagram (see Exercise 7) suggests that a curvilinear modle may be more appropriate.

20. a. The summations needed in this problem are:

$$\sum x_i = 7.045 \quad \sum y_i = 367 \quad \sum x_i y_i = 552.250 \quad \sum x_i^2 = 9.500 \quad \sum y_i^2 = 34{,}529$$

$$b_1 = \frac{\sum x_i y_i - \left(\sum x_i \sum y_i\right)/n}{\sum x_i^2 - \left(\sum x_i\right)^2/n} = \frac{552.25 - (7.045)(367)/6}{9.500 - (7.045)^2/6} = 98.8039$$

$$b_0 = \bar{y} - b_1\bar{x} = 61.1667 - (98.8039)(1.1742) = -54.8488$$

$$\hat{y} = -54.85 + 98.80\,x$$

b. $\quad$ SSR = 11,987.97 $\quad\quad$ SST = 12,080.83 $\quad\quad r^2 = .992$

With $r^2 = .992$ we should feel comfortable using the model.

c. $\quad \hat{y} = -54.85 + 98.80(.941) = 38.13$ mgs.

21. a. $\quad$ The summations needed in this problem are:

$$\sum x_i = 76.3 \quad \sum y_i = 1753 \quad \sum x_i y_i = 16,342.1 \quad \sum x_i^2 = 770.67 \quad \sum y_i^2 = 389,993$$

$$b_1 = \frac{\sum x_i y_i - \left(\sum x_i \sum y_i\right)/n}{\sum x_i^2 - \left(\sum x_i\right)^2/n} = \frac{16342.1 - (76.3)(1753)/8}{770.67 - (76.3)^2/8} = -8.7791$$

$$b_0 = \bar{y} - b_1\bar{x} = 219.125 - (-8.7791)(9.5375) = 302.8557$$

$$\hat{y} = 302.86 - 8.78\,x$$

b. $\quad$ SSR = 3310.91 $\quad\quad$ SST = 5866.88 $\quad\quad r^2 = .564$

We see that 56.4% of the variability in y has been explained by the estimated regression equation.

22. a. $\quad s^2 = $ MSE $ = $ SSE $/(n - 2) = 12.4/3 = 4.133$

b. $\quad s = \sqrt{\text{MSE}} = \sqrt{4.133} = 2.033$

c. $\quad \sum x_i = 15 \quad\quad\quad\quad \sum x_i^2 = 55$

$$s_{b_1} = \frac{s}{\sqrt{\sum x_i^2 - \left(\sum x_i\right)^2/n}}$$

$$= \frac{2.033}{\sqrt{55 - (15)^2/5}} = .643$$

d. $\quad t = \dfrac{b_1 - B_1}{s_{b_1}} = \dfrac{2.6 - 0}{.643} = 4.04$

$t_{.025} = 3.182$ (3 degrees of freedom)

Since $t = 4.04 > t_{.05} = 3.182$ we reject H_0: $B_1 = 0$

e. $MSR = SSR / 1 = 67.6$

$F = MSR / MSE = 67.6 / 4.133 = 16.36$

$F_{.05} = 10.13$ (1 degree of freedom numerator and 3 denominator)

Since $F = 16.36 > F_{.05} = 10.13$ we reject H_0: $B_1 = 0$

23. a. $s^2 = MSE = SSE / (n - 2) = 6.33 / 3 = 2.11$

b. $s = \sqrt{MSE} = \sqrt{2.11} = 1.453$

c. $\sum x_i = 19$ $\qquad\qquad \sum x_i^2 = 103$

$$s_{b_1} = \frac{s}{\sqrt{\sum x_i^2 - \left(\sum x_i\right)^2 / n}}$$

$$= \frac{1.453}{\sqrt{103 - (19)^2 / 5}} = .262$$

d. $t = \dfrac{b_1 - B_1}{s_{b_1}} = \dfrac{-1.88 - 0}{.262} = -7.18$

$t_{.025} = 3.182$ (3 degrees of freedom)

Since $t = -7.18 < -t_{.05} = -3.182$ we reject H_0: $B_1 = 0$

e. $MSR = SSR / 1 = 108.47$

$F = MSR / MSE = 108.47 / 2.11 = 51.41$

$F_{.05} = 10.13$ (1 degree of freedom numerator and 3 denominator)

Since $F = 51.41 > F_{.05} = 10.13$ we reject H_0: $B_1 = 0$

24. a. $s^2 = MSE = SSE / (n - 2) = 5.30 / 3 = 1.77$

b. $s = \sqrt{MSE} = \sqrt{1.77} = 1.33$

c. $\sum x_i = 26$ $\qquad\qquad \sum x_i^2 = 158$

$$s_{b_1} = \frac{s}{\sqrt{\sum x_i^2 - \left(\sum x_i\right)^2 / n}}$$

$$= \frac{1.33}{\sqrt{158 - (26)^2 / 5}} = \frac{1.33}{\sqrt{22.8}} = .28$$

d. $\quad t = \dfrac{b_1 - B_1}{s_{b_1}} = \dfrac{.51 - 0}{.28} = 1.82$

$t_{.025} = 3.182$ (3 degrees of freedom)

Since $t = 1.82 < t_{.05} = 3.182$ we cannot reject H_0: $B_1 = 0$; x and y do not appear to be related.

25. a. $s^2 = \text{MSE} = \text{SSE} / (n - 2) = 85{,}135.14 / 4 = 21{,}283.79$

$s = \sqrt{\text{MSE}} = \sqrt{21{,}283.79} = 145.89$

$\sum x_i = 19.2 \qquad\qquad \sum x_i^2 = 62.18$

$$s_{b_1} = \frac{s}{\sqrt{\sum x_i^2 - \left(\sum x_i\right)^2 / n}}$$

$$= \frac{145.89}{\sqrt{62.18 - (19.2)^2 / 6}} = 169.59$$

$$t = \frac{b_1 - B_1}{s_{b_1}} = \frac{581.08 - 0}{169.59} = 3.43$$

$t_{.025} = 2.776$ (4 degrees of freedom)

Since $t = 3.43 > t_{.025} = 2.776$ we reject H_0: $B_1 = 0$

b. $\text{MSR} = \text{SSR} / 1 = 249{,}864.86 / 1 = 249.864.86$

$F = \text{MSR} / \text{MSE} = 249{,}864.86 / 21{,}283.79 = 11.74$

$F_{.05} = 7.71$ (1 degree of freedom numerator and 4 denominator)

Since $F = 11.74 > F_{.05} = 7.71$ we reject H_0: $B_1 = 0$

26. $\quad \sum x_i = 12 \qquad\qquad \sum y_i = 580 \qquad \sum x_i y_i = 1425.8$

$\sum x_i^2 = 29.54 \qquad\qquad \sum y_i^2 = 68{,}920$

$$SSR = \frac{\left[\sum x_i y_i - \left(\sum x_i \sum y_i\right)/n\right]^2}{\sum x_i^2 - \left(\sum x_i\right)^2 / n}$$

$$= \frac{[1425.8 - (12)(580)/5]^2}{29.54 - (12)^2/5} = 1543.84$$

$MSR = SSR / 1 = 1543.84 / 1 = 1543.84$

$$SST = \sum y_i^2 - \frac{\left(\sum y_i\right)^2}{n}$$

$$= 68,920 - \frac{(580)^2}{5} = 1640$$

$s^2 = MSE = SSE / (n - 2) = 96.16 / 3 = 32.05$

$F = MSR / MSE = 1543.84 / 32.05 = 48.17$

$F_{.01} = 34.12$ (1 degree of freedom numerator and 3 denominator)

Since $F = 48.17 > F_{.05} = 34.12$ we reject H_0: $B_1 = 0$.

Selling price and square footage are related.

27. $\sum x_i = 282$　　　　　　$\sum y_i = 191$　　$\sum x_i y_i = 11,378$

$\sum x_i^2 = 16,268$　　　　　$\sum y_i^2 = 8413$

$$SSR = \frac{\left[\sum x_i y_i - \left(\sum x_i \sum y_i\right)/n\right]^2}{\sum x_i^2 - \left(\sum x_i\right)^2 / n}$$

$$= \frac{[11,378 - (282)(191)/5]^2}{16,268 - (282)^2/5} = 1009.78$$

$MSR = SSR / 1 = 1009.78 / 1 = 1009.78$

$$SST = \sum y_i^2 - \frac{\left(\sum y_i\right)^2}{n}$$

$$= 8413 - \frac{(191)^2}{5} = 116.8$$

$SSE = SST - SSR = 1,116.8 - 1,009.78 = 107.02$

$MSE = SSE / (n - 2) = 107.02 / 3 = 35.67$

$F = MSR / MSE = 1,009.78 / 35.67 = 28.31$

$F_{.05} = 10.13$ (1 degree of freedom numerator and 3 denominator)

Since $F = 28.31 > F_{.05} = 10.13$ we reject H_0: $B_1 = 0$.

The percentage of management jobs held by women and the percentage of women employed are related.

28. $\sum x_i = 70$ $\sum y_i = 1,080$ $\sum x_i y_i = 8,128$

$\sum x_i^2 = 632$ $\sum y_i^2 = 119,082$

$$SSR = \frac{\left[\sum x_i y_i - \left(\sum x_i \sum y_i\right)/n\right]^2}{\sum x_i^2 - \left(\sum x_i\right)^2/n}$$

$$= \frac{[8.128 - (70)(1,080)/10]^2}{632 - (70)^2/10} = 2,272$$

MSR = SSR / 1 = 2,272

$$SST = \sum y_i^2 - \frac{\left(\sum y_i\right)^2}{n}$$

$$= 119,082 - \frac{(1,080)^2}{10} = 2,442$$

SSE = SST - SSR = 2,442 - 2,272 = 170

MSE = SSE / $(n - 2)$ = 170 / 8 = 21.25

F = MSR / MSE = 2,272 / 21.25 = 106.92

$F_{.05} = 5.32$ (1 degree of freedom numerator and 8 denominator)

Since $F = 106.92 > F_{.05} = 5.32$ we reject H_0: $B_1 = 0$.

Years of experience and sales are related.

29. SST = 12,080.83

SSR = 11,987.97

MSR = SSR / 1 = 11,987.97

SSE = SST - SSR = 12,080.83 - 11,987.97 = 92.86

MSE = SSE / $(n - 2)$ = 92.86 / 4 = 23.22

F = MSR / MSE = 11,987.97 / 23.22 = 516.28

$F_{.01}$ = 7.71 (1 degree of freedom numerator and 4 denominator)

Since F = 516.28 > $F_{.01}$ = 7.71 we reject H_0: B_1 = 0.

The absorbance readings are amount of protein present are related.

30. a. s = 2.033

$$\sum x_i = 15 \qquad\qquad \sum x_i^2 = 55$$

$$s_{\hat{y}_p} = s \sqrt{\frac{1}{n} + \frac{(x_p - \bar{x})^2}{\sum x_i^2 - \left(\sum x_i\right)^2 / n}}$$

$$= 2.033 \sqrt{\frac{1}{5} + \frac{(4-3)^2}{55 - (15)^2/5}} = 1.11$$

b. $\hat{y}$ = .2 + 2.6 x = .2 + 2.6 (4) = 10.6

$$\hat{y}_p \pm t_{\alpha/2} \, s_{\hat{y}_p}$$

10.6 $\pm$ 3.182 (1.11) = 10.6 $\pm$ 3.53

or 7.07 to 14.13

c.
$$s_{ind} = s \sqrt{1 + \frac{1}{n} + \frac{(x_p - \bar{x})^2}{\sum x_i^2 - \left(\sum x_i\right)^2 / n}}$$

$$= 2.033 \sqrt{1 + \frac{1}{5} + \frac{(4-3)^2}{55 - (15)^2/5}} = 2.32$$

d. $\hat{y}_p \pm t_{\alpha/2} \, s_{ind}$

10.6 $\pm$ 3.182 (2.32) = 10.6 $\pm$ 7.38

or 3.22 to 17.98

31. a. s = 1.453

$$\sum x_i = 19 \qquad\qquad \sum x_i^2 = 103$$

$$s_{\hat{y}_p} = s \sqrt{\frac{1}{n} + \frac{(x_p - \bar{x})^2}{\sum x_i^2 - (\sum x_i)^2 / n}}$$

$$= 1.453 \sqrt{\frac{1}{5} + \frac{(3 - 3.8)^2}{103 - (19)^2 / 5}} = .68$$

b. $\hat{y} = 30.33 - 1.88 \, x = 30.33 - 1.88 \, (3)) = 24.69$

$$\hat{y}_p \pm t_{\alpha/2} \, s_{\hat{y}_p}$$

$24.69 \pm 3.182 \, (68) = 24.69 \pm 2.16$

or 22.53 to 26.85

c.

$$s_{ind} = s \sqrt{1 + \frac{1}{n} + \frac{(x_p - \bar{x})^2}{\sum x_i^2 - (\sum x_i)^2 / n}}$$

$$= 1.453 \sqrt{1 + \frac{1}{5} + \frac{(3 - 3.8)^2}{103 - (19)^2 / 5}} = 1.61$$

$$\hat{y}_p \pm t_{\alpha/2} \, s_{ind}$$

$24.69 \pm 3.182 \, (1.61) = 24.69 \pm 5.12$

or 19.57 to 29.81

32. $s = 1.33$

$$\sum x_i = 26 \qquad\qquad \sum x_i^2 = 158$$

$$s_{\hat{y}_p} = s \sqrt{\frac{1}{n} + \frac{(x_p - \bar{x})^2}{\sum x_i^2 - (\sum x_i)^2 / n}}$$

$$= 1.33 \sqrt{\frac{1}{5} + \frac{(3 - 5.2)^2}{158 - (26)^2 / 5}} = .85$$

$\hat{y} = .75 + .51 \, x = .75 + .51 \, (3) = 2.28$

$$\hat{y}_p \pm t_{\alpha/2} \, s_{\hat{y}_p}$$

$2.28 \pm 3.182 \, (.85) = 2.28 \pm 2.70$

or -.40 to 4.98

$$s_{ind} = s \sqrt{1 + \frac{1}{n} + \frac{(x_p - \bar{x})^2}{\sum x_i^2 - \left(\sum x_i\right)^2 / n}}$$

$$= 1.33 \sqrt{1 + \frac{1}{5} + \frac{(3 - 5.2)^2}{158 - (26)^2 / 5}} = 1.58$$

$$\hat{y}_p \pm t_{\alpha/2} \, s_{ind}$$

$$2.28 \pm 3.182 (1.58) = 2.28 \pm 5.03$$

or -2.27 to 7.31

33. $\quad s = \sqrt{MSE} = \sqrt{35.67} = 5.97$

$$\sum x_i = 282 \qquad\qquad \sum x_i^2 = 16,268$$

$$\hat{y} = -55.84 + 1.67 (60) = 44.36$$

$$s_{\hat{y}_p} = s \sqrt{\frac{1}{n} + \frac{(x_p - \bar{x})^2}{\sum x_i^2 - \left(\sum x_i\right)^2 / n}}$$

$$= 5.97 \sqrt{\frac{1}{5} + \frac{(60 - 56.4)^2}{16.268 - (282)^2 / 5}} = 2.90$$

$$\hat{y}_p \pm t_{\alpha/2} \, s_{\hat{y}_p}$$

$$44.36 \pm 3.182 (2.90) = 44.36 \pm 9.23$$

or 35.13% to 53.59%

34. $\quad s = 145.89$

$$\sum x_i = 19.2 \qquad\qquad \sum x_i^2 = 62.18$$

$$\hat{y} = -109.46 + 581.08 \, (x) = -109.46 + 581.08 \, (3) = 1,633.78$$

$$s_{\hat{y}_p} = s \sqrt{\frac{1}{n} + \frac{(x_p - \bar{x})^2}{\sum x_i^2 - \left(\sum x_i\right)^2 / n}}$$

$$= 145.89 \sqrt{\frac{1}{6} + \frac{(3 - 3.2)^2}{62.18 - (19.2)^2 / 6}} = 68.54$$

$$\hat{y}_p \pm t_{\alpha/2} \, s_{\hat{y}_p}$$

$$1{,}633.78 \pm 2.776 \, (68.54) = 1{,}633.78 \pm 190.27$$

or $1,443.51 to $1,824.05

35. $s = \sqrt{MSE} = \sqrt{32.05} = 5.66$

$$\sum x_i = 12 \qquad\qquad \sum x_i^2 = 29.54$$

$$\hat{y} = 6.38 + .45.68 \, (2.2) = 106.88$$

$$s_{\hat{y}_p} = s \sqrt{\frac{1}{n} + \frac{(x_p - \bar{x})^2}{\sum x_i^2 - \left(\sum x_i\right)^2 / n}}$$

$$= 5.66 \sqrt{\frac{1}{5} + \frac{(2.2 - 2.4)^2}{29.54 - (12)^2 / 5}} = 2.85$$

$$\hat{y}_p \pm t_{\alpha/2} \, s_{\hat{y}_p}$$

$$106.88 \pm 3.182 \, (2.85) = 106.88 \pm 9.07$$

or $97.810 to $115,950

36. $s = 145.89$

$$\sum x_i = 19.2 \qquad\qquad \sum x_i^2 = 62.18$$

$$\hat{y} = -109.46 + 581.08 \, (x) = -109.46 + 581.08 \, (3) = 1{,}633.78$$

$$s_{ind} = s \sqrt{1 + \frac{1}{n} + \frac{(x_p - \bar{x})^2}{\sum x_i^2 - \left(\sum x_i\right)^2 / n}}$$

$$= 145.89 \sqrt{1 + \frac{1}{6} + \frac{(3 - 3.2)^2}{62.18 - (19.2)^2 / 6}} = 161.19$$

$$\hat{y}_p \pm t_{\alpha/2}\, s_{\text{ind}}$$

$$1{,}633.78 \pm 2.776\,(161.19) = 1{,}633.78 \pm 447.46$$

or $1,186.32 to $2,081.24

37. $s = \sqrt{\text{MSE}} = 5.66$

$$\sum x_i = 12 \qquad\qquad \sum x_i^2 = 29.54$$

$$\hat{y} = 6.38 + 45.68\,x = 6.38 + 45.68\,(2.8) = 134.28$$

$$s_{\text{ind}} = s\sqrt{1 + \frac{1}{n} + \frac{(x_p - \bar{x})^2}{\sum x_i^2 - \left(\sum x_i\right)^2 / n}}$$

$$= 5.66\sqrt{1 + \frac{1}{5} + \frac{(2.8 - 2.4)^2}{29.54 - (12)^2 / 5}} = 6.74$$

$$\hat{y}_p \pm t_{\alpha/2}\, s_{\text{ind}}$$

$$134.28 \pm 3.182\,(6.74) = 134.28 \pm 21.45$$

or $112,830 to $155,730

38. a. $\sum x_i = 420 \qquad\qquad \sum y_i = 270 \qquad \sum x_i y_i = 10{,}865$

$$\sum x_i^2 = 19{,}300 \qquad\qquad \sum y_i^2 = 7454$$

$$b_1 = \frac{\sum x_i y_i - \left(\sum x_i \sum y_i\right)/n}{\sum x_i^2 - \left(\sum x_i\right)^2 / n}$$

$$= \frac{10{,}865 - (420)\,(270)/10}{19{,}300 - (420)^2/10} = -.2861$$

$$b_0 = 27 - (-.2861)\,(42) = 39.0162$$

$$\hat{y} = 39.0162 - .2861\,x$$

b.

$$SSR = \frac{\left[\sum x_i y_i - \left(\sum x_i \sum y_i\right)/n\right]^2}{\sum x_i^2 - \left(\sum x_i\right)^2/n}$$

$$= \frac{[10,865 - (420)\,(270)\,/\,10]^2}{19,300 - (420)^2\,/\,10} = 135.92$$

$$SST = \sum y_i^2 - \frac{\left(\sum y_i\right)^2}{n}$$

$$= 7454 - \frac{(270)^2}{10} = 164$$

$$SSE = 164 - 135.92 = 28.08$$

$$MSE = SSE\,/\,(n-2) = 28.08\,/\,8 = 3.51$$

$$F = MSR\,/\,MSE = 135.92\,/\,3.51 = 38.72$$

$F_{.05} = 5.32$ (1 degree of freedom numerator and 8 denominator)

Since $F = 38.72 > F_{.05} = 5.32$ we reject H_0: $B_1 = 0$.

Mileage and driving speed are related.

c. $r^2 = SSR\,/\,SST = 135.92\,/\,164 = .829$

82.9% of the variability in y has been explained by the estimates regression line; a good fit.

d. $\hat{y} = 39.0162 - .2861\,(50) = 24.71$

$$s = \sqrt{MSE} = \sqrt{3.51} = 1.87$$

$$s_{\hat{y}_p} = s\sqrt{\frac{1}{n} + \frac{(x_p - \bar{x})^2}{\sum x_i^2 - \left(\sum x_i\right)^2/n}}$$

$$= 1.87\sqrt{\frac{1}{10} + \frac{(50-42)^2}{19,300 - (420)^2/10}} = .70$$

$$\hat{y}_p \pm t_{\alpha/2}\, s_{\hat{y}_p}$$

$$24.71 \pm 2.306\,(.70) = 24.71 \pm 1.61$$

or 23.10 to 26.32

e.

$$s_{ind} = s \sqrt{1 + \frac{1}{n} + \frac{(x_p - \bar{x})^2}{\sum x_i^2 - (\sum x_i)^2 / n}}$$

$$= 1.87 \sqrt{1 + \frac{1}{10} + \frac{(50 - 42)^2}{19,300 - (420)^2 / 10}} = 2.00$$

$$\hat{y}_p \pm t_{\alpha/2} \, s_{ind}$$

$24.71 \pm 2.306 \, (2.00) = 24.71 \pm 4.61$

or 20.10 to 29.32

39.

Source of Variation	Sum of Squares	Degrees of Freedom	Mean Square	F
Regression	67.6	1	67.6	16.36
Error	12.4	3	4.133	
Total	80.0	4		

40.

Source of Variation	Sum of Squares	Degrees of Freedom	Mean Square	F
Regression	108.47	1	108.47	51.41
Error	6.33	3	2.11	
Total	114.80	5		

41.

Source of Variation	Sum of Squares	Degrees of Freedom	Mean Square	F
Regression	5.9	1	5.9	3.33
Error	5.3	3	1.77	
Total	11.2	5		

42. a. 9

b. $\hat{y} = 20.0 + 7.21 \, x$

c. 1.3626

d. $SSE = SST - SSR = 51,984.1 - 41,587.3 = 10,396.8$

$MSE = 10,396.8 / 7 = 1,485.3$

$F = MSR / MSE = 41,587.3 / 1,485.3 = 28.00$

$F_{.05} = 5.59$ (1 degree of freedom numerator and 7 denominator)

Since $F = 28 > F_{.05} = 5.59$ we reject $H_0: B_1 = 0$.

e. $\hat{y} = 20.0 + 7.21 (50) = 380.5$ or $\$380,500$

43. a. $\hat{y} = 6.1092 + .8951 x$

   b. $t = \dfrac{b_1 - B_1}{s_{b_1}} = \dfrac{.8951 - 0}{.149} = 6.01$

   $t_{.025} = 2.306$ (1 degree of freedom numerator and 8 denominator)

   Since $t = 6.01 > t_{.025} = 2.306$ we reject H_0: $B_1 = 0$

   c. $\hat{y} = 6.1092 + .8951 (25) = 28.49$ or $\$28.49$ per month

44. a. $\hat{y} = 80.0 + 50.0 x$

   b. 30

   c. $F = MSR / MSE = 6828.6 / 82.1 = 83.17$

   $F_{.05} = 4.20$ (1 degree of freedom numerator and 28 denominator)

   Since $F = 87.17 > F_{.05} = 4.20$ we reject H_0: $B_1 = 0$.

   Branch office sales are related to the salespersons.

   d. $\hat{y} = 80 + 50 (12) = 680$ or $\$680,000$

45. a. The scatter diagram is shown below:

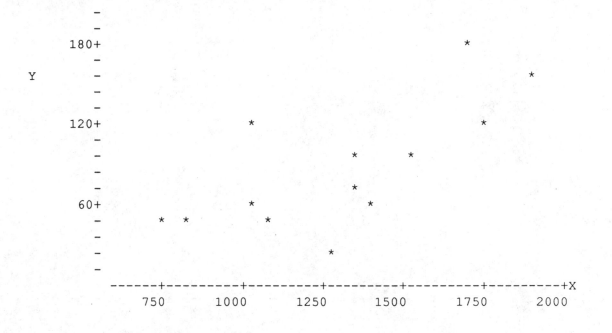

b. Yes, there appears to ba a relationship between these two variables

c. $\hat{y}$ = -33.88 + .09253 x

Note: the estimated regression line was developing using MINITAB. A portion of the regression output is shown below.

```
Analysis of Variance

SOURCE        DF           SS           MS          F          p
Regression    1          13209        13209      11.02      0.007
Error         11         13184        1199
Total         12         26393
```

d. $F_{.05}$ = 4.84 (1 degree of freedom numerator and 11 denominator)

Since F = 11.02 > $F_{.05}$ = 4.84 we reject H_0: B_1 = 0.

Alternatively, since the p-value of .007 is less than α = .05, we can reject H_0: B_1 = 0.

e. The 95% prediction interval is 24.90 to 184.93. With this wide a prediction interval, the use of the model for prediction is very limited.

46.

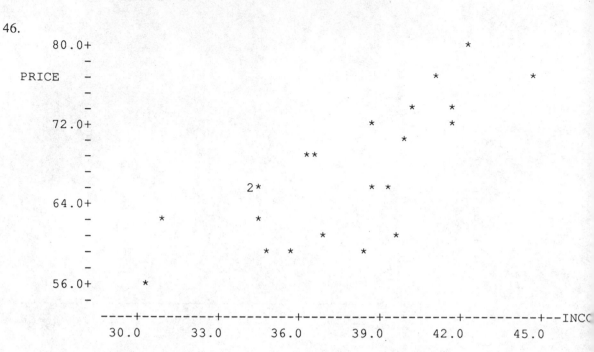

```
       80.0+                                                    *
           -
PRICE      -                                        *              *
           -
           -                                      *       *
       72.0+                                  *       *
           -                                      *
           -                        **
           -
           -              2*                *  *
       64.0+
           -        *              *
           -                             *        *
           -                      *   *        *
           -
       56.0+     *
           -
           ----+---------+---------+---------+---------+---------+---------+--INCC
              30.0      33.0      36.0      39.0      42.0      45.0
```

b. Yes, there does appear to be a relationship between these two variables.

Note: the MINITAB regression output for these data is shown below

```
The regression equation is
PRICE = 17.3 + 1.32 INCOME

Predictor          Coef        Stdev      t-ratio          p
Constant          17.25        10.11         1.71      0.103
INCOME           1.3192       0.2673         4.93      0.000

s = 4.621          R-sq = 53.7%        R-sq(adj) = 51.5%

Analysis of Variance

SOURCE          DF           SS           MS           F          p
Regression       1       519.98       519.98       24.35      0.000
Error           21       448.50        21.36
Total           22       968.48

        Fit   Stdev.Fit          95% C.I.            95% P.I.
     63.421        1.193    ( 60.940, 65.903)   ( 53.493, 73.349)
```

c. $\hat{y}$ 17.3 + 1.32 x

d. Since the p-value corresponding to the F test (0.000) is less than α = .05, we reject H_0: $B_1 = 0$.

e. r^2 = .537; since only 53.7% of the variability in y has been explained by the estimated regression equation, the fit is not very good.

f. The 95% confidence interval is 60.940 to 65.903 or $60,940 to $65,903

g. The 95% prediction interval for Elmira, NY is 53.493 to 65.903 or $53,493 to $65,903.

47. a. $\sum x_i$ = 70 $\sum y_i$ = 76 $\sum x_i y_i$ = 1264 $\sum x_i^2$ = 1106

$$b_1 = \frac{\sum x_i y_i - \left(\sum x_i \sum y_i\right)/n}{\sum x_i^2 - \left(\sum x_i\right)^2/n}$$

$$= \frac{1264 - (70)(65)/5}{1106 - (70)^2/5} = 1.5873$$

b_0 = 15.2 - 1.5873 (14) = -7.0222

$\hat{y}$ = -7.02 + 1.59 x

b. The residuals are 3.48, -2.47, -4.83, -1.60, and 5.22

c.

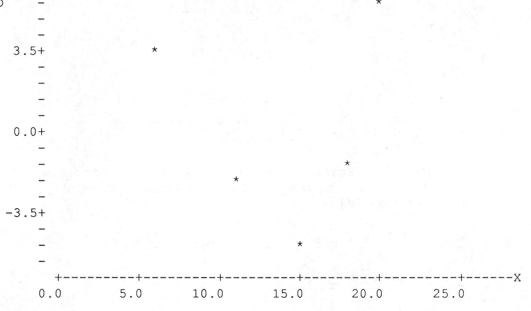

With only 5 observations it is difficult to determine if the assumptions are satisfied; however, the plot does suggest curvature in the residuals which would indicate that the error team assumptions are not satisfied. The scatter diagram for these data also indicates that the underlying relationship between x and y may be curvilinear.

d. $s^2 = 23.78$

$$h_i = \frac{1}{n} + \frac{(x_i - \bar{x})^2}{\sum x_i^2 - (\sum x_i)^2 / n}$$

$$= \frac{1}{5} + \frac{(x_i - 14)^2}{1106 - (70)^2 / 5} = \frac{1}{5} + \frac{(x_i - 14)^2}{126}$$

The standardized residuals are: 1.32, -.59, -1.11, -.40, 1.49

e.

```
            -
            -                                                        *
STDRESID-
            -         *
            -
       1.0+
    •       -
            -
            -                                       •
            -
            -
       0.0+
            -
            -                                                   *
            -                          *
            -
            -
      -1.0+
            -                                  *
            -
            -
            +---------+---------+---------+---------+---------+------YHAT
           0.0       5.0      10.0      15.0      20.0      25.0
```

The plot of the standardized residuals has the same shape as the original residual plot. As stated in part c, the curvature observed indicates that the assumptions regarding the error term may not be satisfied.

48. a. $\sum x_i = 52 \qquad \sum y_i = 54 \qquad \sum x_i y_i = 341 \qquad \sum x_i^2 = 346$

$$b_1 = \frac{\sum x_i y_i - (\sum x_i \sum y_i) / n}{\sum x_i^2 - (\sum x_i)^2 / n}$$

$$= \frac{341 - (52)(54)/9}{346 - (52)^2/9} = .6366$$

$b_0 = 6 - (.6366)(5.7778) = 2.3219$

$\hat{y} = 2.32 + .64\,x$

b.

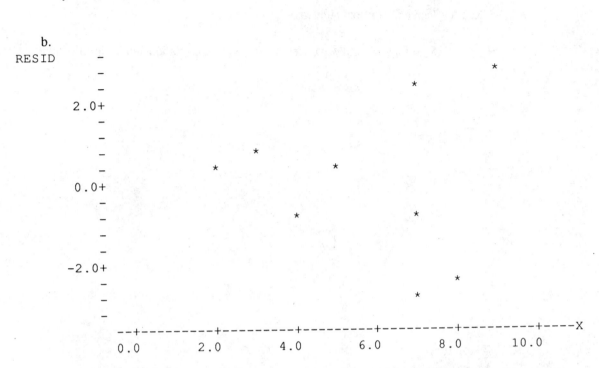

The assumption that the variance is the same for all values of x is questionable. The variance appears to increase for larger values of x.

49. $\sum x_i = 57 \qquad \sum y_i = 294 \qquad \sum x_i\, y_i = 2841$

$\sum x_i^2 = 753 \qquad \sum y_i^2 = 13,350$

$$b_1 = \frac{\sum x_i\, y_i - \left(\sum x_i \sum y_i\right)/n}{\sum x_i^2 - \left(\sum x_i\right)^2/n}$$

$$= \frac{2841 - (57)(294)/7}{753 - (57)^2/7} = \frac{447}{288.857} = 1.5475$$

$b_0 = 42 - (1.5475)(8.1429) = 29,3989$

$\hat{y} = 29.40 + 1.55\,x$

b. From Exercise 19 we have SSR = 691.72 and SST = 1002. Therefore SSE = 1002 - 691.72 = 310.28

$$F = \frac{MSR}{MSE} = \frac{691.72}{310.28 \, / \, 5} = \frac{691.72}{62,0554} = 11.15$$

$F_{.05} = 6.61$ (1 degree of freedom numerator and 5 denominator)

Since $F = 11.15 > F_{.05} = 6.61$ we reject $H_0: B_1 = 0$; the relationship is significant at the .05 level

c.

```
       -                 *
   7.0+                                 *
       -
RESID  -
       -
       -           *           *
   0.0+      *
       -
       -
       -
       -
  -7.0+                                         *
       -
       -
       -
       -   *
 -14.0+
      --+---------+---------+---------+---------+---------+----YHAT
        30.0      36.0      42.0      48.0      54.0      60.0
```

d. The residual plot here leads us to question the assumption of a linear relationship between x and y. Even though the relationship is significant at the $\alpha = .05$ level, it would be extremely dangerous to extrapolate beyond the range of the data. (e.g. $x > 20$).

50. From the solution to Exercise 9 we know that $\hat{y} = 80 + 4x$

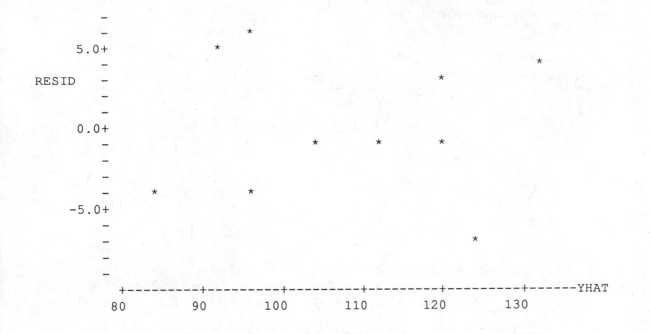

b. The assumptions concerning the error terms appear reasonable.

51. a. Using MINITAB we obtained thee estimated regression equation $\hat{y} = 343 + .051\ x$.

    b. The standardized residuals are: 2.52, .43, -.86, .53, -.59, -.85, -.62, -.25, -.05.

    c. The assumptions concerning the error term should be questioned. Note the large standardized residual corresponding to $x = 9500$; there is also an unusual trend in the standardized residuals.

52. a. The MINITAB output is shown below:

```
The regression equation is
Y = 66.1 + 0.402 X

Predictor          Coef        Stdev      t-ratio          p
Constant          66.10        32.06         2.06      0.094
X                0.4023       0.2276         1.77      0.137

s = 12.62        R-sq = 38.5%      R-sq(adj) = 26.1%

Analysis of Variance

SOURCE          DF            SS            MS          F          p
Regression       1         497.2         497.2       3.12      0.137
Error            5         795.7         159.1
Total            6        1292.9

Unusual Observations
Obs.        X            Y         Fit Stdev.Fit   Residual    St.Resid
  1       135       145.00      120.42      4.87      24.58       2.11R

R denotes an obs. with a large st. resid.
```

The standardized residuals are: 2.11, -1.08, .14, -.38, -.78, -.04, -.41
The first observation appears to be an outlier since it has a large standardized residual.

b.
```
      2.4+
         -                                    *
STDRESID-
         -
         -
      1.2+
         -
         -
         -
         -                   *
      0.0+                                              *
         -
         -         *                    *
         -                                                        *
         -
     -1.2+    *
         -
           --+---------+---------+---------+---------+---------+----YHA
          110.0     115.0     120.0     125.0     130.0     135.0
```

The standardized residual plot indicates that the observation $x = 135, y = 145$ may be an outlier;

note that this observation has a standardized residual of 2.11.

c.   The scatter diagram is shown below

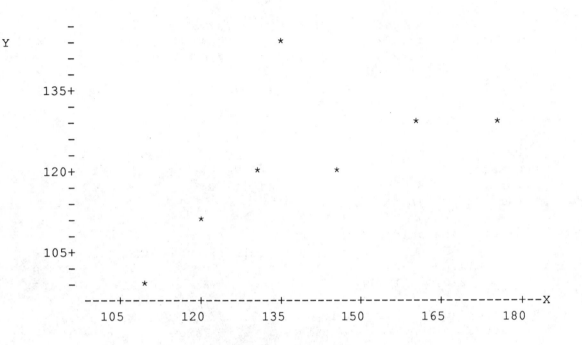

The scatter diagram also indicates that the observation $x = 135, y = 145$ may be an outlier; the implication is that for simple linear regression an outlier can be identified by looking at the scatter diagram.

53. a. The Minitab output is shown below:

```
The regression equation is
Y = 13.0 + 0.425 X

Predictor          Coef        Stdev      t-ratio          p
Constant         13.002        2.396         5.43      0.002
X                0.4248       0.2116         2.01      0.091

s = 3.181         R-sq = 40.2%       R-sq(adj) = 30.2%

Analysis of Variance

SOURCE           DF            SS           MS          F          p
Regression        1         40.78        40.78       4.03      0.091
Error             6         60.72        10.12
Total             7        101.50

Unusual Observations
Obs.       X            Y        Fit  Stdev.Fit   Residual   St.Resid
  7      12.0        24.00      18.10      1.20       5.90      2.00R
  8      22.0        19.00      22.35      2.78      -3.35     -2.16RX

R denotes an obs. with a large st. resid.
X denotes an obs. whose X value gives it large influence.
```

The standardized residuals are: -1.00, -.41, .01, -.48, .25, .65, -2.00, -2.16

The last two observations in the data set appear to be outliers since the standardized residuals for these observations are 2.00 and -2.16, respectively.

b. Using MINITAB, we obtained the following leverage values:

.28, .24, .16, .14, .13, .14, .14, .76

MINITAB identifies an observation as having high leverage if $h_i > 6/n$; for these data, $6/n = 6/8 = .75$. Since the leverage for the observation $x = 22, y = 19$ is .76, MINITAB would identify observation 8 as a high leverage point. Thus, we conclude that observation 8 is an influential observation.

c.

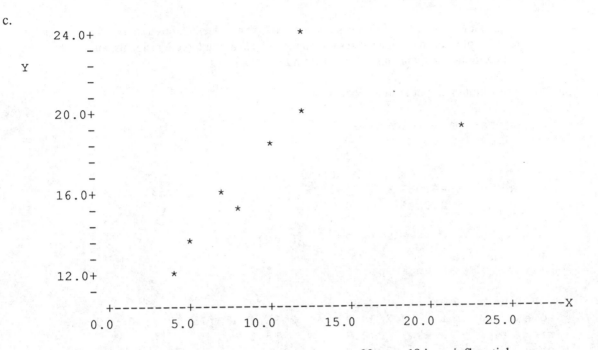

The scatter diagram indicates that the observation $x = 22, y = 19$ is an influential observation.

54. b. The Minitab output is shown below:

```
The regression equation is
Y = - 0.230 + 0.0490 X


Predictor         Coef        Stdev      t-ratio         p
Constant       -0.2303       0.1138       -2.02       0.078
X             0.048987     0.002769       17.69       0.000


s = 0.1086      R-sq = 97.5%      R-sq(adj) = 97.2%


Analysis of Variance


SOURCE         DF         SS          MS         F         p
Regression      1     3.6946      3.6946    313.04     0.000
Error           8     0.0944      0.0118
Total           9     3.7890


Unusual Observations
Obs.        X           Y       Fit Stdev.Fit   Residual   St.Resid
  10     67.0      3.0000    3.0518    0.0843    -0.0518      -0.76 X


X denotes an obs. whose X value gives it large influence.
```

Note that MINITAB identifies observation a 10 as an influential observation. The standardized residual plot for theses data also shows a very unusual trend in the residuals, an indication that the assumptions for Σ may not be satisfied for these data.

55. b. The Minitab output is shown below:

```
The regression equation is
Y = - 9.04 + 2.03 X

Predictor        Coef         Stdev     t-ratio          p
Constant       -9.037         9.108       -0.99      0.331
X               2.0348        0.2337       8.71      0.000

s = 5.787        R-sq = 76.7%      R-sq(adj) = 75.7%

Analysis of Variance

SOURCE          DF            SS            MS          F          p
Regression       1         2538.9        2538.9      75.81      0.000
Error           23          770.3         33.5
Total           24         3309.1

Unusual Observations
Obs.         X            Y         Fit Stdev.Fit   Residual    St.Resid
  16       52.9       111.00       98.60      3.52      12.40       2.70RX

R denotes an obs. with a large st. resid.
X denotes an obs. whose X value gives it large influence.
```

MINITAB identifies observation 16 as a potential outlier (standardized residual = 2.70 > 2) and an influential observation.

56. b.   The Minitab output is shown below:

```
The regression equation is
Y = - 10.9 + 1.04 X

Predictor         Coef         Stdev      t-ratio           p
Constant       -10.871         3.692        -2.94       0.015
X              1.04344       0.04948        21.09       0.000

s = 1.943        R-sq = 97.8%      R-sq(adj) = 97.6%

Analysis of Variance

SOURCE          DF            SS            MS           F           p
Regression       1        1679.2        1679.2      444.74       0.000
Error           10          37.8           3.8
Total           11        1716.9

Unusual Observations
Obs.          X            Y         Fit Stdev.Fit   Residual    St.Resid
 10        75.0       72.000      67.388     0.564      4.612       2.48R

R denotes an obs. with a large st. resid.
```

MINITAB identifies observation 10 as a potential outlier. Visual support for this conclusion is provided by the standardized residual plot as well as the scatter diagram.

57. a.

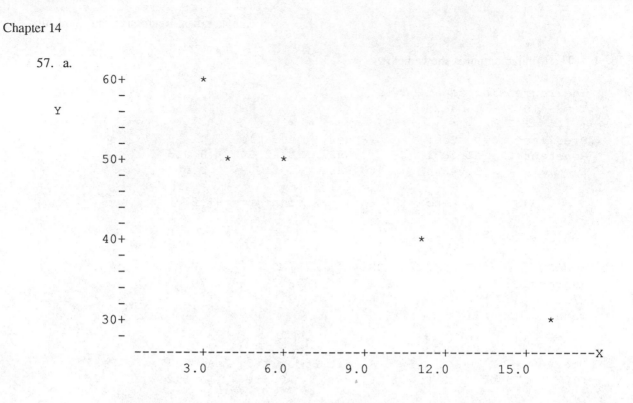

b. There appears to be a negative linear relationship between x and y; that is, as x increase the value of y appears to decrease.

c.

$$s_{xy} = \frac{\sum (x_i - \bar{x})(y_i - \bar{y})}{n - 1} = \frac{-240}{4} = -60$$

The sample covariance is indicative of a negative linear association between x and y.

d. $r_{xy} = \dfrac{-60}{(5.43)(11.40)} = \dfrac{-60}{61.90} = -.97$

The sample correlation coefficient of -.97 is indicative of a reasonably strong negative linear relationship.

58. a.

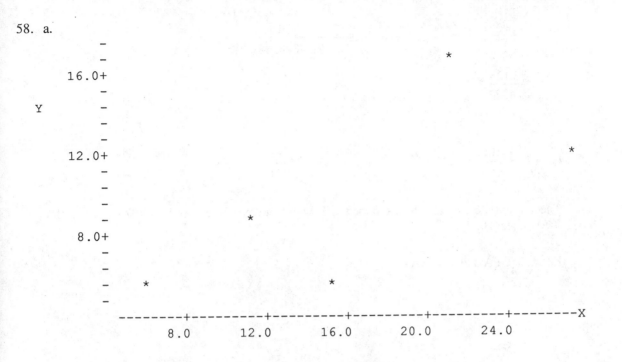

b.   There appears to ba a linear relationship between x and y.

c. $\sum x_i = 80$ $\sum y_i = 50$ $\sum x_i^2 = 1552$

   $\sum y_i^2 = 586$ $\sum (x_i - \bar{x})(y_i - \bar{y}) = 106$

   $\bar{x} = 16$ $\bar{y} = 10$ $s_x = 8.25$ $s_y = 4.64$

   $s_{xy} = \dfrac{106}{4} = 26.5$

d. $r_{xy} = \dfrac{s_{xy}}{s_x \, s_y} = \dfrac{26.5}{(8.25)(4.64)} = .69$

   The sample correlation coefficient provides support for a positive linear relationship between x and y.

59. $\sum x_i = 47$ $\sum y_i = 55$ $\sum x_i y_i = 285$

   $\sum x_i^2 = 311$ $\sum y_i^2 = 425$

$$r = \frac{285 - (47)(55)/8}{\sqrt{311 - (47)^2/8}\ \sqrt{425 - (55)^2/8}} = \frac{-38.125}{\sqrt{34.875}\ \sqrt{46.875}}$$

$$= \frac{-38.125}{40.4322}$$

$$= -.94$$

b. $r_{xy}\sqrt{\dfrac{n-1}{1-r_{xy}^2}} = -.94\sqrt{\dfrac{8-2}{1-(-.94)^2}} = -.94\sqrt{\dfrac{6}{.1164}} = -6.75$

The appropriate critical value from the t table with 6 degree of freedom is -3.707. Since -6.75 < -3.707 reject H_0.

60. a. Let x = GPA and y = SAT

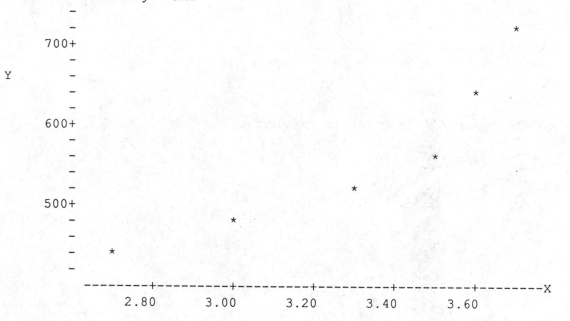

b. Yes, it appears that the relationship between GPA and the SAT score can be approximated by a linear relationship. Note, however that some type of curvilinear relationship may also be appropriate.

c. $\sum (x_i - \bar{x})(y_i - \bar{y}) = 184$

$$s_{xy} = \frac{\sum (x_i - \bar{x})(y_i - \bar{y})}{n-1} = \frac{184}{5} = 36.8$$

The sample covariance of 36.8 is indicative of a positive linear association between x and y.

d. $\sum x_i^2 = 66.08$ $\sum y_i^2 = 1,936,000$

$s_x = 0.385$ $\qquad s_y = 104.31$

$$r_{xy} = \frac{s_{xy}}{s_x\, s_y} = \frac{36.8}{(.385)\,(104.31)} = \frac{36.8}{39.64} = .92$$

The correlation coefficient of .92 is indicative of a strong positive linear association.

61. a. Let $x = $ driving speed and $y = $ mileage

Using MINITAB we obtained the estimate regression equation $\hat{y} = 39 - .286\,x$. The value of r^2 was .829. Thus, the sample correlation coefficient is $-\sqrt{.829} = -.91$

b. $$r_{xy}\sqrt{\frac{n-2}{1-r_{xy}^2}} = -.91\sqrt{\frac{10-2}{1-.829}} = -6.22$$

$t_{.005} = 3.355$ (8 degrees of freedom)

Since $-6.22 < -t_{.005} = -3.555$, we reject H_0:

62. a. Let $x = $ wife's age and $y = $ husband's age.

b. The scatter diagram indicated that the two variables are related.

c. $\sum x_i = 150$ $\sum y_i = 140$ $\sum x_i^2 = 4830$

$\sum y_i^2 = 4050 = 1806$

$s_x = 9.08$ $s_y = 5.7$

$s_{xy} = 180/4 = 45$

$r_{xy} = \dfrac{s_{xy}}{s_x \, s_y} = \dfrac{45}{(9.08)(5.7)} = \dfrac{45}{51.76} = .87$

The sample correlation coefficient indicates a strong positive linear relationship between x and y.

63. $r_{xy} = b_1 \left(\dfrac{s_x}{s_y}\right) = 3.2 \dfrac{10}{35} = .91$

64. a.

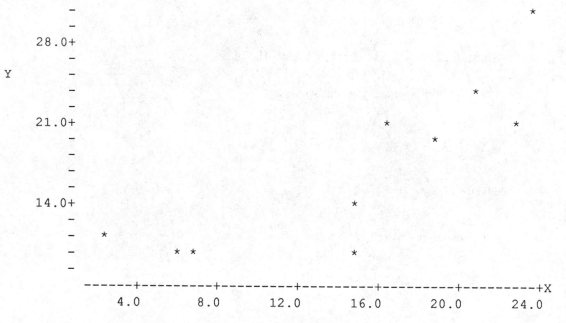

The two variables appear to be related.

b. $\sum x_i = 147.4$ $\sum y_i = 170.8$ $\sum x_i y_i = 2916.79$

$\sum x_i^2 = 2655.06$ $\sum y_i^2 = 3370.8$

$$r_{xy} = \frac{2916.79 - (147.4)\,(170.8)\,/\,10}{\sqrt{2655.06 - (147.4)^2 / 10}\ \sqrt{3370.8 - (170.8)^2 / 10}} = .85$$

c. $.85 \sqrt{\dfrac{8}{1 - (.85)^2}} = 4.56$

$t_{.005} = 3.355$

Since $4.56 > t_{.005} = 3.355$ we reject H_0

65. a. Let x = high temperature and y = low temperature

Using MINITAB we obtained the estimated regression equation $\hat{y} = -8.52 + .783\,x$. The value of r^2 was .66. Thus, the sample correlation coefficient is $+ \sqrt{66} = .81$.

   b. $r_{xy} \sqrt{\dfrac{n - 2}{1 - r_{xy}^2}} = .81 \sqrt{\dfrac{24 - 2}{1 - .81}} = 8.72$

$t_{.025} = 2.074$ (22 degrees of freedom)

Since $8.72 > t_{.025} = 2.074$, the relationship is significant.

66. In regression analysis we are interested in developing a model of the relationship between a dependent variable and one or more independent variables in order to help estimate values of the dependent variable. In correlation analysis we are only concerned with determining if two variables are linearly related.

67. No. Regression or correlation analysis can never prove that two variables are casually related.

68. The estimate of a mean value is an estimate of the average of all y values associated with the same x. The estimate of an individual y value is an estimate of only one of the y values associated with a particular x.

69. To determine whether or not there is a significant relationship between x and y.

70. a. $\sum x_i = 210 \qquad \sum y_i = 102 \qquad \sum x_i y_i = 3400 \qquad \sum x_i^2 = 8500$

$$b_1 = \frac{\sum x_i y_i - \left(\sum x_i \sum y_i\right) / n}{\sum x_i^2 - \left(\sum x_i\right)^2 / n}$$

$$= \frac{3400 - (210)\,(102)\,/\,6}{8500 - (210)^2 / 6} = -.1478$$

$b_0 = 17 - (-.1478)\, 35 = 22.173$

$\hat{y} = 22.173 - .1478\, x$

b.

$$SSR = \frac{\left[\sum x_i y_i - \left(\sum x_i \sum y_i\right)/n\right]^2}{\sum x_i^2 - \left(\sum x_i\right)^2 / n}$$

$$= \frac{[3400 - (210)\,(102)\,/\,6]^2}{8500 - (210)^2 / 6} = 25.13$$

$$SST = \sum y_i^2 - \frac{\left(\sum y_i\right)^2}{n}$$

$$= 1768 - \frac{(102)^2}{6} = 34$$

$SSE = 34 - 25.1304 = 8.87$

$MSE = 8.87 / 4 = 2.218$

$MSR = 25.13$

$F = 25.13 / 2.218 = 11.33$

$F_{.05} = 7.71$ (1 degree of freedom numerator and 4 denominator)

Since $F = 11.33 > F_{.05} = 7.71$, we reject $H_0 : B_1 = 0$; there is significant relationship between line speed and the number of defective parts.

c. $r^2 = SSR / SST = .739.$

This is a reasonably good fit.

d. $s = \sqrt{MSE} = \sqrt{2.218} = 1.489$

$\hat{y}_{50} = 22.173 - .1478\,(50)$

$= 22.173 - 7.39$

$= 14.783$

$$s_{\hat{y}_p} = s \sqrt{\frac{1}{n} + \frac{(x_p - \bar{x})^2}{\sum x_i^2 - \left(\sum x_i\right)^2 / n}}$$

$$= 1.489 \sqrt{\frac{1}{6} + \frac{(50 - 35)^2}{8500 - (210)^2 / 6}} = .896$$

$t_{.025} = 2.776$ (4 degrees of freedom)

$$\hat{y}_p \pm t_{\alpha/2} \, s_{\hat{y}_p}$$

$14.783 \pm 2.776(.896) = 14.783 \pm 2.487$

or 12.296 to 17.270

71. a. $r^2 = $ SSR / SST $ = .78$

SSR $= .78$ (SST) $= .78$ (45) $= 35.1$

SSE $= $ SST $-$ SSR $= 45 - 35.1 = 9.9$

b. $F = \dfrac{\text{MSR}}{\text{MSE}} = \dfrac{35.1 / 1}{9.9 / 28} = 99.27$

$F_{.01} = 7.64$ (1 degree of freedom numerator and 28 denominator)

Since $F = 99.27 > F_{.01} = 7.64$, we reject $H_0 : B_1 = 0$.

c.   Note that $b_1 = +.42$; that is, the slope is positive

$$r_{xy} = +\sqrt{r^2} = +.88$$

72.   The following values are provided in case a calculator is used to perform the computations.

$\sum x_i = 253$ $\sum y_i = 346.5$ $\sum x_i y_i = 9668.5$

$\sum x_i^2 = 7347$ $\sum y_i^2 = 13010.75$

The MINITAB output is shown below:

```
The regression equation is
Y = 10.5 + 0.953 X

Predictor        Coef        Stdev      t-ratio          p
Constant       10.528        3.745         2.81      0.023
X              0.9534       0.1382         6.90      0.000

s = 4.250        R-sq = 85.6%       R-sq(adj) = 83.8%

Analysis of Variance

SOURCE          DF           SS           MS          F          p
Regression       1        860.05       860.05      47.62      0.000
Error            8        144.47        18.06
Total            9       1004.53


        Fit   Stdev.Fit            95% C.I.            95% P.I.
       39.13        1.49      (  35.69,   42.57)  (  28.74,   49.52)
```

a. $\hat{y} = 10.5 + .953\,x$

b. Since the p-value corresponding to $F = 47.62 = .000 < \alpha = .05$, we reject $H_0 : B_1 = 0$.

c. The 95% prediction interval is 28.74 to 49.52 or $2874 to $4952

d. Yes, since the expected expense is $3913.

73. a. There appears to be a negative linear relationship between distance to work and number of days absent.

The following values are provided in case a calculator is used to perform the calculations.

$\sum x_i = 90$ $\qquad\qquad$ $\sum y_i = 50$ $\qquad$ $\sum x_i y_i = 355$

$\sum x_i^2 = 1086$ $\qquad\qquad$ $\sum y_i^2 = 296$

The MINITAB output is shown below:

```
The regression equation is
Y = 8.10 - 0.344 X

Predictor          Coef        Stdev     t-ratio         p
Constant         8.0978       0.8088       10.01     0.000
X               -0.34420      0.07761      -4.43     0.002

s = 1.289        R-sq = 71.1%      R-sq(adj) = 67.5%

Analysis of Variance

SOURCE           DF           SS          MS         F         p
Regression       1         32.699      32.699     19.67     0.002
Error            8         13.301       1.663
Total            9         46.000


     Fit    Stdev.Fit           95% C.I.            95% P.I.
   6.377       0.512    (  5.195,   7.559)  (  3.176,   9.577)
```

c.   Since the p-value corresponding to F = 419.67 is .002 < α = .05

We reject $H_0 : B_1$ - 0.

d. r^2 = .711. The estimated regression equation explained 71.1% of the variability in y; this is a reasonably good fit.

e.   The 95% confidence interval is 5.195 to 7.559 or approximately 5.2 to 7.6 days.

74.   Let x = the number of competitors within 1 mile and y = the daily sales volume.

The following values are provided in case a calculator is used to perform the calculations.

$\sum x_i = 24$ $\sum y_i = 90$ $\sum x_i y_i = 61,400$

$\sum x_i^2 = 90$ $\sum y_i^2 = 64,700,000$

The MINITAB output is shown below:

```
The regression equation is
Y = 3767 - 322 X

Predictor          Coef        Stdev      t-ratio         p
Constant         3766.7        107.6        35.01     0.000
X               -322.22        32.08       -10.05     0.000

s = 136.1         R-sq = 94.4%      R-sq(adj) = 93.5%

Analysis of Variance

SOURCE          DF           SS          MS          F         p
Regression       1       1868889     1868889     100.92     0.000
Error            6        111111       18519
Total            7       1980000


     Fit   Stdev.Fit          95% C.I.              95% P.I.
  2477.8        57.8    ( 2336.2, 2619.3)    ( 2115.9, 2839.7)
```

a. $\hat{y} = 3767 - 322\,x$

b. Since the p-value corresponding to $F = 100.92$ is .002 $< \alpha = .05$, we reject $H_0 : B_1 = 0$.

c. $r^2 = .944$. This is an excellent fit.

d. The 95% prediction interval is 2115.9 to 2839.7 or $2,115.90 to $2,839.70.

75.   Let x = engine revolutions per minute (rpm) and y = boat speed (mph)

       The MINITAB output is shown below:

```
The regression equation is
Y = 0.30 + 0.00919 X

Predictor          Coef         Stdev      t-ratio           p
Constant          0.297         2.838         0.10       0.920
X            0.0091950     0.0008779        10.47       0.000

s = 3.312          R-sq = 94.0%       R-sq(adj) = 93.1%

Analysis of Variance

SOURCE          DF           SS           MS          F           p
Regression       1        1203.6       1203.6     109.71       0.000
Error            7          76.8         11.0
Total            8        1280.4
```

a. $\hat{y} = .30 + .00919\,x$

b. Since the p-value corresponding to $F = 109.71$ is .000 $< \alpha = .05$, we reject $H_0 : B_1 = 0$.

c.
```
STDRESID-
       -                           *
       -                                *
    1.0+
       -                    *
       -
       -                                        *
       -                                            *
    0.0+
       -
       -
       -                                                    *
       -
   -1.0+
       -          *
       -     *                                                  *
       -
        +---------+---------+---------+---------+---------+------YHAT
       7.0      14.0      21.0      28.0      35.0      42.0
```

The standardized residual plot indicates a possible curvilinear relationship between x and y. The scatter diagram also provides support for concluding that a linear relationship may not be appropriate.

76.   Let x = age and y = qualifying time

The MINITAB output is shown below:

```
The regression equation is
Y = 20.7 - 0.234 X


Predictor          Coef        Stdev      t-ratio          p
Constant         20.686        3.477         5.95      0.001
X               -0.2339        0.1188        -1.97      0.096


s = 0.9999       R-sq = 39.3%       R-sq(adj) = 29.1%

Analysis of Variance


SOURCE           DF            SS            MS          F          p
Regression        1        3.8763        3.8763       3.88      0.096
Error             6        5.9987        0.9998
Total             7        9.8750
```

a. $\hat{y}$ = .20.7 - .234 x

b.   Since the p-value corresponding to F = 3.88 is .096 > α = .05, we cannot reject $H_0 : B_1$ = 0.

c.

```
STDRESID
      -                                          *
      -
      -                              *
      -
    1.0+
      -
      -
      -
      -
    0.0+
      -
      -      *                *
      -                                                              *
      -                                               *
    -1.0+      *                                      *
      -
      -
      --+---------+---------+---------+---------+---------+---------+----YHAT
      12.95     13.30     13.65     14.00     14.35     14.70
```

The standardized residual plot indicates that the assumption of a linear relationship is not appropriate;

the scatter diagram also provides support for this conclusion.

77. Let x the age of a bus and y = the annual maintenance cost.

$$\sum x_i = 30 \qquad\qquad \sum y_i = 108 \qquad \sum x_i y_i = 20{,}820$$

$$\sum x_i^2 = 108 \qquad\qquad \sum y_i^2 = 4{,}139{,}900$$

$$b_1 = \frac{\sum x_i y_i - \sum x_i \sum y_i / n}{\sqrt{\sum x_i^2 - \left(\sum x_i\right)^2 / n} \sqrt{\sum y_i^2 - \left(\sum y_i\right)^2 / n}}$$

$$= \frac{20{,}820 - (30)(6150)/10}{\sqrt{108 - (30)^2/10} \sqrt{4{,}139{,}900 - (6150)^2/10}} = .934$$

78. Let x = the age of a bus and y = the annual maintenance cost

The MINITAB output is shown below:

```
The regression equation is
Y = 220 + 132 X

Predictor        Coef        Stdev      t-ratio          p
Constant       220.00        58.48         3.76      0.006
X              131.67        17.80         7.40      0.000

s = 75.50        R-sq = 87.3%       R-sq(adj) = 85.7%

Analysis of Variance

SOURCE         DF          SS          MS         F          p
Regression      1      312050      312050     54.75      0.000
Error           8       45600        5700
Total           9      357650
```

```
       Fit   Stdev.Fit         95% C.I.            95% P.I.
     746.7        29.8   (  678.0,   815.4)   (  559.5,   933.9)
```

a. $\hat{y} = .220 + 132 x$

b. Since the p-value corresponding to $F = 54.75$ is .000 $< \alpha = .05$, we reject $H_0 : B_1 = 0$.

c. $r^2 = .873$. The least squares line provided a very good fit.

d. The 95% prediction interval is 559.5 to 933.9 or $559.50 to $933.90

79. Let x = hours spent studying and y = total points earned

$$\sum x_i = 695 \qquad \sum y_i = 635 \qquad \sum x_i y_i = 48050$$

$$\sum x_i^2 = 53025 \qquad \sum y_i^2 = 44025$$

$$b_1 = \frac{\sum x_i y_i - \sum x_i \sum y_i / n}{\sqrt{\sum x_i^2 - \left(\sum x_i\right)^2 / n} \sqrt{\sum y_i^2 - \left(\sum y_i\right)^2 / n}}$$

$$= \frac{48{,}050 - (695)(635) / 10}{\sqrt{53{,}025 - (695)^2 / 10} \sqrt{44{,}025 - (635)^2 / 10}} = .937$$

80. Let x = the hours spent studying and y = the total points earned

The MINITAB output is shown below:

```
The regression equation is
Y = 5.85 + 0.830 X

Predictor        Coef        Stdev      t-ratio          p
Constant        5.847        7.972         0.73      0.484
X              0.8295       0.1095         7.58      0.000


s = 7.523        R-sq = 87.8%       R-sq(adj) = 86.2%

Analysis of Variance

SOURCE          DF           SS           MS            F          p
Regression       1       3249.7       3249.7        57.42      0.000
Error            8        452.8         56.6
Total            9       3702.5




      Fit   Stdev.Fit          95% C.I.            95% P.I.
    84.65        3.67    ( 76.19,   93.11)    ( 65.35, 103.96)
```

a. $\hat{y} = 5.85 + .830\, x$

b. Since the p-value corresponding to $F = 57.42$ is $.000 < \alpha = .05$, we reject $H_0 : B_1 = 0$.

c. 84.65 points

d. The 95% prediction interval is 65.35 to 103.96

81. a.   The MINITAB output is shown below

```
The regression equation is
ACTMARG = 14.4 + 0.112 PREDMARG


Predictor        Coef         Stdev      t-ratio          p
Constant       14.379         6.714         2.14      0.065
PREDMARG       0.1116        0.3076         0.36      0.726


s = 8.721         R-sq = 1.6%        R-sq(adj) = 0.0%

Analysis of Variance

SOURCE          DF           SS           MS          F          p
Regression       1        10.01        10.01       0.13      0.726
Error            8       608.39        76.05
Total            9       618.40
```

b.   Sample correlation coefficient $= \sqrt{.016} = .126$

c. $r_{xy} \sqrt{\dfrac{n-2}{1-r_{xy}^2}} = .126 \sqrt{\dfrac{10-2}{1-.126}} = .381$

$t_{.005} = 3.355$ (8 degrees of freedom)

Since $.381 < 3.355$ the relationship is not significant.

d.   The estimates regression equation is

$$ACTMARG = 14.4 + 0.112 \ PREDMARG$$

d. $b_0 = 14.4 \quad b_1 = 0.112$

For an ideal system we would like the predicted victory margin to equal the actual victory margin. Thus, for an ideal system $B_0 = 0$ and $B_1 = 1$.

Solution to Computer Case

Descriptive statistics for these data are shown below:

	N	MEAN	MEDIAN	TRMEAN	STDEV	SEMEAN
Percent	42	12.262	12.000	12.184	3.132	0.483
# Fatal	42	1.922	1.881	1.906	1.071	0.165

	MIN	MAX	Q1	Q3
Percent	8.000	18.000	9.000	15.000
# Fatal	0.039	4.100	0.992	2.824

The following scatter diagram suggests a linear relationship between these two variables:

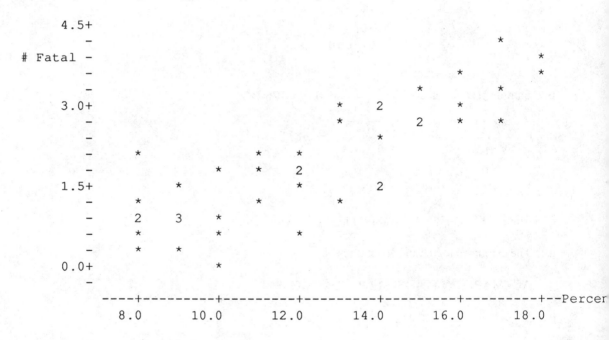

Minitab was used to develop the following regression analysis output:

```
The regression equation is
# Fatal = - 1.60 + 0.287 Percent

Predictor         Coef        Stdev      t-ratio          p
Constant       -1.5974       0.3717        -4.30      0.000
Percent        0.28705      0.02939         9.77      0.000

s = 0.5894       R-sq = 70.5%      R-sq(adj) = 69.7%

Analysis of Variance

SOURCE          DF           SS           MS         F         p
Regression       1       33.134       33.134     95.40     0.000
Error           40       13.893        0.347
Total           41       47.028

Unusual Observations
Obs. Percent   # Fatal       Fit Stdev.Fit   Residual    St.Resid
  15     10.0    0.0390    1.2731    0.1126    -1.2341      -2.13R
  23      8.0    2.1900    0.6990    0.1548     1.4910       2.62R

R denotes an obs. with a large st. resid.
```

There is a significant relationship between the two variables. Two observations are identified as having a large standardized residual and should be treated as possible outliers; the following standardized residual plot does not indicate any other problems with the residuals.

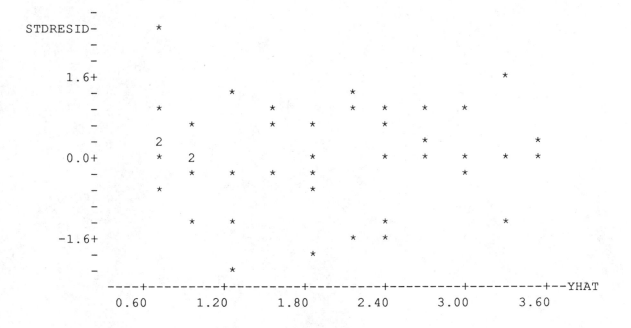

Conclusion: It appears that the number of fatal accidents per 1000 licenses is linearly related to the percentage of licensed drivers under the age of 21; that is, the higher the percentage of drivers under 21, the larger the number of total accidents.

Chapter 15
Multiple Regression

Learning Objectives

1. Understand how multiple regression analysis can be used to develop relationships involving one dependent variable and several independent variables.

2. Be able to interpret the coefficients in a multiple regression analysis.

3. Know the assumptions necessary to conduct statistical tests involving the hypothesized regression model.

4. Understand the role of computer packages in performing multiple regression analysis.

5. Be able to interpret and use computer output to develop the estimated regression equation.

6. Be able to determine how good a fit is provided by the estimated regression equation.

7. Be able to test for the significance of the regression equation.

8. Understand how multicollinearity affects multiple regression analysis.

9. Know how residual analysis can be used to make a judgement as to the appropriateness of the model, identify outliers, and determine which observations are influential.

Solutions:

1. a. $b_1 = .5906$ is an estimate of the change in y corresponding to a 1 unit change in x_1 when x_2 is held constant.

   $b_2 = .4980$ is an estimate of the change in y corresponding to a 1 unit change in x_2 when x_1 is held constant.

2. a. The estimated regression equation is

   $$\hat{y} = 45.06 + 1.94\, x_1$$

   An estimate of y when $x_1 = 45$ is

   $$\hat{y} = 45.06 + 1.94(45) = 132.36$$

   b. The estimated regression equation is

   $$\hat{y} = 85.22 + 4.32\, x_2$$

   An estimate of y when $x_2 = 15$ is

   $$\hat{y} = 85.22 + 4.32(15) = 150.02$$

   c. The estimated regression equation is

   $$\hat{y} = -18.37 + 2.01\, x_1 + 4.74\, x_2$$

   An estimate of y when $x_1 = 45$ and $x_2 = 15$ is

   $$\hat{y} = -18.37 + 2.01(45) + 4.74(15) = 143.18$$

3. a. $b_1 = 3.8$ is an estimate of the change in y corresponding to a 1 unit change in x_1 when x_2, x_3, and x_4 are held constant.

   $b_2 = -2.3$ is an estimate of the change in y corresponding to a 1 unit change in x_2 when x_1, x_3, and x_4 are held constant.

   $b_3 = 7.6$ is an estimate of the change in y corresponding to a 1 unit change in x_3 when x_1, x_2, and x_4 are held constant.

   $b_4 = 2.7$ is an estimate of the change in y corresponding to a 1 unit change in x_4 when x_1, x_2, and x_3 are held constant.

4. a. $\hat{y} = 235 + 10\,(15) + 8\,(10) = 255$

Sales estimate: $255,000

  b. Sales can be expected to increase by $10 for every dollar increase in inventory investment when advertising expenditure is held constant. Sales can be expected to increase by $8 for every dollar increase in advertising expenditure when inventory investment is held constant.

5. a. The Minitab output is shown below:

The regression equation is

REVENUE = 88.6 + 1.60 TVADV

Predicator	Coef	Stdev	t - ratio	p
Constant	88.638	1.582	56.02	0.000
TVADV	1.6039	0.4778	3.36	0.015

$s = 1.215$ R-sq = 65.3%   R-sq (adj) = 59.5%

Analysis of Variance

SOURCE	DF	SS	MS	F	p
Regression	1	16.640	16.640	11.27	0.015
Error	6	8.860	1.477		
Total	7	25.500			

  b. $\hat{y} = 88.6 + 1.60\,(3.5) = 94.2$

In dollars $94,200

6. a. The Minitab output is shown below:

The regression equation is

REVENUE = 83.2 + 2.29 TVADV + 1.30 NEWSADV

Predicator	Coef	Stdev	t - ratio	p
Constant	83.230	1.574	52.88	0.000
TVADV	2.2902	0.3041	7.53	0.001
NEWSADV	1.3010	0.3207	4.06	0.010

$s = 0.6426$ R-sq = 91.9%   R-sq (adj) = 88.7%

Analysis of Variance

SOURCE	DF	SS	MS	F	p
Regression	2	23.435	11.718	28.38	0.002
Error	5	2.065	0.413		
Total	7	25.500			

b. No, it is 1.60 in 2a and 2.99 above. In this exercise it represents the marginal change in revenue due to an increase in television advertising with newspaper advertising held constant.

7. a. The Minitab output is shown below:

The regression equation is

$Y = 66.5 + 0.414 X1 - 0.270 X2$

Predicator	Coef	Stdev	t - ratio	p
Constant	66.52	41.88	1.59	0.156
X1	0.4139	0.2604	1.59	0.156
X2	-0.26978	0.08091	-3.33	0.013

$s = 18.74$ R-sq = 65.3%   R-sq (adj) = 88.7%

Analysis of Variance

SOURCE	DF	SS	MS	F	p
Regression	2	4618.8	2309.4	6.58	0.025
Error	7	25457.3	351.0		
Total	9	7076.1			

b. $b_1 = .414$ is an estimate of the change in the quantity sold (1000s) of the Heller mower with respect to a $1 change in price in competitor's mower with the price if the Heller mower held constant.

$b_2 = -.270$ is an estimate of the change in the quantity sold (1000s) of the Heller mower with respect to a $1 change in its price with the prices of the competitor's mower held constant.

c. $\hat{y} = 66.5 + 0.414 (170) - 0.270 (160) = 93.68$

Therefore, 93,680 units

8. a. The Minitab output is shown below:

The regression equation is

$Y = 2.1 + 0.0138 X1 + 0.00584 X2$

Predicator	Coef	Stdev	t - ratio	p
Constant	2.14	14.71	0.15	0.887
X1	0.01385	0.01410	0.98	0.349
X2	0.0058414	0.0007050	8.29	0.000

$s = 12.95$ R-sq = 93.6%   R-sq (adj) = 92.4%

Analysis of Variance

SOURCE	DF	SS	MS	F	p
Regression	2	24717	12358	73.73	0.000
Error	10	1676	168		
Total	12	26393			

b.   Advertising expenditure, per capita income in the city, store size.

9.   a.   The Minitab output is shown below:

The regression equation is

%COLLEGE = 26.7 - 1.43 SIZE + 0.0757 SAT

Predicator	Coef	Stdev	t - ratio	p
Constant	26.71	51.67	0.52	0.613
SIZE	-1.4298	0.9931	-1.44	0.170
SAT	0.07574	0.03906	1.94	0.072

$s = 12.42$ R-sq = 38.2%   R-sq (adj) = 30.0%

Analysis of Variance

SOURCE	DF	SS	MS	F	p
Regression	2	1430.4	715.2	4.64	0.027
Error	15	2312.7	154.2		
Total	17	3743.1			

b. $\hat{y} = 26.7 - 1.43 (20) + 0.0757 (1000) = 73.8$

Estimate is 73.8%

10.   a.   The Minitab output is shown below:

The regression equation is

COST = -5.7 + 1.54 STARTS + 1.81 INCOME

Predicator	Coef	Stdev	t - ratio	p
Constant	-5.73	51.86	-0.11	0.914
SIZE	1.536	1.191	1.29	0.219
SAT	1.808	1.017	1.78	0.099

$s = 24.56$ R-sq $= 37.7\%$ R-sq (adj) $= 28.2\%$

Analysis of Variance

SOURCE	DF	SS	MS	F	p
Regression	2	4750.6	2375.3	3.94	0.046
Error	13	7838.9	603.0		
Total	15	12589.5			

b. $\hat{y} = -5.73 + 1.536\,(8) + 1.808\,(50) = 96.96$

11. a. SSE $=$ SST - SSR $= 6,724.125 - 6,216.375 = 507.75$

b. $R^2 = \dfrac{SSR}{SST} = \dfrac{6,216.375}{6,724.125} = .924$

c. $R_a^2 = 1 - (1 - R^2)\dfrac{n-1}{n-p-1}$

$= 1 - (1 - .924)\dfrac{10-1}{10-2-1} = .902$

d. The estimated regression equation provided an excellent fit.

12. a. $R^2 = \dfrac{SSR}{SST} = \dfrac{14,052.2}{15,182.9} = .926$

b. $R_a^2 = 1 - (1 - R^2)\dfrac{n-1}{n-p-1}$

$= 1 - (1 - .926)\dfrac{10-1}{10-2-1} = .905$

c. Yes; after adjusting for the number of independent variables in the model, we see that 90.5% of the variability in y has been accounted for.

13. a. $R^2 = \dfrac{SSR}{SST} = \dfrac{1760}{1805} = .975$

b. $R_a^2 = 1 - (1 - R^2)\dfrac{n-1}{n-p-1}$

$= 1 - (1 - .975)\dfrac{30-1}{30-4-1} = .971$

c. The estimated regression equation provided an excellent fit.

14. a. $R^2 = \dfrac{SSR}{SST} = \dfrac{12,000}{16,000} = .75$

b. $R_a^2 = 1 - (1 - R^2)\dfrac{n-1}{n-p-1}$

$= 1 - .25\dfrac{9}{7} = .68$

c. The adjusted coefficient of determination shows that 68% of the variability has been explained by the two independent variables; thus, we conclude that the model does not explain a large amount of variability.

15. Note: The Minitab output is shown with the solution to Exercise 9.

a. $R^2 = .382,\ R_a^2 = .30$

b. The fit is not very good.

16. Note: The Minitab output is shown with the solution to Exercise 10.

a. $R^2 = .377,\ R_a^2 = .282$

b. The fit is not very good.

17. a. MSR = SSR / p = 6,216.375 / 2 = 3,108.188

MSE = $\dfrac{SSE}{n-p-1} = \dfrac{507.75}{10-2-1} = 72.536$

b. F = MSR / MSE = 3,108.188 / 72.536 = 42.85

$F_{.05}$ = 4.74 (2 degrees of freedom numerator and 7 denominator)

Since F = 42.85 > $F_{.05}$ = 4.74 the overall model is significant.

c. t = .5906 / .0813 = 7.26

$t_{.025}$ = 2.365 (7 degrees of freedom)

Since t = 2.365 > $t_{.025}$ = 2.365, β_1 is significant.

d. t = .4980 / .0567 = 8.78

Since $t = 8.78 > t_{.025} = 2.365$, β_2 is significant.

18.   A portion of the Minitab output is shown below.

The regression equation is

Y1 = -18.4 + 2.01 X1 + 4.74 X2

Predicator	Coef	Stdev	t - ratio	p
Constant	-18.37	17.97	-1.02	0.341
X1	2.0102	0.2471	8.13	0.000
X2	4.7378	0.9484	5.00	0.000

s = 12.71   R-sq = 92.6%   R-sq (adj) = 90.4%

Analysis of Variance

SOURCE	DF	SS	MS	F	p
Regression	2	1405.2	7026.1	43.50	0.000
Error	7	1130.7	161.5		
Total	9	15182.9	161.5		

a.   Since the p-value corresponding to $F = 43.50$ is .000 $< \alpha = .05$, we reject H_0: $\beta_1 = \beta_2 = 0$; there is a significant relationship.

b.   Since the p-value corresponding to $t = 8.13$ is .000 $< \alpha = .05$, we reject H_0: $\beta_1 = 0$; β_1 is significant.

c.   Since the p-value corresponding to $t = 5.00$ is .000 $< \alpha = .05$, we reject H_0: $\beta_2 = 0$; β_2 is significant.

19. a.   In the two independent variable case the coefficient of x_1 represents the expected change in y corresponding to a one unit increase in x_1 when x_2 is held constant.

In the single independent variable case the coefficient of x_1 represents the expected change in y corresponding to a one unit increase in x_1.

b.   Yes. If x_1 and x_2 are correlated one would expect a change in x_1 to be accompanied by a change in x_2.

20. a.   SSE = SST - SSR = 16000 - 12000 = 4000

$$s^2 = \frac{SSE}{n - p - 1} = \frac{4000}{7} = 571.43$$

$$MSR = \frac{SSR}{p} = \frac{12000}{2} = 6000$$

b. $F = MSR / MSE = 6000 / 571.43 = 10.50$

$F_{.05} = 4.74$ (2 degrees of freedom numerator and 7 denominator)

Since $F = 10.50 > F_{.05} = 4.74$, we reject H_0. There is a significant relationship among the variables.

21. a. $F = 28.38$

$F_{.01} = 13.27$ (2 degrees of freedom, numerator and 1 denominator)

Since $F > F_{.01} = 13.27$, reject H_0.

Alternatively, the p-value of .002 leads to the same conclusion.

b. $t = 7.53$

$t_{.025} = 2.571$

Since $t > t_{.025} = 2.571$, β_1 is significant and x_1 should not be dropped from the model.

c. $t = 4.06$

$t_{.025} = 2.571$

Since $t > t_{.025} = 2.571$, β_2 is significant and x_2 should not be dropped from the model.

22.   Note: The Minitab output is shown with the solution to Exercise 7

$F = 6.58$

$F_{.05} = 4.74$ (2 degrees of freedom numerator and 7 denominator)

Since $F > F_{.05} = 4.74$, the overall model is significant.

Alternatively, the p-value os .025 leads to the same conclusion.

23. a.   The Minitab output is shown below:

The regression equation is

P/E $= 5.56 + 0.465$ %PROFIT $+ 0.204$ %GROWTH

Predicator	Coef	Stdev	t - ratio	p
Constant	5.560	1.600	3.47	0.003
%PROFIT	0.4654	0.1431	3.25	0.005
%GROWTH	0.2038	0.1403	1.45	0.165

s = 2.499   R-sq = 59.1%   R-sq (adj) = 54.0%

Analysis of Variance

SOURCE	DF	SS	MS	F	p
Regression	2	144.592	72.296	11.57	0.001
Error	16	99.944	6.247		
Total	18	244.537			

b. $H_0 : \beta_1 = \beta_2 = 0$

H_a : One or more of the coefficients is not equal to zero.

$F = 11.57$

$F_{.05}$ = 3.63 (2 degrees of freedom numerator and 16 denominator)

Since $F > F_{.05}$ = 3.63, reject H_0.

Alternatively, the p-value of .001 leads to the same conclusion.

c. The sample correlation coefficient between the two independent variables is 0.498 (from Minitab output not shown). Although somewhat high, it is less than the .7 critical value for the "rule of thumb" test.

24.   Note: The Minitab output is shown with the solution to Exercise 10.

a. Since the p-value corresponding to F = 3.94 is .046 < α = .05, the overall model is significant.

c. Since the p-value corresponding to t = 1.78 is .219 > α = .05, B_1 is not significant.

c. Since the p-value corresponding to t = 1.78 is .099 > α = .05, B_2 is not significant

d. Although the sample correlation coefficient between x_1 and x_2 is .396, considerably less than the critical value given by the "rule of thumb test" for multicollinearity, the correlation between x_1 and x_2 has resulted in the conclusion that none of the individual parameters are significantly different from zero (parts b and c) when an overall F test indicates a significant relationship (part a).

25. a. $\hat{y}$ = 29.1270 + .5906 (180) + .4980 (310) = 289.8150

b. The point estimate for an individual value is $\hat{y}$ = 289.8150, the same as the point estimate of the mean value.

26. a. Using Minitab, the 95% confidence interval is 132.16 to 154.15.

    b. Using Minitab, the 95% prediction interval is 111.15 to 175.17.

27. a. $\hat{y} = 160 + 8(3) + 15(0) = 184$

    b. $\hat{y} = 160 + 8(2) + 15(1) = 191$

    c, $b_2 = 15$ or $\$15,000$

28. a. Using Minitab the 95% confidence interval is 71.13 to 112.35.

    In terms of units: 71,130 to 112,350

    b. Using Minitab the 95% prediction interval is 42.87 to 140.61.

    In terms of units: 42,870 to 140,610.

    This prediction interval estimate would probably most be of interest to Heller since they are a manufacturer of mowers and not a retailer.

29. a. Using Minitab the 95% confidence interval is 58.37% to 75.03%.

    b. Using Minitab the 95% prediction interval is 35.23% to 90.60%.

30. a. $E(y) = \beta_0 + \beta_1 x_1 + \beta_2 x_2$ where

    $x_2 = 0$ if level 1 and 1 if level 2

    b. $E(y) = \beta_0 + \beta_1 x_1 + \beta_2 (0) = \beta_0 + \beta_1 x_1$

    c.. $E(y) = \beta_0 + \beta_1 x_1 + \beta_2 (1) = \beta_0 + \beta_1 x_1 + \beta_1$

    d. $\beta_2 = E(y \mid \text{level 2}) - E(y \mid \text{level 1})$

    β_1 is the change in $E(y)$ for a 1 unit change in x_1 holding x_2 constant.

31. a. two

    b. $E(y) = \beta_0 + \beta_1 x_1 + \beta_2 x_2 + \beta_3 x_3$ where

x_2	x_3	Level
0	0	1
1	0	2
0	1	3

c. $E (y \mid \text{level 1}) = \beta_0 + \beta_1 x_1 + \beta_2 (0) + \beta_3 (0) = \beta_0 + \beta_1 x_1$

$E (y \mid \text{level 2}) = \beta_0 + \beta_1 x_1 + \beta_2 (1) + \beta_3 (0) = \beta_0 + \beta_1 x_1 + \beta_2$

$E (y \mid \text{level 3}) = \beta_0 + \beta_1 x_1 + \beta_2 (0) + \beta_3 (0) = \beta_0 + \beta_1 x_1 + \beta_3$

$\beta_2 = E (y \mid \text{level 2}) - E (y \mid \text{level 1})$

$\beta_3 = E (y \mid \text{level 3}) - E (y \mid \text{level 1})$

β_1 is the change in E (y) for a 1 unit change in x_1 holding x_2 and x_3 constant.

32 a. $15,300

b. Estimate of sales = 10.1 - 4.2(2) + 6.8(8) + 15.3(0) = 56.1 or $56,100

c. Estimate of sales = 10.1 - 4.2(1) + 6.8(3) + 15.3(1) = 41.6 or $41,600

33. a. The Minitab output is shown below:

The regression equation is

HOURS = 3.45 + 0.617 TYPE

Predicator	Coef	Stdev	t - ratio	p
Constant	3.4500	0.5467	6.31	0.000
Type	0.6167	0.7058	0.87	0.408

$s = 1.093$ R-sq = 8.7%   R-sq (adj) = 0.0%

Analysis of Variance

SOURCE	DF	SS	MS	F	p
Regression	1	0.913	0.913	0.76	0.408
Error	8	9.563	1.195		
Total	9	10.476			

b. The estimate regression equation did not provide a good fit. In fact, there p-value of .408 shows that the relationship is not significant for any reasonable value of α.

c. PERSON = 0 if Bob Jones performed the service and PERSON = 1 if Dave Newton performed the service. The Minitab output is shown below:

The regression equation is

HOURS = 4.62 - 1.60 PERSON

Predicator	Coef	Stdev	t - ratio	p
Constant	4.6200	0.3192	14.47	0.000
PERSON	-1.6000	0.4514	-3.54	0.008

s = 0.7138   R-sq = 61.1%   R-sq (adj) = 56.2%

Analysis of Variance

SOURCE	DF	SS	MS	F	p
Regression	1	6.4000	6.4000	12.56	0.008
Error	8	4.0760	0.5095		
Total	9	10.4760			

d. We see that 61.1% of the variability in repair time has been explained by the repairson that performed the service; an acceptable, but not good, fit.

34. a. The Minitab output is shown below:

The regression equation is

HOURS = 1.86 + 0.291 MONTHS + 1.10 TYPE - 0.609 PERSON

Predicator	Cocf	Stdcv	t - ratio	p
Constant	1.8602	0.7286	2.55	0.043
MONTHS	0.29144	0.08360	3.49	0.013
TYPE	1.1024	0.3033	3.63	0.011
PERSON	-0.6091	0.3879	-1.57	0.167

s = 0.4174   R-sq = 90.0%   R-sq (adj) = 85.0%

Analysis of Variance

SOURCE	DF	SS	MS	F	p
Regression	3	9.4305	3.1435	18.04	0.002
Error	6	1.0455	0.1743		
Total	9	10.4760			

b. Since the p-value corresponding to F = 18.04 is .002 < α = .05, the overall model is statistically significant.

c. The p-value corresponding to t = -1.57 is .167 > α = .05; thus, the addition of PERSON is not statistically significant. PERSON is highly correlated with MONTHS (the sample correlation coefficient is -.691); thus, once the effect of MONTHS has been accounted for, PERSON will not add much to the model.

35. a. D1 = 1 if Industry 2 and D2 = 1 if Industry 3; the Minitab output is shown below:

```
The regression equation is
P/E = 7.54 + 0.183 %PROFIT + 0.213 %GROWTH + 2.98 D1 - 0.84 D2


Predictor        Coef        Stdev      t-ratio         p
Constant         7.539       1.736       4.34        0.001
%PROFIT          0.1827      0.2092      0.87        0.397
%GROWTH          0.2128      0.1311      1.62        0.127
D1               2.984       2.231       1.34        0.202
D2              -0.835       1.509      -0.55        0.589


s = 2.309        R-sq = 69.5%      R-sq(adj) = 60.8%


Analysis of Variance


SOURCE        DF          SS          MS          F          p
Regression     4       169.887      42.472       7.97     0.001
Error         14        74.650       5.332
Total         18       244.537
```

b. The Minitab output including the interaction terms is shown below:

```
The regression equation is
P/E = 8.90 - 0.017 %PROFIT + 0.199 %GROWTH + 0.20 D1 + 0.18 D2 + 0.305
%PROFXD1
           - 0.052 %PROFXD2


Predictor        Coef        Stdev      t-ratio         p
Constant         8.896       3.492       2.55        0.026
%PROFIT         -0.0175      0.5170     -0.03        0.974
%GROWTH          0.1991      0.1406      1.42        0.182
D1               0.204       5.248       0.04        0.970
D2               0.181       6.407       0.03        0.978
%PROFXD1         0.3053      0.5759      0.53        0.606
%PROFXD2        -0.0523      0.7874     -0.07        0.948


s = 2.445        R-sq = 70.7%      R-sq(adj) = 56.0%


Analysis of Variance


SOURCE        DF          SS          MS          F          p
Regression     6       172.823      28.804       4.82     0.010
Error         12        71.713       5.976
Total         18       244.537
```

Interaction is not a significant factor for this model.

36. a. The Minitab output is shown below:

The regression equation is

RISK = -91.8 + 1.08 AGE + 0.252 PRESSURE + 8.74 SMOKER

Predicator	Coef	Stdev	t - ratio	p
Constant	-91.76	15.22	-6.03	0.000
AGE	1.0767	0.1660	6.49	0.000
PRESSURE	0.25181	0.4523	5.57	0.000
SMOKER	8.740	3.001	2.91	0.010

s = 5.757   R-sq = 87.3%   R-sq (adj) = 85.0%

Analysis of Variance

SOURCE	DF	SS	MS	F	p
Regression	3	3660.7	1220.2	36.82	0.000
Error	16	530.2	33.1		
Total	19	4190.9			

b. Since the p-value corresponding to t = 2.91 is .01 < α = .05, smoking is a significant factor.

c. Using Minitab, the point estimate is 34.27; the 95% prediction interval is 21.35 to 47.19. Thus, the probability of a stroke (.2135 to .4719 at the 95% confidence level) appears to be quite high. The physician would probably recommend that Art quit smoking and begin some type of treatment designed to reduce his blood pressure.

37. a. The Minitab output is shown below:

The regression equation is

Y = 0.20 + 2.60 X

Predicator	Coef	Stdev	t - ratio	p
Constant	0.200	2.132	0.09	0.931
X	2.6000	0.6429	4.040.008	0.027

s = 2.033   R-sq = 84.5%   R-sq (adj) = 79.3%

Analysis of Variance

SOURCE	DF	SS	MS	F	p
Regression	1	67.600	6.4000	16.35	0.027
Error	3	12.400	4.133		
Total	4	80.000			

b. Using Minitab we obtained the following values:

x_i	y_i	$\hat{y}_i$	Standardized Residual
1	3	2.8	.16
2	7	5.4	.94
3	5	8.0	-1.65
4	11	10.6	.24
5	14	13.2	.62

The point (3,5) does not appear to follow the trend of remaining data; however, the value of the standardized residual for this point, -1.65, is not large enough for us to conclude that (3, 5) is an outlier.

c. Using Minitab, we obtained the following values:

x_i	y_i	Studentized Deleted Residual
1	3	.13
2	7	.92
3	5	- 4.42
4	11	.19
5	14	.54

$t_{.025} = 4.303$ ($n - p - 2 = 5 - 1 - 2 = 2$ degrees of freedom)

Since the studentized deleted residual for (3, 5) is -4.42 < -4.303, we conclude that the 3rd observation is an outlier.

38. a. The Minitab output is shown below:

The regression equation is

$Y = -53.3 + 3.11 X$

Predicator	Coef	Stdev	t - ratio	p
Constant	-53.280	5.786	-9.21	0.003
X	3.1100	0.2016	15.43	0.001

$s = 2.851$ R-sq = 98.8%   R-sq (adj) = 98.3%

Analysis of Variance

SOURCE	DF	SS	MS	F	p
Regression	1	1934.4	1934.4	238.03	0.001
Error	3	24.4	8.1		
Total	4	1598.8			

b. Using the Minitab we obtained the following values:

x_i	y_i	Studentized Deleted Residual
22	12	- 1.40
24	21	- .15
26	31	1.36
28	35	.47
40	70	- 1.39

$t_{.025} = 4.303$ $(n - p - 2 = 5 - 1 - 2 = 2$ degrees of freedom)

Since none of the studentized deleted residuals are less than -4.303 or greater than 4.303, none of the observations can be classified as an outlier.

c. Using Minitab we obtained the following values:

x_i	y_i	h_i
22	12	.38
24	21	.28
26	31	.22
28	35	.20
40	70	.98

The critical value is

$$\frac{3 (p + 1)}{n} = \frac{3 (1 + 1)}{5} = 1.2$$

Since none of the values exceed 1.2, we conclude that there are no influential observations in the data.

d. Using Minitab we obtained the following values:

x_i	y_i	D_i
22	12	.60
24	21	.00
26	31	.26
28	35	.03
40	70	11.09

Since $D_5 = 11.09 > 1$ (rule of thumb critical value), we conclude that the fifth observation is influential.

39. a. The Minitab output appears in the solution to Exercise 6; the estimated regression equation is
REVENUE $= 83.2 + 2.29 +$ TVADV $+ 1.30$ NEWSADV

b. Using Minitab we obtained the following values:

$\hat{y}_i$	Standardized Residual
96.63	-1.62
90.41	-1.08
94.34	1.22
92.21	- .37
94.39	1.10
94.24	- .40
94.42	-1.12
93.35	1.08

With the relatively few observations, it is difficult to determine if any of the assumptions regarding the error term have been violated. For instance, an argument could be made that there does not appear to be any pattern in the plot; alternatively an argument could be made that there is a curvilinear pattern in the plot.

c. The values of the standardized residuals are greater than -2 and less than +2; thus, using test, there are no outliers.

As a further check for outliers, we used Minitab to compute the following studentized deleted residuals:

Observation	Studentized Deleted Residual
1	-2.11
2	-1.10
3	1.31
4	- .33
5	1.13
6	- .36
7	-1.16
8	1.10

$t_{.025} = 2.776$ ($n - p - = 8 - 2 - 2 = 4$ degrees of freedom)

Since none of the studentized deleted residuals is less tan -2.776 or greater than 2.776, we conclude that there are no outliers in the data.

d. Using Minitab we obtained the following values:

Observation	h_i	D_i
1	.63	1.52
2	.65	.70
3	.30	.22
4	.23	.01
5	.26	.14
6	.14	.01
7	.66	.81
8	.13	.06

The critical average value is

$$\frac{3\,(p + 1)}{n} = \frac{3\,(2 + 1)}{8} = 1.125$$

Since none of the values exceed 1.125, we conclude that there are no influential observations.

However, using Cook's distance measure, we see that $D_1 > 1$ (rule of thumb critical value); thus, we conclude the first observation is influential.

Final Conclusion: observations 1 is an influential observation.

40. a. The Minitab output appears in the solution to Exercise 23; the estimate regression equation is

   P/E = 5.56 + 0.465 %PROFIT + 0.204 %GROWTH

   b. The following Minitab output was also provided as part of the regression output.

   Unusual Observations

Obs.	%PROFIT	P/E	Fit	Stdev.Fit	Residual	St.Resid
13	8.7	16.000	11.036	0.695	4.964	2.07R

   R denotes an obs. with a large st. resid.

   Thus, we conclude that observation 13 is an outlier.

   Alternatively, Minitab shows that the studentized deleted residual for observation 13 is 2.34. Since $2.34 > t_{.025} = 2.131$ ($n - p - 2 = 19 - 2 - 2 = 15$ degrees of freedom), we conclude that observation 13 is an outlier.

   c. The values of D_i are all less than 1 for these data; thus, using Cook's distance measure, there are no influential observations.

41. a. The Minitab output is shown below:

The regression equation is

%COLLEGE = - 26.6 + 0.0970 SAT

Predicator	Coef	Stdev	t - ratio	p
Constant	-26.61	37.22	-0.72	0.485
SAT	0.09703	0.03734	2.60	0.019

s = 12.83   R-sq = 29.78%   R-sq (adj) = 25.3%

Analysis of Variance

SOURCE	DF	SS	MS	F	p
Regression	1	1110.8	1110.8	6.75	0.019
Error	16	2632.3	164.5		
Total	17	3743.1			

Unusual Observations

Obs.	%PROFIT	P/E	Fit	Stdev.Fit	Residual	St.Resid
3	716	40.00	42.86	10.79	-2.86	-0.41 X

b. The Minitab output shown in part a identifies observation 3 as an influential observation.

c. The Minitab output appears in the solution to Exercise 9; the estimates regression equation is
%COLLEGE = 26.7 - 1.43 SIZE + 0.0757 SAT

d. The following Minitab output was also provided as part of the regression output for part c.

Unusual Observations

Obs.	SIZE	%COLLEGE	Fit	Stdev.Fit	Residual	St.Resid
3	30.0	40.00	38.04	10.97	1.96	0.34 X

X denotes an obs. whose X value gives it large influence.

Observation 3 is still identified as an influential observation.

42. a. The expected increase in final college grade point average corresponding to a one point increase in high school grade point average is .0235 when SAT mathematics score does not change. Similarly, the expected increase in final college grade point average corresponding to a one point increase in the SAT mathematics score is .00486 when the high school grade point average does not change.

b. $\hat{y}$ = -1.41 + .0235 (84) + .00486 (540) = 3.19

43. a. Job satisfaction can be expected to decrease by 8.69 units with a one unit increase in length of service if the wage rate does not change. A dollar increase in the wage rate is associated with a 13.5 point increase in the job satisfaction score when the length of service does not change.

b. $\hat{y} = 14.4 - 8.69\ (4) + 13.5\ (6.5) = 67.39$

44. SST $= 18051.63 + 1014.30 = 19,065.93$

a. $R^2 = \dfrac{18,051.63}{19,065.93} = .95$

$R_a^2 = 1 - (1 - 95)\left(\dfrac{18 - 1}{18 - 4 - 1}\right) = 1 - (.05)\left(\dfrac{17}{13}\right)$

$= .93$

b. MSR $= 18,051.63 / 4 = 4512.91$

MSE $= 1014 / 13 = 78.02$

$F =$ MSR / MSE $= 4512.91 / 78.02 = 57.84$

$F_{.01} = 5.21$ (4 numerator DF, 13 denominator DF)

Since $57.84 > 5.21$ we reject H_0. The relationship is significant.

45. a. $t = \dfrac{b_1}{s_{b_1}} = \dfrac{8.12}{2.1} = 3.87$

$t_{.025} = 2.201$ (11 DF)

Since $3.87 > 2.201$ we reject $H_0: \beta_1 = 0$.

b. $t = \dfrac{b_2}{s_{b_2}} = \dfrac{17.9}{9.72} = 1.84$

Since $1.84 < 2.201$ we cannot reject $H_0: \beta_2 = 0$.

c. $t = \dfrac{b_3}{s_{b_3}} = \dfrac{-3.6}{.71} = -5.07$

Since $-5.07 < -2.201$ we reject $H_0: \beta_3 = 0$.

d. Yes, x_2 should be dropped since the hypothesis test indicated β_2 is not significantly different than zero.

46.   The computer output with the missing values filled in is as follows:

The regression equation is

$Y = 8.103 + 7.602\ X1 + 3.111\ X2$

Predicator	Coef	Stdev	t - ratio
Constant	8.103	2.667	3.04
X1	7.602	2.105	3.61
X2	3.111	0.613	5.08

$s = 3.35$ R-sq $= 92.3\%$ R-sq (adj) $= 91.0\%$

Analysis of Variance

SOURCE	DF	SS	MS	F
Regression	2	1612	806	71.82
Error	12	134,67	11.2225	
Total	14	1746.67		

a.   See computer output.

b. $t_{.025} = 2.179$ (12 DF)

for β_1: 3.61 > 2.179; reject $H_0 : \beta_1 = 0$

for β_2: 3.61 > 2.179; reject $H_0 : \beta_2 = 0$

c.   See computer output.

d. $R_a^2 = 1 - (1 - 923)\left(\dfrac{14}{12}\right) = .91$

47. a.   The regression equation is

$Y = -1.41 + .0235\ X1 + .00486\ X2$

Predicator	Coef	Stdev	t - ratio
Constant	-1.4053	0.4848	-2.90
X1	0.023467	0.008666	2.71
X2	.00486	0.001077	4.51

$s = 0.1298$ R-sq $= 93.7\%$ R-sq (adj) $= 91.9\%$

Analysis of Variance

SOURCE	DF	SS	MS	F
Regression	2	1.76209	.881	52.44
Error	7	.1179	.0168	
Total	9	1.88000		

b. $F_{.05} = 4.74$ (2 DF numerator, 7 DF denominator)

$F = 523.44 > F.05$; significant relationship.

c. $R^2 = \dfrac{SSR}{SST} = .937$

$R_a^2 = 1 - (1 - 937)\left(\dfrac{9}{7}\right) = .919$

good fit

d. $t_{.025} = 2.365$ (7 DF)

for $B_1 : t = 2.71 > 2.365$; reject $H_0 : B_1 = 0$

for $B_2 : t = 4.51 > 2.365$; reject $H_0 : B_2 = 0$

48. a. The regression equation is

$Y = 14.4 - 8.69\ X1 + 13.52\ X2$

Predicator	Coef	Stdev	t - ratio
Constant	14.448	8.191	1.76
X1	-8.69	1.555	-5.59
X2	13.517	2.085	6.48

$s = 3.773$ R-sq = 90.1%   R-sq (adj) = 86.1%

Analysis of Variance

SOURCE	DF	SS	MS	F
Regression	2	648.83	324.415	22.79
Error	5	71.17	14.234	
Total	7	720.00		

b. $F_{.05} = 5.79$ (5 DF)

$F = 22.79 > F.05$; significant relationship.

c. $R^2 = \dfrac{SSR}{SST} = .901$

$R_a^2 = 1 - (1 - 901)\left(\dfrac{7}{5}\right) = .861$

good fit

d. $t_{.025} = 2.571$ (5 DF)

for $\beta_1 : t = -5.59 < -2.571$; reject $H_0 : \beta_1 = 0$

for $\beta_2 : t = 6.48 > 2.571$; reject $H_0 : \beta_2 = 0$

49. a. $\hat{y} = 80 + 45\,(50) - 3\,(70) = 2120$

In dollars: \$2,120,000.

b. SSE = 21533 - 19780 = 1753

MSR = 197.80 / 2 = 9890

MSE = 1753 / 12 = 146.08

F = 9890 / 146.08 = 67.70

$F_{.01} = 6.93$ (2 numerator DF, 12 denominator DF)

Since 67.70 > 6.93 we conclude that the relationship is significant.

50. a.   The Minitab output is shown below:

```
The regression equation is
%MGTJOBS = - 16.7 + 1.02 %WOMEN

Predictor          Coef        Stdev      t-ratio          p
Constant        -16.697        3.918        -4.26      0.000
%WOMEN          1.01549       0.08255       12.30       0.000

s = 6.223         R-sq = 86.8%      R-sq(adj) = 86.2%

Analysis of Variance

SOURCE           DF            SS           MS           F          p
Regression        1        5859.4       5859.4      151.31      0.000
Error            23         890.6        38.7
Total            24        6750.0

Unusual Observations
Obs.   %WOMEN    %MGTJOBS         Fit Stdev.Fit   Residual    St.Resid
  9     47.0       18.00        31.03      1.26     -13.03       -2.14R
 14     47.0       16.00        31.03      1.26     -15.03       -2.47R

R denotes an obs. with a large st. resid.
```

b.   The coefficient of determination is .868; a very good fit.

c.   Let D1 = 1 if Technology, D2 = 1 if Consumer, D3 = 1 if Retailing, D4 = 1 if Media, D5 = 1 if Financial; the Minitab output is shown below:

```
The regression equation is
%MGTJOBS = 11.5 + 7.75 D1 + 7.75 D2 + 26.7 D3 + 24.8 D4 + 33.5 D5

Predictor          Coef        Stdev     t-ratio          p
Constant         11.500        6.177        1.86       0.078
D1                7.750        8.736        0.89       0.386
D2                7.750        8.736        0.89       0.386
D3               26.700        8.288        3.22       0.004
D4               24.833        9.436        2.63       0.016
D5               33.500        8.288        4.04       0.001


s = 12.35        R-sq = 57.0%      R-sq(adj) = 45.7%

Analysis of Variance

SOURCE         DF          SS          MS          F          p
Regression      5      3850.0       770.0       5.04      0.004
Error          19      2900.0       152.6
Total          24      6750.0

Unusual Observations
Obs.        D1    %MGTJOBS       Fit Stdev.Fit   Residual    St.Resid
 13       0.00      61.00      38.20      5.53      22.80       2.06R
 14       0.00      16.00      38.20      5.53     -22.20      -2.01R

R denotes an obs. with a large st. resid.
```

d.   %WOMEN is a better predictor than the type of industry.

e.   The Minitab output is shown below:

The regression equation is
%MGTJOBS = - 20.0 + 1.18 %WOMEN - 1.96 D1 - 5.49 D2 - 8.20 D3 + 3.74 D4
          - 7.99 D5

```
Predictor        Coef      Stdev     t-ratio        p
Constant      -19.989      4.773      -4.19      0.001
%WOMEN         1.1771     0.1420       8.29      0.000
D1             -1.961      4.253      -0.46      0.650
D2             -5.493      4.389      -1.25      0.227
D3             -8.202      5.724      -1.43      0.169
D4              3.743      5.096       0.73      0.472
D5             -7.994      6.331      -1.26      0.223
```

s = 5.782   R-sq = 91.1%   R-sq(adj) = 88.1%

Analysis of Variance

Unusual Observations
```
Obs.   %WOMEN   %MGTJOBS       Fit  Stdev.Fit   Residual   St.Resid
  9     47.0      18.00      29.84       3.16     -11.84      -2.45R
 14     47.0      16.00      27.13       2.91     -11.13      -2.23R
```

R denotes an obs. with a large st. resid.

f. Although the model involving %WOMEN and industry is significant, the additional variation explained by type of industry given the effect of %WOMEN is not sisgnificant.

51. a. The pattern of the standard residual plot is acceptable.

b. The Minitab output shown in Exercise 50 identifies observation 9 and observation 14 as having a large standardized residual; on this basis we could classify these two observations as outliers.

c. There does not appear to be any influential observations.

52. a. The Minitab output is shown below:

The regression equation is

POINTS = 170 + 6.61 TEAMINT

```
Predicator       Coef       Stdev     t - ratio        p
Constant       170.13       44.02        3.86      0.002
TEAMINT         6.613        2.258       2.93      0.013
```

s = 43.93   R-sq = 41.7%   R-sq (adj) = 36.8%

Analysis of Variance

SOURCE	DF	SS	MS	F	p
Regression	1	16546	16546	8.57	0.013
Error	12	23157	1930		
Total	13	39703			

Unusual Observations

Obs.	%PROFIT	P/E	Fit	Stdev.Fit	Residual	St.Resid
13	33.0	340.0	388.4	34.2	-48.4	-1.75 X

X denotes an obs. whose X value gives it large influence.

b. Although the pattern of the plot is acceptable, observation 13 appears to be an unusual looking observation.

c. Observation 13 appears to be an outlier in the sense that it does not fit the trend exhibited by the remaining data. However, the value of its standardized residual, -1.75, does not result in Minitab identifying it as an observation with a larger standardized residual and thus an outlier. At the .05 level of significance, the studentized deleted residual for this observation is also not significant and hence observation 13 is not classified as an outlier.

Note: Even though observation 13 is not classified as an outlier based upon the value of its standardized residual or studentized deleted residual, it is clear from the standardized residual plot that this observation is unusual and warrants more investigation. Since there is only one independent variable, the scatter diagram of the number of points scored versus the number of team interceptions will also verify this conclusion.

d. Minitab classifies observation 13 as an influential observation. The value of Cook's distance measure for observation 13 is $D_{13} = 2.356$; thus, we would conclude that observation 13 is an influential observation.

53. a. The Minitab output is shown below:

The regression equation is

POINTS = 394 - 5.10 OPPININT

Predicator	Coef	Stdev	t - ratio	p
Constant	394.23	37.38	10.55	0.000
OPPONINT	-5.103	1.810	-2.82	0.015

$s = 44.61$ R-sq = 39.8%   R-sq (adj) = 34.8%

Analysis of Variance

SOURCE	DF	SS	MS	F	p
Regression	1	15819	15819	7.95	0.015
Error	12	23884	1990		
Total	13	39703			

Unusual Observations

Obs.	OPPONINT	POINTS	Fit	Stdev.Fit	Residual	St.Resid
2	24.0	187.0	271.8	14.4	-84.8	-2.01R
7	35.0	206.0	215.6	30.4	-9.6	-0.29 X

R denotes an obs. with a large st. resid.

X denotes an obs. whose X value gives it large influence.

b. The general pattern of the plot looks acceptable.

c. Observation 2 has a standardized residual of -2.01; thus, we could classify this observation as an outlier.

d. Minitab identifies observation 7 as an influential observation.

Note: Since there is only one independent variable, it is useful to examine the scatter diagram of points scored versus the number of interceptions made by the opponents in order to see what effect this point has. It is also instructive to delete observation 7 from the data set and fit a new estimated regression equation involving 13 observations.

Solution to Computer Case

Descriptive statistics for these data are shown below:

	N	MEAN	MEDIAN	TRMEAN	STDEV	SEMEAN
INCOME	50	43.48	42.00	43.41	14.55	2.06
SIZE	50	3.420	3.000	3.341	1.739	0.246
AMOUNT	50	3964	4090	3973	933	132

	MIN	MAX	Q1	Q3
INCOME	21.00	67.00	30.00	55.00
SIZE	1.000	7.000	2.000	5.000
AMOUNT	1864	5678	3109	4747

The following scatter diagrams suggest a linear relationship.

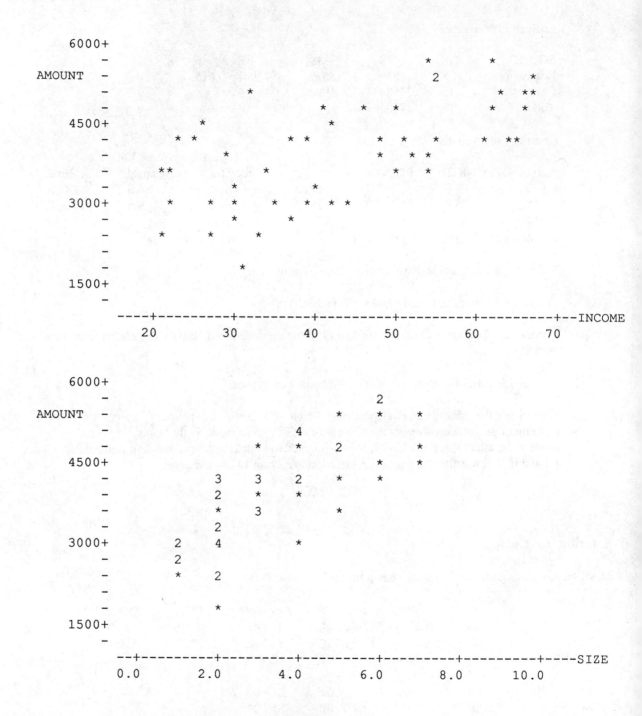

Minitab was used to obtain the following regrssion analysis output:

The regression equation is
AMOUNT = 2204 + 40.5 INCOME

Predictor	Coef	Stdev	t-ratio	p
Constant	2204.0	329.0	6.70	0.000
INCOME	40.480	7.184	5.63	0.000

s = 731.7   R-sq = 39.8%   R-sq(adj) = 38.6%

Analysis of Variance

SOURCE	DF	SS	MS	F	p
Regression	1	16999744	16999744	31.75	0.000
Error	48	25699404	535404		
Total	49	42699148			

Unusual Observations

Obs.	INCOME	AMOUNT	Fit	Stdev.Fit	Residual	St.Resid
3	32.0	5100	3499	132	1601	2.22R
5	31.0	1864	3459	137	-1595	-2.22R

R denotes an obs. with a large st. resid.

The regression equation is
AMOUNT = 2582 + 404 SIZE

Predictor	Coef	Stdev	t-ratio	p
Constant	2581.9	195.3	13.22	0.000
SIZE	404.13	51.00	7.92	0.000

s = 620.8   R-sq = 56.7%   R-sq(adj) = 55.8%

Analysis of Variance

SOURCE	DF	SS	MS	F	p
Regression	1	24200718	24200718	62.80	0.000
Error	48	18498432	385384		
Total	49	42699152			

Unusual Observations

Obs.	SIZE	AMOUNT	Fit	Stdev.Fit	Residual	St.Resid
5	2.00	1864.0	3390.2	113.8	-1526.2	-2.50R

R denotes an obs. with a large st. resid.

```
The regression equation is
AMOUNT = 1305 + 33.1 INCOME + 356 SIZE

Predictor        Coef        Stdev      t-ratio          p
Constant        1304.9       197.7         6.60      0.000
INCOME          33.133       3.968         8.35      0.000
SIZE            356.30       33.20        10.73      0.000

s = 398.1        R-sq = 82.6%      R-sq(adj) = 81.8%

Analysis of Variance

SOURCE        DF           SS           MS          F          p
Regression     2       35250756     17625378     111.22     0.000
Error         47        7448393       158476
Total         49       42699148

SOURCE        DF        SEQ SS
INCOME         1       16999744
SIZE           1       18251010

Unusual Observations
Obs.   INCOME      AMOUNT        Fit  Stdev.Fit    Residual    St.Resid
  3      32.0      5100.0     3790.3      76.9      1309.7        3.35R
  5      31.0      1864.0     3044.6      83.9     -1180.6       -3.03R
 11      25.0      4208.0     3202.1      91.6      1005.9        2.60R

R denotes an obs. with a large st. resid.
```

The standardized residual plot for the model involving both independent variables is shown below:

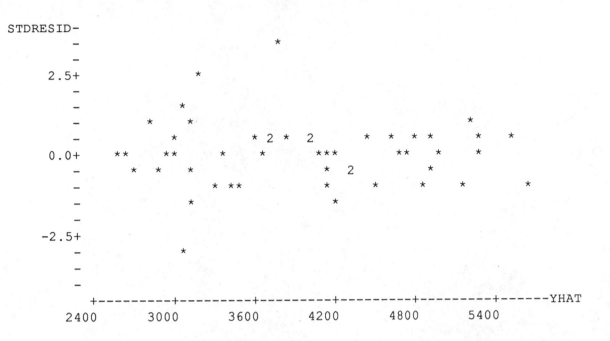

Although the multiple regression model explains a high percentage of the variability in the dependent variable, the output identifies three observations as having a large standardized residual; thus, these 3 observations should be treated as possible outliers.

Chapter 16
Regression Analysis: Model Building

Learning Objectives

1. Learn how the general linear model can be used to model problems involving curvilinear relationships.

2. Understand the concept of interaction and how it can be accounted for in the general linear model.

3. Understand how an F test can be used to determine when to add or delete one or more variables.

4. Develop an appreciation for the complexities involved in solving larger regression analysis problems.

5. Understand how variable selection procedures can be used to choose a set of independent variables for an estimated regression equation.

6. Know how the Durban-Watson test can be used to test for autocorrelation.

7. Learn how residual analysis can be used to identify observations that can be classified as an outlier or as being especially influential in determining the estimated regression equation.

8. Learn how analysis of variance and experimental design problems can be analyzed using a regression model.

Solutions:

1. a. The Minitab output is shown below:

```
The regression equation is
Y = - 6.8 + 1.23 X

Predictor          Coef        Stdev      t-ratio          p
Constant          -6.77        14.17        -0.48      0.658
X                1.2296       0.4697         2.62      0.059

s = 7.269         R-sq = 63.1%      R-sq(adj) = 53.9%

Analysis of Variance

SOURCE         DF           SS           MS           F          p
Regression      1       362.13       362.13        6.85      0.059
Error           4       211.37        52.84
Total           5       573.50
```

b. Since the *p*-value corresponding to F= 6.85 is 0.59 > α = .05, the relationship is not significant.

c.

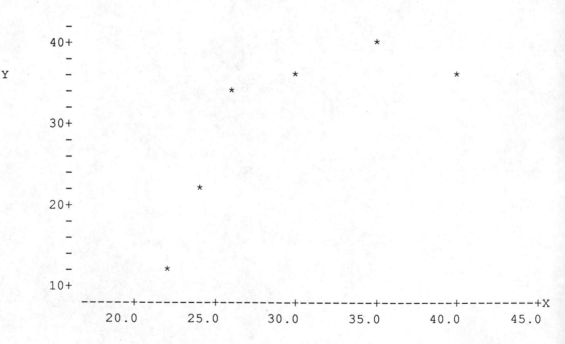

The scatter diagram suggests that a curvilinear relationship may be appropriate.

d. The Minitab output is shown below:

```
The regression equation is
Y = - 169 + 12.2 X - 0.177 XSQ


Predictor          Coef          Stdev       t-ratio          p
Constant        -168.88          39.79         -4.24      0.024
X                12.187           2.663          4.58      0.020
XSQ             -0.17704         0.04290        -4.13      0.026


s = 3.248          R-sq = 94.5%       R-sq(adj) = 90.8%


Analysis of Variance


SOURCE          DF          SS            MS          F          p
Regression       2        541.85        270.92      25.68      0.013
Error            3         31.65         10.55
Total            5        573.50
```

e. Since the p-value corresponding to F = 25.68 is .013 < α = .05, the relationship is significant.

f. $\hat{y} = -168.88 + 12.187(25) - 0.17704(25)^2 = 25.145$

2. a. The Minitab output is shown below:

```
The regression equation is
Y = 9.32 + 0.424 X


Predictor          Coef          Stdev       t-ratio          p
Constant         9.315          4.196          2.22       0.113
X                0.4242         0.1944         2.18       0.117


s = 3.531          R-sq = 61.4%       R-sq(adj) = 48.5%


Analysis of Variance


SOURCE          DF          SS            MS          F          p
Regression       1         59.39         59.39       4.76      0.117
Error            3         37.41         12.47
Total            4         96.80
```

The high *p*-value (.117) indicates a weak relationship; note that 61.4% of the variability in *y* has been explained by *x*.

b. The Minitab output is shown below:

```
The regression equation is
Y = - 8.10 + 2.41 X - 0.0480 XSQ

Predictor        Coef        Stdev      t-ratio          p
Constant       -8.101        4.104        -1.97      0.187
X               2.4127       0.4409        5.47      0.032
XSQ            -0.04797      0.01050      -4.57      0.045


s = 1.279          R-sq = 96.6%      R-sq(adj) = 93.2%

Analysis of Variance

SOURCE          DF           SS          MS          F          p
Regression      2         93.529      46.765      28.60      0.034
Error           2          3.271       1.635
Total           4         96.800
```

At the .05 level of significance, the relationship is significant; the fit is excellent.

c. $\hat{y} = -8.101 + 2.4127(20) - 0.04797(20)^2 = 20.965$

3. a. The scatter diagram shows some evidence of a possible linear relationship.

b. The Minitab output is shown below:

```
The regression equation is
Y = 2.32 + 0.637 X

Predictor        Coef        Stdev      t-ratio          p
Constant        2.322       1.887        1.23      0.258
X               0.6366      0.3044       2.09      0.075


s = 2.054          R-sq = 38.5%      R-sq(adj) = 29.7%

Analysis of Variance

SOURCE          DF           SS          MS          F          p
Regression      1         18.461      18.461      4.37       0.075
Error           7         29.539       4.220
Total           8         48.000
```

c. The following standardized residual plot indicates that the constant variance assumption is not satisfied.

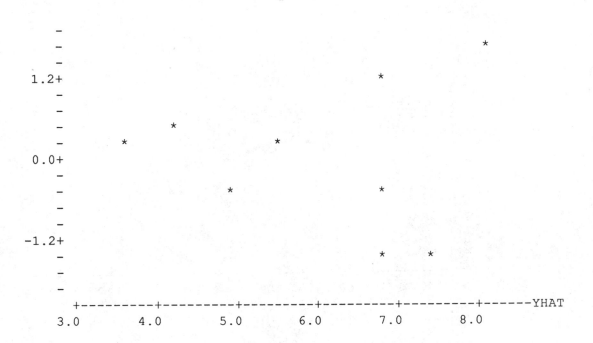

d. The logarithmic transformation does not appear to eliminate the wedged-shaped pattern in the above residual plot. The reciprocal transformation does, however, remove the wedge-shaped pattern. Neither transformation provides a good fit. The Minitab output for the reciprocal transformation and the corresponding standardized residual pot are shown below.

```
The regression equation is
1/Y = 0.275 - 0.0152 X

Predictor        Coef        Stdev      t-ratio        p
Constant       0.27498      0.04601       5.98       0.000
X             -0.015182     0.007421     -2.05       0.080

s = 0.05009     R-sq = 37.4%      R-sq(adj) = 28.5%

Analysis of Variance

SOURCE          DF         SS           MS          F         p
Regression       1      0.010501     0.010501      4.19     0.080
Error            7      0.017563     0.002509
Total            8      0.028064
```

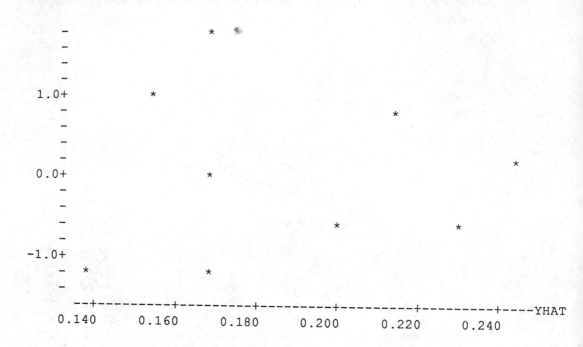

```
         -
         -
         -
         -
    1.0+            *
         -               *
         -
         -
         -                                              *
    0.0+                 *
         -                                                        *
         -
         -                           *
         -                                        *
   -1.0+
         -   *
         -            *
         --+---------+---------+---------+---------+---------+---------+----YHAT
         0.140    0.160     0.180     0.200     0.220     0.240
```

4. a. The Minitab output is shown below:

```
The regression equation is
Y = 943 + 8.71 X

Predictor        Coef        Stdev     t-ratio           p
Constant       943.05        59.38       15.88       0.000
X               8.714        1.544        5.64       0.005

s = 32.29        R-sq = 88.8%      R-sq(adj) = 86.1%

Analysis of Variance

SOURCE          DF           SS          MS         F         p
Regression       1        33223       33223     31.86     0.005
Error            4         4172        1043
Total            5        37395
```

b. The p-value of $.005 < \alpha = .01$; reject H_0

5. The Minitab output is shown below:

```
The regression equation is
Y = 433 + 37.4 X - 0.383 1/Y

Predictor          Coef        Stdev      t-ratio          p
Constant          432.6        141.2         3.06      0.055
X                37.429        7.807         4.79      0.017
1/Y             -0.3829       0.1036        -3.70      0.034


s = 15.83         R-sq = 98.0%       R-sq(adj) = 96.7%

Analysis of Variance

SOURCE          DF           SS          MS          F          p
Regression       2        36643       18322      73.15      0.003
Error            3          751         250
Total            5        37395
```

b. Since the linear relationship was significant (Exercise 4), this relationship must be significant. Note also that since the p-value of .005 < α = .05, we can reject H_0.

c. The fitted value is 1302.01, with a standard deviation of 9.93. The 95% confidence interval is 1270.41 to 1333.61; the 95% prediction interval is 1242.55 to 1361.47.

6. a. The scatter diagram is shown below:

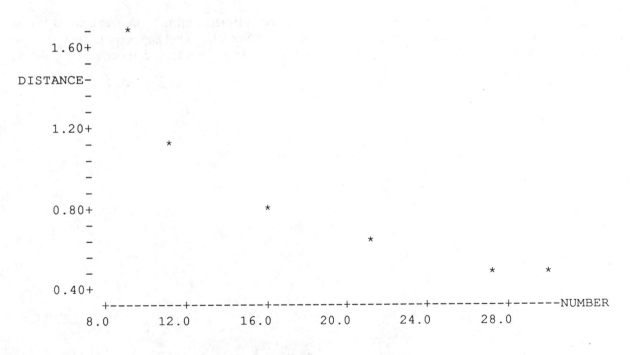

b. No; the relationship appears to be curvilinear.

c. Several possible models can be fitted to these data, as shown below:

$$\hat{y} = 2.90 - 0.185x + .00351x^2 \quad R_a^2 = .91$$

$$\hat{y} = -0.0468 + 14.4\left(\frac{1}{x}\right) \quad R_a^2 = .91$$

7. The Minitab output using just engine rpm to predict boat speed is shown below:

```
The regression equation is
SPEED = 0.30 + 0.00919 RPM

Predictor        Coef        Stdev      t-ratio        p
Constant        0.297       2.838         0.10    0.920
RPM        0.0091950   0.0008779        10.47    0.000

s = 3.312      R-sq = 94.0%      R-sq(adj) = 93.1%

Analysis of Variance

SOURCE         DF          SS          MS         F        p
Regression      1      1203.6      1203.6    109.71    0.000
Error           7        76.8        11.0
Total           8      1280.4
```

Although the estimated regression equation provides an excellent fit, the standardized residual plot indicates that the assumption of a linear relationship is not appropriate. As a result, we developed a model which also uses the square of rpm to predict y; the corresponding Minitab output is shown below:

```
The regression equation is
SPEED = - 13.9 + 0.0210 RPM -0.000002 RPMSQ

Predictor          Coef          Stdev      t-ratio          p
Constant        -13.890          2.737       -5.08      0.002
RPM            0.021040       0.002087       10.08      0.000
RPMSQ       -0.00000202     0.00000035       -5.77      0.001


s = 1.399         R-sq = 99.1%       R-sq(adj) = 98.8%

Analysis of Variance

SOURCE          DF            SS           MS         F          p
Regression       2       1268.64       634.32    324.22      0.000
Error            6         11.74         1.96
Total            8       1280.38
```

b. $\hat{y} = -13.890 + 0.021040(2800) - 0.00000202(2800)^2 = 29.185$ mph

8. a. The scatter diagram is shown below:

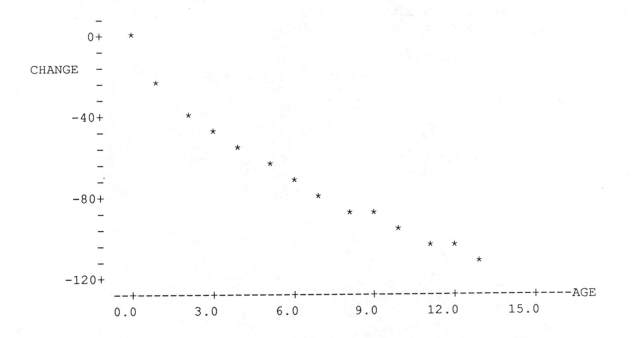

b. Although a simple linear model does appear to be appropriate, there may be some curvilinear effect in the data.

c. Although the simple liner model provides an excellent fit, the standardized residual plot indicates that the assumption of a linear relationship may not be appropriate. As a result we developed a model which also uses the square of the film age to predict the change in the film speed; the corresponding Minitab output is shown below:

```
The regression equation is
CHANGE = - 6.60 - 14.2 AGE + 0.508 AGESQ

Predictor        Coef        Stdev      t-ratio         p
Constant       -6.603        3.151       -2.10      0.060
AGE           -14.211        1.125      -12.63      0.000
AGESQ         0.50824      0.08347        6.09      0.000

s = 4.504          R-sq = 98.4%       R-sq(adj) = 98.1%

Analysis of Variance

SOURCE         DF            SS           MS          F         p
Regression      2       13906.3       6953.1     342.74     0.000
Error          11         223.2         20.3
Total          13       14129.4
```

9. a. A scatter diagram of cost versus the number of housing starts shows that observation 3 is influential; in fact, the plot suggests a curvilinear relationship between these two variables. The corresponding Minitab output is shown below:

```
The regression equation is
COST = 52.9 + 11.8 STARTS - 0.398 STARTSSQ

Predictor        Coef        Stdev      t-ratio         p
Constant        52.86       12.29         4.30      0.001
STARTS         11.836       2.970         3.99      0.002
STARTSSQ      -0.3984      0.1192        -3.34      0.005

s = 20.08          R-sq = 58.4%       R-sq(adj) = 51.9%
```

Analysis of Variance

SOURCE	DF	SS	MS	F	p
Regression	2	7346.1	3673.1	9.11	0.003
Error	13	5243.3	403.3		
Total	15	12589.5			
4501.6					

Unusual Observations

Obs.	STARTS	COST	Fit	Stdev.Fit	Residual	St.Resid
1	12.9	181.80	139.25	10.40	42.55	2.48R
3	24.2	100.60	105.99	19.87	-5.39	-1.84 X
12	8.0	82.10	122.05	7.51	-39.95	-2.15R

R denotes an obs. with a large st. resid.
X denotes an obs. whose X value gives it large influence.

The standardized residual plot indicates that the constant variance assumption does not appear to be satisfied. In an attempt to solve this problem, we fitted a model using the reciprocal of COST as the dependent variable. The estimated regression equation for this model is

$$1/\text{COST} = 0.0149 - 0.00105 \text{ STARTS} + .000035 \text{ STARTSSQ}$$

Although the reciprocal transformation does eliminate the wedged-shape pattern in the residual plot, observation 3 is still identified as being influential and observation 12 has a large standardized residual.

Conclusion: INCOME does not appear to be a very strong predictor of COST for these data.

Cautionary Note: The wide range for the number of housing starts suggests that we may have insufficient data to fit a model that covers a range from 1.0 housing starts (Mobile, Ala.) to 24.2 housing starts (Atlanta). One possible approach would be to reduce the range to at most 12.9 housing starts by dropping the Atlanta observation, or to at most 10 housing starts by dropping the Chicago, Atlanta, and Baltimore observations. We should also investigate the effect of adding one or more other independent variables, such as the population of the city, to the current model.

b. $1/\text{COST} = 0.0149 - 0.00105\,(8) + .000035\,(8)^2 = .087$

Thus, an estimate of the cost is 1/.0087 = 114.94 or $114,940

10. a. $t = \dfrac{b_1}{s_{b_1}} = \dfrac{2.3}{.53} = 4.34$

$t_{.025} = 2.069$ (23 DF)

Since $4.34 > 2.069$ we reject H_0: $\beta_1 = 0$ and conclude that x_1 is significant.

b.　$t = \dfrac{b_2}{s_{b_2}} = \dfrac{12.1}{8.15} = 1.48$

$t_{.025} = 2.069$

Since $1.48 < 2.069$ we cannot reject H_0: $\beta_2 = 0$

c.　$t = \dfrac{b_3}{s_{b_3}} = \dfrac{-5.8}{1.30} = -4.46$

$t_{.025} = 2.069$

Since $-4.46 < -2.069$ we reject H_0: $\beta_3 = 0$ and conclude that x_3 is significant.

d.　x_2 can be dropped since it does not make a significant addition to a model involving x_1 and x_3

11. a.　$R^2 = \dfrac{SSR}{SST} = \dfrac{1760}{1805} = .975$

b.　$R_a^2 = 1 - \left(1 - R^2\right)\left(\dfrac{n-1}{n-p-1}\right) = 1 - (.025)\left(\dfrac{29}{25}\right) = .971$

c.　SSE $= 1805 - 1760 = 45$

$F = \dfrac{MSR}{MSE} = \dfrac{1760/4}{45/25} = 244.44$

$F_{.05} = 2.76$ (4 numerator and 25 denominator DF)

Since $244.44 > 2.76$ we reject H_0 and conclude that the relationship is significant.

12. a. The Minitab output is shown below.

```
The regression equation is
POINTS = 170 + 6.61 TEAMINT

Predictor          Coef        Stdev      t-ratio        p
Constant         170.13        44.02         3.86    0.002
TEAMINT           6.613         2.258        2.93    0.013

s = 43.93        R-sq = 41.7%      R-sq(adj) = 36.8%

Analysis of Variance

SOURCE          DF          SS          MS          F         p
Regression       1        16546       16546       8.57    0.013
Error           12        23157        1930
Total           13        39703

Unusual Observations
Obs.  TEAMINT      POINTS       Fit Stdev.Fit  Residual    St.Resid
 13      33.0       340.0     388.4      34.2     -48.4     -1.75 X

X denotes an obs. whose X value gives it large influence.
```

b. The Minitab output is shown below.

```
The regression equation is
POINTS = 280 + 5.18 TEAMINT - 0.0037 RUSHING - 3.92 OPPONINT

Predictor          Coef        Stdev      t-ratio        p
Constant         280.34        81.42         3.44    0.006
TEAMINT           5.176         2.073        2.50    0.032
RUSHING        -0.00373        0.03336      -0.11    0.913
OPPONINT         -3.918         1.651       -2.37    0.039

s = 37.84        R-sq = 63.9%      R-sq(adj) = 53.1%

Analysis of Variance

SOURCE          DF          SS          MS          F         p
Regression       3        25386        8462       5.91    0.014
Error           10        14317        1432
Total           13        39703

SOURCE          DF      SEQ SS
TEAMINT          1       16546
RUSHING          1         776
OPPONINT         1        8064
```

16-13

c.
$$F = \frac{\dfrac{\text{SSE(reduced) - SSE(full)}}{\text{\# extra terms}}}{\text{MSE(full)}} = \frac{\dfrac{23{,}157 - 14{,}317}{2}}{1432} = 3.09$$

$F_{.05} = 4.10$ (2 numerator and 10 denominator DF)

Since $3.09 < 4.10$ the addition of the two independent variables is not significant.

Note: Suppose that we considered adding only the number of interceptions made by the opponents; the corresponding Minitab output is shown below:

```
The regression equation is
POINTS = 274 + 5.23 TEAMINT - 3.96 OPPONINT

Predictor        Coef        Stdev      t-ratio           p
Constant       273.77        53.81         5.09       0.000
TEAMINT         5.227         1.931        2.71       0.020
OPPONINT       -3.965         1.524       -2.60       0.025

s = 36.10        R-sq = 63.9%      R-sq(adj) = 57.3%

Analysis of Variance

SOURCE          DF          SS           MS          F          p
Regression       2        25368        12684       9.73      0.004
Error           11        14335         1303
Total           13        39703

SOURCE          DF       SEQ SS
TEAMINT          1        16546
OPPONINT         1         8822
```

In this case,

$$F = \frac{\dfrac{23{,}157 - 14{,}335}{1}}{1303} = 6.77$$

$F_{.05} = 4.84$ (1 numerator and 11 denominator DF)

Since $6.77 > 4.84$ the addition of the number of interceptions made by the opponents is significant.

13. a.   The Minitab output is shown below:

```
The regression equation is
POINTS = 218 + 0.0252 PASSING + 4.39 TEAMINT - 4.38 OPPONINT

Predictor        Coef        Stdev      t-ratio         p
Constant        218.38       69.07         3.16      0.010
PASSING         0.02520      0.02039       1.24      0.245
TEAMINT          4.387       2.005         2.19      0.053
OPPONINT        -4.376       1.525        -2.87      0.017


s = 35.26        R-sq = 68.7%       R-sq(adj) = 59.3%


Analysis of Variance

SOURCE          DF           SS           MS          F         p
Regression       3         27269         9090       7.31      0.007
Error           10         12435         1243
Total           13         39703
```

b.   The Minitab output is shown below:

```
The regression equation is
POINTS = 235 + 0.0266 PASSING + 4.18 TEAMINT - 4.26 OPPONINT - 0.0115 RUSHING

Predictor        Coef        Stdev      t-ratio         p
Constant        235.40       87.52         2.69      0.025
PASSING         0.02663      0.02174       1.22      0.252
TEAMINT          4.185       2.180         1.92      0.087
OPPONINT        -4.256       1.635        -2.60      0.029
RUSHING         -0.01145     0.03316      -0.35      0.738


s = 36.93        R-sq = 69.1%       R-sq(adj) = 55.4%


Analysis of Variance

SOURCE          DF           SS           MS          F         p
Regression       4         27431         6858       5.03      0.021
Error            9         12272         1364
Total           13         39703
```

c. $$F = \frac{\dfrac{\text{SSE(reduced) - SSE(full)}}{\text{\# extra terms}}}{\text{MSE(full)}} = \frac{\dfrac{12{,}435 - 12{,}272}{1}}{1364} = .1195$$

$F_{.05} = 5.12$ (1 numerator and 9 denominator DF)

Since $.1195 < 5.12$ the addition of RUSHING is not significant.

Note: Since only 1 variable was added to the model in part (a), the test can also be performed using the t-ratio for RUSHING in the Minitab output.

14. a. The Minitab output is shown below:

```
The regression equation is
RISK = - 111 + 1.32 AGE + 0.296 PRESSURE

Predictor          Coef          Stdev       t-ratio          p
Constant        -110.94          16.47         -6.74      0.000
AGE               1.3150         0.1733          7.59      0.000
PRESSURE          0.29640       0.05107          5.80      0.000

s = 6.908          R-sq = 80.6%       R-sq(adj) = 78.4%

Analysis of Variance

SOURCE           DF            SS           MS           F          p
Regression        2        3379.6       1689.8       35.41      0.000
Error            17         811.3         47.7
Total            19        4191.0
```

b. The Minitab output is shown below:

```
The regression equation is
RISK = - 123 + 1.51 AGE + 0.448 PRESSURE + 8.87 SMOKER - 0.00276 AGEXPRES

Predictor          Coef          Stdev       t-ratio          p
Constant        -123.16          56.94         -2.16      0.047
AGE               1.5130         0.7796          1.94      0.071
PRESSURE          0.4483         0.3457          1.30      0.214
SMOKER            8.866          3.074           2.88      0.011
AGEXPRES         -0.002756       0.004807       -0.57      0.575

s = 5.881          R-sq = 87.6%       R-sq(adj) = 84.3%

Analysis of Variance

SOURCE           DF            SS           MS           F          p
Regression        4        3672.11       918.03       26.54      0.000
Error            15         518.84        34.59
Total            19        4190.95
```

c.
$$F = \frac{\dfrac{SSE(\text{reduced}) - SSE(\text{full})}{\text{\# extra terms}}}{MSE(\text{full})} = \frac{\dfrac{811.3 - 518.84}{2}}{34.59} = 4.23$$

$F_{.05} = 3.68$ (2 numerator and 15 denominator DF)

Since 4.23 > 3.68 the addition of the two terms is significant.

15. a. The Minitab output is shown below:

```
The regression equation is
%COLLEGE = - 26.6 + 0.0970 SATSCORE

Predictor         Coef          Stdev      t-ratio          p
Constant        -26.61          37.22       -0.72       0.485
SATSCORE        0.09703        0.03734        2.60       0.019

s = 12.83       R-sq = 29.7%      R-sq(adj) = 25.3%

Analysis of Variance

SOURCE          DF            SS           MS          F          p
Regression       1         1110.8       1110.8       6.75      0.019
Error           16         2632.3        164.5
Total           17         3743.1
```

b.
```
    STEPWISE REGRESSION OF %COLLEGE ON  5 PREDICTORS,
WITH N =    18

        STEP          1          2
CONSTANT        -26.61     -26.93

SATSCORE          0.097      0.084
T-RATIO           2.60       2.46

%TAKESAT                     0.204
T-RATIO                      2.21

S                 12.8       11.5
R-SQ             29.68      46.93
```

c.   Backward elimination procedure:

```
        STEP          1         2         3         4
      CONSTANT     33.71     17.46    -32.47    -26.93

      SIZE         -1.56     -1.39
      T-RATIO      -1.43     -1.42

      STUDENT$   -0.0024   -0.0026   -0.0019
      T-RATIO      -1.47     -1.75     -1.31

      SALARY    -0.00026
      T-RATIO      -0.40

      SATSCORE     0.077     0.081     0.095     0.084
      T-RATIO       2.06      2.36      2.77      2.46

      %TAKESAT     0.285     0.274     0.291     0.204
      T-RATIO       2.47      2.53      2.60      2.21

      S             11.2      10.9      11.2      11.5
      R-SQ         59.65     59.10     52.71     46.93
```

d.

```
      Best Subsets Regression of %COLLEGE
```

					S	S	%
					T	A	T
					U	S	A
					D	A	K
					S	L	C	E
					I	A	O	S
		Adj.			Z	T	R	R	A
Vars	R-sq	R-sq	C-p	s	E	$	Y	E	T
1	29.7	25.3	6.9	12.826			X		
1	25.5	20.8	8.2	13.203					X
2	46.9	39.9	3.8	11.508				X	X
2	38.2	30.0	6.4	12.417	X			X	
3	52.7	42.6	4.1	11.244		X		X	X
3	49.5	38.7	5.0	11.618	X			X	X
4	59.1	46.5	4.2	10.852	X	X		X	X
4	52.8	38.3	6.0	11.660		X	X	X	X
5	59.6	42.8	6.0	11.219	X	X	X	X	X

16. a.   The sample correlation coefficients are as follows:

```
            SATSCORE       SIZE STUDENT$    SALARY %TAKESAT
SIZE        -0.379
STUDENT$     0.302     -0.509
SALARY       0.029     -0.517     0.576
%TAKESAT     0.176     -0.376     0.606     0.512
%COLLEGE     0.545     -0.477     0.212     0.164     0.505
```

The variable most highly correlated with SATSCORE is %COLLEGE; thus, the best one variable model involves %COLLEGE. The Minitab output is shown below:

```
The regression equation is
SATSCORE = 780 + 3.06 %COLLEGE

Predictor        Coef        Stdev      t-ratio          p
Constant       780.02        83.87         9.30      0.000
%COLLEGE        3.059         1.177        2.60      0.019

s = 72.02       R-sq = 29.7%      R-sq(adj) = 25.3%

Analysis of Variance

SOURCE          DF           SS           MS          F          p
Regression       1        35018        35018       6.75      0.019
Error           16        82979         5186
Total           17       117996
```

b.   Stepwise procedure:

```
      STEP          1
CONSTANT       780.0

%COLLEGE         3.1
T-RATIO         2.60

S               72.0
R-SQ           29.68
```

c. Backward elimination procedure:

STEP	1	2	3	4	5
CONSTANT	892.6	798.6	724.0	756.7	780.0
SIZE	-2.4				
T-RATIO	-0.31				
STUDENT$	0.0155	0.0166	0.0142	0.0068	
T-RATIO	1.40	1.66	1.56	0.90	
SALARY	-0.0029	-0.0024			
T-RATIO	-0.70	-0.65			
%TAKESAT	-0.89	-0.96	-1.10		
T-RATIO	-0.98	-1.13	-1.38		
%COLLEGE	3.4	3.6	3.7	2.8	3.1
T-RATIO	2.06	2.65	2.77	2.33	2.60
S	74.5	71.9	70.4	72.4	72.0
R-SQ	43.54	43.08	41.25	33.31	29.68

d.

Best Subsets Regression of SATSCORE

Vars	R-sq	Adj. R-sq	C-p	s	S T U D S E I N Z E	% T A K E S A T $	% C O L L E G E Y T		
1	29.7	25.3	0.9	72.015					X
1	14.3	9.0	4.2	79.483	X				
2	33.3	24.4	2.2	72.431		X			X
2	31.5	22.4	2.6	73.403	X				X
3	41.2	28.7	2.5	70.371		X		X	X
3	37.5	24.1	3.3	72.606		X	X		X
4	43.1	25.6	4.1	71.877		X	X	X	X
4	41.3	23.2	4.5	73.020	X	X		X	X
5	43.5	20.0	6.0	74.512	X	X	X	X	X

17. a. The correlation coefficients are as follows:

```
              WINS    POINTS  RUSHING  PASSING  TEAMINT
POINTS      -0.664
RUSHING      0.527   -0.318
PASSING      0.206    0.293    0.133
TEAMINT     -0.671    0.646   -0.285    0.290
OPPONINT     0.506   -0.631    0.312    0.120   -0.276
```

The variable most highly correlated with WINS is TEAMINT. The Minitab output for this model using TEAMINT to predict WINS is shown below:

```
The regression equation is
WINS = 14.3 - 0.373 TEAMINT

Predictor          Coef        Stdev     t-ratio          p
Constant         14.294        2.318        6.17      0.000
TEAMINT         -0.3730       0.1189       -3.14      0.009

s = 2.313        R-sq = 45.1%      R-sq(adj) = 40.5%

Analysis of Variance

SOURCE          DF           SS           MS          F          p
Regression       1       52.652       52.652       9.84      0.009
Error           12       64.205        5.350
Total           13      116.857
```

b. Stepwise regression procedure:

```
        STEP          1           2           3
CONSTANT        14.294       7.585      11.199

TEAMINT          -0.37       -0.44       -0.28
T-RATIO          -3.14       -4.14       -2.45

PASSING                    0.00256     0.00288
T-RATIO                       2.27        3.02

POINTS                                  -0.026
T-RATIO                                  -2.37

S                 2.31        1.99        1.67
R-SQ             45.06       62.63       76.04
```

c. Backward elimination procedure:

```
       STEP          1          2          3
       CONSTANT    8.072      7.827     11.199

       POINTS     -0.024     -0.023     -0.026
       T-RATIO     -1.54      -2.08      -2.37

       RUSHING    0.0018     0.0018
       T-RATIO      1.13       1.19

       PASSING   0.00261    0.00257    0.00288
       T-RATIO      2.36       2.65       3.02

       TEAMINT    -0.26      -0.26      -0.28
       T-RATIO     -2.11      -2.30      -2.45

       OPPONINT   -0.01
       T-RATIO     -0.08

       S            1.74       1.64       1.67
```

d.

Best Subsets Regression of WINS

		Adj.			R P T P

Vars	R-sq	Adj. R-sq	C-p	s	P U A E P O S S A O I H S M N N I I I I T N N N N S G G T T
1	45.1	40.5	11.3	2.3131	X
1	44.0	39.4	11.7	2.3344	X
2	62.6	55.8	6.5	1.9925	X X
2	61.6	54.7	6.8	2.0187	X X
3	76.0	68.9	3.3	1.6732	X X X
3	69.3	60.1	5.9	1.8932	X X X
4	79.3	70.1	4.0	1.6389	X X X X
4	76.0	65.4	5.3	1.7637	X X X X
5	79.3	66.4	6.0	1.7377	X X X X X

18. a. The variable most highly correlated with POINTS is WINS (sample correlation coefficient is -0.664). The Minitab output for the model corresponding to WINS is shown below:

```
The regression equation is
POINTS = 383 - 12.2 WINS

Predictor        Coef       Stdev      t-ratio        p
Constant        383.48      31.20       12.29      0.000
WINS           -12.232       3.980      -3.07      0.010

s = 43.03       R-sq = 44.0%     R-sq(adj) = 39.4%

Analysis of Variance

SOURCE          DF           SS          MS          F          p
Regression       1         17485       17485       9.44      0.010
Error           12         22218        1852
Total           13         39703
```

b. Stepwise regression procedure:

```
       STEP          1          2          3
CONSTANT         383.5      244.0      278.6

WINS             -12.2      -13.9      -10.2
T-RATIO          -3.07      -4.06      -3.01

PASSING                     0.048      0.049
T-RATIO                      2.41       2.86

OPPONINT                               -3.3
T-RATIO                                -2.25

S                 43.0       36.4       31.1
R-SQ             44.04      63.38      75.71
```

c. Backward elimination procedure:

STEP	1	2	3
CONSTANT	258.1	266.8	278.6
WINS	−9.5	−8.9	−10.2
T-RATIO	−1.54	−1.65	−3.01
RUSHING	0.008		
T-RATIO	0.24		
PASSING	0.045	0.045	0.049
T-RATIO	1.92	2.02	2.86
TEAMINT	0.8	0.9	
T-RATIO	0.27	0.31	
OPPONINT	−3.4	−3.3	−3.3
T-RATIO	−2.06	−2.17	−2.25
S	34.4	32.6	31.1

d.

Best Subsets Regression of POINTS

Vars	R-sq	Adj. R-sq	C-p	s	WINS	RUSHING	PASSING	TEAMINT	OPPONINT
1	44.0	39.4	8.8	43.029	X				
1	41.7	36.8	9.6	43.929			X		
2	63.9	57.3	4.1	36.099			X		X
2	63.4	56.7	4.3	36.355	X		X		
3	75.7	68.4	2.1	31.056	X		X		X
3	68.7	59.3	4.5	35.263			X	X	X
4	76.0	65.3	4.1	32.560	X		X	X	X
4	75.9	65.2	4.1	32.592	X	X	X		X
5	76.1	61.2	6.0	34.414	X	X	X	X	X

19.   See the solution to Exercise 35 in Chapter 15. The Minitab output using the best subsets regression procedure is shown below:

```
Best Subsets Regression of P/E
                                                        %  %
                                                  %  %  P  P
                                                  P  G  R  R
                                                  R  R  O  O
                                                  O  O  F  F
                          Adj.                    F  W  X  X
                                                  I  T  D  D  D  D
   Vars   R-sq   R-sq    C-p        s             T  H  1  2  1  2

     1    65.6   63.6   -0.9     2.2249                       X
     1    59.7   57.4    1.5     2.4067              X
     2    70.5   66.8   -0.9     2.1236           X           X
     2    67.6   63.5    0.3     2.2254           X  X
     3    70.7   64.8    1.0     2.1874           X           X  X
     3    70.6   64.7    1.0     2.1883           X  X        X
     4    70.7   62.3    3.0     2.2634           X  X        X  X
     4    70.7   62.3    3.0     2.2636              X  X     X  X
     5    70.7   59.4    5.0     2.3488           X  X  X     X  X
     5    70.7   59.4    5.0     2.3488              X  X  X  X  X
     6    70.7   56.0    7.0     2.4446           X  X  X  X  X  X
```

We see that a variety of models with approximately the same vale for the adjusted coefficient of determination can be obtained. Note that how well the model involving just the interaction between the net profit margin and the dummy variable D! does. The value of the best subsets regression output is that it quickly shows us the results from a great many possible models.

20. a.   See the solution to Exercise 14 in this chapter. The Minitab output using the best subsets regression procedure is shown below:

Best Subsets Regression of RISK

Vars	R-sq	Adj. R-sq	C-p	s	P R E S S U R E	A G E	S M O K E R	P R E S S U R E S
1	63.3	61.3	28.5	9.2430		X		
1	46.3	43.3	49.1	11.182			X	
2	80.6	78.4	9.5	6.9083	X	X		
2	79.5	77.1	10.8	7.1058	X			X
3	87.3	85.0	3.3	5.7566	X	X	X	
3	86.2	83.7	4.7	6.0051	X		X	X
4	87.6	84.3	5.0	5.8813	X	X	X	X

This output suggests that the model involving AGE, PRESSURE, and SMOKER is the preferred model; the Minitab output for this model is shown below:

```
The regression equation is
RISK = - 91.8 + 1.08 AGE + 0.252 PRESSURE + 8.74 SMOKER
```

Predictor	Coef	Stdev	t-ratio	p
Constant	-91.76	15.22	-6.03	0.000
AGE	1.0767	0.1660	6.49	0.000
PRESSURE	0.25181	0.04523	5.57	0.000
SMOKER	8.740	3.001	2.91	0.010

s = 5.757   R-sq = 87.3%   R-sq(adj) = 85.0%

Analysis of Variance

SOURCE	DF	SS	MS	F	p
Regression	3	3660.7	1220.2	36.82	0.000
Error	16	530.2	33.1		
Total	19	4190.9			

21. a.   The Minitab output is shown below:

```
The regression equation is
P/E = 6.51 + 0.569 %PROFIT

Predictor         Coef        Stdev      t-ratio          p
Constant         6.507        1.509         4.31      0.000
%PROFIT         0.5691       0.1281         4.44      0.000

s = 2.580        R-sq = 53.7%      R-sq(adj) = 51.0%

Analysis of Variance

SOURCE          DF            SS           MS          F          p
Regression       1        131.40       131.40      19.74      0.000
Error           17        113.14         6.66
Total           18        244.54
```

b.   The residual plot as a function of the order in which the data are presented is shown below:

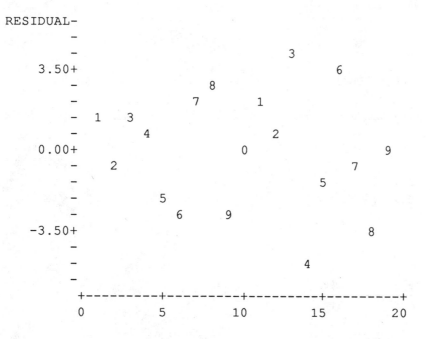

There does not appear to be any pattern indicative of positive autocorrelation.

c.   The Durban-Watson statistic (obtained from Minitab) is $d = 2.34$. At the .05 level of significance, $d_L = 1.18$ and $d_U = 1.39$. Since $d > d_U$ there is no significant positive autocorrelation.

22. From Minitab, $d = 1.60$. At the .05 level of significance, $d_L = 1.04$ and $d_U = 1.77$. Since $d_L \leq d$, the test is inconclusive.

23. The dummy variables are defined as follows:

x_1	x_2	x_3	Treatment
0	0	0	A
1	0	0	B
0	1	0	C
0	0	1	D

$$E(y) = \beta_0 + \beta_1 x_1 + \beta_2 x_2 + \beta_3 x_3$$

24. The dummy variables are defined as follows:

x_1	x_2	Treatment
0	0	1
1	0	2
0	1	3

$x_3 = 0$ if block 1 and 1 if block 2

$$E(y) = \beta_0 + \beta_1 x_1 + \beta_2 x_2 + \beta_3 x_3$$

25. Factor A

$x_1 = 0$ if level 1 and 1 if level 2

Factor B

x_2	x_3	Level
0	0	1
1	0	2
0	1	3

$$E(y) = \beta_0 + \beta_1 x_1 + \beta_2 x_2 + \beta_3 x_1 x_2 + \beta_4 x_1 x_3$$

26. a. The dummy variables are defined as follows:

x_2	x_3	Mfg.
0	0	1
1	0	2
0	1	3

$$E(y) = \beta_0 + \beta_1 D_1 + \beta_2 D_2$$

b. The Minitab output is shown below:

```
The regression equation is
TIME = 23.0 + 5.00 D1 - 2.00 D2

Predictor       Coef        Stdev      t-ratio        p
Constant      23.000        1.106       20.80     0.000
D1             5.000        1.563        3.20     0.011
D2            -2.000        1.563       -1.28     0.233

s = 2.211        R-sq = 70.3%       R-sq(adj) = 63.7%

Analysis of Variance

SOURCE          DF          SS           MS          F          p
Regression       2       104.000       52.000      10.64      0.004
Error            9        44.000        4.889
Total           11       148.000
```

c. $H_0\colon \beta_1 = \beta_2 = 0$

d. The p-value of .004 is less than $\alpha = .05$; therefore, we can reject H_0 and conclude that the mean time to mix a batch of material is most the same for each manufacturer.

27. a. The dummy variables are defined as follows:

D1	D2	D3	Paint
0	0	0	1
1	0	0	2
0	1	0	3
0	0	1	4

The Minitab output is shown below:

```
The regression equation is
TIME = 133 + 6.00 D1 + 3.00 D2 + 11.0 D3

Predictor         Coef        Stdev      t-ratio         p
Constant       133.000        2.941        45.22     0.000
D1               6.000        4.159         1.44     0.168
D2               3.000        4.159         0.72     0.481
D3              11.000        4.159         2.64     0.018

s = 6.576        R-sq = 32.3%      R-sq(adj) = 19.6%

Analysis of Variance

SOURCE         DF          SS           MS         F        p
Regression      3      330.00       110.00      2.54    0.093
Error          16      692.00        43.25
Total          19     1022.00
```

The appropriate hypothesis test is:

$$H_0: \beta_1 = \beta_2 = \beta_3 = 0$$

The p-value of .093 is greater than $\alpha = .05$; therefore, at the 5% level of significance we can not reject H_0.

b. D1 = 1 D2 = 0 D3 = 0

TIME = 133 + 6(1) + 3(0) +11(0) = 139

28.   X1 = 0 if computerized analyzer, 1 if electronic analyzer

X2 and X3 are defined as follows:

X2	X3	Car
0	0	1
1	0	2
0	1	3

The complete data set and the Minitab output are shown below:

```
        Y    X1   X2   X3

        50   0    0    0
        55   0    1    0
        63   0    0    1
        42   1    0    0
        44   1    1    0
        46   1    0    1
```

The regression equation is
Y = 52.0 - 12.0 X1 + 3.50 X2 + 8.50 X3

```
Predictor        Coef      Stdev    t-ratio        p
Constant       52.000      2.646      19.65    0.003
X1            -12.000      2.646      -4.54    0.045
X2              3.500      3.240       1.08    0.393
X3              8.500      3.240       2.62    0.120

s = 3.240      R-sq = 93.2%     R-sq(adj) = 83.1%
```

Analysis of Variance

```
SOURCE        DF          SS         MS        F        p
Regression     3      289.00      96.33     9.17    0.100
Error          2       21.00      10.50
Total          5      310.00
```

To test for any significant difference between the two analyzers we must test the hypothesis $H_0: \beta_1 = 0$. Since the p-value corresponding to $t = -4.54$ is .045 $< \alpha = .05$, we reject $H_0: \beta_0 = 0$; the time to do a tuneup is not the same for the two analyzers.

29.   X1 = 0 if a small advertisement and 1 if a large advertisement

X2 and X3 are defined as follows:

X2	X3	Design
0	0	A
1	0	B
0	1	C

The complete data set and the Minitab output are shown below:

Y	X1	X2	X3	X1X2	X1X3
8	0	0	0	0	0
12	0	0	0	0	0
12	1	0	0	0	0
8	1	0	0	0	0
22	0	1	0	0	0
14	0	1	0	0	0
26	1	1	0	1	0
30	1	1	0	1	0
10	0	0	1	0	0
18	0	0	1	0	0
18	1	0	1	0	1
14	1	0	1	0	1

The regression equation is
$Y = 10.0 + 0.00\ X1 + 8.00\ X2 + 4.00\ X3 + 10.0\ X1X2 + 2.00\ X1X3$

Predictor	Coef	Stdev	t-ratio	p
Constant	10.000	2.828	3.54	0.012
X1	0.000	4.000	0.00	1.000
X2	8.000	4.000	2.00	0.092
X3	4.000	4.000	1.00	0.356
X1X2	10.000	5.657	1.77	0.128
X1X3	2.000	5.657	0.35	0.736

s = 4.000   R-sq = 82.4%   R-sq(adj) = 67.6%

Analysis of Variance

SOURCE	DF	SS	MS	F	p
Regression	5	448.00	89.60	5.60	0.029
Error	6	96.00	16.00		
Total	11	544.00			

30. a.   A scatter diagram is shown below:

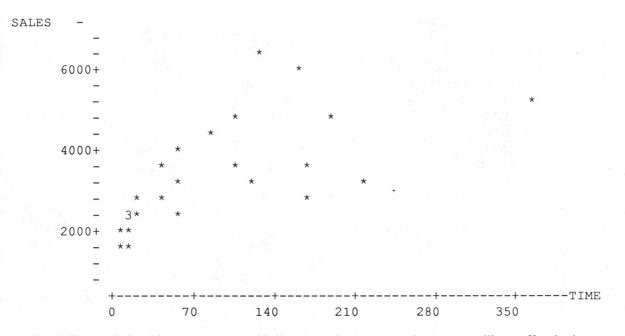

```
SALES     -
          -
          -                      *
   6000+                              *
          -
          -                                                                    *
          -                 *              *
          -             *
   4000+           *
          -      *        *         *
          -      *    *         *
          -   *    *                  *
          -   3*      *            *
   2000+   **
          -  **
          -
          -
          +---------+---------+---------+---------+---------+---------+------TIME
          0        70        140       210       280       350
```

b.   A linear relationship appears reasonable, but there also appears to be some curvilinear effect in the data.

c.   One possibility is to add another variable by squaring the value of TIME. The Minitab output with the addition of the square of TIME, denoted as TIMESQ, is shown below:

```
The regression equation is
SALES = 2081 + 21.9 TIME - 0.0417 TIMESQ

Predictor         Coef        Stdev      t-ratio         p
Constant        2081.3        348.6         5.97     0.000
TIME            21.853        6.029         3.62     0.001
TIMESQ        -0.04170      0.01873        -2.23     0.036

s = 969.2       R-sq = 50.1%       R-sq(adj) = 45.5%

Analysis of Variance

SOURCE         DF          SS          MS          F         p
Regression      2    20713548    10356774      11.03     0.000
Error          22    20666002      939364
Total          24    41379552
```

31. a.   The Minitab output is shown below:

```
The regression equation is
AUDELAY = 80.4 + 11.9 INDUS - 4.82 PUBLIC - 2.62 ICQUAL -
4.07 INTFIN

Predictor        Coef        Stdev     t-ratio          p
Constant       80.429        5.916       13.60      0.000
INDUS          11.944        3.798        3.15      0.003
PUBLIC         -4.816        4.229       -1.14      0.263
ICQUAL         -2.624        1.184       -2.22      0.033
INTFIN         -4.073        1.851       -2.20      0.035

s = 10.92        R-sq = 38.3%      R-sq(adj) = 31.2%

Analysis of Variance

SOURCE          DF          SS          MS          F          p
Regression       4      2587.7       646.9       5.42      0.002
Error           35      4176.3       119.3
Total           39      6764.0
```

b.   The low value of the adjusted coefficient of determination (31.2%) does not indicate a good fit.

c.   The scatter diagram is shown below:

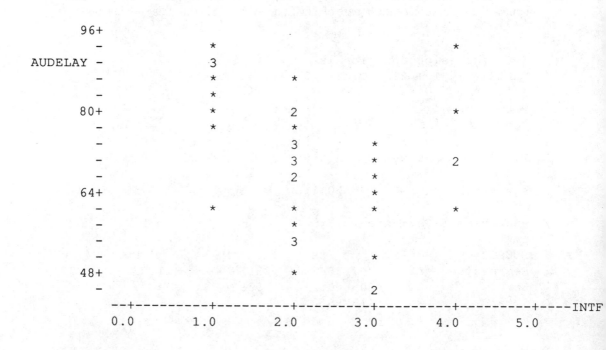

The scatter diagram suggests a curvilinear relationship between these two variables.

d. The output from the stepwise procedure is shown below, where INTFINSQ is the square of INTFIN.

STEP	1	2	3	4
CONSTANT	63.00	70.63	79.73	112.79
INDUS	11.1	12.7	12.6	11.6
T-RATIO	2.68	3.21	3.36	3.80
ICQUAL		-2.92	-2.82	-2.49
T-RATIO		-2.36	-2.40	-2.60
INTFIN			-4.2	-36.6
T-RATIO			-2.26	-4.91
INTFINSQ				6.6
T-RATIO				4.44
S	12.2	11.6	11.0	8.90
R-SQ	15.91	26.89	35.97	59.05

32. a. The dummy variables are defined as follows:

D1	D2	D3	D4	D5	Industry
0	0	0	0	0	Industrial
1	0	0	0	0	Technology
0	1	0	0	0	Consumer
0	0	1	0	0	Retailing
0	0	0	1	0	Media
0	0	0	0	1	Financial

The Minitab output is shown below:

```
The regression equation is
%MGTJOBS = - 16.7 + 1.02 %WOMEN
```

Predictor	Coef	Stdev	t-ratio	p
Constant	-16.697	3.918	-4.26	0.000
%WOMEN	1.01549	0.08255	12.30	0.000

```
s = 6.223        R-sq = 86.8%      R-sq(adj) = 86.2%
```

Analysis of Variance

SOURCE	DF	SS	MS	F	p
Regression	1	5859.4	5859.4	151.31	0.000
Error	23	890.6	38.7		
Total	24	6750.0			

Unusual Observations

Obs.	%WOMEN	%MGTJOBS	Fit	Stdev.Fit	Residual	St.Resid
9	47.0	18.00	31.03	1.26	-13.03	-2.14R
14	47.0	16.00	31.03	1.26	-15.03	-2.47R

R denotes an obs. with a large st. resid.

b. Stepwise regression procedure:

STEP	1	2
CONSTANT	-16.70	-17.81
%WOMEN	1.015	1.017
T-RATIO	12.30	13.69
D4		8.7
T-RATIO		2.53
S	6.22	5.60
R-SQ	86.81	89.78

c. Backward elimination procedure:

STEP	1	2	3	4	5	6
CONSTANT	-19.99	-20.41	-21.40	-22.06	-17.57	-16.70
%WOMEN	1.177	1.159	1.227	1.201	1.050	1.015
T-RATIO	8.29	8.68	10.10	9.48	11.79	12.30
D1	-2.0					
T-RATIO	-0.46					
D2	-5.5	-4.4	-6.0			
T-RATIO	-1.25	-1.22	-1.78			
D3	-8.2	-6.8	-9.6	-7.5	-3.5	
T-RATIO	-1.43	-1.44	-2.36	-1.83	-1.03	
D4	3.7	5.0				
T-RATIO	0.73	1.17				
D5	-8.0	-6.5	-9.7	-7.4		
T-RATIO	-1.26	-1.23	-2.13	-1.62		
S	5.78	5.66	5.71	6.00	6.21	6.22
R-SQ	91.09	90.98	90.33	88.81	87.42	86.81

33.   The computer output is shown below:

```
The regression equation is
AUDELAY = 63.0 + 11.1 INDUS

Predictor          Coef        Stdev       t-ratio         p
Constant          63.000       3.393        18.57       0.000
INDUS             11.074       4.130         2.68       0.011

s = 12.23        R-sq = 15.9%      R-sq(adj) = 13.7%

Analysis of Variance

SOURCE          DF          SS           MS          F          p
Regression       1        1076.1       1076.1       7.19      0.011
Error           38        5687.9        149.7
Total           39        6764.0

Unusual Observations
Obs.    INDUS    AUDELAY      Fit  Stdev.Fit  Residual   St.Resid
  5      0.00     91.00     63.00     3.39      28.00       2.38R
 38      1.00     46.00     74.07     2.35     -28.07      -2.34R

R denotes an obs. with a large st. resid.

Durban-Watson statistic = 1.55
```

At the .05 level of significance, $d_L = 1.44$ and $d_U = 1.54$. Since $d = 1.55 > d_U$, there is no significant positive autocorrelation.

34. a. The Minitab output is shown below:

```
The regression equation is
AUDELAY = 70.6 + 12.7 INDUS - 2.92 ICQUAL


Predictor         Coef        Stdev      t-ratio         p
Constant        70.634        4.558        15.50     0.000
INDUS           12.737        3.966         3.21     0.003
ICQUAL          -2.919        1.238        -2.36     0.024


s = 11.56      R-sq = 26.9%      R-sq(adj) = 22.9%

Analysis of Variance

SOURCE          DF           SS           MS          F          p
Regression       2       1818.6        909.3       6.80      0.003
Error           37       4945.4        133.7
Total           39       6764.0


SOURCE          DF        SEQ SS
INDUS            1        1076.1
ICQUAL           1         742.4

Unusual Observations
Obs.     INDUS     AUDELAY       Fit Stdev.Fit   Residual    St.Resid
  5       0.00       91.00     67.71      3.78      23.29       2.13R
 38       1.00       46.00     71.70      2.44     -25.70      -2.27R

R denotes an obs. with a large st. resid.

Durban-Watson statistic = 1.43
```

b. The residual plot as a function of the order in which the data are presented is shown below:

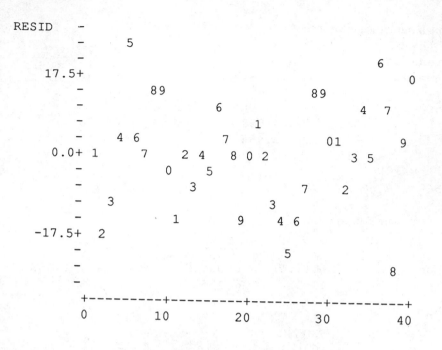

There is no obvious pattern in the data indicative of positive autocorrelation.

c. At the .05 level of significance, $d_L = 1.44$ and $d_U = 1.54$. Since $d = 1.55 > d_U$, there is no significant positive autocorrelation.

35. a. The Minitab output is shown below:

```
The regression equation is
%MGTJOBS = - 16.7 + 1.02 %WOMEN

Predictor         Coef        Stdev      t-ratio         p
Constant        -16.697       3.918        -4.26     0.000
%WOMEN          1.01549      0.08255       12.30      0.000

s = 6.223        R-sq = 86.8%      R-sq(adj) = 86.2%

Analysis of Variance

SOURCE          DF          SS           MS          F         p
Regression       1        5859.4       5859.4     151.31     0.000
Error           23         890.6        38.7
Total           24        6750.0

Unusual Observations
Obs.   %WOMEN   %MGTJOBS       Fit  Stdev.Fit   Residual   St.Resid
  9      47.0     18.00       31.03      1.26     -13.03      -2.14R
 14      47.0     16.00       31.03      1.26     -15.03      -2.47R

R denotes an obs. with a large st. resid.

Durban-Watson statistic = 2.07
```

b. The residual plot a function of the order in which the data are presented is shown below:

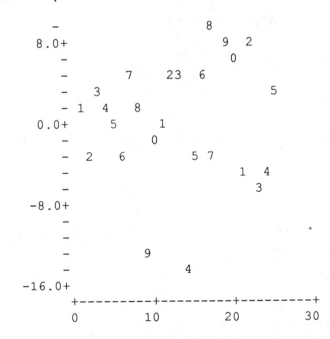

There is no obvious pattern in the data.

c. At the .05 level of significance, $d_L = 1.29$ and $d_U = 1.45$. Since $d = 2.07 > d_U$, there is no significant positive autocorrelation.

36. The dummy variables are defined as follows:

D1	D2	Type
0	0	Non
1	0	Light
0	1	Heavy

The Minitab output is shown below:

```
The regression equation is
SCORE = 4.25 + 1.00 D1 + 1.50 D2

Predictor        Coef        Stdev      t-ratio          p
Constant       4.2500      0.3819        11.13      0.000
D1             1.0000      0.5401         1.85      0.078
D2             1.5000      0.5401         2.78      0.011

s = 1.080       R-sq = 27.6%       R-sq(adj) = 20.7%

Analysis of Variance

SOURCE        DF          SS          MS         F          p
Regression     2       9.333       4.667      4.00      0.034
Error         21      24.500       1.167
Total         23      33.833
```

Since the p-value = .034 is less than $\alpha = .05$, there are significant differences between comfort levels for the three types of browsers.

Solution to Computer Case

The sample correlation coefficients are as follows:

	WEEKS	AGE	EDUC	MARRIED	HEAD	TENURE	MGT
AGE	0.577						
EDUC	0.007	0.100					
MARRIED	-0.130	-0.209	-0.151				
HEAD	-0.205	0.027	-0.156	-0.449			
TENURE	0.398	0.459	0.174	-0.057	-0.046		
MGT	-0.198	0.097	0.160	0.073	-0.200	-0.113	
SALES	-0.134	0.137	0.124	-0.148	-0.013	0.097	-0.156

Using the stepwise regression procedure the following output was obtained:

```
STEPWISE REGRESSION OF   WEEKS    ON  7 PREDICTORS, WITH N =    50

     STEP         1         2         3         4
 CONSTANT  -8.86002  -9.09741  -0.10922  -0.06890

 AGE          1.51      1.57      1.61      1.73
 T-RATIO      4.90      5.30      5.74      6.51

 MGT                   -20.1     -24.6     -28.7
 T-RATIO               -2.26     -2.88     -3.53

 HEAD                            -14.3     -15.1
 T-RATIO                         -2.61     -2.95

 SALES                                     -17.4
 T-RATIO                                   -2.79

 S            19.5      18.7      17.7      16.5
 R-SQ        33.34     39.87     47.64     55.38
```

The Minitab best subset regression procedure was used to obtain the following results:

Best Subsets Regression of WEEKS

```
                                     M
                                     A
                                     R         T
                                     E    E    N         S
                                   E R H  N              A
                          Adj.     A D I  E  U M     L
                                   G U E  A  R G     E
  Vars  R-sq  R-sq   C-p     s     E C D  D  E T     S
     1  33.3  32.0  22.5  19.534   X
     1  15.8  14.0  40.6  21.954              X
     2  39.9  37.3  17.8  18.749   X                 X
     2  38.2  35.6  19.5  19.005   X    X
     3  47.6  44.2  11.8  17.686   X    X  X
     3  46.8  43.3  12.7  17.831   X                 X X
     4  55.4  51.4   5.9  16.507   X       X         X X
     4  49.1  44.6  12.3  17.628   X  X X  X
     5  58.1  53.3   5.1  16.179   X  X X        X X
     5  56.0  51.0   7.3  16.582   X        X X  X X
     6  58.7  53.0   6.4  16.241   X  X X X X X


     6  58.3  52.5   6.8  16.318   X X X X      X X
     7  59.1  52.3   8.0  16.350   X X X X X X X
```

These results suggest a model using four independent variables: AGE, HEAD, MGT, and SALES.

```
The regression equation is
WEEKS = - 0.07 + 1.73 AGE - 15.1 HEAD - 28.7 MGT - 17.4 SALES
```

Predictor	Coef	Stdev	t-ratio	p
Constant	-0.069	9.843	-0.01	0.994
AGE	1.7252	0.2651	6.51	0.000
HEAD	-15.086	5.121	-2.95	0.005
MGT	-28.672	8.117	-3.53	0.001
SALES	-17.421	6.236	-2.79	0.008

```
s = 16.51      R-sq = 55.4%     R-sq(adj) = 51.4%
```

Analysis of Variance

SOURCE	DF	SS	MS	F	p
Regression	4	15216.0	3804.0	13.96	0.000
Error	45	12261.5	272.5		
Total	49	27477.5			

SOURCE	DF	SEQ SS
AGE	1	9161.4
HEAD	1	1339.8
MGT	1	2588.1
SALES	1	2126.7

Unusual Observations

Obs.	AGE	WEEKS	Fit	Stdev.Fit	Residual	St.Resid
24	23.0	7.00	39.61	5.29	-32.61	-2.09R
39	62.0	80.00	89.47	9.36	-9.47	-0.70 X

R denotes an obs. with a large st. resid.
X denotes an obs. whose X value gives it large influence.

The standardized residual plot for this model is shown below:

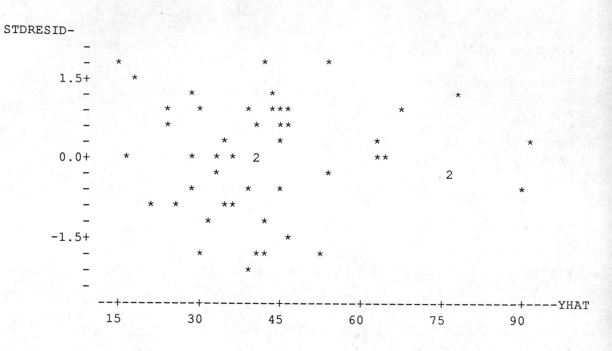

Chapter 17
Index Numbers

Learning Objectives

1. Know how to compute price relatives and understand how they represent price changes over time.

2. Know how to compute aggregate price indexes and understand how the choice of a base period affects the index.

3. Become familiar with the Consumer Price Index, the Producer Price Index and the Dow Jones averages.

4. Learn how to deflate a time series to measure changes over time in constant dollars.

5. Learn how to compute an aggregate quantity index and how to interpret it.

Solutions:

1. a.

Item	Price Relative
A	103
B	238

   b. $I_{1991} = \dfrac{7.75 + 1500.00}{7.50 + 630.00}(100) = \dfrac{1507.75}{637.50}(100) = 237$

   c. $I_{1991} = \dfrac{7.75(1500) + 1500.00(2)}{7.50(1500) + 630.00(2)}(100) = \dfrac{14,625.00}{12,510.00}(100) = 117$

   d. $I_{1991} = \dfrac{7.75(1800) + 1500.00(1)}{7.50(1800) + 630.00(1)}(100) = \dfrac{15,450.00}{14,130.00}(100) = 109$

2. a. From the price relative we see the percentage increase was 32%.

   b. Divide the current cost by the price relative and multiply by 100.

$$1986 \text{ cost} = \frac{\$10.75}{132}(100) = \$8.14.$$

3. a. Price Relatives $\quad A = (6.00 / 5.45)\,100 = 110$

$$B = (5.95 / 5.60)\,100 = 106$$

$$C = (6.20 / 5.50)\,100 = 113$$

   b. $I_{1991} = \dfrac{6.00 + 5.95 + 6.20}{5.45 + 5.60 + 5.50}(100) = 110$

   c. $I_{1991} = \dfrac{6.00(150) + 5.95(200) + 6.20(120)}{5.45(150) + 5.60(200) + 5.50(120)}(100) = 109$

   9% increase over the two year period.

4. $I_{1991} = \dfrac{13.00(35,000) + 50.00(5000) + 8.00(60,000)}{12.00(35,000) + 47.00(5000) + 7.85(60,000)}(100) = 105$

5. $I = \dfrac{.19(500) + 1.80(50) + 4.20(100) + 13.20(40)}{.15(500) + 1.60(50) + 4.50(100) + 12.00(40)}(100) = 104$

   Paasche index

6.

Item	Price Relative	Base Period Price	Base Period Usage	Weight	Weighted Price Relatives
A	150	22.00	20	440	66,000
B	90	5.00	50	250	22,500
C	120	14.00	40	560	67,200
				1250	155,700

$$I = \frac{155,700}{1250} = 125$$

7. a. Price Relatives   A $= (3.95 / 2.50)\ 100\ = 158$

B $= (9.90 / 8.75)\ 100\ = 113$

C $= (.95 / .99)\ 100\quad = 96$

b.

Item	Price Relatives	Base Price	Quantity	Weight $P_{i0}Q_i$	Weighted Price Relatives
A	158	2.50	25	62.5	9875
B	113	8.75	15	131.3	14837
C	96	.99	60	59.4	5702
				253.2	30414

$$I = \frac{30414}{253.2} = 120$$

Cost up 20% for the chemical.

8.

Stock	Price Relatives	Base Price	Quantity	Weight	Weighted Price Relatives
Holiday	110	15.50	500	7750	852500
NY Electric	109	18.50	200	3700	403300
KY Gas	97	26.75	500	13375	1297375
PQ Soaps	108	42.25	300	12675	1368900
				37500	3922075

$$I = \frac{3922075}{37500} = 105$$

Portfolio up 5%

9.

Item	Price Relatives	Base Price	Quantity	Weight	Weighted Price Relatives
Beer	108	12.00	35,000	420000	45,360,000
Wine	106	47.00	5,000	235000	24,910,000
Soft Drink	102	7.85	60,000	471000	48,042,000
				1,126,000	118,312,000

$$I = \frac{118,312,000}{1,126,000} = 105$$

10. a. $\frac{\$10.83}{159} (100) = \$6.81$

b. $\frac{10.83}{7.00} (100) = 154.7$ The actual percentage increase is 54.7%

c. $\frac{6.81}{7.00} (100) = 97.3$ The change in real wages is a 2.7% decrease.

11.
        1976   1,300
        1977   1,440 (100 / 105) = 1371
        1978   1,605 (100 / 113) = 1420
        1979   1,800 (100 / 122) = 1475
        1980   2,050 (100 / 138) = 1486

        1486 / 1300 = 1.14   14% increase.

12. a.
        1976   155
        1977   163 (100 / 105)   = 155
        1978   178 (100 / 113)   = 158
        1979   198 (100 / 122)   = 162
        1980   227 (100 / 138)   = 164

    In constant dollars, inventories are rather stable.

    b.
        1976   155
        1977   163 (100 / 103)   = 158
        1978   178 (100 / 110)   = 162
        1979   198 (100 / 120)   = 165
        1980   227 (100 / 135)   = 168

    c.   PPI, on the basis that inventory is in this category rather than consumer products.

13.

Year	Retail Sales ($)	CPI	Deflated Retail Sales ($)
1975	380,000	53.8	706,320
1980	520,000	82.4	631,068
1985	700,000	107.6	650,558
1990	870,000	130.7	665,647

14. $$I_{1992} = \frac{300(18.00) + 400(4.90) + 850(15.00)}{350(18.00) + 220(4.90) + 730(15.00)} (100) = \frac{20,110}{18,328} (100) = 110$$

15. $$I = \frac{95(1200) + 75(1800) + 50(2000) + 70(1500)}{120(1200) + 86(1800) + 35(2000) + 60(1500)} (100) = 99$$

Quantities down slightly.

16.

Model	Quantity Relatives	Base Quantity	Price ($)	Weight	Weighted Quantity Relatives
Sedan	85	200	15,200	3,040,000	258,400,000
Sport	80	100	17,000	1,700,000	136,000,000
Wagon	80	75	16,800	1,260,000	100,800,000
				6,000,000	495,200,000

$$I = \frac{495,200,000}{6,000,000} = 83$$

17. a,b.

	Price Index	
Year	1982 Base	1985 Base
1982	100.0	90.0
1983	101.6	91.4
1984	102.4	92.1
1985	111.1	100.0
1986	124.8	112.3
1987	136.6	122.9

18. a. Price Relatives   A = (15.90 / 10.50) (100) = 151

   B = (32.00 / 16.25) (100) = 197

   C = (17.40 /12.20) (100) = 143

   D = (35.50 / 20.00) (100) = 178

b. $$I = \frac{15.90(2000) + 32.00(5000) + 17.40(6500) + 35.50(2500)}{10.50(2000) + 16.25(5000) + 12.20(6500) + 20.00(2500)} (100) = 170$$

19. $$I = \frac{15.90(4000) + 32.00(3000) + 17.40(7500) + 35.50(3000)}{10.50(4000) + 16.25(3000) + 12.20(7500) + 20.00(3000)} (100) = 164$$

20. $$I_{Jan} = \frac{32.75(100) + 59(150) + 42(75) + 16.5(50)}{31.50(100) + 65(150) + 40(75) + 18(50)} (100) = 96$$

$$I_{Mar} = \frac{32.50(100) + 57.5(150) + 39.5(75) + 13.75(50)}{31.50(100) + 65(150) + 40(75) + 18(50)} (100) = 92$$

Market is down compared to 1988.

21. Price Relatives:

			Jan	Mar
Oil	(32.75 / 31.50) (100)	=	104	103
Computer	(59.00 / 65.00) (100)	=	91	88
Steel	(42.00 / 40.00) (100)	=	105	99
Real Estate	(16.5 / 18.00) (100)	=	92	76

$I_{Jan} = 96$ $I_{Mar} = 92$

22.

Product	Relatives	Base Price	Quantity	Weight	Weighted Price Relatives
Corn	79	2.02	1707	3448	272,392
Soybeans	107	4.99	310	1547	165,529
				4995	437,921

$$I = \frac{437,921}{4995} = 88$$

23. a.

Product	Price Relatives
Milk	(2.09 / .79) (100) = 265
Eggs	(.95 / .49) (100) = 194
Butter	(.91 / .60) (100) = 152
Cheese	(1.49 / .79) (100) = 189

b. $$I = \frac{2.09(125) + .95(50) + .91(50) + 1.49(25)}{.79(125) + .49(50) + .60(50) + .79(25)} (100) = 226$$

24.

1970	$14,000 (38.8 / 38.8)	= $14,000
1975	$17,500 (38.8 / 53.8)	= $12,621
1980	$23,000 (38.8 / 82.4)	= $10,830
1985	$37,000 (38.8 / 107.6)	= $13,342
1990	$53,000 (38.8 / 130.7)	= $15,734

In constant dollars, starting salaries decreased through 1980 but increased significantly during the 1980's.

25.   1983 $51.00 (100 / 99.6)   = $51.20
      1984 $54.00 (100 / 103.9)   = $51.97
      1985 $58.00 (100 / 107.6)   = $53.90
      1986 $59.50 (100 / 109.6)   = $54.29
      1987 $59.00 (100 / 113.6)   = $51.94

1987 Price: $51 (113.6 / 99.6) = $58.17

The stock price has barely increased by more than the cost of living ($59.00 vs. $58.17).

26. $$I = \frac{1200(30) + 500(20) + 500(25)}{800(30) + 600(20) + 200(25)} (100) = 143$$

Quantity is up 43%.

Chapter 18
Time Series Analysis and Forecasting

Learning Objectives

1.   Understand that the long-run success of an organization is often closely related to how well management is able to predict future aspects of the operation.

2.   Know the various components of a time series.

3.   Be able to use smoothing techniques such as moving averages and exponential smoothing.

4.   Be able to use the least squares method to identify the trend component of a time series.

5.   Understand how the classical time series model can be used to explain the pattern or behavior of the data in a time series and to develop a forecast for the time series.

6.   Be able to determine and use seasonal indexes for a time series.

7.   Know how regression models can be used in forecasting.

8.   Know the definition of the following terms:

time series	mean squared error
forecast	moving averages
trend component	weighted moving averages
cyclical component	smoothing constant
seasonal component	seasonal constant
irregular component	

Chapter 18

Solutions:

1. a.

Week	Time-Series Value	Forecast	Forecast Error	(Error)^2
1	8			
2	13			
3	15			
4	17	12	5	25
5	16	15	1	1
6	9	16	-7	49
				75

Forecast for week 7 is $(17 + 16 + 9)/3 = 14$

b. MSE = 75 / 3 = 25

c. Smoothing constant = .3.

Week t	Time-Series Value Y_t	Forecast F_t	Forecast Error $Y_t - F_t$	Squared Error $(Y_t - F_t)^2$
1	8			
2	13	8.00	5.00	25.00
3	15	9.00	6.00	36.00
4	17	10.20	6.80	46.24
5	16	11.56	4.44	19.71
6	9	12.45	-3.45	11.90
				138.85

Forecast for week 7 is $.2(9) + .8(12.45) = 11.76$

d. For the $\alpha = .2$ exponential smoothing forecast MSE = 138.85 / 5 = 27.77. Since the three-week moving average has a smaller MSE, it appearsa to provide the better forecasts.

e. Smoothing constant = .4.

Week t	Time-Series Value Y_t	Forecast F_t	Forecast Error $Y_t - F_t$	Squared Error $(Y_t - F_t)^2$
1	8			
2	13	8.0	5.0	25.00
3	15	10.0	5.0	25.00
4	17	12.0	5.0	25.00
5	16	14.0	2.0	4.00
6	9	14.8	-5.8	33.64
				112.64

MSE = 112.64 / 5 = 22.53. A smoothing constant of .4 appaears to provide better forecasts.

Forecast for week 7 is .4(9) + .6(14.8) = 12.48

2. a.

Week	Time-Series Value	4-Week Moving Average Forecast	(Error)^2	5-Week Moving Average Forecast	(Error)^2
1	17				
2	21				
3	19				
4	23				
5	18	20.00	4.00		
6	16	20.25	18.06	19.60	12.96
7	20	19.00	1.00	19.40	0.36
8	18	19.25	1.56	19.20	1.44
9	22	18.00	16.00	19.00	9.00
10	20	19.00	1.00	18.80	1.44
11	15	20.00	25.00	19.20	17.64
12	22	18.75	10.56	19.00	9.00
			77.18		51.84

b. MSE(4-Week) = 77.18 / 8 = 9.65

MSE(5-Week) = 51.84 / 7 = 7.41

c. For the limited data provided, the 5-week moving average provides the smallest MSE.

3. a.

Week	Time-Series Value	Weighted Moving Average Forecast	Forecast Error	(Error)^2
1	17			
2	21			
3	19			
4	23	19.33	3.67	13.47
5	18	21.33	-3.33	11.09
6	16	19.83	-3.83	14.67
7	20	17.83	2.17	4.71
8	18	18.33	-0.33	0.11
9	22	18.33	3.67	13.47
10	20	20.33	-0.33	0.11
11	15	20.33	-5.33	28.41
12	22	17.83	4.17	17.39
				103.43

b. MSE = 103.43 / 9 = 11.49

Prefer the unweighted moving average here.

c. You could always find a weighted moving average at least as good as the unweighted one. Actually the unweighted moving average is a special case of the weighted ones where the weights are equal.

4.

Week	Time-Series Value	Forecast	Error	(Error)^2
1	17			
2	21	17.00	4.00	16.00
3	19	17.40	1.60	2.56
4	23	17.56	5.44	29.59
5	18	18.10	-0.10	0.01
6	16	18.09	-2.09	4.37
7	20	17.88	2.12	4.49
8	18	18.10	-0.10	0.01
9	22	18.09	3.91	15.29
10	20	18.48	1.52	2.31
11	15	18.63	-3.63	13.18
12	22	18.27	3.73	13.91
				101.72

MSE = 101.72 / 11 = 9.25

α = .2 provided a lower MSE; therefore α = .2 is better than α = .1

5. a. $F_{13} = .2Y_{12} + .16Y_{11} + .64(.2Y_{10} + .8F_{10}) = .2Y_{12} + .16Y_{11} + .128Y_{10} + .512F_{10}$

$F_{13} = .2Y_{12} + .16Y_{11} + .128Y_{10} + .512(.2Y_9 + .8F_9) = .2Y_{12} + .16Y_{11} + .128Y_{10} + .1024Y_9 + .4096F_9$

$F_{13} = .2Y_{12} + .16Y_{11} + .128Y_{10} + .1024Y_9 + .4096(.2Y_8 + .8F_8) = .2Y_{12} + .16Y_{11} + .128Y_{10} + .1024Y_9$
$\quad + .08192Y_8 + .32768F_8$

b. The more recent data receives the greater weight or importance in determining the forecast. The moving averages method weights the last n data values equally in determining the forecast.

6. a.

Year	Time-Series Value	$\alpha = .2$ Forecasts	$\alpha = .3$ Forecasts
1	2.49		
2	2.82	2.49	2.49
3	2.72	2.56	2.59
4	2.60	2.59	2.63
5	2.81	2.59	2.62
6	2.98	2.63	2.68
7	2.86	2.70	2.77
8	3.13	2.74	2.80
9	2.98	2.81	2.90
10	3.16	2.85	2.92
11	3.20	2.91	2.99
12	2.85	2.97	3.05

MSE($\alpha = .2$) = 0.06

MSE($\alpha = .3$) = 0.05

b. Consider $\alpha = ..3$ the better smoothing constant. The forecast of park attendance in year 13 (1992) is:

$$F_{13} = .3(2.85) + .7(3.05) = 2.99 \text{ million people}$$

7. a.

Month	Time-Series Value	3-Month Moving Average Forecast	(Error)^2	4-Month Moving Average Forecast	(Error)^2
1	9.5				
2	9.3				
3	9.4				
4	9.6	9.40	0.04		
5	9.8	9.43	0.14	9.45	0.12
6	9.7	9.60	0.01	9.53	0.03
7	9.8	9.70	0.01	9.63	0.03
8	10.5	9.77	0.53	9.73	0.59
9	9.9	10.00	0.01	9.95	0.00
10	9.7	10.07	0.14	9.98	0.08
11	9.6	10.03	0.18	9.97	0.14
12	9.6	9.73	0.02	9.92	0.10
			1.08		1.09

MSE(3-Month) = 1.08 / 9 = .12

MSE(4-Month) = 1.09 / 8 = .14

Use 3-Month moving averages.

b. Forecast = (9.7 + 9.6 + 9.6) / 3 = 9.63

c. For the limited data provided, the 5-week moving average provides the smallest MSE.

8. a.

Month	Time-Series Value	3-Month Moving Average Forecast	(Error)^2	$\alpha = .2$ Forecast	(Error)^2
1	240				
2	350			240.00	12100.00
3	230			262.00	1024.00
4	260	273.33	177.69	255.60	19.36
5	280	280.00	0.00	256.48	553.19
6	320	256.67	4010.69	261.18	3459.79
7	220	286.67	4444.89	272.95	2803.70
8	310	273.33	1344.69	262.36	2269.57
9	240	283.33	1877.49	271.89	1016.97
10	310	256.67	2844.09	265.51	1979.36
11	240	286.67	2178.09	274.41	1184.05
12	230	263.33	1110.89	267.53	1408.50
			17,988.52		27,818.49

MSE(3-Month) = 17,988.52 / 9 = 1998.72

MSE($\alpha = .2$) = 27,818.49 / 11 = 2528.95

Based on the above MSE values, the 3-month moving averages appears better. However, exponential smoothing was penalized by including month 2 which was difficult for any method to forecast. Using only the errors for months 4 to 12, the MSE for exponential smoothing is revised to

$$\text{MSE}(\alpha = .2) = 14,694.49 / 9 = 1632.72$$

Thus, exponential smoothing was better considering months 4 to 12.

b. Using exponential smoothing,

$$F_{13} = \alpha Y_{12} + (1 - \alpha)F_{12} = .20(230) + .80(267.53) = 260$$

9. a. Smoothing constant = .3.

Month t	Time-Series Value Y_t	Forecast F_t	Forecast Error $Y_t - F_t$	Squared Error $(Y_t - F_t)^2$
1	105.0			
2	135.0	105.00	30.00	900.00
3	120.0	114.00	6.00	36.00
4	105.0	115.80	-10.80	116.64
5	90.0	112.56	-22.56	508.95
6	120.0	105.79	14.21	201.92
7	145.0	110.05	34.95	1221.50
8	140.0	120.54	19.46	378.69
9	100.0	126.38	-26.38	695.90
10	80.0	118.46	-38.46	1479.17
11	100.0	106.92	-6.92	47.89
12	110.0	104.85	5.15	26.52
			Total	5613.18

MSE = 5613.18 / 11 = 510.29

Forecast for month 13:
$$F_{13} = .3(110) + .7(104.85) = 106.4$$

b. Smoothing constant = .5

Month t	Time-Series Value Y_t	Forecast F_t	Forecast Error $Y_t - F_t$	Squared Error $(Y_t - F_t)^2$
1	105			
2	135	105	30.00	900.00
3	120	.5(135) + .5(105) = 120	0.00	0.00
4	105	.5(120) + .5(120) = 120	-15.00	225.00
5	90	.5(105) + .5(120) = 112.50	-22.50	506.25
6	120	.5(90) + .5(112.5) = 101.25	18.75	351.56
7	145	.5(120) + .5(101.25) =110.63	34.37	1181.30
8	140	.5(145) + .5(110.63) = 127.81	12.19	148.60
9	100	.5(140) + .5(127.81) = 133.91	-33.91	1149.89
10	80	.5(100) + .5(133.91) = 116.95	-36.95	1365.30
11	100	.5(80) + .5(116.95) = 98.48	1.52	2.31
12	110	.5(100) + .5(98.48) = 99.24	10.76	115.78
				5945.99

MSE = 5945.99 / 11 = 540.55

Forecast for month 13:

$$F_{13} = .5(110) + .5(99.24) = 104.62$$

Conclusion: a smoothing constant of .3 is better than a smoothing constant of .5 since the MSE is less for 0.3.

10. a & b.

Week	Time-Series Value	$\alpha = .2$ Forecasts	$\alpha = .3$ Forecasts
1	2480		
2	2470	2480.00	2480.00
3	2475	2478.00	2477.00
4	2510	2477.40	2476.40
5	2500	2483.92	2486.48
6	2480	2487.14	2490.54
7	2520	2485.71	2487.38
8	2470	2492.57	2497.16
9	2440	2488.05	2489.01
10	2480	2478.44	2474.31
11	2530	2478.75	2476.02
12	2550	2489.00	2492.21

$MSE(\alpha = .2) = 11,825.31 / 11 = 1075$

$MSE(\alpha = .3) = 12,016.45 / 11 = 1092$

Consider $\alpha = .2$ the better smoothing constant.

$$F_{13} = .2(2550) + .8(2489) = 2501.2$$

11. The following values are needed to compute the slope and intercept:

$$\sum t = 15 \quad \sum t^2 = 15 \quad \sum Y_t = 55 \quad \sum t\, Y_t = 186$$

Computation of slope:

$$b_1 = \frac{\sum t\, Y_t - \left(\sum t \sum Y_t\right)/n}{\sum t^2 - \left(\sum t^2\right)/n} = \frac{186 - (15)(55)/5}{55 - (15)^2/5} = 2.1$$

Computation of intercept:

$$b_0 = \overline{Y} - b_1 \overline{t} = 11 - 2.1(3) = 4.7$$

Equation for linear trend:

$$T_t = 4.7 + 2.1t$$

Forecast:

$$T_6 = 4.7 + 2.1(6) = 17.3$$

12.   The following values are needed to compute the slope and intercept:

$$\sum t = 21 \quad \sum t^2 = 91 \quad \sum Y_t = 1171 \quad \sum t\, Y_t = 4037$$

Computation of slope:

$$b_1 = \frac{\sum t\, Y_t - \left(\sum t \sum Y_t\right)/n}{\sum t^2 - \left(\sum t^2\right)/n} = \frac{4037 - (21)(1171)/6}{91 - (21)^2/6} = -3.5143$$

Computation of intercept:

$$b_0 = \overline{Y} - b_1\, \overline{t} = 195.1667 - (-3.5143)(3.5) = 207.4668$$

Equation for linear trend: $T_t = 207.467 - 3.514t$

Forecast: $T_6 = 207.467 - 3.514(7) = 182.87$

13. a   The following values are needed to compute the slope and intercept:

$$\sum t = 15 \quad \sum t^2 = 55 \quad \sum Y_t = 19.7 \quad \sum t\, Y_t = 74.3$$

Computation of slope:

$$b_1 = \frac{\sum t\, Y_t - \left(\sum t \sum Y_t\right)/n}{\sum t^2 - \left(\sum t^2\right)/n} = \frac{74.3 - (15)(19.7)/5}{55 - (15)^2/5} = 1.52$$

Computation of intercept:

$$b_0 = \overline{Y} - b_1\, \overline{t} = 3.94 - 1.52(3) = -.62$$

Equation for linear trend: $T_t = -.62 + 1.52t$

b.   An estimate of the increase in the number of subscriptions per year is 1.52 million per year

14. The following values are needed to compute the slope and intercept:

$$\sum t = 15 \quad \sum t^2 = 55 \quad \sum Y_t = 66.9 \quad \sum t\, Y_t = 222.1$$

Computation of slope:

$$b_1 = \frac{\sum t\, Y_t - \left(\sum t \sum Y_t\right)/n}{\sum t^2 - \left(\sum t\right)^2/n} = \frac{222.1 - (15)(66.9)/5}{55 - (15)^2/5} = 2.14$$

Computation of intercept:

$$b_0 = \overline{Y} - b_1 \bar{t} = 13.38 - 2.14(3) = 6.96$$

Equation for linear trend: $T_t = 6.96 + 2.14\, t$

Forecast: $T_6 = 6.96 + 2.14(6) = 19.8$ or 19.8 million working couples

15. The following values are needed to compute the slope and intercept:

$$\sum t = 28 \quad \sum t^2 = 140 \quad \sum Y_t = 213{,}400 \quad \sum t\, Y_t = 865{,}400$$

Computation of slope:

$$b_1 = \frac{\sum t\, Y_t - \left(\sum t \sum Y_t\right)/n}{\sum t^2 - \left(\sum t\right)^2/n} = \frac{865{,}400 - (28)(213{,}400)/7}{140 - (28)^2/7} = 421.429$$

Computation of intercept:

$$b_0 = \overline{Y} - b_1 \bar{t} = 30{,}485.714 - 421.429(4) = 28{,}800$$

Equation for linear trend: $T_t = 28{,}800 + 421.429\, t$

16. A linear trend model is not appropriate. A nonlinear model would provide a better approximation.

17. a. A linear trend appears to be reasonable.

   b. The following values are needed to compute the slope and intercept:

$$\sum t = 36 \quad \sum t^2 = 204 \quad \sum Y_t = 223.8 \quad \sum t\, Y_t = 1081.6$$

Computation of slope:

$$b_1 = \frac{\sum t\, Y_t - \left(\sum t \sum Y_t\right)/n}{\sum t^2 - \left(\sum t\right)^2/n} = \frac{1081.6 - (36)(223.8)/8}{204 - (36)^2/8} = 1.7738$$

Computation of intercept:

$$b_0 = \overline{Y} - b_1\, \bar{t} = 27.975 - 1.7738(4.5) = 19.993$$

Equation for linear trend: $T_t = 19.993 + 1.774\, t$

Conclusion: The firm has been realizing an average cost increase of $1.77 per unit per year.

18. a. The following values are needed to compute the slope and intercept:

$$\sum t = 55 \quad \sum t^2 = 385 \quad \sum Y_t = 14.26 \quad \sum t\, Y_t = 94.34$$

Computation of slope:

$$b_1 = \frac{\sum t\, Y_t - \left(\sum t \sum Y_t\right)/n}{\sum t^2 - \left(\sum t\right)^2/n} = \frac{94.35 - (55)(14.26)/10}{385 - (55)^2/10} = .19297$$

Computation of intercept:

$$b_0 = \overline{Y} - b_1\, \bar{t} = 1.426 - .19297(5.5) = .365$$

Equation for linear trend: $T_t = .365 + .193\, t$

Forecast: $T_t = .365 + .193(11) = \$2.49$

b. Over the past ten years the earnings per share have been increasing at the average rate of $.193 per year. Althouogh this is a positive indicator of Walgreen's performance. More information would be necessary to conclude "good investment".

19. a. The following values are needed to compute the slope and intercept:

$$\sum t = 36 \quad \sum t^2 = 204 \quad \sum Y_t = 250.9 \quad \sum t\, Y_t = 1997.7$$

Computation of slope:

$$b_1 = \frac{\sum t\, Y_t - \left(\sum t \sum Y_t\right)/n}{\sum t^2 - \left(\sum t^2\right)/n} = \frac{1197.7 - (36)(250.9)/8}{204 - (36)^2/8} = 1.6345$$

Computation of intercept:

$$b_0 = \bar{Y} - b_1\, \bar{t} = 31.3625 - 1.6345(4.5) = 24.007$$

Equation for linear trend: $T_t = 24.007 + 1.635\,t$

The number of applications is increasing by approximately 1630 per year.

b. $T_t = 24.007 + 1.635(9) = 38.722$ or 38,722

20. a. The following values are needed to compute the slope and intercept:

$$\sum t = 55 \quad \sum t^2 = 385 \quad \sum Y_t = 41841 \quad \sum t\, Y_t = 262,923$$

Computation of slope:

$$b_1 = \frac{\sum t\, Y_t - \left(\sum t \sum Y_t\right)/n}{\sum t^2 - \left(\sum t^2\right)/n} = \frac{262,923 - (55)(41,841)/10}{385 - (55)^2/10} = 397.545$$

Computation of intercept:

$$b_0 = \bar{Y} - b_1\, \bar{t} = 4184.1 - 397.545(5.5) = 1997.6$$

Equation for linear trend: $T_t = 1997.6 + 397.545\,t$

b. $T_{11} = 1997.6 + 397.545(11) = 6371$

$T_{12} = 1997.6 + 397.545(12) = 6768$

21. a.

Year	Quarter	Y_t	Four-Quarter Moving Average	Centered Moving Averagae
1	1	4		
	2	2		
			3.50	
	3	3		3.750
			4.00	
	4	5		4.125
			4.25	
2	1	6		4.500
			4.75	
	2	3		5.000
			5.25	
	3	5		5.375
			5.50	
	4	7		5.875
			6.25	
3	1	7		6.375
			6.50	
	2	6		6.625
			6.75	
	3	6		
	4	8		

b.

Year	Quarter	Y_t	Centered Moving Average	Seasonal-Irregular Component
1	1	4		
	2	2		
	3	3	3.750	0.8000
	4	5	4.125	1.2121
2	1	6	4.500	1.3333
	2	3	5.000	0.6000
	3	5	5.375	0.9302
	4	7	5.875	1.1915
3	1	7	6.375	1.0980
	2	6	6.625	0.9057
	3	6		
	4	8		

Quarter	Seasonal-Irregular Component Values	Seasonal Index	Adjusted Seasonal Index
1	1.3333,1.0980	1.2157	1.2050
2	.60000,.9057	0.7529	0.7463
3	.80000,.9032	0.8651	0.8675
4	1.2121,1.1915	1.2018	1.1912
		4.0355	

Note: Adjustment for seasonal index = 4.000 / 4.0355 = 0.9912

22. a. Four quarter moving averages beginning with

$$(1690 + 940 + 2625 + 2500) / 4 = 1938.75$$

Other moving averages are

1966.25	2002.50
1956.25	2052.50
2025.00	2060.00
1990.00	2123.75

b.

Quarter	Seasonal-Irregular Component Values		Seasonal Index	Adjusted Seasonal Index
1	0.904	0.900	0.9020	0.900
2	0.448	0.526	0.4970	0.486
3	1.344	1.453	1.3985	1.396
4	1.275	1.164	1.2195	1.217
			4.0070	

Note: Adjustment for seasonal index = 4.000 / 4.007 = 0.9983

c   The largest seasonal effect is in the third quarter which corresponds to the back-to-school demand during July, August, and September of each year.

23.

Month	Seasonal-Irregular Component Values		Seasonal Index	Adjusted Seasonal Index
1	0.72	0.70	0.71	0.707
2	0.80	0.75	0.78	0.777
3	0.83	0.82	0.83	0.827
4	0.94	0.99	0.97	0.966
5	1.01	1.02	1.02	1.016
6	1.25	1.36	1.31	1.305
7	1.49	1.51	1.50	1.494
8	1.19	1.26	1.23	1.225
9	0.98	0.97	0.98	0.976
10	0.98	1.00	0.99	0.986
11	0.93	0.94	0.94	0.936
12	0.78	0.80	0.79	0.787
			12.05	

Notes: 1. Adjustment for seasonal index = 12 / 12.05 = 0.996

2. The adjustment is really not necessary in this problem since it imples more accuracy than is warranted. That is, the seasonal component values and the seasonal index were rounded to two decimal places.

24. a. Use a twelve period moving averages. After centering the moving averages, you should obtain the following seasonal indexes:

Hour	Seasonal Index	Hour	Seasonal Index
1	0.771	7	1.207
2	0.864	8	0.994
3	0.954	9	0.850
4	1.392	10	0.647
5	1.571	11	0.579
6	1.667	12	0.504

b. The hours of July 18 are number 37 to 48 in the time series. Thus the trend component for 7:00 a.m. on July 18 (period 37) would be

$$T_{37} = 32.983 + .3922(37) = 47.49$$

A summary of the trend components for the twelve hours on July 18 is as follows:

Hour	Trend Component	Hour	Trend Component
1	47.49	7	49.85
2	47.89	8	50.24
3	48.28	9	50.63
4	48.67	10	51.02
5	49.06	11	51.42
6	49.46	12	51.81

c. Multiply the trend component in part b by the seasonal indexes in part a to obtain the twelve hourly forecasts for July 18. For example, 47.49 x (.771) = 36.6 or rounded to 37, would be the forecast for 7:00 a.m. on July 18th.

The seasonally adjusted hourly forecasts for July 18 are as follows:

Hour	Forecast	Hour	Forecast
1	37	7	60
2	41	8	50
3	46	9	43
4	68	10	33
5	77	11	30
6	82	12	26

25. a.

Month	Y_t	3-Month Moving Averages Forecast	(Error)^2	$\alpha = 2$ Forecast	(Error)^2
1	80				
2	82			80.00	4.00
3	84			80.40	12.96
4	83	82.00	1.00	81.12	3.53
5	83	83.00	0.00	81.50	2.25
6	84	83.33	0.45	81.80	4.84
7	85	83.33	2.79	82.24	7.62
8	84	84.00	0.00	82.79	1.46
9	82	84.33	5.43	83.03	1.06
10	83	83.67	0.45	82.83	0.03
11	84	83.00	1.00	82.86	1.30
12	83	83.00	0.00	83.09	0.01
			11.12		39.06

MSE(3-Month) = 11.12 / 9 = 1.24

MSE(α = .2) = 39.06 / 11 = 3.55

Use 3-month moving averages.

b. (83 + 84 + 83) / 3 = 83.3

26.

Week t	Time-Series Value Y_t	Forecast F_t	Forecast Error $Y_t - F_t$	Squared Error $(Y_t - F_t)^2$
1	200			
2	350	200.00	150.00	22,500.00
3	250	237.50	12.50	156.25
4	360	240.63	119.37	14,249.20
5	250	270.47	-20.47	419.02
6	210	265.35	-55.35	3,063.62
7	280	251.51	28.49	811.68
8	350	258.64	91.36	8,346.65
9	290	281.48	8.52	72.59
10	320	283.61	36.39	1,324.23
				50,943.24

MSE = 50,943.24 / 9 = 5,660.36

Forecast for week 11:

$$F_{11} = 0.25(320) + 0.75(283.61) = 292.71$$

27. a.

Period	Time Series Value	$\alpha = .2$ Forecasts	$\alpha = .3$ Forecasts	$\alpha = .4$ Forecasts
1	27.0			
2	26.0	27.00	27.00	27.00
3	26.5	26.80	26.70	26.60
4	27.5	26.74	26.64	26.56
5	25.5	26.89	26.90	26.94
6	30.0	26.61	26.48	26.36
7	28.0	27.29	27.54	27.82
8	30.5	27.43	27.67	27.89
9	32	28.05	28.52	28.93

MSE($\alpha = .2$) = 5.08

MSE($\alpha = .3$) = 4.55

MSE($\alpha = .4$) = 4.18 $\alpha = .4$ provides the best forecast

b. Using $\alpha = .4$, $F_{10} = .4(32) + .6(28.93) = 30.16$

28.

Week t	Time-Series Value Y_t	Forecast F_t	Forecast Error $Y_t - F_t$	Squared Error $(Y_t - F_t)^2$
1	22			
2	18	22.00	-4.00	16.00
3	23	21.20	1.80	3.24
4	21	21.56	-0.56	0.31
5	17	21.45	-4.45	19.80
6	24	20.56	3.44	11.83
7	20	21.25	-1.25	1.56
8	19	21.00	-2.00	4.00
9	18	20.60	-2.60	6.76
10	21	20.08	0.92	0.85
			Total	64.35

MSE = 64.35 / 9 = 7.15

Forecast for week 11:

$$F_{11} = 0.2(21) + 0.8(20.08) = 20.26$$

29.

t	Y_t	F_t	$Y_t - F_t$	$(Y_t - F_t)^2$
1	2,750			
2	3,100	2,750.00	350.00	122,500.00
3	3,250	2,890.00	360.00	129,600.00
4	2,800	3,034.00	-234.00	54,756.00
5	2,900	2,940.40	-40.40	1,632.16
6	3,050	2,924.24	125.76	15,815.58
7	3,300	2,974.54	325.46	105,924.21
8	3,100	3,104.73	-4.73	22.37
9	2,950	3,102.84	-152.84	23,260.07
10	3,000	3,041.70	-41.70	1,738.89
11	3,200	3,025.02	174.98	30,618.00
12	3,150	3,095.01	54.99	3,023.90
			Total	488,991.18

MSE = 488,991.18 / 11 = 44,453.74

Forecast for week 13:

$$F_{13} = 0.4(3,150) + 0.6(3,095.01) = 3,117.01$$

30. a & b.

Week	Time-Series Value	$\alpha = .2$ Forecast	(Error)^2	$\alpha = .3$ Forecast	(Error)^2
1	7.35				
2	7.40	7.35	.0025	7.35	.0025
3	7.55	7.36	.0361	7.36	.0361
4	7.56	7.40	.0256	7.42	.0196
5	7.60	7.43	.0289	7.46	.0196
6	7.52	7.46	.0036	7.50	.0004
7	7.52	7.48	.0016	7.51	.0001
8	7.70	7.48	.0484	7.51	.0361
9	7.62	7.53	.0081	7.57	.0025
10	7.55	7.55	.0000	7.58	.0009
			.1548		.1178

c. $MSE(\alpha = .2) = .1548 / 9 = .0172$

$MSE(\alpha = .3) = .1178 / 9 = .0131$

Use $\alpha = .3$.

$$F_{11} = .3Y_{10} + .7F_{10} = .3(7.55) + .7(7.58) = 7.57$$

31. a. The following values are needed to compute the slope and intercept:

$$\sum t = 36 \quad \sum t^2 = 204 \quad \sum Y_t = 66.9 \quad \sum t Y_t = 338.9$$

Computation of slope:

$$b_1 = \frac{\sum t Y_t - \left(\sum t \sum Y_t\right)/n}{\sum t^2 - \left(\sum t^2\right)/n} = \frac{338.9 - (36)(66.9)/8}{204 - (36)^2/8} = .9012$$

Computation of intercept:

$$b_0 = \bar{Y} - b_1 \bar{t} = (66.9/8) - .9012(36/8) = 4.3071$$

Equation for linear trend: $T_t = 4.3071 + .9012t$

b. 1988 forecast: $T_9 = 4.3071 + .9012(9) = 12.4$

c. 1989 forecast: $T_{10} = 4.3071 + .9012(10) = 13.3$

d. 1990 forecast: $T_{11} = 4.3071 + .9012(11) = 14.2$

32.   The following values are needed to compute the slope and intercept:

$$\sum t = 21 \quad \sum t^2 = 91 \quad \sum Y_t = 201.2 \quad \sum t\, Y_t = 766.8$$

Computation of slope:

$$b_1 = \frac{\sum t\, Y_t - \left(\sum t \sum Y_t\right)/n}{\sum t^2 - \left(\sum t^2\right)/n} = \frac{766.8 - (21)(201.2)/6}{91 - (21)^2/6} = 3.5771$$

Computation of intercept:

$$b_0 = \overline{Y} - b_1\, \overline{t} = 33.5333 - 3.5771(3.5) = 21.0135$$

Equation for linear trend: $T_t = 21.0135 + 3.5771t$

Forecast: $T_7 = 21.0135 + 3.5771(7) = 46.05$ or $46.05 billion

33.   The following values are needed to compute the slope and intercept:

$$\sum t = 45 \quad \sum t^2 = 285 \quad \sum Y_t = 798.3 \quad \sum t\, Y_t = 4275.6$$

Computation of slope:

$$b_1 = \frac{\sum t\, Y_t - \left(\sum t \sum Y_t\right)/n}{\sum t^2 - \left(\sum t^2\right)/n} = \frac{4275.6 - (45)(798.3)/9}{285 - (45)^2/9} = 4.735$$

Computation of intercept:

$$b_0 = \overline{Y} - b_1\, \overline{t} = (798.3/9) - 4.735(45/9) = 65.025$$

Equation for linear trend: $T_t = 65.025 + 4.735t$

Forecast: $T_{10} = 65.025 + 4.735(10) = 112.4$

$T_{11} = 65.025 + 4.735(11) = 117.1$

34.   The following values are needed to compute the slope and intercept:

$$\sum t = 28 \quad \sum t^2 = 140 \quad \sum Y_t = 1575 \quad \sum t\, Y_t = 6491$$

Computation of slope:

$$b_1 = \frac{\sum t\,Y_t - \left(\sum t \sum Y_t\right)/n}{\sum t^2 - \left(\sum t\right)^2/n} = \frac{6491 - (28)(1575)/7}{140 - (28)^2/7} = 6.8214$$

Computation of intercept:

$$b_0 = \overline{Y} - b_1\,\overline{t} = 225 - 6.8214(4) = 197.714$$

Equation for linear trend: $T_t = 197.714 + 6.821t$

Forecast: $T_8 = 197.714 + 6.821(8) = 252.28$

$$T_9 = 65.025 + 4.735(9) = 259.10$$

35. a. The following values are needed to compute the slope and intercept:

$$\sum t = 78 \quad \sum t^2 = 650 \quad \sum Y_t = 343 \quad \sum t\,Y_t = 2441$$

Computation of slope:

$$b_1 = \frac{\sum t\,Y_t - \left(\sum t \sum Y_t\right)/n}{\sum t^2 - \left(\sum t\right)^2/n} = \frac{2441 - (78)(343)/12}{650 - (78)^2/12} = 1.479$$

Computation of intercept:

$$b_0 = \overline{Y} - b_1\,\overline{t} = (343/12) - 1.479(78/12) = 18.97$$

Equation for linear trend: $T_t = 18.97 + 1.479t$

Forecast: $T_{10} = 65.025 + 4.735(10) = 112.4$

$$T_{11} = 65.025 + 4.735(11) = 117.1$$

b.

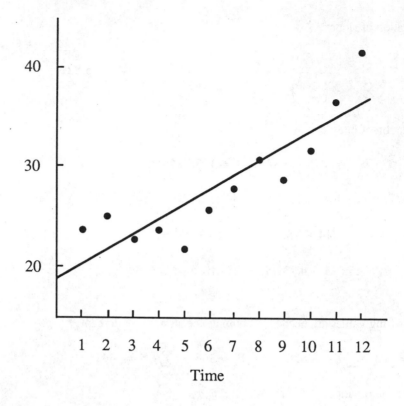

Time

36. a.   A graph of these data shows a linear trend.

b   The following values are needed to compute the slope and intercept:

$$\sum t = 15 \quad \sum t^2 = 55 \quad \sum Y_t = 200 \quad \sum t\, Y_t = 750$$

Computation of slope:

$$b_1 = \frac{\sum t\, Y_t - \left(\sum t \sum Y_t\right)/n}{\sum t^2 - \left(\sum t^2\right)/n} = \frac{750 - (15)(200)/5}{55 - (15)^2/5} = 15$$

Computation of intercept:

$$b_0 = \overline{Y} - b_1\, \overline{t} = 40 - 15(3) = -5$$

Equation for linear trend: $T_t = -5 + 15t$

Conclusion: average increase in sales is 15 units per year

37. a. Yes, a linear trend appears to exist.

    b The following values are needed to compute the slope and intercept:

    $$\sum t = 28 \quad \sum t^2 = 140 \quad \sum Y_t = 595 \quad \sum t\, Y_t = 2815$$

    Computation of slope:

    $$b_1 = \frac{\sum t\, Y_t - \left(\sum t \sum Y_t\right)/n}{\sum t^2 - \left(\sum t^2\right)/n} = \frac{2815 - (28)(595)/7}{140 - (28)^2/7} = 15.5357$$

    Computation of intercept:

    $$b_0 = \overline{Y} - b_1\, \overline{t} = 85 - 15.5357(4) = 22.857$$

    Equation for linear trend: $T_t = 22.857 + 15.536t$

    c. Forecast: $T_8 = 22.857 + 15.536(8) = 147.15$

38. a. PC Systems: $T_t = -31.267 + 60.314t$
    Mainframe Systems: $T_t = 140.467 + 15.629t$

    b. PC Systems: $T_7 = -31.267 + 60.314(7) = 390.93$
    Mainframe Systems: $T_7 = 140.467 + 15.629(7) = 249.87$

    c. The estimate of the change in software spending per year is much greater for the PC Systems; in other words, PC Systems sales are growing much more rapidly than Mainframe Systems sales.

39. a.

t	Sales	Centered Moving Average	Seasonal-Irregular Component
1	6		
2	15		
3	10	9.250	1.081
4	4	10.125	0.395
5	10	11.125	0.899
6	18	12.125	1.485
7	15	13.000	1.154
8	7	14.500	0.483
9	14	16.500	0.848
10	26	18.125	1.434
11	23	19.375	1.187
12	12	20.250	0.593
13	19	20.750	0.916
14	28	21.750	1.287
15	25	22.875	1.093
16	18	24.000	0.750
17	22	25.125	0.876
18	34	25.875	1.314
19	28	26.500	1.057
20	21	27.000	0.778
21	24	27.500	0.873
22	36	27.625	1.303
23	30	28.000	1.071
24	20	29.000	0.690
25	28	30.125	0.929
26	40	31.625	1.265
27	35		
28	27		

b.

Quarter	Seasonal-Irregular Component Values	Seasonal Index
1	0.899, 0.848, 0.916, 0.876, 0.873, 0.929	0.890
2	1.485, 1.434, 1.287, 1.314, 1.303, 1.265	1.348⁻
3	1.081, 1.154, 1.187, 1.093, 1.057, 1.071	1.107
4	0.395, 0.483, 0.593, 0.750, 0.778, 0.690	0.615
	Total	3.960

Quarter	Adjusted Seasonal Index
1	0.899
2	1.362
3	1.118
4	0.621

Note: Adjustment for seasonal index = 4.00 / 3.96 = 1.0101

c.   Hudson Marine experiences the largest seasonal increase in quarter 2. Since this quarter occurs prior to the peak summer boating season, this result seems reasonable.

40. a.

t	Sales	Centered Moving Average	Seasonal-Irregular Component
1	4		
2	2		
3	1	3.250	0.308
4	5	3.750	1.333
5	6	4.375	1.371
6	4	5.875	0.681
7	4	7.500	0.533
8	14	7.875	1.778
9	10	7.875	1.270
10	3	8.250	0.364
11	5	8.750	0.571
12	16	9.750	1.641
13	12	10.750	1.116
14	9	11.750	0.766
15	7	13.250	0.528
16	22	14.125	1.558
17	18	15.000	1.200
18	10	17.375	0.576
19	13		
20	35		

Quarter	Seasonal-Irregular Component Values	Seasonal Index
1	1.371, 1.270, 1.116, 1.200	1.239
2	0.681, 0.364, 0.776, 0.576	0.597
3	0.308, 0.533, 0.571, 0.528	0.485
4	1.333, 1.778, 1.641, 1.558	1.578
	Total	3.899

Quarter	Adjusted Seasonal Index
1	1.271
2	0.613
3	0.498
4	1.619

Note: Adjustment for seasonal index = 4 / 3.899 = 1.026

b. The largest effect is in quarter 4; this seems reasonable since retail sales are generally higher during October, November, and December.

41 a. Note: To simplify the calculations the seasonal indexes calculated in problem 19 have been rounded to two decimal places.

Year	Quarter	Sales Y_t	Seasonal Factor S_t	Deseasonalized Sales $Y_t / S_t = T_t I_t$
1	1	6	0.90	6.67
	2	15	1.36	11.03
	3	10	1.12	8.93
	4	4	0.62	6.45
2	1	10	0.90	11.11
	2	18	1.36	13.24
	3	15	1.12	13.39
	4	7	0.62	11.29
3	1	14	0.90	15.56
	2	26	1.36	19.12
	3	23	1.12	20.54
	4	12	0.62	19.35
4	1	19	0.90	21.11
	2	28	1.36	20.59
	3	25	1.12	22.32
	4	18	0.62	29.03
5	1	22	0.90	24.44
	2	34	1.36	25.00
	3	28	1.12	25.00
	4	21	0.62	33.87
6	1	24	0.90	26.67
	2	36	1.36	26.47
	3	30	1.12	26.79
	4	20	0.62	32.26
7	1	28	0.90	31.11
	2	40	1.36	29.41
	3	35	1.12	31.25
	4	27	0.62	43.55

t	Y_t (deseasonalized)	tY_t	t^2
1	6.67	6.67	1
2	11.03	22.06	4
3	8.93	26.79	9
4	6.45	25.80	16
5	11.11	55.55	25
6	13.24	79.44	36
7	13.39	93.73	49
8	11.29	90.32	64
9	15.56	140.04	81
10	19.12	191.20	100
11	20.54	225.94	121
12	19.35	232.20	144
13	21.11	274.43	169
14	20.59	288.26	196
15	22.32	334.80	225
16	29.03	464.48	256
17	24.44	415.48	289
18	25.00	450.00	324
19	25.00	475.00	361
20	33.87	677.40	400
21	26.67	560.07	441
22	26.47	582.34	484
23	26.79	616.17	529
24	32.26	774.24	576
25	31.11	777.75	625
26	29.41	764.66	676
27	31.25	843.75	729
28	43.55	1,219.40	784
406	605.55	10,707.34	7,714

$$\bar{t} = 14.5 \quad \bar{Y} = 21.627 \quad b_1 = 1.055 \quad b_0 = 6.329 \quad T_t = 6.329 + 1.055\, t$$

b.

t	Trend Forecast
29	36.92
30	37.98
31	39.03
32	40.09

c.

Year	Quarter	Trend Forecast	Seasonal Index	Quarterly Forecast
8	1	36.92	0.90	33.23
	2	37.98	1.36	51.65
	3	29.03	1.12	43.71
	4	40.09	0.62	24.86

42. a Note: To simplify the calculations the seasonal indexes in problem 20 have been
roundd to two decimal places.

Year	Quarter	Sales Y_t	Seasonal Factor S_t	Deseasonalized Sales $Y_t / S_t = T_t I_t$
1	1	4	1.27	3.15
	2	2	0.61	3.28
	3	1	0.50	2.00
	4	5	1.62	3.09
2	1	6	1.27	4.72
	2	4	0.61	6.56
	3	4	0.50	8.00
	4	14	1.62	8.64
3	1	10	1.27	7.87
	2	3	0.61	4.92
	3	5	0.50	10.00
	4	16	1.62	9.88
4	1	12	1.27	9.45
	2	9	0.61	14.75
	3	7	0.50	14.00
	4	22	1.62	13.58
5	1	18	1.27	14.17
	2	10	0.61	16.39
	3	13	0.50	26.00
	4	35	1.62	21.60

t	Y_t (deseasonalized)	tY_t	t^2
1	3.15	3.15	1
2	3.28	6.56	4
3	2.00	6.00	9
4	3.09	12.36	16
5	4.72	23.60	25
6	6.56	39.36	36
7	8.00	56.00	49
8	8.64	69.12	64
9	7.87	70.83	81
10	4.92	49.20	100
11	10.00	110.00	121
12	9.88	118.56	144
13	9.45	122.85	169
14	14.75	206.50	196
15	14.00	210.00	225
16	13.58	217.28	256
17	14.17	240.89	289
18	16.39	295.02	324
19	26.00	494.00	361
20	21.60	432.00	400
210	202.05	2783.28	2870

$$\bar{t} = 10.5 \quad \bar{Y} = 10.1025 \quad b_1 = .995 \quad b_0 = -.345 \quad T_t = -.345 + .995\,t$$

b.

y	Trend Forecast
21	20.55
22	21.55
23	22.54
24	23.54

c.

Year	Quarter	Trend Forecast	Seasonal Index	Quarterly Forecast
6	1	20.55	1.27	26.10
	2	21.55	0.61	13.15
	3	22.54	0.50	11.27
	4	23.54	1.62	38.13

Chapter 19
Nonparametric Methods

Learning Objectives

1. Learn the difference between parametric and nonparametric methods.

2. Know the particular advantages of nonparametric methods and when they are and when they are not applicable.

3. Learn how to use the sign test for the analysis of paired comparisons.

4. Be able to use the sign test to conduct hypothesis tests about a median.

5. Be able to use the Wilcoxon signed-rank test and the Mann-Whitney-Wilcoxon test to determine whether or not two populations have the same distribution.

6. Be able to use the Kruskal-Wallis tests for the comparison of k populations.

7. Be able to compute the Spearman rank correlation coefficient and test for a significant correlation between two sets of rankings.

Solutions:

1.   Binomial Probabilities for $n = 10$, $p = .50$.

x	Probability	x	Probability
0	.0010	6	.2051
1	.0098	7	.1172
2	.0439	8	.0439
3	.1172	9	.0098
4	.2051	10	.0010
5	.2461		

$P(0) + P(1) = .0108$; adding $P(2)$, exceeds .025 required in the tail. Therefore, reject H_0 if the number of plus signs is less than 2 or greater than 8.

Number of plus signs is 7.

Do not reject H_0; conclude that there is no indication that a difference exists.

2.   There are $n = 27$ cases in which a value different from 150 is obtained.

Use the normal approximation with $\mu = np = .5(27) = 13.5$ and

$$\sigma = \sqrt{.25\, n} = \sqrt{.25(27)} = 2.6$$

Use $x = 22$ as the number of plus signs and obtain the following test statistic:

$$z = \frac{x - \mu}{\sigma} = \frac{22 - 13.5}{2.6} = 3.27$$

With $\alpha = .01$, we reject if $z > 2.33$; since $z = 3.27 > 2.33$ we reject H_0.

Conclusion: the median is greater than 150.

3.   a. $H_0: p = .50$
            $H_a: p \neq .50$

        If H_0 cannot be rejected, there is no evidence to conclude that mothers and fathers are touched more or less frequently.

    b.   Let x be the number of plus signs (mothers touched more).

        Use the binomial probability tables with $n = 18$ (there were 2 ties in the 20 cases)

$$P(x < 5) + P(x > 13) = .0310$$

Reject H_0 if the number of + signs is less than 5 or greater than 13.

c. With $x = 14$, we reject H_0. The results support the conclusion that mothers and fathers are not touched with the same frequency.

Conclusion: mothers are touched more often.

4. We need to determine the number who said better and the number who said worse. The sum of the two is the sample size used for the study.

$$n = .34(1253) + .29(1253) = 789.4$$

Use the large sample test using the normal distribution. This means the value of n ($n = 789.4$ above) need not be integer. Hence,

$$\mu = .5 n = .5(789.4) = 394.7$$

$$\sigma = \sqrt{.25\, n} = \sqrt{.25(789.4)} = 14.05$$

Let p = proportion of adults who feel children will have a better future.

$$H_0:\ p \le .50$$

$$H_a:\ p > .50$$

With $x = .34(1253) = 426$

$$z = \frac{x - \mu}{\sigma} = \frac{426 - 394.7}{14.05} = 2.23$$

With $\alpha = .05$, we reject H_0 if $z > 1.645$

Since $z = 2.23 > 1.645$, we reject H_0

Conclusion: more than half of the adults feel their children will have a better future.

5. $\mu = .5 n = .5(165) = 82.5$

$\sigma = \sqrt{.25\, n} = \sqrt{.25(165)} = 6.42$

Reject H_0 if $z < -1.96$ or if $z > 1.96$

$$z = \frac{100 - 82.5}{6.42} = 2.73$$

Reject H_0; conclude that a significant difference exists.

6. $\mu = .5\, n = .5(250) = 125$

$\sigma = \sqrt{.25\, n} = \sqrt{.25(250)} = 7.91$

Reject H_0 if $z < -1.96$ or if $z > 1.96$

For 140 + signs

$$z = \frac{140 - 125}{7.91} = 1.90$$

Do not reject H_0; a preference differential cannot be concluded.

7. $\mu = .5\, n = .5(188) = 94$

$\sigma = \sqrt{.25\, n} = \sqrt{.25(188)} = 6.86$

Reject H_0 if $z < -2.33$ or if $z > 2.33$

For 54 + signs

$$z = \frac{54 - 94}{6.86} = -5.83$$

Reject H_0; conclude that the median hourly wage is different from the nationwide median hourly wage.

8. $\mu = .5\, n = .5(150) = 75$

$\sigma = \sqrt{.25\, n} = \sqrt{.25(150)} = 6.12$

One tailed test: reject H_0 if $z > 1.645$

For 98 + signs

$$z = \frac{98 - 75}{6.12} = 3.76$$

Reject H_0; conclude that a home team advantage exists.

9. H_0: Median ≤ 15
H_a: Median > 15

Use binomial probabilities with $n = 8$ and $p = .50$:

One tail test with $\alpha = .05$,

$$P(8 +\text{'s}) = .0039$$
$$P(7 +\text{'s}) = \underline{.0312}$$
$$.0351$$

$$P(6 +\text{'s}) = .1094$$

Reject H_0 if 7 or 8 +'s. With 7 +'s in the sample, reject H_0. Data does enable us to conclude that there has been an increase in the median number of part-time employees.

10. H_0: Median $= 25.9$
         H_a: Median $\neq 25.9$

$$\mu = .5 \, n = .5(225) = 112.5$$

$$\sigma = \sqrt{.25 \, n} = \sqrt{.25(225)} = 7.5$$

Reject H_0 if $z < -1.96$ or if $z > 1.96$

For 122 cases

$$z = \frac{122 - 112.5}{7.5} = 1.27$$

Do not reject H_0; we are unable to conclude that the median age for men differs from the reported 25.9 years.

11. H_0: Median ≤ 9
         H_a: Median > 9 One tailed test

$$\mu = .5 \, n = .5(25) = 12.5$$

$$\sigma = \sqrt{.25 \, n} = \sqrt{.25(25)} = 2.5$$

Reject H_0 if $z > 1.645$

18 had hourly wages greater than \$9.00
$$z = \frac{18 - 12.5}{2.5} = 2.2$$

Reject H_0; conclude that the median hourly wage in the Los Angeles area is greater than \$9.00.

12. H_0: The populations are identical

        H_a: The populations are not identical

Additive 1	Additive 2	Difference	Absolute Value	Rank	Signed Rank
20.12	18.05	2.07	2.07	9	+9
23.56	21.77	1.79	1.79	7	+7
22.03	22.57	-.54	.54	3	-3
19.15	17.06	2.09	2.09	10	+10
21.23	21.22	.01	.01	1	+1
24.77	23.80	.97	.97	4	+4
16.16	17.20	-1.04	1.04	5	-5
18.55	14.98	3.57	3.57	12	+12
21.87	20.03	1.84	1.84	8	+8
24.23	21.15	3.08	3.08	11	+11
23.21	22.78	.43	.43	2	+2
25.02	23.70	1.32	1.32	6	+6

Total 62

$\mu_T = 0$

$$\sigma_T = \sqrt{\frac{n(n+1)(2n+1)}{6}} = \sqrt{\frac{12(13)(25)}{6}} = 25.5$$

$$z = \frac{T - \mu_T}{\sigma_T} = \frac{62 - 0}{25.5} = 2.43$$

Two-tailed test. Reject H_0 if $z < -1.96$ or if $z > 1.96$

Since $z = 2.43 > 1.96$ we reject H_0.

Conclusion: there is a significant difference in the additives.

13.

Without Relaxant	With Relaxant	Difference	Rank of Absolute Difference	Signed Rank
15	10	5	9	9
12	10	2	3	3
22	12	10	10	10
8	11	-3	6.5	-6.5
10	9	1	1	1
7	5	2	3	3
8	10	-2	3	-3
10	7	3	6.5	6.5
14	11	3	6.5	6.5
9	6	3	6.5	6.5
				Total 36

$\mu_T = 0$

$$\sigma_T = \sqrt{\frac{n\,(n+1)\,(2n+1)}{6}} = \sqrt{\frac{10(11)(21)}{6}} = 19.62$$

$$z = \frac{T - \mu_T}{\sigma_T} = \frac{36}{19.62} = 1.83$$

One-tailed test. Reject H_0 if $z > 1.645$

Since $z = 1.83 > 1.645$ we reject H_0.

Conclusion: there is a significant difference in favor of the relaxant.

14. Formulate as a one-tail test with H_a corresponding to January complaints being less than December complaints. If H_0 can be rejected, conclude that complaints are lower in January.

Difference	Absolute Difference	Rank	Signed Rank
.9	.9	8	+8
.3	.3	4	+4
-.3	.3	4	-4
-.3	.3	4	-4
3.1	3.1	10	+10
-.1	.1	1	-1
1.3	1.3	9	+9
.3	.3	4	+4
.3	.3	4	+4
.7	.7	7	+7
		Total	+37

Note: the five differences of .3 are assigned the average rank of 4.

Mean $\mu_T = 0$

Standard deviation:

$$\sigma_T = \sqrt{\frac{n(n+1)(2n+1)}{6}} = \sqrt{\frac{10(11)(21)}{6}} = 19.62$$

$$z = \frac{T - \mu_T}{\sigma_T} = \frac{37 - 0}{19.62} = +1.89$$

One-tailed test with $\alpha = .05$; reject H_0 if $z > 1.645$

Reject H_0; we can conclude that the baggage complaints have decreased in January.

15.

Service #1	Service #2	Difference	Rank of Absolute Difference	Signed Rank
24.5	28.0	-3.5	7.5	-7.5
26.0	25.5	0.5	1.5	1.5
28.0	32.0	-4.0	9.5	-9.5
21.0	20.0	1.0	4	4.0
18.0	19.5	-1.5	6	-6.0
36.0	28.0	8.0	11	11.0
25.0	29.0	-4.0	9.5	-9.5
21.0	22.0	-1.0	4	-4.0
24.0	23.5	0.5	1.5	1.5
26.0	29.5	-3.5	7.5	-7.5
31.0	30.0	1.0	4	4.0
			T =	-22.0

$\mu_T = 0$

$$\sigma_T = \sqrt{\frac{n\,(n+1)\,(2n+1)}{6}} = \sqrt{\frac{11(12)(23)}{6}} = 22.49$$

$$z = \frac{T - \mu_T}{\sigma_T} = \frac{-22}{22.49} = -.98$$

Reject H_0 if $z < -1.96$ or if $z > 1.96$. Do not reject H_0; there is no significant difference.

16.

Pretest	Post-test	Difference	Rank of Absolute Difference	Signed Rank
45	65	-20	10	-10
60	70	-10	8	-8
65	63	2	1	1
60	67	-7	5	-5
52	60	-8	6.5	-6.5
62	58	4	2.5	2.5
57	70	-13	9	-9
70	65	5	4	4
72	80	-8	6.5	-6.5
66	88	-22	11	-11
78	74	4	2.5	2.5
				T = -46

$\mu_T = 0$

$$\sigma_T = \sqrt{\frac{n\,(n+1)\,(2n+1)}{6}} = \sqrt{\frac{11(12)(23)}{6}} = 22.49$$

$$z = \frac{T - \mu_T}{\sigma_T} = \frac{-46}{22.49} = -2.05$$

Since $z = -2.05 < -1.645$ we reject H_0; test scores differ in favor of post-test scores.

17.

Precampaign	Postcampaign	Difference	Rank of Absolute Difference	Signed Rank
130	160	-30	10	-10
100	105	-5	2.5	-2.5
120	140	-20	9	-9
95	90	5	2.5	2.5
140	130	10	4.5	4.5
80	82	-2	1	-1
65	55	10	4.5	4.5
90	105	-15	7.5	-7.5
140	152	-12	6	-6
125	140	-15	7.5	-7.5
				$T = -32$

$$\mu_T = 0$$

$$\sigma_T = \sqrt{\frac{n(n+1)(2n+1)}{6}} = \sqrt{\frac{10(11)(21)}{6}} = 19.62$$

$$z = \frac{T - \mu_T}{\sigma_T} = \frac{-32}{19.62} = -1.63$$

Reject H_0 if $z < -1.645$

Do not reject H_0; the difference is not significant at the $\alpha = .05$ level.

18.   Rank the combined samples and find the rank sum for each sample.

This is a small sample test since $n_1 = 7$ and $n_2 = 9$

Additive 1		Additive 2	
MPG	Rank	MPG	Rank
17.3	2	18.7	8.5
18.4	6	17.8	4
19.1	10	21.3	15
16.7	1	21.0	14
18.2	5	22.1	16
18.6	7	18.7	8.5
17.5	3	19.8	11
	34	20.7	13
		20.2	12
			102

$T = 34$

With $\alpha = .05$, $n_1 = 7$ and $n_2 = 9$

$$T_L = 41 \text{ and } T_U = 7(7 + 9 + 1) - 41 = 78$$

Since $T = 34 < 41$, we reject H_0

Conclusion: there is a significant difference in gasoline mileage

19. a. Rank the combined samples and find the rank sum for each sample. With $n_1 = 12$ and $n_2 = 12$, this is a large sample case.

H_0: There are no differences in the distribution of starting salaries

H_a: There is a difference between the distributions of starting salaries

We reject H_0 if $z < -1.96$ or $z > 1.96$

Accounting		Finance	
Salary	Rank	Salary	Rank
28.8	20	26.3	13
25.3	9	23.6	3
26.2	11	25.0	7
27.9	17.5	23.0	1
27.0	15	27.9	17.5
26.2	11	24.5	5
28.1	19	29.0	21
24.7	6	27.4	16
25.2	8	23.5	2
29.2	22	26.9	14
29.7	24	26.2	11
29.3	23	24.0	4
327.6	185.5	307.3	114.5

$$\mu_T = \frac{1}{2} n_1(n_1 + n_2 + 1)) = \frac{1}{2} 12(12 + 12 + 1)) = 150$$

$T = 185.5$

$$\sigma_T = \sqrt{\frac{1}{12} n_1 n_2(n_1 + n_2 + 1))} = \sqrt{\frac{1}{12}(12)(12)(25)} = 17.32$$

$$z = \frac{T - \mu_T}{\sigma_T} = \frac{185.5 - 150}{17.32} = 2.05$$

Since $z = 2.05 > 1.96$, we reject H_0

Conclusion: there is a significant difference in starting salaries

20. The ranks of the 13 employees relative to each other can be computed from the class ranks.

Data Processing	Typists
1	4
2	6
3	7
5	9.5
8	11
9.5	12
	13
28.5	62.5

Let $T = 28.5$. Using Table 10 of Appendix B

$$T_L = 30$$

$$T_U = n_1(n_1 + n_2 + 1) - T_L = 6(6 + 7 + 1) - 30 = 54$$

Reject H_0 if $T < 30$ or if $T > 54$

Since $T = 28.5$ we reject H_0

Conclusion: there is a significant performance difference in favor of the data processing group.

21. Sum of ranks (Model 1) = 185.5

Sum of ranks (Model 2) = 114.5

Use $T = 185.5$

$$\mu_T = \frac{1}{2} n_1(n_1 + n_2 + 1)) = \frac{1}{2} 12(12 + 12 + 1)) = 150$$

$$\sigma_T = \sqrt{\frac{1}{12} n_1 n_2(n_1 + n_2 + 1))} = \sqrt{\frac{1}{12}(12)(12)(25)} = 17.32$$

$$z = \frac{T - \mu_T}{\sigma_T} = \frac{185.5 - 150}{17.32} = 2.05$$

Reject H_0 if $z > 1.645$

Since $z = 2.05 > 1.645$ we reject H_0

Conclusion: there is a significant difference between the populations.

22.

Men	Rank	Women	Rank
167	14	146	3
175	17	162	9
160	8	164	11
165	12	148	4
172	16	166	13
180	18	158	7
185	20	150	5.5
170	15	150	5.5
163	10	140	1
184	19	142	2
	149		61

$$\mu_T = \frac{1}{2} n_1(n_1 + n_2 + 1) = \frac{1}{2} 10(10 + 10 + 1) = 105$$

$$\sigma_T = \sqrt{\frac{1}{12} n_1 n_2(n_1 + n_2 + 1)} = \sqrt{\frac{1}{12}(10)(10)(21)} = 13.23$$

$$z = \frac{T - \mu_T}{\sigma_T} = \frac{149 - 105}{13.232} = 3.33$$

Reject H_0 if $z < -1.96$ or if $z > 1.96$

Since $z = 3.33 > 1.96$, we reject H_0.

Conclusion: insurance costs differ for men and women.

23.   Sum of ranks (Winter) = 71.5

Sum of ranks (Summer) = 138.5

Use T = 71.5

$$\mu_T = \frac{1}{2} n_1(n_1 + n_2 + 1) = \frac{1}{2} 10(21) = 105$$

$$\sigma_T = \sqrt{\frac{1}{12} n_1 n_2(n_1 + n_2 + 1)} = \sqrt{\frac{1}{12}(10)(10)(21)} = 13.23$$

$$z = \frac{T - \mu_T}{\sigma_T} = \frac{71.5 - 105}{13.23} = -2.53$$

Reject H_0 if $z < -1.96$ or if $z > 1.96$

Reject H_0; there is a significant difference

24.   Sum of ranks (Dallas) = 116   Sum of ranks (San Antonio) = 160

Use T = 116

$$\mu_T = \frac{1}{2} n_1(n_1 + n_2 + 1)) = \frac{1}{2} 10(24) = 120$$

$$\sigma_T = \sqrt{\frac{1}{12} n_1 n_2 (n_1 + n_2 + 1))} = \sqrt{\frac{1}{12}(10)(13)(24)} = 16.12$$

$$z = \frac{T - \mu_T}{\sigma_T} = \frac{116 - 120}{16.12} = -.25$$

Reject H_0 if $z < -1.96$ or if $z > 1.96$

Do not reject H_0; there is not significant evidence to conclude that there is a difference.

25.   Sum of ranks (MIS) = 106   Sum of ranks (Gen. Bus.) = 47

Use T = 106

From Table 10 of Appendix B, we get

   $T_L = 58$ $T_U = 104$

Reject H_0 if $T < 58$ if $T > 104$

Since T = 106 > 104, reject H_0.

Conclusion: there is a significant difference in favor of the management information systems major.

26.

A	B	C
4	11	7
8	14	2
10	15	1
3	12	6
9	13	5
34	65	21

$$W = \frac{12}{(15)(16)} \left[\frac{(34)^2}{5} + \frac{(65)^2}{5} + \frac{(21)^2}{5} \right] - 3(16) = 10.22$$

$\chi^2_{.05} = 5.99147$ (2 degrees of freedom)

Reject H_0; conclude that the ratings for the products differ.

27.

A	B	C
11.5	5.0	17.0
2.5	11.5	20.0
8.0	2.5	15.0
10.0	4.0	8.0
8.0	6.0	16.0
18.0	1.0	19.0
	13.0	14.0
58.0	43.0	109.0

$$W = \frac{12}{(20)(21)} \left[\frac{(58)^2}{6} + \frac{(43)^2}{7} + \frac{(109)^2}{7} \right] - 3(21) = 9.06$$

$\chi^2_{.01} = 9.21034$ (2 degrees of freedom)

Do not reject H_0; we cannot conclude that there is a significant difference in test preparation programs.

28.

Surgery	Radiology	Obstetrics
16	17	7.5
10.5	2	1
18	12	3
7.5	15	14
6	5	4
10.5	13	9
68.5	64	38.5

$$W = \frac{12}{(18)(19)} \left[\frac{(68.5)^2}{6} + \frac{(64)^2}{6} + \frac{(38.5)^2}{6} \right] - 3(19) = 3.06$$

$\chi^2_{.05} = 5.99147$ (2 degrees of freedom)

Since $3.06 < 5.99147$ do not reject H_0; for these specialties we cannot conclude that there are significant differences in salary.

29. a.

A	B	C
2	2	12
7	4.5	14
4.5	9	10.5
2	7	13
7	10.5	15
22.5	33	64.5

$$W = \frac{12}{(15)(16)} \left[\frac{(22.5)^2}{5} + \frac{(33)^2}{5} + \frac{(64.5)^2}{5} \right] - 3(16) = 9.555$$

$\chi^2_{.05} = 5.99147$ (2 degrees of freedom)

Since $9.555 > 5.99147$ we reject H_0 and conclude that there is a significant difference in gas mileage among the three automobiles.

b. The ANOVA procedure uses the actual mileage results (ratio data). The Kruskal-wallis procedure only uses the rank order of the data. Thus, the magnitude of the differences is not considered in the Kruskal-Wallis test.

30.

Course 1	Course 2	Course 3	Course 4
3	2	19	20
14	7	16	4
10	1	9	15
12	5	18	6
13	11	17	8
52	26	79	53

$$W = \frac{12}{(20)(21)} \left[\frac{(52)^2}{5} + \frac{(26)^2}{5} + \frac{(79)^2}{5} + \frac{(53)^2}{5} \right] - 3(21) = 8.03$$

$\chi^2_{.05} = 7.81473$ (3 degrees of freedom)

Since $8.03 > 7.81473$, we reject H_0 and conclude that there is a significant difference in the quality of courses offered by the four management development centers.

31.

M&Ms	Kit Kat	Milky Way II
10.5	9	3
7	5	6
13	14	4
15	12	2
10.5	8	1
56	48	16

$$W = \frac{12}{(15)(16)}\left[\frac{(56)^2}{5} + \frac{(48)^2}{5} + \frac{(16)^2}{5}\right] - 3(16) = 8.96$$

$\chi^2_{.05} = 5.99147$ (2 degrees of freedom)

Since 8.96 > 5.99147 we reject H_0

There are significant differences in calorie content among the three candies.

32. a. $\sum d_i^2 = 52$

$$r_s = 1 - \frac{6 \sum d_i^2}{n(n^2 - 1)} = 1 - \frac{6(52)}{10(99)} = .68$$

b. $\sigma_{r_s} = \sqrt{\frac{1}{n-1}} = \sqrt{\frac{1}{9}} = .33$

$$z = \frac{r_s - 0}{\sigma_{r_s}} = \frac{.68}{.33} = 2.06$$

Reject if $z < -1.96$ or if $z > 1.96$

Since $z = 2.06 > 1.96$, we reject H_0.

Conclude that significant rank correlation exists.

33. Case 1:

$$\sum d_i^2 = 0$$

$$r_s = 1 - \frac{6 \sum d_i^2}{n(n^2 - 1)} = 1 - \frac{6(0)}{6(36 - 1)} = 1$$

Case 2:

$$\sum d_i^2 = 70$$

$$r_s = 1 - \frac{6 \sum d_i^2}{n(n^2 - 1)} = 1 - \frac{6(70)}{6(36 - 1)} = -1$$

With perfect agreement, $r_s = 1$.

With exact opposite ranking, $r_s = -1$.

34. $\sum d_i^2 = 170$

$$r_s = 1 - \frac{6 \sum d_i^2}{n(n^2 - 1)} = 1 - \frac{6(170)}{11(120)} = .23$$

$$\sigma_{r_s} = \sqrt{\frac{1}{n - 1}} = \sqrt{\frac{1}{10}} = .32$$

$$z = \frac{r_s - 0}{\sigma_{r_s}} = \frac{.23}{.32} = .72$$

Reject if $z < -1.96$ or if $z > 1.96$

Since $z = .72$, we cannot reject H_0.

Conclude that there is not a significant relationship between the rankings.

35. a. $\sum d_i^2 = 66$

$$r_s = 1 - \frac{6 \sum d_i^2}{n(n^2 - 1)} = 1 - \frac{6(66)}{10(100 - 1)} = .60$$

indicating a positive correlation in rank order.

b. $\mu_{r_s} = 0$

$$\sigma_{r_s} = \sqrt{\frac{1}{n - 1}} = \sqrt{\frac{1}{9}} = .33$$

$$z = \frac{r_s - \mu_{r_s}}{\sigma_{r_s}} = \frac{.6 - 0}{.33} = 1.82$$

Reject H_0 if $z < -1.96$ or if $z > 1.96$

Since $z = 1.82$, we cannot reject H_0 ; conclude that a non-zero rank correlation exists.

36. $\sum d_i^2 = 158$

$$r_s = 1 - \frac{6 \sum d_i^2}{n(n^2 - 1)} = 1 - \frac{6(158)}{10(99)} = .04$$

$$\mu_{r_s} = 0$$

$$\sigma_{r_s} = \sqrt{\frac{1}{n-1}} = \sqrt{\frac{1}{9}} = .3333$$

Reject H_0 if $z < -1.645$ or if $z > 1.645$

$$z = \frac{r_s - \mu_{r_s}}{\sigma_{r_s}} = \frac{.04 - 0}{.3333} = .12$$

Do not reject H_0; the rankings of men and women are not significantly related.

37. $\sum d_i^2 = 38$

$$r_s = 1 - \frac{6 \sum d_i^2}{n(n^2 - 1)} = 1 - \frac{6(38)}{10(99)} = .77$$

$$\mu_{r_s} = 0$$

$$\sigma_{r_s} = \sqrt{\frac{1}{n-1}} = \sqrt{\frac{1}{9}} = .3333$$

Reject H_0 if $z < -1.645$ or if $z > 1.645$

$$z = \frac{r_s - 0}{\sigma_{r_s}} = \frac{.77}{.3333} = 2.31$$

Reject H_0; there is a significant rank correlation between current students and recent graduates.

38. $u = .5n = .5(24) = 12$

Chapter 19

$$\sigma = \sqrt{.25\,n} = \sqrt{.25(24)} = 2.45$$

Reject H_0 if $z < -1.96$ or if $z > 1.96$

For 14 plus signs,

$$z = \frac{14 - 12}{2.45} = .82$$

Do not reject H_0; the difference in preferences is not significant at the .05 level of significance.

39.   With $n = 12$ use the small-sample sign test.

Using the binomial distribution with $n = 12$ and $p = .50$, $P(0) + P(1) + P(2) = .0002 + .0029 + .0161 = .0192$

Reject H_0 if the number of plus signs is less than 3 or greater than 9.

Since the number of plus signs is 9, we cannot reject H_0. We cannot conclude that there is a significant difference.

40. $u = .5\,n = .5(44) = 22$

$$\sigma = \sqrt{.25\,n} = \sqrt{.25(44)} = 3.32$$

Reject H_0 if $z < -1.645$ or if $z > 1.645$

For 28,
$$z = \frac{28 - 22}{3.32} = 1.81$$

Reject H_0; conclude that there is a significant difference in the preference for the two brands.

41.   Use $n = 10$ since the data for worker 8 provides a tie.

With $n = 10$, use the small-sample sign test.

Using the binomial distribution with $n = 10$ and $p = .50$, $P(0) + P(1) = .0108$.

Reject H_0 if the number of plus signs is less than 2 or greater than 8.

Since the number of plus signs is 8, we cannot reject H_0. The data do not allow us to conclude that a significant difference exists for the two methods.

42.   Chicago $n = 55 + 28 = 83$

$u = .50\, n = .50(83) = 41.5$

$\sigma = \sqrt{.25\, n} = \sqrt{.25(83)} = 4.56$

$z = \dfrac{55 - 41.5}{4.56} = 2.96$

Reject if $z < -1.96$ or if $z > 1.96$

Conclude that the median price of new homes in Chicago is not equal to the national median price.

Dallas-F. Worth $n = 42 + 36 = 78$

$u = .50\, n = .50(78) = 39$

$\sigma = \sqrt{.25\, n} = \sqrt{.25(78)} = 4.42$

$z = \dfrac{42 - 39}{4.42} = .68$

Do not reject H_0; we cannot reject the hypothesis that the median price of new homes in Dallas-Ft. Worth is the national median of $123,500.

43. Using binomial probabilities for $n = 12$ and $p = .50$, the rejection region is reject H_0 if the number of plus signs is less than 3 or greater than 9. With 8 plus signs, do not reject H_0. There is not evidence of a difference in preference.

44. Use the Wilcoxon Signed Rank Test

Homemaker	Difference	Signed Rank
1	-250	-11
2	40	2
3	50	3
4	-150	-6
5	-330	-12
6	-180	-7
7	-190	-8.5
8	-230	-10
9	-100	-5
10	-190	-8.5
11	-90	-4
12	20	1
		$T = -66$

$\mu_T = 0$

$$\sigma_T = \sqrt{\frac{n(n+1)(2n+1)}{6}} = \sqrt{\frac{12(13)(25)}{6}} = 25.5$$

Reject H_0 if $z < -1.96$ or if $z > 1.96$

$$z = \frac{T - \mu_T}{\sigma_T} = \frac{-66}{25.5} = -2.59$$

Reject H_0; conclude that the models differ in terms of selling prices.

45.

Difference	Rank of Absolute Difference	Signed Ranks
1.5	10	10.0
1.2	9	9.0
-0.2	2.5	-2.5
0.0	—	—
0.5	4	4.0
0.7	6	6.0
0.8	7	7.0
1.0	8	8.0
0.0	—	—
0.6	5	5.0
0.2	2.5	2.5
-.01	1	-1.0
		$T = 48$

$$\sigma_T = \sqrt{\frac{n(n+1)(2n+1)}{6}} = \sqrt{\frac{10(11)(21)}{6}} = 19.62$$

Reject H_0 if $z > 1.645$

$$z = \frac{T - \mu_T}{\sigma_T} = \frac{48}{19.62} = 2.45$$

Reject H_0; conclude that there is a significant weight gain.

46. Use the MWW test.

Sum of ranks (line 1) = 70

Sum of ranks (line 2) = 183

T = 70

$$\mu_T = \frac{1}{2} n_1(n_1 + n_2 + 1)) = \frac{1}{2} 10(23)) = 115$$

$$\sigma_T = \sqrt{\frac{1}{12} n_1 n_2(n_1 + n_2 + 1))} = \sqrt{\frac{1}{12}(10)(12)(23)} = 15.17$$

Reject H_0 if z < -1.645 or if if z > 1.645

$$z = \frac{T - \mu_T}{\sigma_T} = \frac{70 - 115}{15.17} = -2.97$$

Reject H_0; conclude that the weights differ for the two production lines.

47.

Method 1	Method 2	Method 3
8.5	4.5	2.0
15.0	14.0	7.0
6.0	16.0	10.0
17.0	8.5	1.0
18.0	12.5	3.0
12.5	11.0	4.5
77.0	66.5	27.5

$$W = \frac{12}{(18)(19)}\left[\frac{(77)^2}{6} + \frac{(66.5)^2}{6} + \frac{(27.5)^2}{6}\right] - 3(19) = 7.956$$

$\chi^2_{.05} = 5.99147$ (3 degrees of freedom)

Since 7.956 > 5.99147, we reject H_0 and conclude that there is a significant difference among the methods.

48.

No Program	Company Program	Off Site Program
16	12	7
9	20	1
10	17	4
15	19	2
11	6	3
13	18	8
	14	5
74	106	30

$$W = \frac{12}{(20)(21)}\left[\frac{(74)^2}{6} + \frac{(106)^2}{7} + \frac{(30)^2}{7}\right] - 3(21) = 12.61$$

$\chi^2_{.05} = 7.37776$ (2 degrees of freedom)

Since $12.61 > 7.37776$, we reject H_0 and conclude that there is a significant difference among the programs.

49.

Black	Jennings	Swanson	Wilson
22.5	20.5	22.5	9.5
9.5	27.0	6.0	17.5
8.0	7.0	2.5	1.0
2.5	17.5	12.5	5.0
26.0	28.5	17.5	24.0
4.0	28.5	12.5	20.5
	17.5	15.0	
	25.0	14.0	
		11.0	
72.5	171.5	113.5	77.5

$$W = \frac{12}{(29)(30)}\left[\frac{(72.5)^2}{6} + \frac{(171.5)^2}{8} + \frac{(113.5)^2}{9} + \frac{(77.5)^2}{6}\right] - 3(30) = 6.344$$

$\chi^2_{.05} = 7.81473$ (3 degrees of freedom)

Since $6.344 < 7.81473$ we cannot reject H_0. We cannot conclude that there is a significant difference among the course evaluation ratings for the 4 instructors.

50. $\sum d_i^2 = 550$

$$r_s = 1 - \frac{6 \sum d_i^2}{n(n^2 - 1)} = 1 - \frac{6(550)}{12(143)} = -.92$$

$$\sigma_{r_s} = \sqrt{\frac{1}{n - 1}} = \sqrt{\frac{1}{11}} = .3015$$

Reject H_0 if $z < -1.96$ or if $z > 1.96$

$$z = \frac{r_s - \mu_{r_s}}{\sigma_{r_s}} = \frac{-.92}{.3015} = -3.05$$

Reject H_0; conclude that there is a significant rank correlation between book value and growth potential

51. $\sum d_i^2 = 550$

$$r_s = 1 - \frac{6 \sum d_i^2}{n(n^2 - 1)} = 1 - \frac{6(20)}{7(48)} = .64$$

52. $\sum d_i^2 = 136$

$$r_s = 1 - \frac{6 \sum d_i^2}{n(n^2 - 1)} = 1 - \frac{6(136)}{15(224)} = .76$$

$$\sigma_{r_s} = \sqrt{\frac{1}{n - 1}} = \sqrt{\frac{1}{14}} = .2673$$

Reject H_0 if $z < -1.645$ or if $z > 1.645$

$$z = \frac{r_s - \mu_{r_s}}{\sigma_{r_s}} = \frac{.76}{.2673} = 2.84$$

Reject H_0; conclude that there is a significant rank correlation between the two exams.

Chapter 20
Statistical Methods for Quality Control

Learning Objectives

1. Learn about the importance of quality control and how statistical methods can assist in the quality control process.

2. Learn about acceptance sampling procedures.

3. Know the difference between consumer's risk and producer's risk.

4. Be able to use the binomial probability distribution to develop acceptance sampling plans.

5. Know what is meant by multiple sampling plans.

6. Be able to construct quality control charts and understand how they are used for statistical process control.

7. Know the definitions of the following terms:

producer's risk	assignable causes
consumer's risk	common causes
acceptance sampling	control charts
acceptance criterion	upper control limit
operating characteristic curve	lower control limit

Solutions:

1. $$f(x) = \frac{n!}{x!\,(n-x)!}\,p^x\,(1-p)^{n-x}$$

    When $p = .02$, the probability of accepting the lot is

    $$f(0) = \frac{25!}{0!\,(25-0)!}\,(.02)^0\,(1-.02)^{25} = .6035$$

    When $p = .06$, the probability of accepting the lot is

    $$f(0) = \frac{25!}{0!\,(25-0)!}\,(.06)^0\,(1-.06)^{25} = .2129$$

2. a. Using binomial probabilities with $n = 20$ and $p_0 = .02$.

    P (Accept lot) $= f(0) = .6676$

    Producer's risk: $\alpha = 1 - .6676 = .3324$

    b. P (Accept lot) $= f(0) = .2901$

    Producer's risk: $\alpha = 1 - .2901 = .7099$

3. At $p_0 = .02$, the $n = 20$ and $c = 1$ plan provides

    P (Accept lot) $= f(0) + f(1) = .6676 + .2725 = .9401$

    Producer's risk: $\alpha = 1 - .9401 = .0599$

    At $p_0 = .06$, the $n = 20$ and $c = 1$ plan provides

    P (Accept lot) $= f(0) + f(1) = .2901 + .3703 = .6604$

    Producer's risk: $\alpha = 1 - .6604 = .3396$

    For a given sample size, the producer's risk decreases as the acceptance number c is increased.

4. a. Using binomial probabilities with $n = 20$ and $p_0 = .03$.

    $P(\text{Accept lot}) = f(0) + f(1)$

    $\qquad\qquad\qquad = .5438 + .3364 = .8802$

    Producer's risk: $\alpha = 1 - .8802 = .1198$

b. With $n = 20$ and $p_1 = .15$.

$P(\text{Accept lot}) = f(0) + f(1)$

$= .0388 + .1368 = .1756$

Consumer's risk: $\beta = .1756$

c. The consumer's risk is acceptable; however, the producer's risk associated with the $n = 20, c = 1$ plan is a little larger than desired.

5.

	c	P (Accept) $p_0 = .05$	Producer's Risk α	P (accept) $p_1 = .30$	Consumer's Risk β
($n = 10$)	0	.5987	.4013	.0282	.0282
	1	.9138	.0862	.1493	.1493
	2	.9884	.0116	.3828	.3828
($n = 15$)	0	.4633	.5367	.0047	.0047
	1	.8291	.1709	.0352	.0352
	2	.9639	.0361	.1268	.1268
	3	.9946	.0054	.2968	.2968
($n = 20$)	0	.3585	.6415	.0008	.0008
	1	.7359	.2641	.0076	.0076
	2	.9246	.0754	.0354	.0354
	3	.9842	.0158	.1070	.1070

The plan with $n = 15, c = 2$ is close with $\alpha = .0361$ and $\beta = .1268$. However, the plan with $n = 20, c = 3$ is necessary to meet both requirements.

6. a. P (Accept) shown for p values below:

c	$p = .01$	$p = .05$	$p = .08$	$p = .10$	$p = .15$
0	.8179	.3585	.1887	.1216	.0388
1	.9831	.7359	.5169	.3918	.1756
2	.9990	.9246	.7880	.6770	.4049

The operating characteristic curves would show the P (Accept) versus p for each value of c.

b. P (Accept)

c	At $p_0 = .01$	Producer's Risk	At $p_1 = .08$	Consumer's Risk
0	.8179	.1821	.1887	.1887
1	.9831	.0169	.5169	.5169
2	.9990	.0010	.7880	.7880

7. a. For $n = 4$

$$UCL = \mu + 3\,(\sigma / \sqrt{n}) = 12.5 + 3\,(.8 / \sqrt{4}) = 13.7$$
$$LCL = \mu + 3\,(\sigma / \sqrt{n}) = 12.5 - 3\,(.8 / \sqrt{4}) = 11.3$$

b. For $n = 8$

$$UCL = \mu + 3\,(.8 / \sqrt{8}) = 13.35$$
$$LCL = \mu - 3\,(.8 / \sqrt{8}) = 11.65$$

For $n = 16$

$$UCL = \mu + 3\,(.8 / \sqrt{16}) = 13.10$$
$$LCL = \mu - 3\,(.8 / \sqrt{16}) = 11.90$$

c. UCL and LCL become closer together as n increases. If the process is in control, the larger samples should have less variance and should fall closer to 12.5.

8. a. $\mu = \dfrac{677.5}{25\,(5)} = 5.42$

b.
$$UCL = \mu + 3\,(\sigma / \sqrt{n}) = 5.42 + 3\,(.5 / \sqrt{5}) = 6.09$$
$$LCL = \mu - 3\,(\sigma / \sqrt{n}) = 5.42 - 3\,(.5 / \sqrt{5}) = 4.75$$

9. a. $p = \dfrac{135}{25\,(100)} = .0540$

b. $\sigma_{\bar{p}} = \sqrt{\dfrac{p\,(1 - p)}{n}} = \sqrt{\dfrac{.0540\,(.9460)}{100}} = .0226$

c.
$$UCL = p + 3\sigma_{\bar{p}} = .0540 + 3\,(.0226) = .1218$$
$$LCL = p - 3\sigma_{\bar{p}} = .0540 - 3\,(.0226) = -.0138$$

Use LCL $= 0$

10. R Chart

$$UCL = \overline{R} D_4 = 1.6 (1.864) = 2.98$$

$$LCL = \overline{R} D_3 = 1.6 (.136) = .22$$

$\overline{x}$ Chart

$$UCL = \overline{\overline{x}} + A_2 \overline{R} = 28.5 + .373 (1.6) = 29.10$$

$$LCL = \overline{\overline{x}} - A_2 \overline{R} = 28.5 - .373 (1.6) = 27.90$$

11. a.
$$UCL = \mu + 3 (\sigma / \sqrt{n}) = 128.5 + 3 (.4 / \sqrt{6}) = 128.99$$
$$LCL = \mu - 3 (\sigma / \sqrt{n}) = 128.5 - 3 (.4 / \sqrt{6}) = 128.01$$

b. $\overline{x} = \dfrac{\sum x_i}{n} = \dfrac{772.4}{6} = 128.73 \quad$ in control

c. $\overline{x} = \dfrac{\sum x_i}{n} = \dfrac{774.3}{6} = 129.05 \quad$ out of control

12. Process Mean $= \dfrac{20.12 + 19.90}{2} = 20.01$

$$UCL = \mu + 3 (\sigma / \sqrt{n}) = 20.01 + 3 (\sigma / \sqrt{5}) = 20.12$$

Solve for σ.

$$\sigma = \dfrac{(20.12 - 20.01) \sqrt{5}}{3} = .082$$

13.

Sample Number	Observations			$\bar{x}_i$	R_i
1	31	42	28	33.67	14
2	26	18	35	26.33	17
3	25	30	34	29.67	9
4	17	25	21	21.00	8
5	38	29	35	34.00	9
6	41	42	36	39.67	6
7	21	17	29	22.33	12
8	32	26	28	28.67	6
9	41	34	33	36.00	8
10	29	17	30	25.33	13
11	26	31	40	32.33	14
12	23	19	25	22.33	6
13	17	24	32	24.33	15
14	43	35	17	31.67	26
15	18	25	29	24.00	11
16	30	42	31	34.33	12
17	28	36	32	32.00	8
18	40	29	31	33.33	11
19	18	29	28	25.00	11
20	22	34	26	27.33	12

$\bar{R}$ = 11.4 and $\bar{\bar{x}}$ = 29.17

R Chart

$$UCL = \bar{R} D_4 = 11.4 (2.575) = 29.3$$

$$LCL = \bar{R} D_3 = 11.4 (0) = 0$$

$\bar{x}$ Chart

$$UCL = \bar{\bar{x}} + A_2 \bar{R} = 29.17 + 1.023 (11.4) = 40.8$$

$$LCL = \bar{\bar{x}} - A_2 \bar{R} = 29.17 - 1.023 (11.4) = 17.5$$

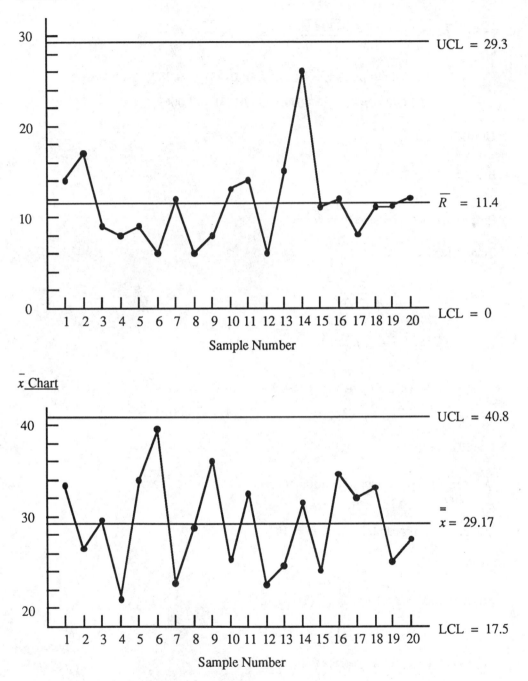

Chapter 20

14. a. $p = \dfrac{141}{20\,(150)} = .0470$

   b. $\sigma_{\bar{p}} = \sqrt{\dfrac{p\,(1-p)}{n}} = \sqrt{\dfrac{.0470\,(.9530)}{150}} = .0173$

$$\text{UCL} = p + 3\sigma_{\bar{p}} = .0470 + 3\,(.0173) = .0989$$
$$\text{LCL} = p - 3\sigma_{\bar{p}} = .0470 - 3\,(.0173) = -.0049$$

   Use LCL $= 0$

   c. $\bar{p} = \dfrac{12}{150} = .08$

   Process should be considered in control.

15. a. Total defectives: 165

$$p = \dfrac{165}{20\,(200)} = .0413$$

   b. $\sigma_{\bar{p}} = \sqrt{\dfrac{p\,(1-p)}{n}} = \sqrt{\dfrac{.0413\,(.9587)}{200}} = .0141$

$$\text{UCL} = p + 3\sigma_{\bar{p}} = .0413 + 3\,(.0141) = .0836$$
$$\text{LCL} = p - 3\sigma_{\bar{p}} = .0413 - 3\,(.0141) = -.0010$$

   Use LCL $= 0$

   c. $\bar{p} = \dfrac{20}{200} = .10$ Out of control

16. a. Use binomial probabilities with $n = 10$.

   At $p_0 = .05$,

   $P(\text{Accept lot}) = f\,(0) + f\,(1) + f\,(2)$

$$= .5987 + .3151 + .0746 = .9884$$

   Producer's Risk: $\alpha = 1 - .9884 = .0116$

At $p_1 = .20$,

$P(\text{Accept lot}) = f(0) + f(1) + f(2)$

$\qquad\qquad = .1074 + .2684 + .3020 = .6778$

Consumer's risk: $\beta = .6778$

b. The consumer's risk is unacceptably high. Too many bad lots would be accepted.

c. Reducing c would help, but increasing the sample size appears to be the best solution.

17. a. P (Accept) are shown below: (Using $n = 15$)

	$p = .01$	$p = .02$	$p = .03$	$p = .04$	$p = .05$
$f(0)$	.8601	.7386	.6333	.5421	.4633
$f(1)$	.1303	.2261	.2938	.3388	.3658
	.9904	.9647	.9271	.8809	.8291
$\alpha = 1 - P$ (Accept)	.0096	.0353	.0729	.1191	.1709

Using $p_0 = .03$ since α is close to .075. Thus, .03 is the fraction defective where the producer will tolerate a .075 probability of rejecting a good lot (only .03 defective).

b.

	$p = .25$
$f(0)$	.0134
$f(1)$	.0668
$\beta =$	.0802

18. a. P (Accept) when $n = 25$ and $c = 0$. Use the binomial probability function with

$$f(x) = \frac{n!}{x!\,(n-x)!}\, p^x (1-p)^{n-x}$$

or

$$f(0) = \frac{25!}{0!\,25!}\, p^0 (1-p)^{25} = (1-p)^{25}$$

If	$f(0)$
$p = .01$	.7778
$p = .03$	.4670
$p = .10$	.0718
$p = .20$	.0038

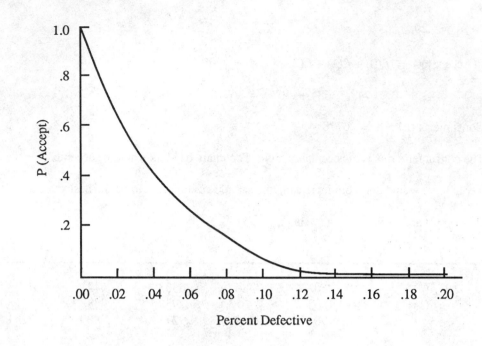

b.

c. $1 - f(0) = 1 - .778 = .222$

19. a. $\mu = np = 250(.02) = 5$

$$\sigma = \sqrt{np(1-p)} = \sqrt{250\,(.02)\,(.98)} = 2.21$$

$P(\text{Accept}) = P(x \leq 10.5)$

$$z = \frac{10.5 - 5}{2.21} = 2.49$$

$P(\text{Accept}) = .5000 + .4936 = .9936$

Producer's Risk: $\alpha = 1 - .9936 = .0064$

b. $\mu = np = 250\,(.08) = 20$

$$\sigma = \sqrt{np(1-p)} = \sqrt{250\,(.08)\,(.92)} = 4.29$$

$P(\text{Accept}) = P(x \leq 10.5)$

$$z = \frac{10.5 - 5}{4.29} = -2.21$$

$P(\text{Accept}) = 1 - .4864 = .0136$

Consumer's Risk: $\beta = .0136$

c. The advantage is the excellent control over the producer's and the consumer's risk. The disadvantage is the cost of taking a large sample.

20. a. $\mu = \dfrac{\sum \bar{x}}{20} = \dfrac{1908}{20} = 95.4$

$\text{UCL} = \mu + 3\,(\sigma/\sqrt{n}) = 95.4 + 3\,(.50/\sqrt{5}) = 96.07$

b. $\text{LCL} = \mu - 3\,(\sigma/\sqrt{n}) = 95.4 - 3\,(.50/\sqrt{5}) = 94.73$

c. No; all were in control

21. a. For $n = 10$,

$\text{UCL} = \mu + 3\,(\sigma/\sqrt{n}) = 350 + 3\,(15/\sqrt{10}) = 364.23$

$\text{LCL} = \mu - 3\,(\sigma/\sqrt{n}) = 350 - 3\,(15/\sqrt{10}) = 335.77$

For $n = 20$

$\text{UCL} = 350 + 3\,(15/\sqrt{20}) = 360.06$

$\text{LCL} = 350 - 3\,(15/\sqrt{20}) = 339.94$

For $n = 30$

$\text{UCL} = 350 + 3\,(15/\sqrt{30}) = 358.22$

$\text{LCL} = 350 - 3\,(15/\sqrt{30}) = 343.78$

b. Both control limits come closer to the process mean as the sample size is increased.

c. The process will be declared out of control and adjusted when the process is in control.

d. The process will be judged in control and allowed to continue when the process is out of control.

e. All have $z = 3$ where area $= .4986$

$P\,(\text{Type I}) = 1 - 2\,(.4986) = .0028$

22. _R Chart_

$\text{UCL} = \bar{R}\,D_4 = 2\,(2.115) = 4.23$

$\text{LCL} = \bar{R}\,D_3 = 2\,(0) = 0$

$\bar{x}$ Chart

$$UCL = \bar{\bar{x}} + A_2 \bar{R} = 5.42 + .577 \,(2) = 6.57$$

$$LCL = \bar{\bar{x}} - A_2 \bar{R} = 5.42 - .577 \,(2) = 4.27$$

Estimate of Standard Deviation

$$\hat{\sigma} = \frac{\bar{R}}{d_2} = \frac{2}{2.326} = .86$$

23. $\bar{R} = .665 \quad \bar{\bar{x}} = 95.398$

R Chart

$$UCL = \bar{R}\, D_4 = .665 \,(2.115) = 1.41$$

$$LCL = \bar{R}\, D_3 = .665 \,(0) = 0$$

$\bar{x}$ Chart

$$UCL = \bar{\bar{x}} + A_2 \bar{R} = 95.398 + .577 \,(.665) = 95.78$$

$$LCL = \bar{\bar{x}} - A_2 \bar{R} = 95.398 - .577 \,(.665) = 95.01$$

24. $\bar{R} = .053 \quad \bar{\bar{x}} = 3.078$

R Chart

$$UCL = \bar{R}\, D_4 = .053 \,(2.115) = .11$$

$$LCL = \bar{R}\, D_3 = .053 \,(0) = 0$$

$\bar{x}$ Chart

$$UCL = \bar{\bar{x}} + A_2 \bar{R} = 3.078 + .577 \,(.053) = 3.11$$

$$LCL = \bar{\bar{x}} - A_2 \bar{R} = 3.078 - .577 \,(.053) = 3.05$$

25. a.

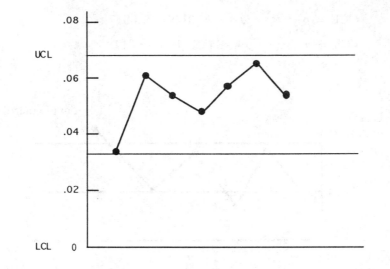

Warning: Process should be checked. All points are within control limits; however, all points are also greater than the process proportion defective.

b.

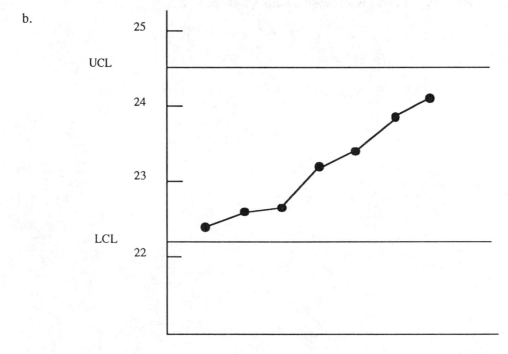

Warning: Process should be checked. All points are within control limits yet the trend in points show a movement or shift toward UCL out-of-control point.

26. a. $p = .04$

$$\sigma_{\bar{p}} = \sqrt{\frac{p\,(1-p)}{n}} = \sqrt{\frac{.04\,(.96)}{200}} = .0139$$

$$\text{UCL} = p + 3\sigma_{\bar{p}} = .04 + 3\,(.0139) = .0817$$

$$\text{LCL} = p - 3\sigma_{\bar{p}} = .04 - 3\,(.0139) = -.0017$$

Use LCL $= 0$

b.

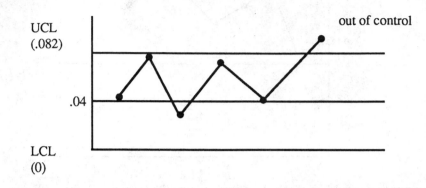

For month 1 $\bar{p} = 10\,/\,200 = .05$. Other monthly values are .075, .03, .065, .04, and .085. Only the last month with $\bar{p} = .085$ is an out-of-control situation.

Chapter 21
Sample Survey

Learning Objectives

1.   Learn what a sample survey is and how it differs from an experiment as a method of collecting data.

2.   Know about the methods of data collection for a survey.

3.   Know the difference between sampling and nonsampling error.

4.   Learn about four sample designs: (1) simple random sampling, (2) stratified simple random sampling, (3) cluster sampling, and (4) systematic sampling.

5.   Lean how to estimate a population mean, a population total, and a population proportion using the above sample designs.

6.   Understand the relationship between sample size and precision.

7.   Learn how to choose the approximate sample size using stratified and simple random sampling.

8.   Learn how to allocate the total sample to the various strata using stratified simple random sampling.

Solutions:

1. a. $\bar{x} = 215$ is an estimate of the population mean.

    b. $s_{\bar{x}} = \dfrac{20}{\sqrt{50}} \sqrt{\dfrac{800 - 50}{800}} = 2.7386$

    c. $215 \pm 2(2.7386)$ or   209.5228 to 220.4772

2. a.   Estimate of population total $= N\bar{x} = 400(75) = 30{,}000$

    b.   Estimate of Standard Error $= Ns_{\bar{x}}$

    $$Ns_{\bar{x}} = 400\left(\dfrac{8}{\sqrt{80}}\right) \sqrt{\dfrac{400 - 80}{400}} = 320$$

    c. $30{,}000 \pm 2(320)$ or   29,360 to 30,640

3. a. $\bar{p} = .30$ is an estimate of the population proportion

    b. $s_{\bar{p}} = \sqrt{\left(\dfrac{1000 - 100}{1000}\right)\left(\dfrac{(.3)(.7)}{99}\right)} = .0437$

    c. $.30 \pm 2(.0437)$ or   .2126 to .3874

4. $B = 15$

    $$n = \dfrac{(70)^2}{\dfrac{(15)^2}{4} + \dfrac{(70)^2}{450}} = \dfrac{4900}{67.1389} = 72.9830$$

    A sample size of 73 will provide an approximate 95% confidence interval of width 30.

5. a. $\bar{x} = 1.8$ and $s = .4$

    $$s_{\bar{x}} = \left(\dfrac{.4}{\sqrt{30}}\right) \sqrt{\dfrac{153 - 30}{153}} = .0655$$

    <u>approximate 95% confidence interval</u>

    $$1.8 \pm 2(0.0655)$$
    or
    1.669 billion to 1.931 billion

b. $\bar{x} = 6$ and $s = 1.4$

$$N\bar{x} = 153(6) = 918 \text{ and } N s_{\bar{x}} = 153\left(\frac{1.4}{\sqrt{30}}\right)\sqrt{\frac{153-30}{153}} = 35.0643$$

approximate 95% confidence interval

$$918 \pm 2(35.0643)$$
or
$$847.8714 \text{ to } 988.1286$$

c. $\bar{p} = .25$ and $s_{\bar{p}} = \sqrt{\left(\frac{153-30}{153}\right)\frac{(.25)(.75)}{29}} = .0721$

approximate 95% confidence interval

$$.25 \pm 2(.0721)$$
or
$$.1058 \text{ to } .3942$$

This is a rather large interval; sample sizes must be rather large to obtain tight confidence intervals on a population proportion.

6. $B = 5000/2 = 2500$ Use the value of s for the previous year in the formula to determine the necessary sample size.

$$n = \frac{(31.3)^2}{\frac{(2.5)^2}{4} + \frac{(31.3)^2}{724}} = \frac{979.69}{2.9157} = 336.0051$$

A sample size of 337 will provide an approximate 95% confidence interval of width no larger than $5000.

7. a. Stratum 1: $\bar{x}_1 = 138$

   Stratum 2: $\bar{x}_2 = 103$

   Stratum 3: $\bar{x}_3 = 210$

   b. Stratum 1

   $\bar{x}_1 = 138$

   $s_{\bar{x}_1} = \left(\frac{30}{\sqrt{20}}\right)\sqrt{\frac{200-20}{200}} = 6.3640$

$$138 \pm 2(6.3640)$$
or

$$125.272 \text{ to } 150.728$$

Stratum 2

$$\bar{x}_2 = 103$$

$$s_{\bar{x}_2} = \left(\frac{25}{\sqrt{30}}\right)\sqrt{\frac{250-30}{250}} = 4.2817$$

$$103 \pm 2(4.2817)$$

$$94.4366 \text{ to } 111.5634$$

Stratum 3

$$\bar{x}_3 = 210$$

$$s_{\bar{x}_3} = \left(\frac{50}{\sqrt{25}}\right)\sqrt{\frac{100-25}{100}} = 8.6603$$

$$210 \pm 2(8.6603)$$
or
$$192.6794 \text{ to } 227.3206$$

c. $$\bar{x}_{st} = \left(\frac{200}{550}\right)138 + \left(\frac{250}{550}\right)103 + \left(\frac{100}{550}\right)210$$

$$= 50.1818 + 46.8182 + 38.1818$$
$$= 135.1818$$

$$s_{\bar{x}_{st}} = \sqrt{\left(\frac{1}{(550)^2}\right)\left(200\,(180)\,\frac{(30)^2}{20} + 250\,(220)\,\frac{(25)^2}{30} + 100\,(75)\,\frac{(50)^2}{25}\right)}$$

$$= \sqrt{\left(\frac{1}{(550)^2}\right)3,515,833.3}$$

$$= 3.4092$$

approximate 95% confidence interval

$$135.1818 \pm 2(3.4092)$$
or
$$128.3634 \text{ to } 142.0002$$

8. a. Stratum 1: $N_1 \bar{x}_1 = 200(138) = 27,600$

    Stratum 2: $N_2 \bar{x}_2 = 250(103) = 25,750$

    Stratum 3: $N_3 \bar{x}_3 = 100(210) = 21,000$

    b. $N \bar{x}_{st} = 27,600 + 25,750 + 21,000 = 74,350$

    Note: the sum of the estimate for each stratum total equals $N \bar{x}_{st}$

    c. $N s_{\bar{x}_{st}} = 550(3.4092) = 1875.06$ (see 7c)

    approximate 95% confidence interval

    $$74,350 \pm 2(1875.06)$$
    or
    $$70,599.88 \text{ to } 78,100.12$$

9. a. Stratum 1

    $\bar{p}_1 = .50$

    $$s_{\bar{p}_1} = \sqrt{\left(\frac{200 - 20}{200}\right)\left(\frac{(.50)\,(.50)}{19}\right)} = .1088$$

    $$.50 \pm 2(.1088)$$
    or
    $$.2824 \text{ to } .7176$$

    Stratum 2

    $\bar{p}_2 = .78$

    $$s_{\bar{p}_2} = \sqrt{\left(\frac{250 - 30}{250}\right)\left(\frac{(.78)\,(.22)}{29}\right)} = .0722$$

    $$.78 \pm 2(.0722)$$
    or
    $$.6356 \text{ to } 9244$$

Stratum 3

$$\overline{p}_3 = .21$$

$$s_{\overline{p}_3} = \sqrt{\left(\frac{100 - 25}{100}\right)\left(\frac{(.21)\,(.79)}{24}\right)} = .0720$$

$$.21 \pm 2(.0720)$$
or
$$.066 \text{ to } .354$$

b. $\overline{p}_{st} = \dfrac{200}{550}\,(.50) + \dfrac{250}{550}\,(.78) + \dfrac{100}{550}\,(.21)$

$$= .5745$$

c. $s_{\overline{p}_{st}} = \sqrt{\left(\dfrac{1}{(550)^2}\right)\left(200\,(180)\,\dfrac{(.5)\,(.5)}{19} + 250\,(220)\,\dfrac{(.78)\,(.22)}{29} + (100)\,(75)\,\dfrac{(.21)\,(.79)}{24}\right)}$

$$= \sqrt{\left(\dfrac{1}{(550)^2}\right)(473.6842 + 325.4483 + 51.8438)}$$

$$= .0530$$

d.

approximate 95% confidence interval

$$.5745 \pm 2(.0530)$$
or
$$.4685 \text{ to } .6805$$

10. a. $n = \dfrac{[\,300(150) + 600\,(75) + 500\,(100)\,]^2}{(1400)^2\left(\dfrac{(20)^2}{4}\right) + [\,300\,(150)^2 + 600\,(75)^2 + 500\,(100)^2\,]}$

$$= \dfrac{(140,000)^2}{196,000,000 + 15,125,000}$$

$$= 92.8359$$

Rounding up we choose a total sample of 93.

$$n_1 = 93 \left(\frac{300\ (150)}{140,000} \right) = 30$$

$$n_2 = 93 \left(\frac{600\ (75)}{140,000} \right) = 30$$

$$n_3 = 93 \left(\frac{500\ (100)}{140,000} \right) = 33$$

b. With $B = 10$, the first term in the denominator in the formula for n changes.

$$n = \frac{(140,000)^2}{(1400)^2 \left(\frac{(10)^2}{4} \right) + 15,125,000}$$

$$= \frac{(140,000)^2}{49,000,000 + 15,125,000}$$

$$= 305.6530$$

Rounding up, we see that a sample size of 306 is needed to provide this level of precision.

$$n_1 = 306 \left(\frac{300\ (150)}{140,000} \right) = 98$$

$$n_2 = 306 \left(\frac{600\ (75)}{140,000} \right) = 98$$

$$n_3 = 306 \left(\frac{500\ (100)}{140,000} \right) = 109$$

Due to rounding, the total of the allocations to each strata only add to 305. Note that even though the sample size is larger, the proportion allocated to each stratum has not changed.

$$n = \frac{(140,000)^2}{\frac{(15,000)^2}{4} + 15,125,000}$$

$$= \frac{(140,000)^2}{56,250,000 + 15,125,000}$$

$$= 274.6060$$

Rounding up, we see that a sample size of 275 will provide the desired level of precision.

The allocations to the strata are in the same proportion as for parts a and b.

$$n_1 = 275\left(\frac{300\,(150)}{140,000}\right) = 88$$

$$n_2 = 275\left(\frac{600\,(75)}{140,000}\right) = 88$$

$$n_3 = 275\left(\frac{500\,(100)}{140,000}\right) = 98$$

Again, due to rounding, the stratum allocations do not add to the total sample size. Another item could be sampled from, say, stratum 3 if desired.

11. a. $\bar{x}_1 = 29.5333$ $\qquad$ $\bar{x}_2 = 64.775$

$\bar{x}_3 = 45.2125$ $\qquad$ $\bar{x}_4 = 53.0300$

b. Indianapolis

$$29.533 \pm 2\left(\frac{13.3603}{\sqrt{6}}\right)\sqrt{\frac{38-6}{38}}$$

$$29.533 \pm 10.9086(.9177)$$
or
$$19.5222 \text{ to } 39.5438$$

Louisville

$$64.775 \pm 2\left(\frac{25.0666}{\sqrt{8}}\right)\sqrt{\frac{45-8}{45}}$$

$$64.775 \pm 17.7248(.9068)$$
or
$$48.7022 \text{ to } 80.8478$$

St. Louis

$$45.2125 \pm 2\left(\frac{19.4084}{\sqrt{8}}\right)\sqrt{\frac{80-8}{80}}$$

$$45.2125 \pm (13.7238)\,(.9487)$$
or
$$32.1927 \text{ to } 58.2323$$

Memphis

$$53.0300 \pm 2\left(\frac{29.6810}{\sqrt{10}}\right)\sqrt{\frac{70-10}{70}}$$

$$53.0300 \pm 18.7719(.9258)$$

$$35.6510 \text{ to } 70.4090$$

c. $\bar{p}_{st} = \left(\dfrac{38}{233}\right)\left(\dfrac{1}{6}\right) + \left(\dfrac{45}{233}\right)\left(\dfrac{5}{8}\right) + \left(\dfrac{80}{233}\right)\left(\dfrac{3}{8}\right) + \left(\dfrac{70}{233}\right)\left(\dfrac{5}{10}\right)$

    $= .4269$

d.

$$N_1 (N_1 - n_1) \dfrac{\bar{p}_1 (1 - \bar{p}_1)}{n_1 - 1} = 38 \, (32) \dfrac{\left(\frac{1}{6}\right)\left(\frac{5}{6}\right)}{5} = 33.7778$$

$$N_2 (N_2 - n_2) \dfrac{\bar{p}_2 (1 - \bar{p}_2)}{n_2 - 1} = 45 \, (37) \dfrac{\left(\frac{5}{8}\right)\left(\frac{3}{8}\right)}{7} = 55.7478$$

$$N_3 (N_3 - n_3) \dfrac{\bar{p}_3 (1 - \bar{p}_3)}{n_3 - 1} = 80 \, (72) \dfrac{\left(\frac{3}{8}\right)\left(\frac{5}{8}\right)}{7} = 192.8571$$

$$N_4 (N_4 - n_4) \dfrac{\bar{p}_4 (1 - \bar{p}_4)}{n_4 - 1} = 70 \, (60) \dfrac{\left(\frac{5}{10}\right)\left(\frac{5}{10}\right)}{9} = 116.6667$$

$$s_{\bar{p}_{st}} = \sqrt{\left(\dfrac{1}{(233)^2}\right) [33.7778 + 55.7478 + 192.8571 + 116.6667]}$$

    $= \sqrt{\dfrac{1}{(233)^2} (399.0494)}$

    $= .0857$

<u>approximate 95% confidence interval</u>

$$.4269 \pm 2(.0857)$$
$$\text{or}$$
$$.2555 \text{ to } .5983$$

12. a.   St. Louis total $= N_1 \, \bar{x}_1 = 80 \, (45.2125) = 3617$

    In dollars: \$3,617,000

  b. Indianapolis total $= N_1 \, \bar{x}_1 = 38 \, (29.5333) = 1122.2654$

    In dollars: \$1,122,265

  c. $\bar{x}_{st} = \left(\dfrac{38}{233}\right) 29.5333 + \left(\dfrac{45}{233}\right)(64.775) + \left(\dfrac{80}{233}\right)45.2125 + \left(\dfrac{70}{233}\right)53.0300$

    $= 48.7821$

$$N_1 (N_1 - n_1) \frac{s_1^2}{n_1} = 38 (32) \frac{(13.3603)^2}{6} = 36,175.517$$

$$N_2 (N_2 - n_2) \frac{s_2^2}{n_2} = 45 (37) \frac{(25.0666)^2}{8} = 130,772.1$$

$$N_3 (N_3 - n_3) \frac{s_3^2}{n_3} = 80 (72) \frac{(19.4084)^2}{8} = 271,213.91$$

$$N_4 (N_4 - n_4) \frac{s_4^2}{n_4} = 70 (60) \frac{(29.6810)^2}{10} = 370,003.94$$

$$s_{\bar{x}_{st}} = \sqrt{\left(\frac{1}{(233)^2}\right)(36,175.517 + 130,772.1 + 271,213.91 + 370,003.94)}$$

$$= \sqrt{\frac{1}{(233)^2}(808,165.47)}$$

$$= 3.8583$$

<u>approximate 95% confidence interval</u>

$$\bar{x}_{st} \pm 2\, s_{\bar{x}_{st}}$$

$$48.7821 \pm 2(3.8583)$$
or
$$41.0655 \text{ to } 56.4987$$

In dollars: $41,066 to $56,499

d.

<u>approximate 95% confidence interval</u>

$$N \bar{x}_{st} \pm 2\, N s_{\bar{x}_{st}}$$

$$233(48.7821) \pm 2(233)(3.8583)$$

$$11,366.229 \pm 1797.9678$$
or
$$9,568.2612 \text{ to } 13,164.197$$

In dollars: $9,568,261 to $13,164,197

13.
$$n = \frac{[\,50(80) + 38\,(150) + 35\,(45)\,]^2}{(123)^2 \left(\dfrac{(30)^2}{4}\right) + [\,50\,(80)^2 + 38\,(150)^2 + 35\,(45)^2\,]}$$

$$= \frac{(11{,}275)^2}{3{,}404{,}025 + 1{,}245{,}875}$$

$$= 27.3394$$

Rounding up we see that a sample size of 28 is necessary to obtain the desired precision..

$$n_1 = 28\left(\frac{50\,(80)}{11{,}275}\right) = 10$$

$$n_2 = 28\left(\frac{38\,(150)}{11{,}275}\right) = 14$$

$$n_3 = 28\left(\frac{35\,(45)}{11{,}275}\right) = 4$$

b.
$$n = \frac{[50\,(100) + 38\,(100) + 35(100)\,]^2}{(123)^2 \left(\dfrac{(30)^2}{4}\right) + [50\,(100)^2 + 38\,(100)^2 + 35\,(100)^2]}$$

$$= \frac{[\,123\,(100)\,]^2}{3{,}404{,}025 + 123\,(100)^2}$$

$$= 33$$

$$n_1 = 33\left(\frac{50\,(100)}{12{,}300}\right) = 13$$

$$n_2 = 33\left(\frac{38\,(100)}{12{,}300}\right) = 10$$

$$n_3 = 33\left(\frac{35\,(100)}{12{,}300}\right) = 9$$

This is the same as proportional allocation . Note that for each stratum
$$n_{\hat{h}} = n\left(\frac{N_h}{N}\right).$$

14. a. $\bar{x}_c = \dfrac{\sum x_i}{\sum M_i} = \dfrac{750}{50} = 15$

$\hat{X} = M\,\bar{x}_c = 300(15) = 4500$

$$\bar{p}_c = \frac{\sum a_i}{\sum M_i} = \frac{15}{50} = .30$$

b. $\sum (x_i - \bar{x}_c\, M_i\,)^2 = [\,95 - 15\,(7)\,]^2 + [\,325 - 15\,(18)\,]^2 + [\,190 - 15\,(15)\,]^2 + [\,140 - 15\,(10)\,]^2$

$$= (-10)^2 + (55)^2 + (-35)^2 + (-10)^2$$

$$= 4450$$

$$s_{\bar{x}_c} = \sqrt{\left(\frac{25-4}{(25)\,(4)\,(12)^2}\right)\left(\frac{4450}{3}\right)} = 1.4708$$

$$s_{\hat{X}} = M\, s_{\bar{x}_c} = 300\,(1.4708) = 441.24$$

$$\sum (a_i - \bar{p}_c\, M_i\,)^2 = [\,1 - .3\,(7)\,]^2 + [\,6 - .3\,(18)\,]^2 + [\,6 - .3\,(15)\,]^2 + [\,2 - .3\,(10)\,]^2$$

$$= (-1.1)^2 + (.6)^2 + (1.5)^2 + (-1)^2$$

$$= 4.82$$

$$s_{\bar{p}_c} = \sqrt{\left(\frac{25-4}{(25)\,(4)\,(12)^2}\right)\left(\frac{4.82}{3}\right)} = .0484$$

c. approximate 95% confidence
Interval for Population Mean:

$$15 \pm 2(1.4708)$$
or
$$12.0584 \text{ to } 17.9416$$

d. approximate 95% confidence
Interval for Population Total:

$$4500 \pm 2(441.24)$$
or
$$3617.52 \text{ to } 5382.48$$

e. approximate 95% confidence
Interval for Population Proportion:

$$.30 \pm 2(.0484)$$
or
$$.2032 \text{ to } .3968$$

15. a. $\bar{x}_c = \dfrac{10,400}{130} = 80$

$$\hat{X} = M\, \bar{x}_c = 600(80) = 48,000$$

$$\bar{p}_c = \frac{13}{130} = .10$$

b. $\sum (x_i - \bar{x}_c M_i)^2 = [\,3500 - 80\,(35)\,]^2 + [\,965 - 80\,(15)\,]^2 + [\,960 - 80\,(12)\,]^2$
$$+ [\,2070 - 80\,(23)\,]^2 + [\,1100 - 80\,(20)\,]^2 + [\,1805 - 80\,(25)\,]^2$$
$$= (700)^2 + (-235)^2 + (0)^2 + (230)^2 + (-500)^2 + (-195)^2$$
$$= 886{,}150$$

$$s_{\bar{x}_c} = \sqrt{\left(\frac{30 - 6}{(30)\,(6)\,(20)^2}\right)\left(\frac{886{,}150}{5}\right)} = 7.6861$$

approximate 95% confidence
Interval for Population Mean:

$$80 \pm 2(7.6861)$$
or
$$64.6278 \text{ to } 95.3722$$

c. $s_{\hat{x}} = 600\,(7.6861) = 4611.66$

approximate 95% confidence
Interval for Population Total:

$$48{,}000 \pm 2(4611.66)$$
or
$$38{,}776.68 \text{ to } 57{,}223.32$$

$\sum (a_i - \bar{p}_c M_i)^2 = [\,3 - .1\,(35)\,]^2 + [\,0 - .1\,(15)\,]^2 + [\,1 - .1\,(12)\,]^2 + [\,4 - .1\,(23)\,]^2$
$$+ [\,3 - .1\,(20)\,]^2 + [\,2 - .1\,(25)\,]^2$$
$$= (-.5)^2 + (-1.5)^2 + (-.2)^2 + (1.7)^2 + (1)^2 + (-.5)^2$$
$$= 6.68$$

$$s_{\bar{p}_c} = \sqrt{\left(\frac{30 - 6}{(30)\,(6)\,(20)^2}\right)\left(\frac{6.68}{5}\right)} = .0211$$

approximate 95% confidence
Interval for Population Proportion:

$$.10 \pm 2(.0211)$$
or
$$.0578 \text{ to } .1422$$

16. a. $\bar{x}_c = \frac{2000}{50} = 40$

Estimate of mean age of mechanical engineers: 40 years

b. $\bar{p}_c = \dfrac{35}{50} = .70$

Estimate of proportion attending local university: .70

c. $\sum (x_i - \bar{x}_c \, M_i)^2 = [\,520 - 40\,(12)\,]^2 + \cdots + [\,462 - 40\,(13)\,]^2$

$\qquad\qquad\quad = (40)^2 + (-7)^2 + (-10)^2 + (-11)^2 + (30)^2 + (9)^2 + (22)^2 + (8)^2 + (-23)^2 + (-58)^2$

$\qquad\qquad\quad = 7292$

$s_{\bar{x}_c} = \sqrt{\left(\dfrac{120 - 10}{(120)\,(10)\,(50/12)^2}\right)\left(\dfrac{7292}{9}\right)} = 2.0683$

approximate 95% confidence
Interval for Mean age:

$$40 \pm 2(2.0683)$$
$$\text{or}$$
$$35.8634 \text{ to } 44.1366$$

d. $\sum (a_i - \bar{p}_c \, M_i)^2 = [\,8 - .7\,(12)\,]^2 + \cdots + [\,12 - .7\,(13)\,]^2$

$\qquad\qquad\quad = (-.4)^2 + (-.7)^2 + (-.4)^2 + (.3)^2 + (-1.2)^2 + (-.1)^2 + (-1.4)^2 + (.3)^2$

$\qquad\qquad\quad\; + (.7)^2 + (2.9)^2$

$\qquad\qquad\quad = 13.3$

$s_{\bar{p}_c} = \sqrt{\left(\dfrac{120 - 10}{(120)\,(10)\,(50/12)^2}\right)\left(\dfrac{13.3}{9}\right)} = .0883$

approximate 95% confidence
Interval for Proportion Attending Local University:

$$.70 \pm 2(.0883)$$
$$\text{or}$$
$$.5234 \text{ to } .8766$$

17. a. $\bar{x}_c = \dfrac{17\,(37) + 35\,(32) + \cdots + 57(44)}{17 + 35 + \cdots + 57} = \dfrac{11{,}240}{304}$

$\qquad = 36.9737$

Estimate of mean age: 36.9737 years

b. Proportion of College Graduates: $128 / 304 = .4211$

Proportion of Males: $112 / 304 = .3684$

c. $\sum (x_i - \bar{x}_c\, M_i)^2 = [\, 17\,(37) - (36.9737)\,(17)\,]^2 + \cdots + [\, 57\,(44) - (36.9737)\,(44)\,]^2$

$$= (.4471)^2 + (-174.0795)^2 + (-25.3162)^2 + (-460.2642)^2 + (173.1309)^2$$
$$+\, (180.3156)^2 + (-94.7376)^2 + (400.4991)^2$$
$$= 474{,}650.68$$

$$s_{\bar{x}_c} = \sqrt{\left(\frac{150 - 8}{(150)\,(8)\,(40)^2}\right)\left(\frac{474{,}650.68}{7}\right)} = 2.2394$$

approximate 95% confidence
Interval for Mean Age of Agents:

$$36.9737 \pm 2(2.2394)$$
$$\text{or}$$
$$32.4949 \text{ to } 41.4525$$

d. $\sum (a_i - \bar{p}_c\, M_i)^2 = [\, 3 - .4211\,(17)\,]^2 + \cdots + [\, 25 - .4211\,(57)\,]^2$
$$= (-4.1587)^2 + (-.7385)^2 + (-2.9486)^2 + (10.2074)^2 + (-.1073)^2 + (-3.0532)^2$$
$$+\, (-.2128)^2 + (.9973)^2$$
$$= 141.0989$$

$$s_{\bar{p}_c} = \sqrt{\left(\frac{150 - 8}{(150)\,(8)\,(40)^2}\right)\left(\frac{141.0989}{7}\right)} = .0386$$

approximate 95% confidence
Interval for Proportion of Agents that are College Graduates:

$$.4211 \pm 2(.0386)$$
$$\text{or}$$
$$.3439 \text{ to } .4983$$

e. $\sum (a_i - \bar{p}_c\, M_i)^2 = [\, 4 - .3684\,(17)\,]^2 + \cdots + [\, 26 - .3684\,(57)\,]^2$
$$= (-2.2628)^2 + (-.8940)^2 + (-2.5784)^2 + (3.6856)^2 + (-3.8412)^2 + (1.5792)^2$$
$$+\, (-.6832)^2 + (5.0012)^2$$
$$= 68.8787$$

$$s_{\bar{p}_c} = \sqrt{\left(\frac{150 - 8}{(150)\,(8)\,(40)^2}\right)\left(\frac{68.8787}{7}\right)} = .0270$$

approximate 95% confidence
Interval for Proportion of Agents that are Male:

$$.3684 \pm 2(.0270)$$
$$\text{or}$$
$$.3144 \text{ to } .4224$$

21 - 15

18. a. $\bar{p} = .80$

$$s_{\bar{p}} = \sqrt{\frac{(.8)\,(.2)}{1420}} = .0106$$

Approximate 95% Confidence Interval:

$$.80 \pm 2(.0106)$$
$$\text{or}$$
$$.7788 \text{ to } .8212$$

b. $\bar{p} = .60$

$$s_{\bar{p}} = \sqrt{\frac{(.6)\,(.4)}{1420}} = .0130$$

Approximate 95% Confidence Interval:

$$.60 \pm 2(.0130)$$
$$\text{or}$$
$$.5740 \text{ to } .6260$$

c. $\bar{p} = .44$

$$s_{\bar{p}} = \sqrt{\frac{(.44)\,(.56)}{1420}} = .0132$$

Approximate 95% Confidence Interval:

$$.44 \pm 2(.0132)$$
$$\text{or}$$
$$.4136 \text{ to } .4664$$

d. The largest standard error is when $\bar{p} = .50$.

At $\bar{p} = .50$, we get

$$s_{\bar{p}} = \sqrt{\frac{(.5)\,(.5)}{1420}} = .0133$$

Multiplying by 2, we get a bound of $B = 2(.0133) = .0266$

So $\pm$ 3% provides a slightly more conservative bound than an approximate 95% confidence interval for any value of $\bar{p}$.

e. If the poll was conducted by calling people at home during the day the sample results would only be representative of adults not working outside the home. It is likely that the Gallup organization took precautions against this and other possible sources of bias.

19. a. Assume $(N - n) / N = 1$

   $\bar{p} = .71$

   $$s_{\bar{p}} = \sqrt{\frac{(.71)\,(.29)}{1082}} = .0138$$

   Approximate 95% Confidence Interval:

   $$.71 \pm 2(.0138)$$
   or
   $$.6824 \text{ to } .7376$$

   b. $\bar{p} = .62$

   $$s_{\bar{p}} = \sqrt{\frac{(.62)\,(.38)}{1082}} = .0148$$

   Approximate 95% Confidence Interval:

   $$.62 \pm 2(.0148)$$
   or
   $$.5904 \text{ to } .6496$$

   c. $\bar{p} = .34$

   $$s_{\bar{p}} = \sqrt{\frac{(.34)\,(.66)}{1082}} = .0144$$

   Approximate 95% Confidence Interval:

   $$.34 \pm 2(.0144)$$
   or
   $$.3112 \text{ to } .3688$$

   d. The largest standard error is for an estimate with $\bar{p} = .50$. With $\bar{p} = .50$, we get

   $$s_{\bar{p}} = \sqrt{\frac{(.50)\,(.50)}{1082}} = .0152$$

   For an approximate 95% confidence interval, the bound would be

   $$B = 2\,(.0152) = .0304.$$

   The percent of error stated (3.1%) added to and subtracted from any proportion estimated from the sample will provide conservative bounds.

Chapter 21

20. a. $s_{\bar{x}} = \sqrt{\dfrac{3000 - 200}{3000}} \dfrac{3000}{\sqrt{200}} = 204.9390$

Approximate 95% Confidence Interval for Mean Annual Salary:

$$23,200 \pm 2(204.9390)$$
or
$$\$22,790 \text{ to } \$23,610$$

b. $N\,\bar{x} = 3000\,(23,200) = 69,600,000$

$s_{\hat{x}} = 3000\,(204.9390) = 614,817$

Approximate 95% Confidence Interval for Population Total Salary:

$$69,600,000 \pm 2(614,817)$$
or
$$\$68,370,366 \text{ to } \$70,829,634$$

c. $\bar{p} = .73$

$$s_{\bar{p}} = \sqrt{\left(\dfrac{3000 - 200}{3000}\right)\left(\dfrac{(.73)\,(.27)}{199}\right)} = .0304$$

Approximate 95% Confidence Interval for Proportion that are Generally Satisfied:

$$.73 \pm 2(.0304)$$
or
$$.6692 \text{ to } .7908$$

d. If management administered the questionnaire and anonymity was not guaranteed we would expect a definite upward bias in the percent reporting they were "generally satisfied" with their job. A procedure for guaranteeing anonymity should reduce the bias.

21. a. $\bar{p} = 1/3$

$$s_{\bar{p}} = \sqrt{\left(\dfrac{380 - 30}{380}\right)\left(\dfrac{(1/3)\,(2/3)}{29}\right)} = .0840$$

Approximate 95% Confidence Interval:

$$.3333 \pm 2(.0840)$$
or
$$.1653 \text{ to } .5013$$

b. $\hat{X}_2 = 760\,(19/45) = 320.8889$

c. $\bar{p} = 19/45 = .4222$

$$s_{\bar{p}} = \sqrt{\left(\frac{760 - 45}{760}\right)\left(\frac{(19/45)(26/45)}{44}\right)} = .0722$$

Approximate 95% Confidence Interval:

$$.4222 \pm 2(.0722)$$
$$\text{or}$$
$$.2778 \text{ to } .5666$$

d. $\bar{p}_{st} = \left(\frac{380}{1400}\right)\left(\frac{10}{30}\right) + \left(\frac{760}{1400}\right)\left(\frac{19}{45}\right) + \left(\frac{260}{1400}\right)\left(\frac{7}{25}\right)$

$\quad = .3717$

$$\sum N_h (N_h - n_h)\left[\frac{\bar{p}_h(1 - \bar{p}_h)}{n_h - 1}\right] = 380(350)\frac{(1/3)(2/3)}{29}$$

$$+ 760(715)\frac{(19/45)(26/45)}{44} + 260(235)\frac{(7/25)(18/25)}{24}$$

$$= 1019.1571 + 3012.7901 + 513.2400$$

$$= 4545.1892$$

$$s_{\bar{p}_{st}} = \sqrt{\left(\frac{1}{(1400)^2}\right)4545.1892} = .0482$$

Approximate 95% Confidence Interval:

$$.3717 \pm 2(.0482)$$
$$\text{or}$$
$$.2753 \text{ to } .4681$$

22. a. $\hat{X} = 380(9/30) + 760(12/45) + 260(11/25)$

$\quad = 431.0667$

Estimate approximately 431 deaths due to beating.

b. $\bar{p}_{st} = \left(\frac{380}{1400}\right)\left(\frac{9}{30}\right) + \left(\frac{760}{1400}\right)\left(\frac{12}{45}\right) + \left(\frac{260}{1400}\right)\left(\frac{11}{25}\right)$

$\quad = .3079$

$$\sum N_h \ (N_h - n_h) \ \frac{\left[\overline{p}_h \left(1 - \overline{p}_h \right) \right]}{n_h - 1}$$

$= (380) (380 - 30) (9 / 30) (21 / 30) / 29 \ + \ (760) (760 - 45) (12 / 45) (33 / 45) / 44 +$
$\quad (260) (260 - 25)(11 / 25) (14 / 25) / 24$

$= 4005.5079$

$$s_{\overline{p}_{st}} = \sqrt{\left(\frac{1}{(1400)^2} \right) 4005.5079} \ = .0452$$

Approximate 95% Confidence Interval:

$$.3079 \ \pm \ 2(.0452)$$
$$\text{or}$$
$$.2175 \text{ to } .3983$$

c. $\overline{p}_{st} = \left(\frac{380}{1400} \right) \left(\frac{21}{30} \right) + \left(\frac{760}{1400} \right) \left(\frac{34}{45} \right) + \left(\frac{260}{1400} \right) \left(\frac{15}{25} \right)$

$\quad = .7116$

$$\sum N_h \ (N_h - n_h) \ \frac{\left[\overline{p}_h \left(1 - \overline{p}_h \right) \right]}{n_h - 1}$$

$= (380) (380 - 30) (21 / 30) (9 / 30) / 29 + (760) (760 - 45) (34 / 45) (11 / 45) / 44 +$
$\quad (260) (260 - 25) (15 / 25) (10 / 25) / 24$

$= 3855.0417$

$$s_{\overline{p}_{st}} = \sqrt{\left(\frac{1}{(1400)^2} \right) 3855.0417} \ = .0443$$

Approximate 95% Confidence Interval:

$$.7116 \ \pm \ 2(.0443)$$
$$\text{or}$$
$$.6230 \text{ to } .8002$$

d. $\widehat{X} = 1400 \ (.7116) = 996.24$

Estimate of total number of black victims ≈ 996

23. a.
$$n = \frac{[\,3000\,(80) + 600\,(150) + 250\,(220) + 100\,(700) + 50\,(3000)\,]^2}{(4000)^2 \left(\dfrac{(20)^2}{4}\right) + 3000\,(80)^2 + 600\,(150)^2 + 250\,(220)^2 + 100\,(700)^2 + 50\,(3000)^2}$$

$$= \frac{366{,}025{,}000{,}000}{1{,}600{,}000{,}000 + 543{,}800{,}000}$$

$$= 170.7365$$

Rounding up, we need a sample size of 171 for the desired precision.

$$n_1 = 171 \left(\frac{3000\,(80)}{605{,}000}\right) = 68$$

$$n_2 = 171 \left(\frac{600\,(150)}{605{,}000}\right) = 25$$

$$n_3 = 171 \left(\frac{250\,(220)}{605{,}000}\right) = 16$$

$$n_4 = 171 \left(\frac{100\,(700)}{605{,}000}\right) = 20$$

$$n_5 = 171 \left(\frac{50\,(3000)}{605{,}000}\right) = 42$$

24. a.
$$\bar{x}_c = \frac{14\,(61) + 7\,(74) + 96\,(78) + 23\,(69) + 71\,(73) + 29\,(84)}{14 + 7 + 96 + 23 + 71 + 29}$$

$$= \frac{18{,}066}{240}$$

$$= 75.275$$

Estimate of mean age is approximately 75 years old.

b.
$$\bar{p}_c = \frac{12 + 2 + 30 + 8 + 10 + 22}{14 + 7 + 96 + 23 + 71 + 29}$$

$$= \frac{84}{240}$$

$$= .35$$

$$
\begin{aligned}
\sum (a_i - \bar{p}_c\, M_i)^2 &= [12 - .35\,(14)\,]^2 + [\,2 - .35\,(7)\,]^2 + [30 - .35\,(96)\,]^2 \\
&\quad + [\,8 - .35\,(23)\,]^2 + [\,10 - .35\,(71)\,]^2 + [\,22 - .35\,(29)\,]^2 \\
&= (7.1)^2 + (-.45)^2 + (-3.6)^2 + (-.05)^2 + (-14.85)^2 + (11.85)^2 \\
&= 424.52
\end{aligned}
$$

$$s_{\bar{p}_c} = \sqrt{\left(\frac{100 - 6}{100\,(6)\,(48)^2}\right)\frac{424.52}{5}} = .0760$$

Approximate 95% Confidence Interval:

$$.35 \pm 2(.0760)$$
or
$$.198 \text{ to } .502$$

$\widehat{X} = 4800 \, (.35) = 1680$

Estimate of total number of Disabled Persons is 1680.

Chapter 22
Decision Analysis

Learning Objectives

1.   Learn how probability information and economic measures can be combined to arrive at decision recommendations.

2.   Understand what is meant by the decision analysis approach to decision making.

3.   Learn how to describe a problem situation in terms of its decision alternatives, states of nature, and payoffs.

4.   Be able to analyze a decision analysis problem from both a payoff table and decision tree point of view.

5.   Be able to use sensitivity analysis to study how changes in the probability estimates for the states of nature affect or alter the recommended decision.

6.   Be able to determine the potential value of additional information.

7.   Learn how new information and revised probability values can be used in the decision analysis approach to problem solving.

8.   Be able to use a Bayesian approach to computing revised probabilities.

9.   Understand what a decision strategy or decision rule is.

10.   Learn how to evaluate the contribution and efficiency of additional decision making information.

11.   Understand the following terms:

decision alternatives	prior and posterior probabilities
states of nature	Bayesian revision
payoff table	decision strategy
decision tree	expected value of sample information
optimistic approach	efficiency of sample information
conservative approach	marginal analysis
minimax regret approach	sensitivity analysis
expected value approach	expected value of perfect information

Solutions:

1. a.

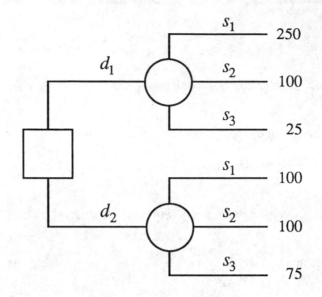

b.

Decision	Maximum Profit	Minimum Profit
d_1	250	25
d_2	100	75

Optimistic approach: select d_1

Conservative approach: select d_2

Regret or opportunity loss table:

	s_1	s_2	s_1
d_1	0	0	50
d_2	150	0	0

Maximum Regret: 50 for d_1 and 150 for d_2; select d_2

2. a.

Decision	Maximum Profit	Minimum Profit
d_1	14	5
d_2	11	7
d_3	11	9
d_4	13	8

Optimistic approach: select d_1

Conservative approach: select d_3

Regret or Opportunity Loss Table with the Maximum Regret

	s_1	s_2	s_3	s_4	Maximum Regret
d_1	0	1	1	8	8
d_2	3	0	3	6	6
d_3	5	0	1	2	5
d_4	6	0	0	0	6

Minimax regret approach: select d_3

b. The choice of which approach to use is up to the decision maker. Since different approaches can result in different recommendations, the most appropriate approach should be selected before analyzing the problem.

c.

Decision	Minimum Cost	Maximum Cost
d_1	5	14
d_2	7	11
d_3	9	11
d_4	8	13

Optimistic approach: select d_1

Conservative approach: select d_2 or d_3

Regret or Opportunity Loss Table

	s_1	s_2	s_3	s_4	Maximum Regret
d_1	6	0	2	0	6
d_2	3	1	0	2	3
d_3	1	1	2	6	6
d_4	0	1	3	8	8

Minimax regret approach: select d_2

3.   a.

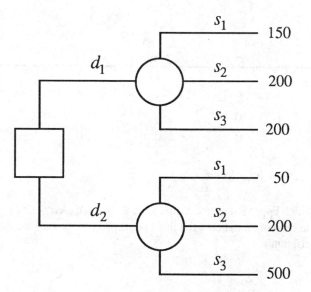

b.

Decision	Maximum Profit	Minimum Profit	Maximum Regret
d_1	200	150	300
d_2	500	50	100

Optimistic approach: select d_2

Conservative approach: select d_1

Minimax regret approach: select d_2

4   a.

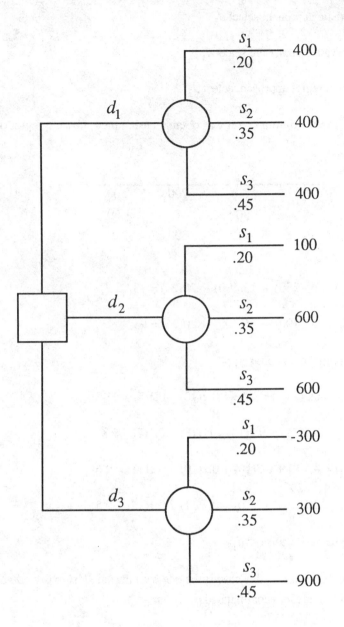

b.

Decision	Maximum Profit	Minimum Profit	Maximum Regret
d_1	400	400	500
d_2	600	100	300
d_3	900	-300	700

Optimistic approach: select d_3

Conservative approach: select d_1

Minimax regret approach: select d_2

Note: The maximum regret was obtained using the following regret or opportunity loss table.

	s_1	s_2	s_3
d_1	0	200	500
d_2	300	0	300
d_3	700	300	0

5. a. $EV(d_1) = .65(250) + .15(100) + .20(25) = 182.5$

    $EV(d_2) = .65(100) + .15(100) + .20(75) = 95$

    The optimal decision is d_1

6 a. $EV(d_1) = 0.5(14) + 0.2(9) + 0.2(10) + 0.1(5) = 11.3$

    $EV(d_2) = 0.5(11) + 0.2(10) + 0.2(8) + 0.1(7) = 9.8$

    $EV(d_3) = 0.5(9) + 0.2(10) + 0.2(10) + 0.1(11) = 9.6$

    $EV(d_4) = 0.5(8) + 0.2(10) + 0.2(11) + 0.1(13) = 9.5$

    Recommended decision: d_1

    b. The best decision in this case is the one with the smallest expected value; thus, d_4, with an expected cost of 9.5, is the recommended decision.

7. $EV(d_1) = 0.2(-100) + 0.3(50) + 0.5(150) = 70$

    $EV(d_2) = 0.2(100) + 0.3(100) + 0.5(100) = 100$

    Recommended decision: d_2 (sell)

8. $EV(d_1) = 0.20(400) + 0.35(400) + 0.45(400) = 400$

    $EV(d_2) = 0.20(100) + 0.35(600) + 0.45(600) = 500$

$$EV(d_3) = 0.20(-300) + 0.35(300) + 0.45(900) = 450$$

Recommended decision: d_2 (medium)

9.   a. d_1 = invest s_1 = heavy $P(s_1) = 0.4$
          d_2 = do not invest s_2 = moderate $P(s_2) = 0.3$
                                           s_3 = light $P(s_3) = 0.3$

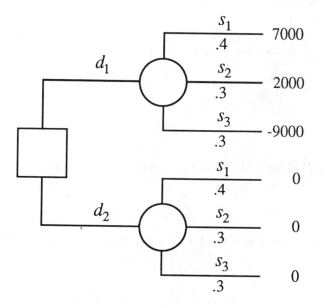

b.   EV(Node 2) = 0.4(7000) + 0.3(2000) + 0.3(-9000) = $700

EV(Node 3) = 0

c.   Recommended decision: d_1 (invest)

10   a.   Let d_1 = develop a prototype
                   d_2 = do not develop a prototype
                   s_1 = failure
                   s_2 = moderate success
                   s_3 = major success

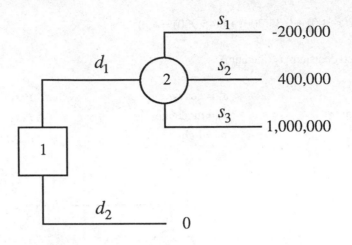

b. $EV(d_1) = 0.7(-200,000) + 0.2(400,000) + 0.1(1,000,000) = 40,000$

$EV(d_2) = 0$

Since the expected value of d_1 is \$40,000 and the expected value of d_2 is 0, JSI should develop the software.

11.   Let d_1 = sell the option
           d_2 = purchase the property, clear the land, and prepare the site for building
           s_1 = real estate market is down
           s_2 = real estate market remains at the current level
           s_3 = real estate market is up

$EV(d_1) = 0.6(250,000) + 0.3(250,000) + 0.1(250,000) = 250,000$

$EV(d_2) = 0.6(-1,500,000) + 0.3(1,000,000) + 0.1(4,000,000) = -200,000$

Doug should sell the option.

12. $EV(d_1) = p(10) + (1 - p)(1) = 9p + 1$
     $EV(d_2) = p(4) + (1 - p)(3) = 1p + 3$

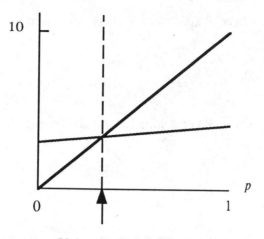

Value of p for
which EVs are equal

$9p + 1 = 1p + 3$ and hence $p = .25$

13.a.　Let p = probability of s_1

$EV(d_1) = p(80) + (1 - p)50 = 30p + 50$

$EV(d_2) = p(65) + (1 - p)85 = -20p + 85$

$EV(d_3) = p(30) + (1 - p)100 = -70p + 100$

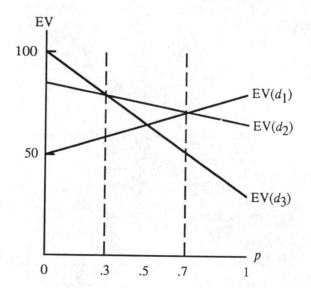

Solving for the point where $EV(d_2)$ and $EV(d_3)$ are equal

$EV(d_2) = EV(d_3)$
$-20p + 85 = -70p + 100$
$\therefore p = 0.3$

Solving for the point where $EV(d_1)$ and $EV(d_2)$ are equal

$EV(d_1) = EV(d_2)$
$30p + 50 = -20p + 85$
$\therefore p = 0.7$

Value(s) of p	Best Decision(s)
$0 \leq p < 0.3$	d_3
$p = 0.3$	d_2 or d_3
$0.3 < p < 0.7$	d_2
$p = 0.7$	d_2 or d_1
$0.7 < p \leq 1.0$	d_1

14. a. $EV(d_1) = 0.4(2000) + 0.6(2000) = 2000$

$EV(d_2) = 0.4(2500) + 0.6(1000) = 1600$

Recommended decision: d_1 (St. Louis)

b. Let p = probability of s_1

$EV(d_1) = 2000$

$EV(d_2) = p(2500) + (1 - p)1000 = 1500p + 1000$

Solving for the point where $EV(d_1)$ and $EV(d_2)$ are equal
$EV(d_1) = EV(d_2)$
$2000 = 1500p + 1000$
$\therefore p = 0.67$

Value(s) of p	Best Decision(s)
$0 \leq p < 0.67$	d_1
$p = 0.67$	d_1 or d_2
$0.67 < p \leq 1.0$	d_2

15.

Probabilities	Expected Value
0.5, 0.3, 0.2	$350,000
0.4, 0.4, 0.2	$600,000

These results suggest that the best decision is influenced a great deal by the probability of s_1.

16. We are given $P(s_3) = 0.1$. First, let us determine the value of $P(s_1)$ that will result in an expected value for d_1 of $250,000, the expected value of selling the option. Denoting the unknown value of $P(s_1)$ as p, we know that

$$p + P(s_2) + 0.1 = 1$$

Thus

$$P(s_2) = 0.9 - p$$

Using p, $0.9 - p$, and 0.1 as the probabilities for s_1, s_2 and s_3, respectively, the expected value for d_2 is

$$EV(d_2) = p(-1,500,000) + (0.9 - p)(1,000,000) + 0.1(400,000)$$
$$= -2,500,000p + 1,300,000$$

Setting the expression equal to $250,000 and solving for p we obtain

$$p = 1,050,000/2,500,000 = 0.42$$

Thus, if the probability that the real estate market is down is equal to 0.42, $EV(d_1)$ and $EV(d_2)$ are equal. However, if $p < 0.42$, $EV(d_2)$ will exceed $250,000 and d_2 will be the best decision.

17. a. If s_1 then d_1 ; if s_2 then d_1 or d_2; if s_3 then d_2

   b. EVwPI = .65(250) + .15(100) + .20(75) = 192.5

   c. From the solution to Exercise 5 we know that $EV(d_1) = 182.5$ and $EV(d_2) = 95$; thus, the recommended decision is d_1. Hence, EVwoPI = 182.5.

   d. EVPI = EVwPI - EVwoPI = 192.5 - 182.5 = 10

18. a. If s_1 then d_1; if s_2 then d_2 , d_3, or d_4 ; if s_3 then d_4; if s_4 then d_4

   b. EVwPI = .5(14) + .2(10) + .2(11) + .1(13) = 12.5

   c. From the solution to Exercise 6 we know that $EV(d_1) = 11.3$, $EV(d_2) = 9.8$, $EV(d_3) = 9.6$, and $EV(d_4) = 95$; thus, the recommended decision is d_1. Hence, EVwoPI = 11.3.

d.   EVPI = EVwPI - EVwoPI = 12.5 - 11.3 = 1.2

19.   Optimal decision strategy with perfect information:

If s_1 then d_2

If s_2 then d_2

If s_3 then d_1

Expected value of this strategy is $0.2(100) + 0.3(100) + 0.5(150) = 125$

EVPI = 125 - 100 = 25

20.   Optimal decision strategy with perfect information:

If s_1 then d_1

If s_2 then d_2

If s_3 then d_3

Expected value of this strategy is

$0.2(400) + 0.35(600) + 0.45(900) = 695$

EVPI = 695 - 500 = 195

21   .a. Let d_3 = purchase blade attachment. Recall that d_1 = purchase snowplow and d_2 = no purchase.

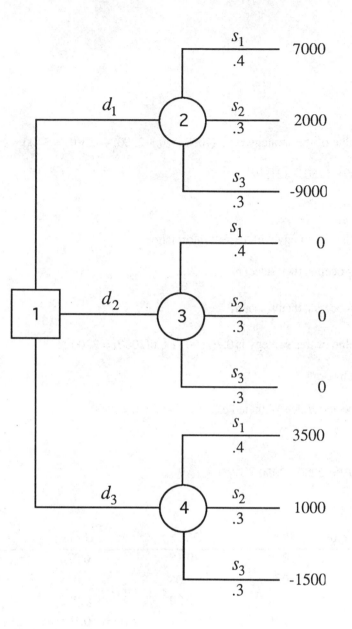

b. From 9 we know that $EV(d_1) = 700$ and $EV(d_2) = 0$

EV(d_3) = 0.4(3500) + 0.3(1000) + 0.3(-1500) = 1250

Recommended decision: d_3 (purchase blade attachment)

c. Optimal decision strategy with perfect information:

If s_1 then d_1

If s_2 then d_1

If s_3 then d_2

Expected value of this strategy is $0.4(7000) + 0.3(2000) + 0.3(0) = 3400$

EVPI = 3400 - 1250 = $2150

22.   Optimal decision strategy with perfect information:

   If s_1 occurs, then select d_2

   If s_2 occurs, then select d_1

Expected value of this strategy is $0.4(2500) + 0.6(2000) = 2200$

From 14 we have

   Expected Value Without Perfect Information = 2000

Therefore,

   EVPI = 2200 - 2000 = $200

23.

State of Nature	$P(s_j)$	$P(I \mid s_j)$	$P(I \cap s_j)$	$P(s_j \mid I)$
s_1	0.2	0.10	0.020	0.1905
s_2	0.5	0.05	0.025	0.2381
s_3	0.3	0.20	0.060	0.5714
	1.0		$P(I) =$ 0.105	1.0000

24. a. $EV(d_1) = 0.8(15) + 0.2(10) = 14$

   $EV(d_2) = 0.8(10) + 0.2(12) = 10.4$

   $EV(d_3) = 0.8(8) + 0.2(20) = 10.4$

   Recommended decision: d_1

   b.   Let p = probability of s_1

$EV(d_1) = p(15) + (1 - p)(10) = 5p + 10$

$EV(d_2) = p(10) + (1 - p)(12) = -2p + 12$

$EV(d_3) = p(8) + (1 - p)(20) = -12p + 20$

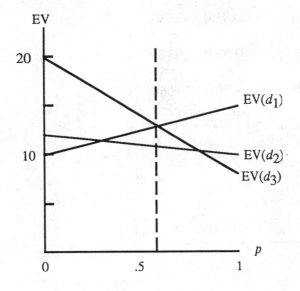

Solving for the point where $EV(d_1)$ and $EV(d_3)$ are equal

$EV(d_1) = EV(d_3)$
$5p + 10 = -12p + 20$
$\therefore p = 0.59$

Value(s) of p	Best Decision
$0 \leq p < 0.59$	d_3
$p = 0.59$	d_1 or d_3
$0.59 < p \leq 1.0$	d_1

c. Optimal decision strategy with perfect information:

If s_1 then d_1

If s_2 then d_3

Expected value of this strategy is $0.8(15) + 0.2(20) = 16$

22 - 15

EVPI = 16 - 14 = 2

d.

State of Nature	$P(s_j)$	$P(I \mid s_j)$	$P(I \cap s_j)$	$P(s_j \mid I)$
s_1	0.8	0.20	0.16	0.5161
s_2	0.2	0.75	0.15	0.4839
			0.31	

$EV(d_1) = 0.5161(15) + 0.4839(10) = 12.5805$

$EV(d_2) = 0.5161(10) + 0.4839(12) = 10.9678$

$EV(d_3) = 0.5161(8) + 0.4839(20) = 13.8068$

Recommended decision: d_3

25.a. & b.

For I_1,

State of Nature	$P(s_j)$	$P(I_1 \mid s_j)$	$P(I_1 \cap s_j)$	$P(s_j \mid I_1)$
s_1	0.4	0.8	0.32	0.57143
s_2	0.6	0.4	0.24	0.42857
		$P(I_1) =$	0.56	

For I_2,

State of Nature	$P(s_j)$	$P(I_2 \mid s_j)$	$P(I_2 \cap s_j)$	$P(s_j \mid I_2)$
s_1	0.4	0.2	0.08	0.18182
s_2	0.6	0.6	0.36	0.81818
		$P(I_2) =$	0.44	

c.

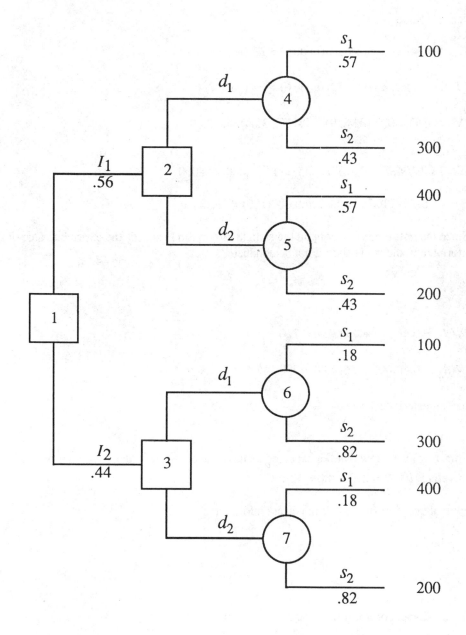

EV(node 4) = 0.5714(100) + 0.4286(300) = 185.71

EV(node 5) = 0.5714(400) + 0.4286(200) = 314.28

EV(node 6) = 0.1818(100) + 0.8182(300) = 263.64

EV(node 7) = 0.1818(400) + 0.8182(200) = 236.36

Decision strategy:

If I_1 then select d_2 since EV(node 5) > EV(node 4)

If I_2 then select d_1 since EV(node 6) > EV(node 7)

EV(node 1) = 0.56(314.29) + 0.44(263.64) = 292.00

26. a.   EVSI = EVwSI - EVwoSI = 45,000 - 37,000 = $8000

   b.   E = EVSI/EVPI(100) = 8000/60,000(100) = 13.13%

   c.   Since the cost required to obtain the sample information exceeds the expected value of the sample information, the study should not be conducted.

27. a. $EV(d_1) = 0.4(100) + 0.6(300) = 220$

   $EV(d_2) = 0.4(400) + 0.6(200) = 280$

   Recommended decision: d_2

   b.   From 16(c) we know that the expected value of the decision strategy which used I_1 and I_2 is 292. Therefore, EVSI = 292 - 280 = 12.

   c.   Optimal decision strategy with perfect information:

   If s_1 then d_2

   If s_2 then d_1

   Expected value of this strategy is 0.4(400) + 0.6(300) = 340

   EVPI = 340 - 280 = 60

   d.   Efficiency = (12/60)100 = 20%

28. a.

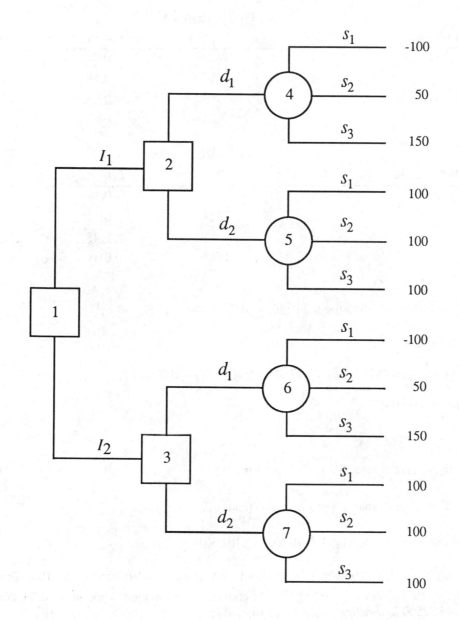

b.

For I_1 - Favorable,

State of Nature	$P(s_j)$	$P(I_1 \mid s_j)$	$P(I_1 \cap s_j)$	$P(s_j \mid I_1)$
s_1	0.2	0.3	0.06	0.08696
s_2	0.3	0.6	0.18	0.26087
s_3	0.5	0.9	0.45	0.65217
		$P(I_2) =$	0.69	

For I_2 - Unfavorable,

State of Nature	$P(s_j)$	$P(I_2 \mid s_j)$	$P(I_2 \cap s_j)$	$P(s_j \mid I_2)$
s_1	0.2	0.7	0.14	0.45161
s_2	0.3	0.4	0.12	0.38710
s_3	0.5	0.1	0.05	0.16129
		$P(I_2) =$	0.31	

EV(node 4) = 0.087(-100) + 0.261(50) + 0.652(150) = 102.17

EV(node 5) = 100

EV(node 6) = 0.452(-100) + 0.387(50) + 0.161(150) = -1.7

EV(node 7) = 100

Decision strategy:

If I_1 then select d_1 since EV(node 4) > EV(node 5)

If I_2 then select d_2 since EV(node 7) > EV(node 6)

EV(node 1) = 0.69(102.17) + 0.31(100) = $101.50

c.   From exercise 7, we know that the expected value of the best decision (d_2) is $100. Thus, EVSI = 101.5 -100 = 1.5, or $1500. The consulting information is not worthwhile; the cost of $2500 is worth more than the expected gain.

29.a.   Revised Probabilities

For I_1,

State of Nature	$P(s_j)$	$P(I_1 \mid s_j)$	$P(I_1 \cap s_j)$	$P(s_j \mid I_1)$
s_1	0.20	0.6	0.120	0.39344
s_2	0.35	0.4	0.140	0.45902
s_3	0.45	0.1	0.045	0.14754
		$P(I_1) =$	0.305	

For I_2,

State of Nature	$P(s_j)$	$P(I_2 \mid s_j)$	$P(I_2 \cap s_j)$	$P(s_j \mid I_2)$
s_1	0.20	0.3	0.060	0.15789
s_2	0.35	0.4	0.140	0.36842
s_3	0.45	0.4	0.180	0.47368
		$P(I_2) =$	0.380	

For I_3,

State of Nature	$P(s_j)$	$P(I_3 \mid s_j)$	$P(I_3 \cap s_j)$	$P(s_j \mid I_3)$
s_1	0.20	0.1	0.020	0.06349
s_2	0.35	0.2	0.070	0.22222
s_3	0.45	0.5	0.225	0.71429
		$P(I_3) =$	0.315	

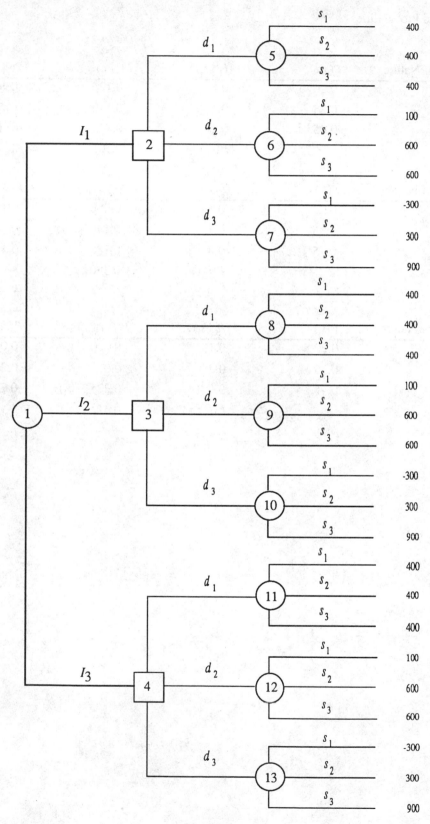

Summary of Calculations

Node	Expected Value
5	400
6	403.28
7	152.46
8	400
9	521.05
10	489.47
11	400
12	568.26
13	690.48

Decision strategy:

If I_1 then d_2 since EV(node 6) > EV(nodes 5 or 7)

If I_2 then d_2 since EV(node 9) > EV(nodes 8 or 10)

If I_3 then d_3 since EV(node 13) > EV(nodes 11 or 12)

EV(node 1) = 0.305(403.28) + 0.380(521.05) + 0.315(690.48) = $538.50

b.   From problem 8 we know that the best decision is d_2 with an expected value of $500

EVSI = 538.50 - 500 = 38.5 or $38,500

c.   Optimal decision strategy with perfect information:

If s_1 then d_1

If s_2 then d_2

If s_3 then d_3

Expected value of this strategy is 0.2(400) + 0.35(600) + 0.45(900) = 695

EVPI = 695 - 500 = 195 or $195,000

Efficiency = (38.500 / 195,000)100 = 19.7%

30.   Let

I_1 = unseasonably cold September

I_2 = not an unseasonably cold September

For I_1,

State of Nature	$P(s_j)$	$P(I_1 \mid s_j)$	$P(I_1 \cap s_j)$	$P(s_j \mid I_1)$
s_1	0.4	0.30	0.120	0.615385
s_2	0.3	0.20	0.060	0.307692
s_3	0.3	0.05	<u>0.015</u>	0.076923
		$P(I_1) =$	0.195	

For I_2,

State of Nature	$P(s_j)$	$P(I_2 \mid s_j)$	$P(I_2 \cap s_j)$	$P(s_j \mid I_2)$
s_1	0.4	0.70	0.280	0.347826
s_2	0.3	0.80	0.240	0.298137
s_3	0.3	0.95	<u>0.285</u>	0.354037
		$P(I_2) =$	0.805	

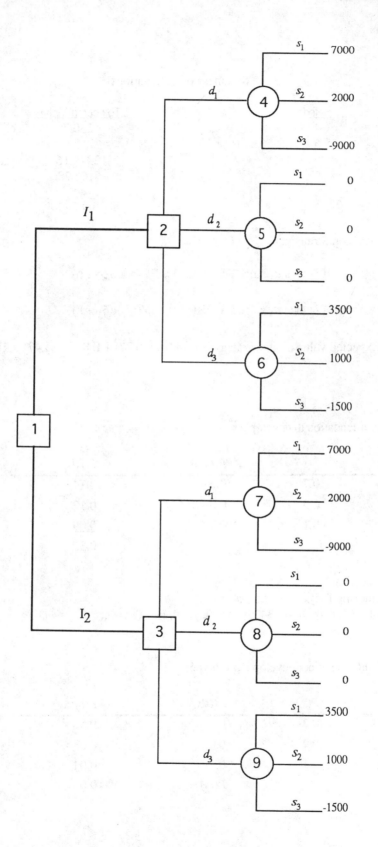

Summary of Calculations

Node	Expected Value
4	4230.77
5	0
6	2346.16
7	-155.28
8	0
9	984.47

Decision Strategy:

If I_1 then d_1 since EV(node 4) > EV(node 5 or 6)

If I_2 then d_3 since EV(node 9) > EV(node 7 or 8)

Expected value of this strategy is $0.195(4230.77) + 0.805(984.47) = 1617.50$

31.   If I_1 (recommendation to develop a prototype)

s_j	$P(s_j)$	$P(I_1 \cap s_j)$	$P(I_1 \vert s_j)$	$P(s_j \vert I_1)$
s_1	0.7	0.2	0.14	0.4000
s_2	0.2	0.6	0.12	0.3429
s_3	0.1	0.9	<u>0.09</u>	<u>0.2571</u>
		$P(I_1) =$	0.35	1.0000

In this case, ignoring for now the $5,000 fee,
  EV(d_1) = 0.4(-200,000) + 0.3429(400,000) + 0.2571(1,000,000)
      = 314,260

If I_1 (recommendation to not develop a prototype)

s_j	$P(s_j)$	$P(I_2 \vert s_j)$	$P(I_2 \cap s_j)$	$P(s_j \vert I_2)$
s_1	0.7	0.8	0.56	0.8615
s_2	0.2	0.4	0.08	0.1231
s_3	0.1	0.1	<u>0.01</u>	<u>0.0154</u>
		$P(I_2) =$	0.65	1.0000

In this case (ignoring for now the $5,000 fee)

$$EV(d_1) = 0.8615(-200,000) + 0.1231(400,000) + 0.0154(1,000,000) = -107,660$$
$$EV(d_2) = 0$$

Decision strategy:

If I_1 then d_1

If I_2 then d_2

The expected value of this decision strategy is $0.35(314,260) + 0.65(0) = 109,991$

Subtracting the fee of $5,000, we obtain an expected value of $104,991. Compared to the expected value of $40,000 using no information (problem 5), JSI's best decision is to hire the consultant.

Note: the consultant's fee of $5,000 could have been subtracted from the payoffs prior to computing $EV(d_1)$ and $EV(d_2)$; the results obtained will be identical to the approach shown.

32.a.   For I_1,

State of Nature	$P(s_j)$	$P(I_1 \mid s_j)$	$P(I_1 \cap s_j)$	$P(s_j \mid I_1)$
s_1	0.40	0.60	0.24	0.57
s_2	0.60	0.30	0.18	0.43
		$P(I_1) =$	0.42	

For I_2,

State of Nature	$P(s_j)$	$P(I_2 \mid s_j)$	$P(I_2 \cap s_j)$	$P(s_j \mid I_2)$
s_1	0.40	0.40	0.16	0.28
s_2	0.60	0.70	0.42	0.72
		$P(I_2) =$	0.58	

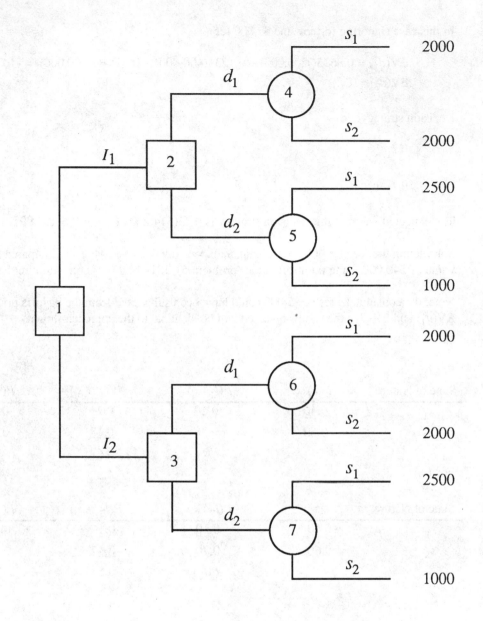

Summary of Calculations

Node	Expected Value
4	2000
5	1855
6	2000
7	1420

Decision strategy:

If I_1 then d_1 since EV(node 4) > EV(node 5)

If I_2 then d_1 since EV(node 6) > EV(node 7)

Expected value of this strategy is 0.42(2000) + 0.58(2000) = 2000

b. $P(s_1 \mid I_1) = 0.57$; nonetheless, Milford should take the St. Louis trip.

c. From problem 9 we know that with no information the recommended decision is d_1 with an expected value of 2000; in addition, EVPI = 200

EVSI = 2000 - 2000 = 0

Efficiency = (0 / 200)100 = 0%

33. a. An estimate of the probability of s_1 is 17/20 = 0.85. An estimate of the probability of s_2 is 3/20 = 0.15. Using the Expected Value Approach we obtain the following results:

EV(d_1) = 0.85(25) + 0.15(45) = 28

EV(d_2) = 0.85(30) + 0.15(30) = 30

Recommended decision: d_1 (expressway)

b. Let p = probability of s_1

EV(d_1) = p(25) + (1 - p)(45) = 25p + 45 - 45p = -20p + 45
EV(d_2) = 30

EV(d_1) = EV(d_2)
-20p + 45 = 30
     20p = 15
       p = 0.75

Thus, whenever p = 0.75 each decision alternative will provide the same expected value. If p < 0.75 then d_2 is the recommended decision; if p > 0.75 then d_1 is the recommended decision.

c. The expected value approach may not be the best approach for this problem since the recommended decision, d_1, also includes a 0.15 probability of a 45 minute trip; if this occurs, Rona and Jerry may be late for work. Thus, the consistent Queen City Avenue route, with a travel time of 30 minutes, may be preferred.

d. The decision tree is shown below:

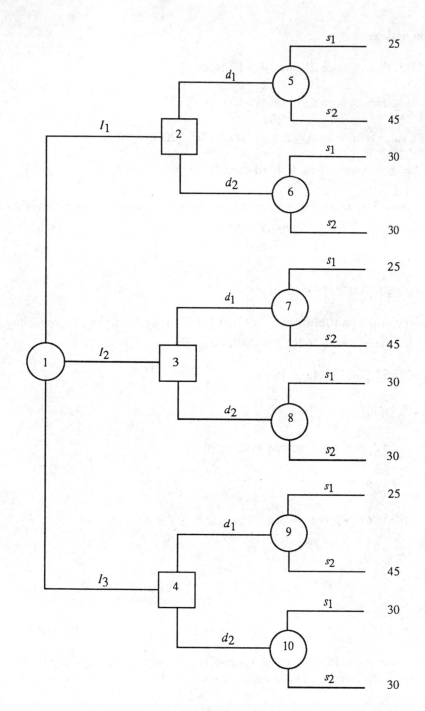

e.

State of Nature	$P(s_j)$	For I_1, $P(I_1 \mid s_j)$	$P(I_1 \cap s_j)$	$P(s_j \mid I_1)$
s_1	0.85	0.8	0.680	0.9784
s_2	0.15	0.1	0.015	0.0216
		$P(I_1) =$	0.695	

For I_2,

State of Nature	$P(s_j)$	$P(I_2 \mid s_j)$	$P(I_2 \cap s_j)$	$P(s_j \mid I_2)$
s_1	0.85	0.2	0.170	0.7907
s_2	0.15	0.3	0.045	0.2093
		$P(I_2) =$	0.215	

For I_3,

State of Nature	$P(s_j)$	$P(I_3 \mid s_j)$	$P(I_3 \cap s_j)$	$P(s_j \mid I_3)$
s_1	0.85	0.0	0.000	0.0000
s_2	0.15	0.6	0.090	1.0000
		$P(I_3) =$	0.090	

Summary of Calculations

Node	Expected Value
5	25.43
6	30
7	29.19
8	30
9	45
10	30

Decision strategy:

If I_1 then d_1 since EV(node 5) < EV(node 6)

If I_2 then d_1 since EV(node 7) < EV(node 8)

If I_3 then d_2 since EV(node 10) < EV(node 9)

EV(node 1) = 0.695(25.43) + 0.215(29.19) + 0.09(30) = 26.65

f.   With no weather information:

EV(d_1) = 0.85(25) + 0.15(45) = 28

EV(d_2) = 30

Recommended decision: d_1

Optimal decision strategy with perfect information:

If s_1 then d_1

If s_2 then d_2

Expected value of this strategy is $0.85(25) + 0.15(30) = 25.75$

EVPI = $28 - 25.75 = 2.25$

EVSI = $28 - 26.65 = 1.35$

Efficiency = $(1.35 / 2.25)100 = 60.0\%$

34. a. d_1 = Manufacture component s_1 = Low demand
        d_2 = Purchase component s_2 = Medium demand
                                              s_3 = High demand

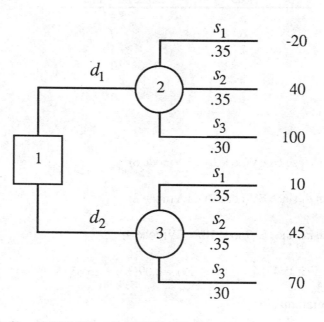

EV(node 2) = $(0.35)(-20) + (0.35)(40) + (0.30)(100) = 37$

EV(node 3) = $(0.35)(10) + (0.35)(45) + (0.30)(70) = 40.25$

Recommended decision: d_2 (purchase component)

b.   Optimal decision strategy with perfect information:

      If s_1 then d_2

      If s_2 then d_2

If s_3 then d_1

Expected value of this strategy is $0.35(10) + 0.35(45) + 0.30(100) = 49.25$

EVPI = $49.25 - 40.25 = 9$ or \$9,000

c. For I_1,

State of Nature	$P(s_j)$	$P(I_1 \mid s_j)$	$P(I_1 \cap s_j)$	$P(s_j \mid I_1)$
s_1	0.35	0.10	0.035	0.09859
s_2	0.35	0.40	0.140	0.39437
s_3	0.30	0.60	0.180	0.50704
		$P(I_1) =$	0.355	

For I_2,

State of Nature	$P(s_j)$	$P(I_2 \mid s_j)$	$P(I_2 \cap s_j)$	$P(s_j \mid I_2)$
s_1	0.35	0.90	0.315	0.48837
s_2	0.35	0.60	0.210	0.32558
s_3	0.30	0.40	0.120	0.18605
		$P(I_2) =$	0.645	

The probability the report will be favorable is $P(I_1) = 0.355$

d. The decision tree is shown below:

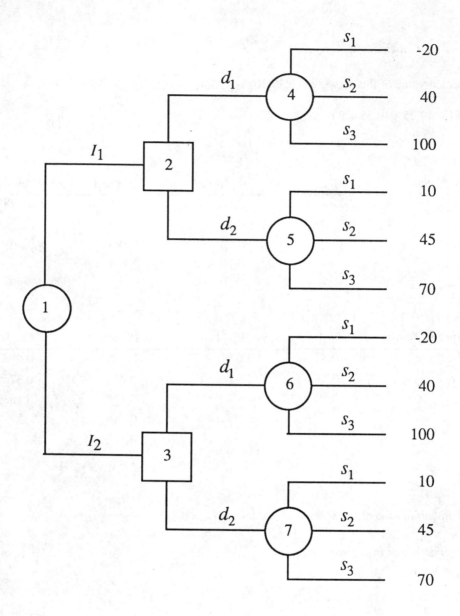

Summary of Calculations

Node	Expected Value
4	64.51
5	54.23
6	21.86
7	32.56

Decision strategy:

If I_1 then d_1 since EV(node 4) > EV(node 5)

If I_2 then d_2 since EV(node 7) > EV(node 6)

EV(node 1) = 0.355(64.51) + 0.645(32.56) = 43.90

e. With no information:

$EV(d_1) = 0.35(-20) + 0.35(40) + 0.30(100) = 37$

$EV(d_2) = 0.35(10) + 0.35(45) + 0.30(70) = 40.25$

Recommended decision: d_2

f. Optimal decision strategy with perfect information:

If s_1 then d_2

If s_2 then d_2

If s_3 then d_1

Expected value of this strategy is

0.35(10) + 0.35(45) + 0.30(100) = 49.25

EVPI = 49.25 - 40.25 = 9 or $9,000

Efficiency = (3650 / 9000)100 = 40.6%

35. a.

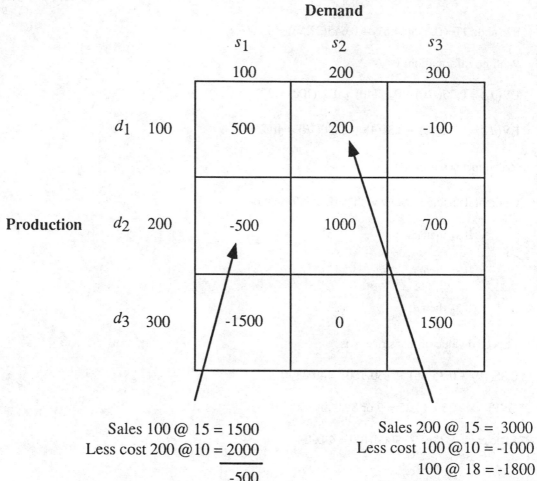

Demand

		s_1	s_2	s_3
		100	200	300
d_1	100	500	200	-100
d_2	200	-500	1000	700
d_3	300	-1500	0	1500

Production

Sales 100 @ 15 = 1500
Less cost 200 @ 10 = 2000
—
-500

Sales 200 @ 15 = 3000
Less cost 100 @ 10 = -1000
100 @ 18 = -1800
—
200

b. $EV(d_1) = .2(500) + .2(200) + .6(-100) = 80$

$EV(d_2) = .2(-500) + .2(1000) + .6(700) = 520$

$EV(d_3) = .2(-1500) + .2(0) + .6(1500) = 600$

Recommended decision: d_3

c. Optimal decision strategy with perfect information:

If s_1 then d_1
If s_2 then d_2
If s_3 then d_3

Expected value of this strategy is .2(500) + .2(1000) + .6(1500) = 1200

EVPI = 1200 - 600 = $600

36. a.

		1000	Demand (lbs) 2000	3000
Amount	1000	50,000	10,000	-30,000
Produced	2000	-50,000	100,000	60,000
(lbs)	3000	-150,000	0	150,000

For example:

Sales	1000 @	$200	=	$200,000
Mfr.Cost	2000 @ -	$150	=	-300,000
Shortage	0 @ -	$240	=	0
Salvage	1000 @	$ 50	=	50,000
Net Profit			=	-$50,000

Sales	3000 @	$200	=	$600,000
Mfr. Cost	2000 @ -	$150	=	-300,000
Shortage	1000 @ -	$240	=	-240,000
Salvage	0 @	$ 50	=	0
Net Profit			=	$ 60,000

b. d_1 = produce 1000 lbs. s_1 = demand is 1000 lbs.

d_2 = produce 2000 lbs. s_2 = demand is 2000 lbs.

d_3 = produce 3000 lbs. s_3 = demand is 3000 lbs.

Given:

$$P(s_1) = 0.3 \qquad P(s_2) = 0.5 \qquad P(s_3) = 0.2$$

EV(d_1) = 0.3(50,000) + 0.5(10,000) + 0.2(-30,000) = $14,000

EV(d_2) = 0.3(-50,000) + 0.5(100,000) + 0.2(60,000) = $47,000

EV(d_3) = 0.3(-150,000) + 0.5(0) + 0.2(150,000) = $-15,000

Recommended decision: d_2 (produce 2000 lbs.)

c. Optimal decision strategy with perfect information:

If s_1 then d_1

If s_2 then d_2

If s_3 then d_3

Expected value of this strategy is 0.3(50,000) + 0.5(100,000) + 0.2(150,000) = 95,000

EVPI = 95,000 - 47,000 = $48,000

Therefore, a discount of up to $48,000 is acceptable.

d.   For I_1,

State of Nature	$P(s_j)$	$P(I_1 \mid s_j)$	$P(I_1 \cap s_j)$	$P(s_j \mid I_1)$
s_1	0.30	0.10	0.03	0.10000
s_2	0.50	0.22	0.11	0.36667
s_3	0.20	0.80	0.16	0.53333
		$P(I_1) =$	0.30	

For I_2,

State of Nature	$P(s_j)$	$P(I_2 \mid s_j)$	$P(I_2 \cap s_j)$	$P(s_j \mid I_2)$
s_1	0.30	0.40	0.12	0.24
s_2	0.50	0.68	0.34	0.68
s_3	0.20	0.20	0.04	0.08
		$P(I_2) =$	0.50	

For I_3,

State of Nature	$P(s_j)$	$P(I_3 \mid s_j)$	$P(I_3 \cap s_j)$	$P(s_j \mid I_3)$
s_1	0.30	0.50	0.15	0.75
s_2	0.50	0.10	0.05	0.25
s_3	0.20	0.00	0.00	0.00
		$P(I_3) =$	0.20	

Summary of
Calculations

EV(Decision)	I_1	I_2	I_3
EV(d_1)	-7,333	16,400	40,000
EV(d_2)	63,667	60,800	- 12,500
EV(d_3)	65,000	-24,000	-112,500

Decision strategy:

If I_1 then d_3

If I_2 then d_2

If I_3 then d_1

Expected value of this strategy is $0.3(65,000) + 0.5(60,800) + 0.2(40,000) = \$57,900$

e. From (b), the best decision with no information is d_2 with an expected value of $47,000.

EVSI = 57,900 - 47,000 = $10,900

f. From (c), EVPI = 48,000

Efficiency = (10,900 /48,000)100 = 22.7%

37 a.

Percent Defective	Number of defects in Batch of 500	Cost @ $25/defective
0%	0	0
1%	5	125
2%	10	250
3%	15	375

	Percent Defective			
	0%	1%	2%	3%
100% Inspect	250	250	250	250
No Inspection	0	125	250	375

b. $EV(d_1) = 0.15(250) + 0.25(250) + 0.40(250) + 0.20(250) = 250$

$EV(d_2) = 0.15(0) + 0.25(125) + 0.40(250) + 0.20(375) = 206.25$

Recommended decision: d_2 (no inspection)

c. The decision tree is shown below:

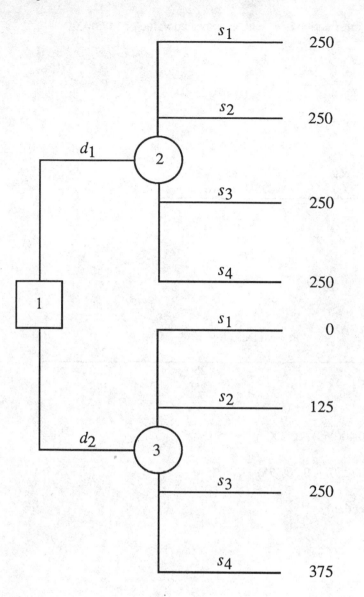

d. Binomial:
   Since the event of interest (I) is one defective part in a sample of 5, $x = 1$ and $n = 5$.

s_j	$p = P(s_j)$	$P(I \mid s_j) = 5p^1(1 - p)^4$
s_1	0.00	$5(0.00)^1(1.00)^4 = 0$
s_2	0.01	$5(0.01)^1(0.99)^4 = 0.048$
s_3	0.02	$5(0.02)^1(0.98)^4 = 0.092$
s_4	0.03	$5(0.03)^1(0.97)^4 = 0.133$

e.

State of Nature	$P(s_j)$	$P(I \mid s_j)$	$P(I \cap s_j)$	$P(s_j \mid I)$
s_1	0.15	0.000	0.0000	0.000
s_2	0.25	0.048	0.0120	0.159
s_3	0.40	0.092	0.0368	0.488
s_4	0.20	0.133	0.0266	0.353
		$P(I) =$	0.0754	

f. $EV(d_1) = 0(250) + 0.159(250) + 0.488(250) + 0.353(250) = \$250$

$EV(d_2) = 0(0) + 0.159(125) + 0.488(250) + 0.353(375) = \$274.25$

Recommended decision: d_1 (100% inspection)

g. cost saving = $\$274.25 - 250 = \$24.25$

38 .a. $EV(d_1) = 0.20(500) + 0.20(200) + 0.60(-100) = 80$

$EV(d_2) = 0.20(-400) + 0.20(800) + 0.60(700) = 500$

$EV(d_3) = 0.20(-1000) + 0.20(-200) + 0.60(1600) = 720$

Recommended decision: d_3

b.

State of Nature	$P(s_j)$	$P(I_2 \mid s_j)$	$P(I_2 \cap s_j)$	$P(s_j \mid I_2)$
s_1	0.20	0.80	0.16	0.5333
s_2	0.20	0.40	0.80	0.2667
s_3	0.60	0.10	0.06	0.2000
		$P(I_2) =$	0.30	

$EV(d_1) = 0.5333(500) + 0.2667(200) + 0.2(-100) = 300$

$$EV(d_2) = 0.5333(-400) + 0.2667(800) + 0.2(700) = 140$$

$$EV(d_3) = 0.5333(-1000) + 0.2667(-200) + 0.2(1600) = -267$$

Recommended decision: d_1

39. a.

		s_1 Major	s_2 Minor	s_3 Failure
Fund	d_1	150,000	10,000	-100,000
Do Not Fund	d_2	0	0	0

$$EV(d_1) = 0.15(150,000) + 0.45(10,000) + 0.40(-100,000) = -13,000$$

$$EV(d_2) = 0$$

Recommended decision: d_2 (do not fund)

b.   Optimal decision strategy with perfect information:

If s_1 then d_1

If s_2 then d_1

If s_3 then d_2

Expected value of this strategy is $0.15(150,000) + 0.45(10,000) + 0.4(0) = 27,000$

EVPI = 27,000 - 0 = \$27,000

Recommendation: Do not hire the consultants

c.   For I_1,

State of Nature	$P(s_j)$	$P(I_1 \mid s_j)$	$P(I \cap s_j)$	$P(s_j \mid I_1)$
s_1	0.15	0.70	0.105	0.552632
s_2	0.45	0.10	0.045	0.236842
s_3	0.40	0.10	0.040	0.210526
		$P(I_1) =$	0.190	

$$EV(d_1) = 64,210.62$$

$EV(d_2) = 0$

Recommended decision: d_1 (fund)

d.   For I_2,

State of Nature	$P(s_j)$	$P(I_2 \mid s_j)$	$P(I_2 \cap s_j)$	$P(s_j \mid I_2)$
s_1	0.15	0.25	0.0375	0.079365
s_2	0.45	0.70	0.3150	0.666667
s_3	0.40	0.30	0.1200	0.253968
		$P(I_2) =$	0.4725	

$EV(d_1) = -6,825.38$

$EV(d_2) = 0$

Recommended decision: d_2 (do not fund)

e.   For I_3

State of Nature	$P(s_j)$	$P(I_3 \mid s_j)$	$P(I_3 \cap s_j)$	$P(s_j \mid I_3)$
s_1	0.15	0.05	0.0075	0.022222
s_2	0.45	0.20	0.0900	0.266667
s_3	0.40	0.60	0.2400	0.711111
		$P(I_3) =$	0.3375	

$EV(d_1) = -65,111.13$

$EV(d_2) = 0$

Recommended decision: d_2 (do not fund)

Decision Strategy:

If I_1 then d_1

If I_2 then d_2

If I_3 then d_2

Expected value of this strategy is $0.19(64,210.62) + 0.4725(0) + 0.3375(0) = \$12,200$

f. From (b) we know that EVPI = $27,000 and that with no information the best decision is d_2 with an expected value of 0.

EVSI = 12,200 - 0 = 12,200

Efficiency = (12,200 / 27,000)100 = 45.2%